TANGLED GOVERNANCE

Tangled Governance

International Regime Complexity, the Troika, and the Euro Crisis

C. RANDALL HENNING

OXFORD
UNIVERSITY PRESS

OXFORD
UNIVERSITY PRESS

Great Clarendon Street, Oxford, OX2 6DP,
United Kingdom

Oxford University Press is a department of the University of Oxford.
It furthers the University's objective of excellence in research, scholarship,
and education by publishing worldwide. Oxford is a registered trade mark of
Oxford University Press in the UK and in certain other countries

First Edition published in 2017
Impression: 1

Published in the United States of America by Oxford University Press
198 Madison Avenue, New York, NY 10016, United States of America

British Library Cataloguing in Publication Data
Data available

Library of Congress Control Number: 2016955312

ISBN 978-0-19-880180-1

Printed and bound by
CPI Group (UK) Ltd, Croydon, CR0 4YY

For Heidi

Acknowledgments

A community of people inspired and supported this study over a number of years and I am deeply grateful to all of those within it. That community comprises several groups of friends, colleagues, and professional partners.

My interviews and conversations with people who were directly involved in the euro crisis were the high points of the research project on which the book is based. The insights gathered from these meetings are, after all, one of the reasons that I study and write about the politics and institutions of global economic governance. People have been generous with their time and intellectual energy, not only over the course of this project but in many cases over a professional lifetime. They placed a significant measure of trust in the professionalism with which I would treat the information conveyed to me. I hope that my interviewees find in this book some measure of compensation for the generosity that they have shown me.

As the title of this book suggests, the European institutions and the International Monetary Fund are central actors in this study. Each of these institutions assisted the project in various ways, such as offering short-term visits, facilitating interviews, participating in professional conferences, and hosting presentations of my research-in-progress. My exchanges with most of these institutions began decades ago on earlier research projects. On all matters, including with respect to competition and cooperation among these institutions, I have endeavored to be objective and believe that I have succeeded in doing so. This endeavor was made easier by the fact that the project has benefited from access to these institutions more or less equally.

The book also benefits from research by fellow travelers through scholarship on the euro crisis, particularly in the early stages of the study. Several excellent books have examined the crisis from various angles and I have done my best to give due credit to these prior contributions. My project also benefited from many conversations over the European Breakfast seminars organized by Nicolas Véron, Jacob Kirkegaard, and Angel Ubide at the Peterson Institute for International Economics in Washington, D.C. Jean Pisani-Ferry and Guntram Wolff hosted me at Bruegel, the Brussels-based research institute, during three of my visits to that city and kindly shared ideas and references. Premela Isaac and her staff at the archives of the International Monetary Fund graciously provided essential assistance in securing access to historical documentation.

At American University's School of International Service, where I have been a member of the faculty for two decades, the SIS Research office organized a meeting to discuss the first full manuscript. Miles Kahler kindly chaired the meeting, which included Robert Kahn, Kathleen McNamara, Sophie Meunier, Alessandro Leipold, Benjamin J. Cohen, Michelle Egan, Tamar Gutner, Wade Jacoby, Louis Pauly, and Randall Stone. They helped me to sharpen and focus the themes in the book. I thank them all for their valuable advice and Shannon Looney and Holly Christensen for their help in organizing the meeting.

I am indebted to several other people for coordinating events at which I received very useful feedback on the project and manuscript. I wish to thank Andrew Moravcsik for inviting me to present to the International Relations Colloquium at the Woodrow Wilson School, Princeton University (November 2014). Randall Stone hosted me at Rochester University for the Seminar on International Political Economy (December 2014). John Wiecking kindly organized my lecture to the Department of State, EB/INR Joint Lecture Series, Washington, D.C. (January 2015). Klaus Regling and Nicola Giammarioli invited me to present the study to the staff of European Stability Mechanism in Luxembourg (May 2015). Sergio Fabbrini organized a seminar for the project at the School of Government at LUISS Guido Carli in Rome (May 2015). Finally, Jim Goldgeier and Nanette Levinson convened our colleagues for an SIS Research Roundtable on the study at the AU campus in Washington, D.C. (March 2016). Criticism of the manuscript at these meetings was uniformly constructive and greatly strengthened the final product.

A number of people provided helpful comments on one or more chapter drafts. They include Moreno Bertoldi, James Boughton, James A. Caporaso, Thanos Catsambas, Ajai Chopra, Jeffrey Chwieroth, Benjamin J. Cohen, Daniel Daco, Servaas Deroose, Gonzalo García, Tamar Gutner, Russell Kincaid, Fernando Jimenez Latorre, Antonio de Lecea, Meg Lundsager, Matthias Matthijs, Sophie Meunier, Georges Pineau, Klaus Regling, Jeremiah Reimer, Edwin M. Truman, Amy Verdun, Martin A. Weiss, Onno de Beaufort Wijnholds, and Norbert Wunner—with my sincere apologies to anyone who I may have unintentionally omitted. A number of readers of the manuscript opted to remain anonymous. Needless to say, some of my readers would have preferred a different rendering of the cases presented here and disagree with some of my conclusions. Certainly, none of these people are responsible for mistakes, oversights, or omissions in this manuscript.

Eight research assistants contributed over the course of the project: Tobias Tesche, Peter Foley, Martin Kessler, Caroline Chumo, Balazs Martonffy, Jeff Eversman, Dimitrije Tasic, and Leticia Donoso. The book represents a large investment of their time and energy as well as mine. I hope they feel that the investment was ultimately worth their diligent and painstaking efforts. They deserve more than the simple thanks conveyed here and I wish them very well in their future endeavors.

At Oxford University Press, Dominic Byatt shepherded the manuscript through the review process and into publication. I am grateful for his support of the project and his advice. Two anonymous reviewers provided very helpful comments, while Olivia Wells and her colleagues managed production.

Personally, I have benefited greatly from the kindness and understanding of family and friends throughout the project. Many have humored me over dinner conversations on regime complexity, institutional interaction, and the politics of financial rescue programs. This book was written during the transition of our boys Nick and Nathaniel to adulthood and college. It occupied me while they were preparing to leave the family nest. Being part of their lives has been my greatest privilege.

Every project like this draws on a deep pool of "patient capital." My wife Heidi accepted an enormous diversion of energy and attention to this project. She never questioned my decision to devote long hours to the book. Our boys have a book dedicated to them already; this one is dedicated to her, with my life-long gratitude for affection and support that go far beyond this book project.

C. Randall Henning
Bethesda, Maryland

November 2016

Contents

List of Figures

List of Tables

List of Abbreviations

BLA	Bilateral Lending Agreement
CAC	Collective Action Clauses
CDS	Credit Default Swap
CDU	Christian Democratic Union
CJEU	Court of Justice of the European Union
CSU	Christian Social Union
DG	Directorate-General
DSA	Debt Sustainability Analysis
DTA	Deferred Tax Asset
EBA	European Banking Authority
EBRD	European Bank for Reconstruction and Development
ECB	European Central Bank
ECCL	Enhanced Conditions Credit Line
ECJ	European Court of Justice
EDP	Excessive Deficit Procedure
EFC	Economic and Financial Committee
EFF	Extended Fund Facility
EFSF	European Financial Stability Facility
EFSM	European Financial Stabilisation Mechanism
EIB	European Investment Bank
ELA	Emergency Liquidity Assistance
EMF	European Monetary Fund
EMS	European Monetary System
EMU	Economic and Monetary Union
ERM	Exchange Rate Mechanism
ESM	European Stability Mechanism
EU	European Union
EWG	Eurogroup Working Group
FCL	Flexible Credit Line
FDI	Foreign Direct Investment
FDP	Free Democratic Party
FSAP	Financial Sector Assessment Program

GDP	Gross Domestic Product
G7	Group of Seven
G20	Group of Twenty
HICP	Harmonized Index of Consumer Prices
HIPC	Heavily Indebted Poor Countries
IBRC	Irish Bank Resolution Corporation
IIF	Institute for International Finance
IMF	International Monetary Fund
IO	International Organization
LTRO	Long-Term Refinancing Operations
MOU	Memorandum of Understanding
MIP	Macroeconomic Imbalances Procedure
NAB	New Arrangements to Borrow
NAMA	National Assets Management Agency
NPL	Non-Performing Loan
OMT	Outright Monetary Transactions
OSI	Official Sector Involvement
PASOK	Panhellenic Socialist Movement
PLL	Precautionary and Liquidity Line
PCL	Precautionary Credit Line
PSI	Private Sector Involvement
QMV	Qualified Majority Voting
SBA	Stand-By Arrangement
SDR	Special Drawing Rights
SGP	Stability and Growth Pact
SME	Small- and Medium-Sized Enterprise
SMP	Securities Market Programme
SOE	State-Owned Enterprise
SPD	Social Democratic Party
SRM	Single Resolution Mechanism
SSM	Single Supervisory Mechanism
SYRIZA	Synaspismós Rizospastikís Aristerás
TALF	Term Asset-Backed Securities Loan Facility
TARP	Troubled Asset Relief Program
TFEU	Treaty on the Functioning of the European Union
WTO	World Trade Organization

1

Introduction

MOMENT OF TRUTH

In the winter of 2010, Europe's monetary union and its leaders stood at the threshold of a profound economic and political crisis. A newly elected government in Greece had announced a few months earlier that the national budget deficits for 2009 and 2010 would be far greater than previously estimated, which shocked financial markets and forced Athens to seek financial assistance from its European partners. Political leaders within the euro area confronted a crucial question: should they include the International Monetary Fund (IMF) in the financial rescue for Greece?

An intelligent observer might have predicted that the answer would be a resounding "no," that Europe would choose to address the crisis on its own, without the help of the international community. Europe was, after all, the richest of the world's regions, possessed more than enough financial resources, and was home to a small army of professional economists who could be harnessed to the task of fighting the crisis. The national finance ministries and central banks, private banks and the European institutions employed more people who had previously served in the IMF than any other region. Europe's institutions were the most highly developed of all the regional organizations around the globe. Moreover, a quarter century had passed since any of the member states that joined the euro area had borrowed from the IMF; in the meantime, the European Union had lent to member countries four times without parallel financing from the Fund.[1]

While the European Union had cooperated with the IMF on programs for countries in Central and Eastern Europe at the high point of the global financial crisis in 2008–9—including Hungary, Latvia, and Romania—financial problems within the euro area were thought to be an entirely different matter. The members of the monetary union had accepted obligations to one another

---

[1] The European Union extended loans to France in 1983, Greece in 1985 and 1991, and Italy in 1993 through the Medium-term Financial Assistance facility. Portugal had been the last Western European country to draw from the IMF, in 1983.

that were supposedly more solemn than those among the countries that had not adopted the euro.

Euro-area leaders had strong personal political incentives to steer clear of the Fund. They were the proud custodians of sixty years of integration; turning to outsiders would be an embarrassing admission that their rules and surveillance had failed, that they and the European institutions could not cope on their own. Most of all, many European officials hoped to use the crisis as a fulcrum on which to leverage a strengthening of those rules and institutions, a time-honored strategy for overcoming political resistance to European integration. Drawing upon the IMF diluted the case for institutional deepening and risked squandering this opportunity.

European policymakers almost universally opposed involving the IMF at the outset of the Greek crisis for these reasons. The finance ministers of Germany and France and the leaders of the European institutions publicly voiced strong opposition in February 2010. The president of the Eurogroup, Jean-Claude Juncker, who would later become president of the European Commission, declared that including the IMF would be "absurd."

Within a matter of weeks, however, these European officials turned a complete about-face. The IMF was invited into the rescue for Greece and began negotiating with the Greek government officials alongside representatives of the European Commission and the European Central Bank (ECB) in April 2010. Their choice was fateful, both for Europe and for the Fund, influencing the policies in the countries that would soon follow Greece into crisis and shaping the future of these institutions.

The decision to include the IMF in the response to the euro crisis is an example of an entrenched and growing phenomenon in international relations: contemporary global problems are now the focus of *sets* of overlapping and intersecting institutions that have been created at the multilateral, regional, and bilateral levels. An increasing number of regional and plurilateral institutions—in East Asia and Latin America and among large emerging market countries—share official international finance with the IMF. This pattern is replicated in a number of other important issue areas. If ever there were a time when we might have understood the global politics of trade, finance, security, development, or human rights by examining a single global institution, that day has long passed. These clusters of institutions provide multiple venues through which states can cooperate. However, they have also become fiendishly complex. Gaps and overlaps among the institutions in these clusters generate a confounding set of political and institutional problems.

The benefits and pitfalls of using multiple institutions to address problems of international cooperation are exemplified by the European sovereign debt crisis of 2010–15. This crisis presents the most important and sustained episode of cooperation between the IMF and a set of regional institutions and a leading episode of cooperation between global and regional institutions generally. Other regional financial arrangements are either still small by comparison with the European institutions or, when large, as in the case of the facilities in East Asia, have not been activated. Europe is the one region where the IMF and regional institutions have worked closely together. If we wish to understand the interactions among institutions in international crisis finance, and how they might interact in the future around the globe, the European debt crisis is the indispensible case.

This book is about the institutions that were deployed to fight the euro crisis, re-establish financial stability, and prevent contagion beyond Europe. It explains the institutional strategy that Europeans adopted to negotiate and administer financial rescue programs for the countries that were stricken by the crisis. It addresses, among other elements of these arrangements, why European leaders chose to include the IMF, not just in the program for Greece in 2010 but for the string of other euro-area countries that were subsequently ensnared by crisis. Providing a detailed account of the decisions of the "troika"—as the IMF, European Commission, and ECB are called—the book places its work in the context of the broader setting of institutions and politics of key member states. The book examines the cluster of overlapping and intersecting institutions (which we call a "complex"), the behavior of the institutions within it, and the strategies of member states in directing them to work together. It also explains why the rest of the world, including the United States, acceded to the deployment of the IMF in the euro crisis.

The book derives lessons for understanding the role of the IMF in Europe, the development of European institutions as regional integration evolves in the coming decades, and the functioning of complex clusters of international institutions generally. It speaks to analysts who wish to discern the impact of institutional overlap and competition on global governance, as well as those who are curious about the impact of global institutions on regional integration. The book addresses the crisis from the perspective of international political economy and international relations, while also seeking to engage economists who are interested in international institutions, practitioners of crisis management, and the broader discourse on the organization of crisis finance and global governance.

DEBATE OVER CRISIS RESPONSE

Virtually nobody is happy with the fashion in which the euro crisis has been prosecuted or with the economic outcomes. The crisis threatened the expulsion of some member countries from the euro area—continuing to do so in the case of Greece—and even brought the viability of the monetary union itself into question. The European economy suffered greatly in the process and its firms and workers continue to be stressed. The pain was most severe in the particular crisis countries, where output fell spectacularly and unemployment rose to extraordinary levels, but was certainly not confined to them.

While most of those countries turned the corner and resumed growth by 2014, Greece descended into yet another crisis in 2015 and growth within the euro area as a whole remained unsatisfactory. Not until the first quarter of 2016 did the euro area return to its level of GDP of the early months of 2008, prior to the global financial crisis. Because growth was uneven, a considerable share of the euro area still remained well below the earlier peak. Economic stagnation was compounded by inflation that was very low and even slipped into deflation briefly during winter 2014–15, far *below* the objective of the European Central Bank (ECB). Although Europe managed to limit the sovereign debt crisis to Greece after 2013, the growth, employment, and banking problems of the monetary union linger.

Some of this economic pain could not have been avoided. The liquidity bubble of the mid-2000s had boosted incomes in the countries of southern Europe and Ireland well above levels that could have been sustained over the long term. Capital flows from the countries of the north to those of the south coincided with deterioration in competitiveness, emergence of large current account deficits, and accumulation of both private and public debt. A fall in income and a period of wrenching adjustment for many sectors was going to be necessary under any realistic scenario after the bubble burst.

Nonetheless, much of the economic pain endured by Europe was indeed avoidable and it is there—the size of the losses, how they might have been avoided, and how the unavoidable losses should have been distributed—where the normative battle among economists is joined.

The European strategy to address the crisis had two major prongs, one for the euro area as a whole and the other for the individual countries that were stricken by financial turmoil. For the euro area as a whole, member states further institutionalized fiscal discipline, constructed a permanent mechanism for providing financial assistance, and bolstered the integration of the banking system—coupled with progressive experimentation with unconventional monetary easing on the part of the ECB. For stricken countries, the creditor governments prescribed fiscal austerity, structural reform, and restructuring of the financial sector in exchange for very large loans from the European institutions and the IMF. Rather than force private creditors to write off the debt of these countries, European authorities lent to allow governments in crisis to repay, shifting the exposure onto the creditor governments. (Only in the case of Greece in 2012 were private creditors forced to write down their claims on the government; but this is getting ahead of the story.) If normal growth and funding conditions were restored—a big "if"—the borrowers would greatly reduce or eliminate their deficits, pay off their loans, and reaccess the private financial markets for whatever continuing financing they might require.

There is a roiling debate over the economic merits of this strategy at both the level of the euro area as a whole and the particular country programs. The debate centers on the (a) origin of the crisis in fiscal profligacy or the banking system, (b) sustainability of debt, (c) wisdom of fiscal austerity, (d) growth potential unleashed by structural reforms, and (e) need for exchange rate adjustment (that is, the viability of membership in the monetary union), among other fundamental matters. But, the choice of the economic response was in very large measure conditioned by the institutional and political arrangements within Europe's monetary union, the views on which can be summarized in two schools of thought, the critics and the defenders.

Policymakers and analysts in the United States, Britain, and many other non-European countries are sharp in their criticism of European governance, which is shared by many Europeans as well. The European Council and Eurogroup responded in what seemed to be a glacially slow fashion, when crisis demanded a rapid one. Some decisions undermined confidence, such as the infamous declaration of German Chancellor Angela Merkel and French President Nicolas Sarkozy that private investors would be required to write down their claims on any government that received official financial assistance. The European Central Bank adopted nonstandard monetary policy measures very cautiously and even raised interest rates briefly in the middle of the crisis. Indeed, European governments and institutions sometimes sought to exploit the crisis to extract concessions from one another.[2] The euro area should have instead addressed the crisis as did the United States, these critics argue with immediate lender-of-last-resort assistance, reduction of interest rates to the zero lower bound, quantitative easing on a large scale, recapitalization of the banks, and a fiscal stimulus.[3]

Defenders of the strategy that was pursued by the European Council and Eurogroup highlight the limits imposed by the political fragmentation of the monetary union among member states. Seeking domestic ratification and democratic consent through national legislatures entailed delay and uncertainty in responding to the crisis that was unavoidable. Under the constitutional structure of decision-making in the monetary union, they suggest, we must be realistic about what European governance can deliver and its performance

---

[2] C. Randall Henning, "The ECB as a Strategic Actor: Central Banking in a Politically Fragmented Monetary Union," in *The Political and Economic Dynamics of the Eurozone Crisis*, eds James A. Caporaso and Martin Rhodes (Oxford: Oxford University Press, 2016), pp. 167–99.

[3] See, for example, Martin Wolf, *The Shifts and the Shocks: What We've Learned—and Have Still to Learn—from the Financial Crisis* (New York: Penguin Press, 2014); Timothy Geithner, *Stress Test: Reflections on Financial Crises* (New York: Broadway Books, 2015); Mark Blyth, *Austerity: The History of a Dangerous Idea* (Oxford: Oxford University Press, 2013). Jean Pisani-Ferry, *The Euro Crisis and Its Aftermath* (Oxford: Oxford University Press, 2014) provides a more nuanced critique. See, also, Peter A. Hall, "Varieties of Capitalism and the Euro Crisis," *West European Politics* 37 (2014), no. (6): 1213–43.

during 2010–15 was as good as should be expected. Because fiscal resources are not mutualized within the euro area, the dominance of national politics in deciding the response to crisis must be accepted, even if those politics are narrowly inward-looking. This defense in effect suggests that the critics have made a "category mistake" of the first order: the euro area is decidedly *not* a *political* union and we cannot expect it to behave like one in a crisis.

Some defenders, notably northern Europeans, add that a swift, effective response to the euro crisis that matched the U.S. government's response to the subprime crisis would have been *undesirable* because it would have undercut incentives for reform of economic policy and institutions in the southern tier. Monetary union had papered over differences in labor markets, structural policies, and competitiveness between the north and south, deep-seated cleavages that were embedded in the institutional features of these economies. By offering leverage for reform in the south, they argue, the crisis was a once-in-a-generation opportunity to establish solid foundations for a stable monetary union. These defenders were loath to spoil the opportunity by riding to the rescue too early.[4] If a more sustainable monetary union could not be forged through reform in the crisis, according to extreme arguments, perhaps the euro was not worth saving in its original form.

My own assessment is that the economies of the monetary union deserved a far more rapid and robust response than the governments and institutions of the euro area delivered. It is certainly true that fiscal deficits must be limited and national economic institutions must be reformed in crisis countries; policy conditionality is a legitimate quid pro quo for financial assistance. I acknowledge the Herculean efforts of many European officials to resolve the crisis, through a seemingly continuous series of frustrating meetings to secure agreements on crisis packages and reforms to the architecture of the euro area. I also accept the danger of moral hazard on the part of both borrowers and lenders in the euro area.

However, the middle of a crisis was not the right time to suddenly prioritize the fight against moral hazard. Stabilizing the economy was a prerequisite for enduring reform. Austerity was not balanced by expansion elsewhere in the euro area. Using the crisis as a tactic to extract reforms from other governments and institutions, as some actors did, was not a viable substitute for the mechanisms that were missing from the euro's architecture. Nor were volatile financial markets, financial fragmentation, recession, and high unemployment ever conceivably likely to yield a stable political foundation on which to complete the institutional architecture in the longer term—quite the opposite.

The monetary union requires not just discipline but also greater solidarity among the members as represented by the projects for "banking union" and

---

[4] Hans-Werner Sinn, *The Euro Trap: On Bursting Bubbles, Budgets, and Beliefs* (Oxford: Oxford University Press, 2015), takes this approach, for example.

"fiscal union." These require in turn greater political integration by strengthening the institutions for democratic consent and accountability. Ultimately, the economic success of the euro area depends on finding a better economic balance among the members, wherein Germany and other creditor countries use the space available to them to sustain economic growth. Adjustment must become more symmetrical across the euro area.

There is indeed a good deal of "category confusion" surrounding the debate over the institutional response. But non-Europeans should be forgiven for this confusion. The *original* category mistake was to create a common currency that required a degree of political integration approaching that of a unified state but endowing it only with *intergovernmental* decision-making on matters of financial assistance. Having solemnly committed to the monetary union, euro-area leaders should accept the logical consequences in terms of providing mutual support in a crisis and the activism of the European Central Bank. Refusing to do so would be worse than never having embarked on the euro project to begin with.

We reviewed this debate over the response to the crisis to place it in perspective as the *backdrop* to the analysis conducted in this book. This book does not provide an original assessment of the economic merits or deficiencies of austerity, structural reform, or debt relief. The principal focus of this study is instead the *interaction among the institutions* and between them and the key *member states*. The economic issues of the euro area are important here because they serve as the substantive terrain over which the member states and financial institutions wrestled when grappling with individual country programs. While this brief review takes a position in the debate, however, the institutional analysis here does not depend on the normative economic orientation of the author. Readers on different sides of the debates over the prosecution of the euro crisis—"austerians" and Keynesians, reform pessimists and optimists, broad and narrow central bankers—will, I hope, be open to this study's conclusions.

TANGLED BY DESIGN?

By joining the financial rescue for Greece in 2010, the IMF entered the debate over the design of crisis programs and inserted itself into the strategic intrigue among European institutions that predated the euro crisis. The IMF designed a rescue program for Greece with the European Commission and the ECB—an institutional mix that was replicated in short order, though not without controversy, for a series of other euro-area countries. These programs joined the expertise and financial contributions of the global community with those of the European institutions. At the same time, however, the introduction of the IMF made the institutional web of euro-area governance even more tangled.

The three institutions that supported the country rescue programs, which came to be known as the "troika," have mandates and objectives that, while partly shared, diverge on important matters. They differ in terms of the amount of financing they can offer, time horizon over which they can lend, tolerance for ambiguity on sustainability of debt, and control over levers that assure repayment, to name a few considerations in program design. The troika institutions have distinct memberships, missions, and capabilities and they negotiated among themselves as they bargained with the governments that borrowed from them. The ECB has responsibility for the euro area, the Commission for the European Union as a whole, and the IMF for financial stability among its nearly universal membership.

This complex bargaining arrangement generated multiple conflicts of incentives and significant conflicts of interest. First, the membership and governance structure of the IMF decidedly favored the European and U.S. governments.[5] But, while the United States holds the largest single share of votes, the European representatives to the executive board are numerous and weightier if they vote as a bloc. Their influence raised concerns on the part of the rest of the membership that the Fund not be "hijacked" for euro-area contingencies.

Second, these arrangements gave rise to potentially conflicted loyalties on the part of the managers of these institutions. Two managing directors of the IMF during the crisis, Dominique Strauss-Kahn and Christine Lagarde, were French nationals with deep prior experience in European integration and were enthusiastically promoted for the presidencies of France and European Commission, respectively. Similar concerns could be raised about the other senior management positions within this cluster of institutions. The problem is endemic to global governance but took an especially vivid form in mid-2010.

Third, while the troika defined the size and conditionality of loans to a crisis-stricken country, one of its members, the ECB, could simultaneously provide liquidity to that country's banking system and buy its government's bonds. The ECB's operations were formally autonomous from the program, but the program's success hinged greatly on the central bank's actions.

This is surely not a system of cooperation in which autonomous institutions negotiated at arm's length according to separate, clearly defined mandates that were developed by distinct sets of member states. The system is comprised of institutions that were created independently for different, unconnected reasons, and were later forced to work together by circumstances that had not been foreseen at the time of their creation. The interactions among

---

[5] Arvind Subramanian and Devesh Kapur, for example, chide the institution for being a "Euro-Atlantic Fund." See "The G-20 and IMF Reform," *Business Standard*, April 1, 2009.

institutions were not understood or were anticipated only vaguely as they were designed. "Build first, reconcile later" could have been the motto of the architects. Nobody proposed decades ago that the system we have now be created by design.

Yet, through the European Council, the national governments of the euro area insisted on this particular institutional mix and the key member states of the IMF accepted it. Under their watchful guidance—an important observation—this complex institutional arrangement negotiated the rescue programs for the crisis countries that included macroeconomic and structural reform notwithstanding these interinstitutional differences. Why member states would downplay or dismiss such conflicts is an important puzzle, the answer to which is critical to understanding how the troika works and the international politics of institutions and complexity more broadly.

The ability of these institutions to work together reasonably effectively much of the time sometimes fed a complacent view of ad hoc arrangements among them. Despite the overlap and differentiated mandates, conflicts among institutions could supposedly be "worked out" informally by reasonable international officials under the guidance of some key finance ministers. No formal mechanisms for interinstitutional cooperation were thought to be needed in advance.[6] In fact, some might argue that the more numerous the institutions that service the area of crisis finance, the greater the number of avenues for solving a particular country's problem. Institutional redundancy could help to avoid deadlock that might arise through institutional monopoly.

Unfortunately, however, the succession of troika programs for Greece, the toughest case among the countries that succumbed to the euro crisis, amounted to a "train wreck" in slow motion. When European leaders finally called upon the IMF in spring 2010, the troika negotiations with the Greek government produced an agreement that went off track within a matter of months. Many of the non-European members of the IMF saw the Fund management as too willing to compromise with the Commission and ECB, arguing that if the IMF managing director and his lieutenants had stuck to their guns, the terms of the loan and the policy adjustments required of the Greek government would have been more realistic and sustainable. Proponents of the first loan to Greece argued that it was critical in order to avoid contagion to the rest of the euro area and indeed the international financial system.

As is now well known, Greece underwent a debt restructuring in 2012 in which private holders of government bonds wrote down their claims by more than fifty percent. But this came after the IMF and euro-area governments disbursed funds that redeemed privately held bonds, replacing private

---

[6] Michael L. Mussa, Economic Counsellor and Director of Research at the IMF during 1991–2001, among other positions, held this view, expressed to the author, through the global financial crisis, for example.

creditors with official credits, thereby shifting risk onto taxpayers and reducing the amount of debt subject to restructuring. Far from ring-fencing Greece
from the rest of the euro area, as this strategy was designed to do, the Greek
program permitted, and the overall crisis strategy of the Eurogroup even
unwittingly contributed to, contagion. The Greek program of 2010 was thus
abandoned and replaced by a second program. The IMF's participation in the
Greek program—regarded by many within the institution as its greatest mistake
since the program for Argentina in 2001–2, notwithstanding key differences—
became the focus of extensive post-mortem evaluation.[7] The second program
was replaced by a third in 2015, by which time the IMF openly argued that
Greece's debt was not sustainable and insisted that European creditors provide
relief beyond the very favorable interest rates and long-term maturities that
they had already extended. The Greek case, the most challenging of the crisis
countries, laid bare the conflicts over the program and the costs of leaving the
institutions to "work it out" in the teeth of crises.

On whose shoulders should the responsibility for these failures fall? My
answer is that, ultimately, neither complexity nor the individual institutions
were the cause of the failures in these programs. Despite the very visible
interinstitutional conflicts in the Greek and subsequent cases, this book will
show, the substantive quality of the response hinged on the preferences and
strategy of the creditor countries in, and the governance of, the monetary
union. Ultimately, the member states of the euro area bear the greatest share of
responsibility for both the failures and successes of governance during the
crisis.[8] Acting through the Council, the Eurogroup, and their financial facilities, the decisions of member states collectively set the timing and financing
envelope within which the crisis could be addressed. Governments' decisions
on design, delegation, and resourcing of the institutions established the landscape for interinstitutional cooperation. Effective action on the part of the
institutions was hostage to the decisions of the member states—creditor and
debtor governments alike—that stood behind them.

In his 2014 book, *The System Worked*,[9] Daniel Drezner sought to correct a
misperception that he attributed to the public and elites that global governance was ineffective during the global financial crisis and its aftermath.

[7] IMF, "Greece: Ex Post Evaluation of Exceptional Access under the 2010 Stand-By Arrangement," IMF Country Report No. 13/156. Washington, D.C.: International Monetary Fund,
2013. See, also, Charles Wyplosz and Silvia Sgherri, "The IMF's Role in Greece in the Context
of the 2010 Stand-By Arrangement," *IEO Background Paper* (BP/16-02/11), Washington, D.C.,
July 8, 2016.
[8] Carlo Bastasin, *Saving Europe: How National Politics Nearly Destroyed the Euro* (Washington, D.C.: Brookings Institution Press, 2012), provides an extended criticism of the parochialism
of national leaders during the crisis.
[9] Daniel Drezner, *The System Worked: How the World Stopped Another Great Depression*
(New York: Oxford University Press, 2014).

Enumerating the accomplishments, Drezner argued that the panoply of international organizations and consultative forums was successful in restoring financial stability and growth and that this success hinged principally on two factors. "First, the United States was still able to exercise effective leadership." Second, although the crisis weakened the European Union and Japan, traditional supporters of international organizations, China, perhaps surprisingly, supported the rules of global economic governance.[10] In contrast to the posture of the United States and United Kingdom during the 1930s—per Charles Kindleberger's famous observation that the absence of hegemony undermined international economic cooperation—there was not a Great Depression in 2008 because the United States and China were willing and able to act and fundamentally agreed on what needed to be done.[11]

Drezner's concept of global governance[12] addresses mainly institutions with broad or universal membership and the conclaves of influential states that back them. Regional institutions have an awkward place in this conception— as they do in many of the treatments of "global" governance elsewhere. Another view worries that, while open regionalism might help underpin a liberal world economy, institutional proliferation fundamentally threatens to fragment governance, spawn forum shopping, and undermine its legitimacy and effectiveness.[13] Drezner's account gives little attention to the interaction between the global and regional institutions—the primary focus of this book and the key to understanding crisis cooperation in the future.

The economic outcomes in Europe, in particular, contrast with Drezner's description of economic success at the global level. My account portrays European policymaking as not at all efficient: many euro-area leaders instead appeared to behave like the Keystone cops of international finance for two and a half years after the onset of the euro crisis. The IMF and the rest of the world helped to fill the gaps in the European architecture until the Europeans themselves might some day do so. Euro-area member states have established a new fiscal regime, common financial facilities, and a banking supervisor,

---

[10] See, separately, Miles Kahler, "Rising Powers and Global Governance: Negotiating Change in a Resilient Status Quo," *International Affairs* 89 (2013): 711–29. He finds that the three largest emerging economies show little sign of mounting "radical challenges to the status quo in global governance."

[11] Drezner, *The System Worked*, pp. 181–3. But see, also, Eric Helleiner, *The Status Quo Crisis: Global Financial Governance After the 2008 Meltdown* (Oxford/New York: Oxford University Press, 2014), which challenges the common view that the G20 was influential in avoiding another Great Depression.

[12] "The 'system' refers to the global economy and the rules of the game that govern it." "Worked" apparently means "good enough at supplying the necessary policies and public goods." Drezner, *The System Worked*, pp. 19 and 15, respectively.

[13] In keeping with Drezner's earlier arguments. See "The Power and Peril of International Regime Complexity," *Perspectives on Politics* 7 (2009): 65–70, which, emphasizing the pitfalls of institutional overlap, cogently argues that complexity is likely to favor the great powers.

while the ECB has eased monetary policy more aggressively. But, important as they are, reforms to date fall short of a completion of the monetary union. In the meantime, domestic political resistance to the next round of reforms that are needed to stabilize the euro area over the long term has strengthened.[14] While the acute phase of the crisis dissipated by late 2013, Greece suffered a relapse in 2015 and the euro area's fundamental economic problems persist. If the "system works" in the next crisis the way it "worked" in Europe during 2010–13, the euro area as we know it could be doomed.

The institutional arrangements examined in this book have been profoundly consequential. Through them, euro-area member states organized the crisis response. The states called upon the institutions to administer programs of macroeconomic and structural reform that affected millions of people, the fate of governments, and the stability of the international financial system. These arrangements affected whose interests were best served, or least harmed, in the crisis response. They determined the quality and effectiveness of international financial cooperation, financial stability, and therefore the economic fortunes of a large swath of the global economy. Institutional patterns affected accountability; they cloaked the actions of some officials and cast the spotlight on the work of others. They affected the evolution of global economic and financial governance.

PUZZLES AND QUESTIONS

The euro crisis presents a number of puzzles or paradoxes for international cooperation, global financial governance, and scholarship in these areas. I group them here into four large questions.

The first, as highlighted in the introduction to this chapter, examines the *choice of the institutional mix* for the financial rescues of the countries of the euro area that were struck by crises during 2010–15. Why did European governments choose this particular institutional form, the troika? Why, despite possessing robust financial resources and technical expertise, did they reject a Europe-only solution and opt instead to include the IMF in the crisis programs? The puzzle is compounded by the development of the European financial facilities over the course of the crisis, after which the governments of the euro area *continued* to include the IMF in the rescues.

The second question addresses the *strategies of key states* in their selection of the institutions for fighting the crises. The chapters that follow consider the

---

[14] See, among others, Matthias Matthijs and Mark Blyth, eds, *The Future of the Euro* (Oxford: Oxford University Press, 2014); Caporaso and Rhodes, *The Political and Economic Dynamics of the Eurozone Crisis*.

question from the standpoint of the European creditors, mainly Germany, and the non-European states, mainly the United States. As the leader of a coalition of creditor states within the euro area, Germany insisted on involving the IMF in one way or another in all of the crisis programs. Why did Germany, the most powerful country in the monetary union, wish to involve an actor that was external to European integration? Why, moreover, did Berlin insist on this choice in the face of sharp substantive conflict with the IMF over some of the critical elements of the rescues?

The involvement of the IMF depended on the consent of the official global community, and a number of non-European officials opposed its use in this way. The support of the United States was critical for the deployment of the Fund for the euro-crisis programs, yet the use of the Fund created financial exposure for all its members, European and non-European alike. Why did the United States permit the use of the IMF despite this exposure—particularly when that exposure threatened political support for the Fund domestically as well as among other advanced and emerging-market countries?

Relatedly, why did the United States and the IMF support with enthusiasm the deepening of European integration and the completion of the architecture of the monetary union? An adherent to realist theory would have expected the United States to oppose the consolidation of the euro area out of fear of currency competition and balance-of-payments constraints. A bureaucratic politics approach would expect the IMF to oppose it on grounds of institutional competition and fear of being closed out of the "business" of crisis finance in an important region. Yet, these two actors consistently advocated fiscal mutualization, banking union, and a robust role for the ECB as part of a sustainable euro-area architecture.

The third question explores the *simultaneous cooperation and competition* among the institutions. The institutional arrangements for these crisis programs appear to many outside observers to be perpetually teetering on the brink of collapse. Conflicts among the members of the troika are well publicized and sometimes very sharp; a number of European officials are on record advocating the expulsion of the IMF. Interinstitutional conflict has fueled predictions of the demise of the troika. But these predictions, like reports of Mark Twain's death, have proven to be "exaggerated," and are likely to remain so for the foreseeable future. Why does substantive conflict not lead to abandonment of the use of the IMF and disintegration of the troika? How can some institutions stand in opposition on critical substantive matters yet nonetheless cooperate on lending programs?

The final set of questions addresses the *normative debate* over development of the European institutional architecture in the future and in particular whether the euro area should create a full-fledged "European Monetary Fund" as a regional alternative to the IMF. Governments of the euro area created new financial facilities over the course of the crisis and deepened institutional capacities for providing financial assistance to members. Many European officials, while accepting the involvement of the IMF during the 2010–15 crises, see the troika as a "one-crisis-only" solution and wish to consolidate new capabilities into an institution that could provide assistance "within the family" in the next crisis, whenever that might be. Others remain deeply skeptical of breaking with the IMF and wary of grand schemes for further political integration that this would entail. We examine the design of interinstitutional cooperation in light of this debate.

This book investigates these questions by conducting a series of case studies of the rescue programs within a structured narrative of the euro crisis. It draws upon, and aims to contribute to, the concepts of an international regime complex and regime complexity. Ultimately, I argue European governments' choice to include the IMF in the rescues inheres in enduring features of the euro area that weakened their faith in European institutions to do the job. By selecting multiple institutions rather than a single institution, creditor states in the euro area could better control the terms and conditions of country programs. Non-European countries, among which the United States remains the most influential, prioritized protection against international financial contagion when acceding to the use of the IMF in this way. Overlapping institutions were bound to create serious complications and inefficiencies in the design and monitoring of programs. But key creditor countries were in a position to arbitrate interinstitutional deadlock, and arbitration presented them with opportunities to restrain institutions from "drifting" beyond their preferences. The regime complex was thus, effectively, tangled by design, and this finding provides insight into several aspects of the crisis that otherwise seem paradoxical. The following chapter previews the main arguments more fully, after developing the theoretical framework.

ORGANIZATION OF THE BOOK

The book organizes the presentation and analysis of the program cases as follows. The next chapter introduces the concepts of regime complexity and locates the book's arguments among some of the leading approaches to the study of international institutions, global governance, and European integration. Chapter 2 also lays out the design of this study. Chapter 3 introduces in more detail the main institutional players in the regime complex: the European Council and Eurogroup, European Commission, ECB, and IMF. It reviews these institutions' membership, governance, rules, and procedures, and highlights the strategic predicaments that confronted each of them as the basis for understanding their distinctive approaches to the crisis. Chapter 4 provides a capsule overview of the economic and financial developments in the euro area over the course of the crisis and the overall response of the governments and European institutions.

The subsequent chapters present the cases of the country programs, embedded in the broader narrative of the crisis, beginning with Greece in 2010. Chapter 5 examines the choice of the political leaders of the euro area to mobilize the troika for that program in the context of the alternative combinations of institutions that they rejected. Chapters 6 and 7 follow the work of the troika as the euro crisis spread to Ireland, Portugal, and the other countries of the southern "periphery."

While Chapters 5, 6, and 7 give substantial attention to the role of Germany and other European creditors in influencing the choice of the institutional mix and Europe's deliberations more broadly, Chapter 8 addresses the United States, its role in the euro crisis, and the role of the IMF in its strategy. Although other non-European countries were more publicly critical of the euro area's strategy during the crisis, the United States was the principal member with which European governments had to deal in order to tap the Fund. U.S. influence over European decision-making was enhanced by its position within the institution.

Chapter 9 addresses the evolution of the institutions of the euro area for crisis finance, the creation of the European Stability Mechanism (ESM) in particular. It also reviews the criticisms of the troika and the alternative proposals for reforming these institutional arrangements now that the ESM is in place. Chapter 10 delves into the debate over debt restructuring by returning the focus to the case of Greece, whose crisis was the most intractable of the program countries. The chapter traces the progress of the Greek crisis through the second program in 2012, during which debt was restructured, as well as of the negotiations surrounding the program for Cyprus in 2013. Chapter 11 examines the tumultuous negotiations that led to the third Greek program in 2015 and the dispute over restructuring official claims on that country through the first review in spring 2016. During these negotiations, Greece was threatened with ejection from the monetary union, "Grexit" as it came to be called. The conclusion, Chapter 12, draws lessons for the analysis of regime complexes and reform of the institutional arrangements for crisis finance in Europe.

skinny love to be [illegible] . better
I told you to be kind

2

Regime Complexity and Main Argument

International regime complexity provides a framework that is useful for analyzing the questions that are addressed in this study. This chapter discusses the origins and development of the regime complexity approach and locates the arguments developed in this book relative to it and other approaches to the study of international organizations and global governance. It reviews the key principles and concepts of the approach, as well as some of its shortcomings, and shows how analysis of regime complexity in international finance can contribute to the regime-complexity research program. We then consider the design of this study and preview the main arguments.

REGIME COMPLEXES AND COMPLEXITY

Scholars of international political economy observe that global governance is becoming more fragmented and debate the consequences and remedies. A growing body of research over the last two decades examines clusters of nested and overlapping institutions—labeled "regime complexes"—rather than simply individual institutions. Whether the involvement of regime complexes improves or degrades substantive outcomes, compared to outcomes under a single global multilateral institution, and the conditions under which multiple institutions cooperate or compete are central questions in this research program.

Genesis and Scope

fragmentation threatens effective int'l cooperation

The first wave of scholarship tended to lament fragmentation as a threat to the effectiveness of international cooperation. Institutional interference in the form of overlaps in substantive jurisdictions, inconsistency of rules and obligations, and forum shopping, among other factors, were expected to weaken the discipline of global governance on member states. These themes

stuff that weaken global governance

were developed in studies devoted to areas particularly prone to fragmentation, such as international trade, development, human rights, and global environmental regulation.[1]

A second wave of studies, on the other hand, counsels against despair over the fragmentation of regime complexes. In their work on the complex for climate change, Robert O. Keohane and David Victor argue that the issue area is itself a collection of different problems with different functional forms and the interests of major states are heterogeneous.[2] In this context, efforts to create a unified climate regime are likely to be wasted. The fragmented regime complex that has emerged has distinct advantages over a unified institutional arrangement, namely adaptability and flexibility, Keohane and Victor maintain. Climate change activists would best channel their energy toward building coherence, substantive validity, and fairness, among other normative criteria, into the existing complex.[3]

Previous scholarly work on regime complexity and institutional interaction gives little if any attention to international finance. This is in part because finance has been a relatively integrated complex, owing to the historical dominance of the IMF in the issue area. Like the World Trade Organization (WTO) in trade policy, the IMF has a near-universal membership and the obligations that states accept as members provide a context in which other regimes have evolved in finance.

But scholarship on regime complexity and institutional interaction should not neglect international finance, for at least two reasons. First, studying the regime complex for finance, which is more integrated than the complex for global environmental issues, for example, is useful in comparative analysis of complexes. It introduces, and can thus help to explain, variation in the degree of separation across complexes in different issue areas. Second, whereas much of the scholarship on complexity examines fragmented complexes out of a desire to integrate them, finance offers a case of a relatively integrated complex that is becoming more fragmented and progressively less hierarchical over time. How and why this happens should interest scholars who advocate integration in complexes in other issue areas.

[1] Vinod Aggarwal, ed., *Institutional Designs for a Complex World: Bargaining, Linkages, and Nesting* (Ithaca, NY: Cornell University Press, 1998); Kal Raustialia and David Victor, "The Regime Complex for Plant Genetic Resources," *International Organization* 58 (2004) (2): 277–310; and Karen Alter and Sophie Meunier, "The Politics of International Regime Complexity," *Perspectives on Politics* 7 (2009) (1): 13–24. See, also, Frank Biermann, Philipp Pattberg, Harro van Asselt, and Fariborz Zelli, "The Fragmentation of Global Governance Architectures: A Framework for Analysis," *Global Environmental Politics* 9 (2009) (4): 14–40.
[2] Robert O. Keohane and David Victor, "The Regime Complex for Climate Change," *Perspectives on Politics* 9 (2011) (1): 7–23.
[3] See, also, Robert O. Keohane, Jeff D. Colgan, and Thijs Van de Graaf, "Punctuated Equilibrium in the Energy Regime Complex," *Review of International Organizations* 7 (2012) (2): 117–43.

The field of international finance hosts a robust normative debate over the threat to the effectiveness of crisis response posed by regional financial arrangements, which parallels the debate in political science over the danger posed by complexity in global governance generally. Some economists who advocate international cooperation, such as Edwin M. Truman and Morris Goldstein, worry that the proliferation of regional institutions undercuts the role and authority of the IMF.[4] Critics of the IMF, on the other hand, cheer the development of alternative sources of crisis finance in order to put the Fund in its place, redress the bias they see in its governance, and circumvent deadlock that might arise from, for example, a refusal by the United States to approve quota increases and reform.

The creation of multiple institutions per se is neither good nor bad for fighting crises effectively; it depends on how and whether these institutions work together. With a number of others, I have argued that institutional proliferation, principally in the form of regional and plurilateral financial facilities, must be accepted as a fact of life. The IMF, dominant in international crisis finance through the 1990s, cooperated with European institutions during the euro crisis and will have to cooperate with other regional institutions in the future.[5] Ideally, we would design interinstitutional cooperation into new institutions as they are created and establish protocols for their cooperation. This book highlights, however, the objections that states are likely to have to that course of action.

Scholarship on regime complexity provides a useful conceptual framework in which to locate analysis of institutional interaction in the euro crisis. It can point us toward testable propositions and can usefully frame the European and international discourse on institutional choice and design. But, while expanding, scholarship on regime complexity is nonetheless incomplete. Much of the literature abstracts from prior decisions by states to cooperate

---

[4] Edwin M. Truman, "The G-20 and International Financial Institutions Governance," *Peterson Institute for International Economics Working Paper* 10–13 (Washington, D.C.: September 2010); Morris Goldstein, "The Role of the IMF in a Reformed International Monetary System," paper for the conference on "The Future of the International Financial System," Bank of Korea, Seoul, May 26–27, 2011.

[5] C. Randall Henning, *East Asian Financial Cooperation*, Policy Analyses in International Economics, No. 68 (Washington, D.C.: Peterson Institute for International Economics, 2002); Henning, "Regional Arrangements and the International Monetary Fund," in *Reforming the IMF for the 21st Century*, Edwin M. Truman, ed. (Washington, D.C: Institute for International Economics, 2006), pp. 171–84; Ulrich Volz, "The Need and Scope for Strengthening Cooperation between Regional Financial Arrangements and the IMF," Deutsches Institut für Entwicklungspolitick Discussion Paper 15/2012 (Bonn: December 2012); Masahiro Kawai and Domenico Lombardi, "Financial Regionalism," *Finance & Development*, September, 2012, pp. 23–5; Toshiyuki Miyoshi et al., "Stocktaking the Fund's Engagement with Regional Financing Arrangements," Washington, D.C.: International Monetary Fund, April 11, 2013; and Changyong Rhee, Lea Sumulong, and Shahin Vallé, "Global and Regional Financial Safety Nets: Lessons from Europe and Asia," *Bruegel Working Paper* 2013/06 (Brussels, November 2013).

and create new institutions, as well as from the broader context of power, private interests, and ideas.[6] We must concede that parts of the research program remain somewhat proto-theoretical. This literature, and the effort to develop a more comprehensive theory of regime complexity in particular, would benefit from (a) common acceptance of basic concepts and definitions, (b) better understanding of what animates institutions, and (c) better understanding of the connections between the institutions and their environments, the mechanisms of informal governance being particularly important. This book's examination of the euro crisis sharpens our understanding of complexity, helps to fill some of these gaps, and proposes new directions for study.

Concepts and Definitions

This book defines a *regime complex* as *a set of international institutions that operate in a common issue area and the informal mechanisms that coordinate them.* The institutions can be legally constituted organizations at the bilateral, plurilateral, regional, or global levels, as well as less formal arrangements. *Fragmentation* occurs when the mechanisms that coordinate different institutions break down. A complex with numerous institutions can be cohesive if coordination is effective. Several institutions can operate in a given area yet not fragment the complex, so long as formal protocols and informal mechanisms sustain and promote cooperation. Conversely, a complex with even just a few institutions could be severely fragmented if these are not coordinated and consequently work at cross purposes.

This definition is both broader and narrower than some other formulations in the field. It is broader in that a complex is not fragmented by definition.[7]

[6] For similar assessments, see Tana Johnson and Johannes Urpelainen, "A Strategic Theory of Regime Integration and Separation," *International Organization* 66 (2012) (no. 4), p. 650; Alexander Ovodenko and Robert O. Keohane, "Institutional Diffusion in International Environmental Affairs," *International Affairs* 88 (2012) (no. 3), pp. 538–40 in particular. Mark Copelovitch and Tonya Putnam, "Design in Context: Existing International Agreements and New Cooperation," *International Organization* 68 (2014): 471–93, is one of a couple of exceptions. Kenneth W. Abbott, Jessica F. Green, and Robert O. Keohane, "Organizational Ecology and Institutional Change in Global Governance," *International Organization* 70 (2016) (no. 2): 247–77, while promising, focuses mainly on configurations of institutions at the systemic level.
[7] This contrasts with Keohane and Victor, "The Regime Complex for Climate Change": "regime complexes are marked by connections between…specific and relatively narrow regimes but the absence of an overall architecture or hierarchy that structures the whole set." For discussion, see John Ruggie, "Global Governance and 'New Governance Theory': Lessons from Business and Human Rights," *Global Governance* 20 (2014): 5–17; Thijs van de Graaf and Ferdi de Ville, "Regime Complexes and Interplay Management," in *Insights from Global Environmental Governance*, eds Jean Frédéric Morin and Amandine Orsini, a special issue of *International Studies Review* 15 (2013) (4): 562–89.

We wish to compare complexes and their ability to generate substantive cooperation among states, substate and private actors, and non-governmental organizations. As conceived here, fragmentation and cohesion is one dimension along which complexes can vary. Our definition is also broader than some others in that a complex may include formal and informal agreements, club groups, and regularized processes.

What falls outside this definition of a complex? This definition stops short of including member states, their ministries, and financial resources, because we want to examine the relationship between state preferences on the one hand and conflict and cooperation within the complex on the other. Nor does the complex as defined include economic beliefs, economic ideology, and analytical frameworks within which adjustment programs are designed. Private actors, such as banks, institutional investors and hedge funds, and capital markets similarly fall outside this definition of a complex. Financial firms and markets are critical to shaping the preferences of states, "capturing" them in some cases, and they can constrain the response of complexes to crises. But, conceptually, they are separate from the institutions.

States and Institutions

brings to life

Our discussion of the euro crisis helps to fill the second gap—what animates institutions—by grounding the actions of institutions in the preferences of member states, key creditor states being the most important. As collective principals, key states compromise with one another in their management of institutions and confront problems in controlling them jointly. Institutions thus exhibit "agency drift," a tendency to deviate from the preferences of member-state principals. But the preferences of key creditors are a fundamental point of departure in understanding their behavior and this study emphasizes this point. Member preferences provide the causal "juice" that animates the institutions, endows them with state and social purpose.

By contrast, a broad swath of the literature on international organizations emphasizes the autonomy of these institutions and their secretariats. Among recent contributions, Johnson,[8] Jinnah,[9] and Abbott, Genschel, Snidal, and Zangl[10] each examine the independent agency of institutional staffs and secretariats, including through the sponsorship of new institutions and non-governmental organizations as a strategy to escape constraints otherwise

---

[8] Tana Johnson, *Organizational Progeny: Why Governments are Losing Control over the Proliferating Structures of Global Governance* (Oxford: Oxford University Press, 2014).

[9] Sikina Jinnah, *Post-Treaty Politics: Secretariat Influence in Global Environmental Governance* (Cambridge, MA: MIT Press, 2014).

[10] Kenneth W. Abbott, Philipp Genschel, Duncan Snidal, and Bernhard Zangl, eds, *International Organizations as Orchestrators* (Cambridge: Cambridge University Press, 2015).

imposed by states. Johnson's subtitle captures a main theme: "Why Governments are Losing Control over the Proliferating Structures of Global Governance." The incubation of new institutions and their use as instruments by other institutions pose an intriguing set of questions, with some resonance in the euro crisis, and extends the work on regime complexity. But the argument advanced in the present book ultimately adopts a different view, one that emphasizes the centrality of states as members in and orchestrators of the institutions.

The substantive responsibilities of institutions and regime complexes stretch across a spectrum on which the main dimension is political priority for member states. At one end, the issues are core priorities that bear on the character of the state and its capacity to govern effectively on matters that are salient in domestic politics. At the other end, issues have relatively low salience. We might believe that issues such as human rights, poverty alleviation, environmental regulation, and climate change should have higher priority; but, regrettably, they might not actually rank highly. Studies emphasizing bureaucratic autonomy often, though not always, address institutions that operate in the low-salience half of the spectrum; the present study makes a foray into the upper half.

This analysis of international institutional interaction and the resolution of the crisis is largely "state-centric." By this phrase I do not mean that the state is the *only* significant actor, dominating markets, private interests, and society in the explanation. Banks and financial markets, for example, played central roles in the euro crisis and influenced the response; social groups resisted austerity. Power and ideas, central causal factors in international relations generally, also played important roles. By "state-centric," I mean that all or most of the main causal factors behind the institutional solutions to the financial crises are best funneled, analytically, through nation states.

This is for two primary reasons. First, vested with the authorities to tax citizens and issue government debt, nation states are the ultimate sources of financial resources with which crises are addressed. The allocation of these resources among competing uses, including capitalization of international financial institutions, is a primary function of states. High on the hierarchy of issues, fiscal matters are jealously guarded and not casually delegated to institutions. Agent autonomy tends to be higher when the stakes are lower.

Second, states are the constitutive members of international financial institutions and the euro-area financial facilities. In other issue contexts, such as development, humanitarian assistance, and the environment, the state might guard its prerogatives less closely. But many of the institutions considered here—the IMF, Eurogroup, and European Stability Mechanism, for example—are creatures of states and official representatives sit in the governing bodies. Differentiating these institutions from some of the others under study in the research program on international organization, these factors make the centrality of the state an inescapable feature of international crisis finance.

This does not mean that bureaucratic autonomy is negligible for the institutions examined here; quite the contrary. Some of the European institutions, such as the European Commission and ECB, are not directly constituted by states, they are supranational.[11] And even those institutions that are constituted intergovernmentally "drift" from time to time away from the preferences of their dominant members. This study devotes considerable attention to the approaches of the secretariats of these institutions and the tension with state preferences. That tension in turn substantially configured the strategies that states pursued with respect to the institutions.

In the end, states choose the institutions that were harnessed to the task of crisis finance, contract with them to negotiate on their behalf, endow them with resources, and, in the case of key states, retain influence or outright control over the disbursement of funds through them. While secretariats retain some room for maneuver, key states ultimately orchestrate the institutions in this issue area, not vice versa. In this issue area, new institutions do not tend to emanate from other institutions or autonomous bureaucrats either, but are rather the creatures of member states and potential competitors of peer institutions. These findings do not necessarily contradict previous studies emphasizing bureaucratic autonomy, but they do suggest that autonomy varies substantially across issue areas.

This approach also has much in common with Andrew Moravcsik's.[12] His liberal theory of international relations privileges the preferences of states and the distribution of those preferences across the system in the analysis of international conflict and cooperation. State preference determination is analytically prior to analysis of institutionalized cooperation. Once we pin down state preferences, according to his method, we can then examine the negotiation of interstate agreements and the delegation of monitoring and enforcement to an international body.

One benefit to this approach, shared with the principal-agent literature, is that it grounds international institutions to the purposes of states: they are not bureaucracies that float freely in their issue space, simply competing for "territorial" advantage and resource allocation with other institutions. These institutions are anchored by the objectives of their members, states, and are

---

[11] For a recent review of supranational and state-centric approaches to European integration, see James A. Caporaso and Min-hyung Kim, "'States Choose but not under Circumstances of Their Own Making': A New Interpretation of the Integration Debate in Light of the European Financial Crisis," in Caporaso and Rhodes, eds, *Political and Economic Dynamics of the Eurozone Crisis*.

[12] Andrew Moravcsik, "Taking Preferences Seriously: A Liberal Theory of International Politics," *International Organization* 51 (1997): 512–53; "The New Liberalism," in *Oxford Handbook of International Relations*, eds Christian Reus-Smit and Duncan Snidal (Oxford/New York: Oxford University Press, 2008), pp. 234–54.

delegated tasks and authorities in order to advance them. One downside to the liberal approach is that multiple layers of analysis are complicated; it requires a good deal of information to "run" this model. But the explanatory benefits are worth the complications and the book embraces this trade-off.

State Strategy

What is especially interesting—under-studied, but illuminated by the case studies presented here—is how institutions relate to state strategy. How do states strategize the choice of institutions for a particular contingency? How do states calculate the benefits of creating new institutions relative to working with existing ones? What effect do decisions on the institutional mix have on outcomes? Do states correctly anticipate the outcomes when making these institutional choices?

We should expect states to create new institutions when they are not satisfied with their existing institutional choices, provided the problem at hand rises above the cost threshold. When existing institutions clash with state preferences, states will be motivated to create new institutions to countervail them. States under certain circumstances pit some institutions against others to advance their goals. The proliferation of institutions yields regime complexity, by definition. To preview the argument developed more fully later on in this book, complexity is a mechanism by which states *control* their institutions—*a strategy to limit agency drift.*

This is a far cry from the conception of institutional proliferation as a strategy to eke out a greater measure of insulation for secretariats from the constraints and control of states. And it is different from, though not necessarily inconsistent with, Keohane's original conception of institutions as solutions to dilemmas of collective action.[13] There are several different ways to solve such dilemmas and some solutions serve the interests of some actors better than others. In the euro crisis, northern, triple-A-rated European countries and their banks preferred institutional solutions that were very different from those sought by borrowing countries and their key stakeholders in the southern tier. States promote some institutions over others to advance their interests while simultaneously solving the cooperation problem.

In their study of international trade, Jupille, Mattli, and Snidal (2013) provide an interesting framework for examining choices to use institutions, reform them, or to create new ones.[14] By emphasizing bounded rationality in state

---

[13] Robert O. Keohane, *After Hegemony: Cooperation and Discord in the World Political Economy* (Princeton, NJ: Princeton University Press, 1984).

[14] Joseph Jupille, Walter Mattli, and Duncan Snidal, *Institutional Choice and Global Commerce* (Cambridge: Cambridge University Press, 2013).

decisions on institutions, they locate their theory midway along a continuum between rational design and historical institutionalism. Lack of information and analytic uncertainty (bounded rationality) impart a strong preference for using existing institutions before considering more ambitious alternatives. This remains true, they find, even when the functional form of the cooperation problem and power relationships among member states change.

The approach taken in the present study shares both Jupille, Mattli, and Snidal's placement of the state at the center of the analysis of institutional choice, as mentioned earlier, and bounded rationality. It also accepts their insight that the use of a particular institution over the course of the crisis generates lessons about the fit with the imperatives of member governments, lessons that could generate momentum for institutional innovation.

This study differs from theirs, however, in at least one important respect. Jupille, Mattli, and Snidal borrow a decision tree from the rational approach in which states proceed through a sequence of decisions. States first each decide whether or not to cooperate; then, assuming cooperation is chosen, they decide whether or not to use institutions.[15] My approach does not see the two options in the second decision to be mutually exclusive: states can choose to cooperate both within and around institutions *simultaneously*. This possibility becomes particularly important in the presence of multiple institutions and regime complexity—where, this book argues, states coordinate the work of institutions *in*formally to overcome deadlocks that arise among them and steer outcomes in their favor. These back channels are vital to navigating tangled governance successfully.

Informalism and Coordination

Examination of the formal interaction among the institutions and the relationship among their rules and obligations is therefore not sufficient for understanding the operation of a regime complex. Our review of the euro crisis shows that institutional interaction must be understood in light of the *informal* influence and bargains. Randall Stone has developed a theory of institutions in which informal governance is balanced with formal rules.[16] The United States, he argues, exercises strong informal influence within the IMF and other organizations because its "outside options" (the unilateral or plurilateral alternatives outside the Fund) are substantial. Small member states

---

[15] Jupille, Mattli, and Snidal, *Institutional Choice*, Figures 2.1 and 2.2, pp. 20 and 29, respectively.

[16] Randall Stone, *Controlling Institutions: International Organizations and the Global Economy* (Cambridge: Cambridge University Press, 2011); "Informal Governance in International Organizations: Introduction to the Special Issue," *Review of International Organization* 8 (2013): 121–36.

generally do not have access to satisfactory outside options. By facilitating temporary or limited departure from explicit rules, informal arrangements keep large states working within the institution.

Mareike Kleine advances an approach that she calls "liberal regime theory" and contrasts it with Stone's, which she labels "power-based institutionalism." The "liberal insight," she writes, is "that for international institutions to be effective, they constantly have to be re-embedded in the interests and values of the member states' societies."[17] Kleine's theory emphasizes the disruption of formal rules and institutions that arises from domestic political problems with implementation and compliance, "political uncertainty." To reconcile regime rules with domestic political imperatives of governments, an informal norm arises whereby the group will defer to individual governments that lack domestic support for adherence. The norm imparts flexibility that avoids an outright breach of the formal rules or arrangements. However, because governments have an incentive to invoke the norm even when domestic politics might in fact be manageable, the system needs to have an actor to differentiate legitimate claims to invoke the escape norm from false claims and render a judgment. Such informalism, Kleine argues, is critical to understanding the politics of European integration from the inception of the European Community to the mid-1990s.

I argue here that informal mechanisms of influence are essential not simply to the operation of individual institutions but to understanding the resolution of conflict *among multiple institutions* and their substantive effectiveness. Interinstitutional cooperation depends on the cooperation of their key shareholders, states, behind the scenes. The argument advanced here shares some of the elements of the approaches of both Stone and Kleine, but differs from each of them in other respects.

With Stone, it emphasizes the importance of key central actors, with the German government being dominant in the case of the euro crisis. Berlin was central to decisions surrounding the choice of institutions in the financial rescues, including through informal, back-channel consultations about how the institutions would operate and how the formal rules would be applied in the crunch. Berlin also exercised outside options that were not available to the smaller member states. Informalism was important in German and U.S. influence over solutions to the euro crisis and the design of rescue programs.

The approach here shares Kleine's liberal approach in emphasizing the importance of domestic politics and institutions. These not only impart social purpose to institutions through states, as mentioned, but also explain why some states were more important than others in shaping the response to the euro crisis. Specifically, domestic political and institutional factors made

---

[17] Mareike Kleine, *Informal Governance in the European Union: How Governments Make International Organizations Work* (Ithaca, NY: Cornell University Press, 2013), p. 18.

Germany pivotal in decisions about which institutions would be included in the financial rescues and the substantive terms on which those rescues were mounted. Germany was also critical because it sat at the nexus of the institutions of the troika.

The type of informalism that helps us to understand the operation of the regime complex for crisis finance and the design of the rescue programs in the euro crisis is different from the types identified by other authors. Different forms of informalism can coexist. Informalism was certainly generated by political uncertainty over the course of the euro crisis; but severe political pressure was placed on the governments of most euro-area member states. The troika deliberately amplified rather than alleviated such pressures on borrowing countries and these pressures broke several of them. Nor did differences in the availability of outside options to large and small states provide impetus to informalism. Creditor states within the euro area were reasonably well aligned on the response to the crisis regardless of whether they were large or small. The informalism in which this study is primarily interested arose instead from conflicts *among* the institutions and—ultimately, as explained below—the need for member states to mediate them. The study adds this new type to the growing list of varieties of informal governance that have been classified by scholars.[18]

Cooperation and Conflict

Interinstitutional interaction during the euro crisis resonates with the scholarly work on regime complexity in another way. Tana Johnson and Johannes Urpelainen provide a testable causal theory of integration and separation of regimes within complexes.[19] States that are committed to cooperation choose between integrating and separating regimes in a given issue area. Their choice depends on the nature of the spillover between the different parts of the issue area, which can be positive or negative. When the spillover is *positive*—that is, when cooperation in one part advances outcomes in a separate part of the issue area—states will choose *not* to integrate the regimes. States can capture the full benefits of cooperation, and thus have incentive to invest, in the two parts separately. When spillover is *negative*—that is, when cooperation in one area, such as ozone depletion, undercuts outcomes in another, such as global warming—states will choose to integrate regimes, because they must do so to secure benefits. "[S]tates integrate not to exploit positive spillovers, but to mitigate negative spillovers," they conclude.

---

[18] Mareike Kleine, "Informal Governance in the European Union," *Journal of European Public Policy* (2013): 1–12; Thomas Christiansen and C. Neuhold, *International Handbook of Informal Governance* (Cheltenham: Edward Elgar, 2012).

[19] Johnson and Urpelainen, "A Strategic Theory of Regime Integration and Separation."

We can adapt the logic used by Johnson and Urpelainen's study to predict where institutions cooperate and where they compete. Regime integration is somewhat different from institutional cooperation, but we should expect negative and positive spillovers to have similar consequences for the willingness of member states to sponsor institutional cooperation or to countenance, or even promote, competition. International crisis finance contains areas of both negative and positive spillover, as discussed in the chapters that follow, and thus provides a test of this thesis. Specifically, where negative spillovers are present—that is, where institutional competition undercuts financial stability and imposes costs on creditor countries—we expect member states to promote, even insist upon, interinstitutional cooperation. Where positive spillovers are present, we expect to observe competition among institutions.

External Actors and European Integration

Analysis of regime complexity has natural connections to the study of regional integration and European integration in particular, but those connections are as yet underdeveloped. Studies of European integration have grappled with institutional overlap and complexity at the regional level for some time.[20] However, the European integration literature is generally not well integrated with global governance in general or regime complexity specifically.

In particular, theories of European integration do not incorporate external actors very well. Historians certainly appreciate the role of the United States in the early decades of the integration movement after the Second World War.[21] Peter Katzenstein derives the concept of "porous regions," including Europe, in which Germany served in a privileged position linking the region with the "American imperium."[22] "New regionalism" saw regional arrangements as

---

[20] See, for example, Henrik Enderlein, Sonja Wälti, and Michael Zürn, eds, *Handbook on Multi-level Governance* (Cheltenham /Northampton, MA: Edward Elgar, 2010); Simona Piattoni, *The Theory of Multi-level Governance: Conceptual, Empirical, and Normative Challenges* (Oxford: Oxford University Press, 2010); Sergio Fabbrini, *Which European Union? Europe after the Euro Crisis* (Cambridge: Cambridge University Press, 2015).

[21] Leading contributions include: Geir Lundestad, *The United States and Western Europe since 1945* (London/New York: Oxford University Press, 2005); John Gillingham and Francis Heller, eds, *The United States and the Integration of Europe: Legacies of the Postwar Era* (New York: Macmillan, 1996); Klaus Larres, "The United States and European Integration, 1945–1990," in *A Companion to Europe Since 1945* (Malden, MA/Oxford: Wiley-Blackwell, 2009), pp. 151–82; and Desmond Dinan, *Europe Recast: A History of the European Union* (London/New York: Palgrave Macmillan, 2004). Relevant economic histories include: Juan Carlos Martinez Oliva, "The EMU versus the EPU," *World Economics* 14 (April–June 2013): 127–43; Barry Eichengreen, *The European Economy Since 1945: Coordinated Capitalism and Beyond* (Princeton, NJ: Princeton University Press, 2007).

[22] Peter J. Katzenstein, *A World of Regions: Asia and Europe in the American Imperium* (Ithaca, NY: Cornell University Press, 2005).

shelter from hyper-globalization and elements of global governance.[23] I have argued that conflicts in the international monetary system substantially drove the process of European monetary integration during the fall of the Bretton Woods regime and for three decades afterward.[24]

These treatments of the role of non-European forces in regional integration tend to be issue-specific or otherwise under-theorized, however. The five chapters on theoretical perspectives in *The Oxford Handbook of the European Union* devote scant attention to external actors.[25] Yet, the IMF played a vitally important role in the stabilization of the euro area during the crises of 2010–15 and the politics of their resolution.[26] Scholarship on European integration would benefit from a theoretical approach that introduces external actors more systematically.

Regime complexity provides a rubric in which the influence of global institutions on regional integration can be examined, and vice versa. Generally, when shocks emanate from outside Europe, member states are likely to seek insulation by reinforcing regional institutions and integration. But when shocks emanate from within the region, European states are likely to look to global multilateral institutions, the United States, and other outside actors for assistance.[27] This is likely to be especially true when regional institutions are not up to the task of stabilization or do not reflect the preferences of key member states within the region.

DESIGN OF THE STUDY

The chapters that follow review the crisis within the euro area from late 2009 through the middle of 2015. During this period, five countries succumbed, secured financial assistance from the European partners and the IMF, and underwent severe economic adjustment. During the acute phase, 2010–13,

---

[23] Mario Telo, ed., *European Union and New Regionalism: Regional Actors and Global Governance in a Post-Hegemonic Era*, 2nd edn (Burlington, VT: Ashgate, 2007).

[24] C. Randall Henning, "Systemic Conflict and Regional Monetary Integration: The Case of Europe," *International Organization* 52 (no. 3, Summer 1998): 537–74; Henning, "Economic Crises and Regional Institutions," in *Integrating Regions: Asia in Comparative Context*, eds Miles Kahler and Andrew MacIntyre, pp. 170–92 (Stanford, CA: Stanford University Press, 2013).

[25] Erik Jones, Anand Menon, and Stephen Weatherill, eds, *The Oxford Handbook of the European Union* (Oxford: Oxford University Press, 2012). See, also, Alberta Sbragia, "Comparative Regionalism," *The JCMS Annual Review of the European Union in 2007*, eds Ulrich Sedelmeier and Alasdair R. Young (Oxford: Wiley-Blackwell, 2008). An exception is: Johannes Mutschick, "Theorising Regionalism and External Influence: A Situation-Structural Approach," *Mainz Papers on International and European Politics*, No. 2, 2012.

[26] A welcome, recent contribution along these lines is Dermot Hodson, "The IMF as a de Facto Institution of the EU: A Multiple Supervisor Approach," *Review of International Political Economy*, No. 3, Vol. 22, 2015.

[27] Henning, "Economic Crises and Regional Institutions."

the crisis migrated sequentially from one country to another. Beginning with Greece, whose program was agreed in May 2010, the crisis metastasized to Ireland in fall 2010, Portugal in spring 2011, Greece again in the second half of 2011, Spain in the first half of 2012, and then Cyprus in winter and spring 2013. Four of the five stricken countries completed their programs and reaccessed international capital markets. Greece—the one country that underwent a debt restructuring and failed to regain sustained access during the period under review—renegotiated its arrangement with the troika twice and accepted yet a third program in the summer of 2015.

The book thus provides a series of cases of country programs—seven in all—that are linked by a structured narrative of the crisis. The case studies are configured by the focus on the institutional questions—examining, for example, the decision by member states to include the IMF in the institutional response to the crisis. The cases also examine the interaction between the Fund and the European institutions, conflicts among them over financing and adjustment, and the preferences and policies of the member states served by them.[28] The case treatments trace the decisions on these matters with some care because that is necessary to address the counterfactual scenario.[29] Counterfactual reasoning involves uncertainty, but is ultimately inescapable in arriving at meaningful conclusions about, for example, the impact of the Fund—how the euro crisis might have progressed had the IMF been excluded from the rescue.

The book develops these cases and the structured narrative through empirical research that draws on multiple sources. These include primary documents and official statements, press and media reports, and other books on the euro crisis, many of which are excellent. The cases are based on a series of more than 200 interviews by the author with officials in national governments, central banks, and European and international institutions over the course of the crisis, some in real time, others retrospectively. The interviews were often conducted on a background basis, on the understanding that the information could be published but the source would not be named. In some cases, the terms of the interview do not allow for any identification of the source but the interview pointed me to specific documents and reports that could be cited instead. Information that was especially relevant to the argument presented here was corroborated by one or more additional sources. Background interviews helped to shape my interpretation of these documents, cross-check

---

[28] Case-study methods are addressed, among others, by Alexander L. George and Andrew Bennett, *Case Studies and Theory Development in the Social Sciences* (Cambridge, MA: Belfer Center for Science and International Affairs, 2005).

[29] Process-tracing methods are developed in Derek Beach and Rasmus B. Pedersen, *Process-Tracing Methods: Foundations and Guidelines* (Ann Arbor, MI: University of Michigan Press, 2013); Andrew Bennett and Jeffrey T. Checkel, eds, *Process Tracing: From Metaphor to Analytic Tool* (Cambridge: Cambridge University Press, 2015).

information gathered in other interviews, separate the "signal" from the "noise" in media reports, and inform my understanding of the case overall.

These program cases are not completely independent of one another. As members of the monetary union, the stricken countries shared some of the causes of the crisis and they shared a common set of institutions and European partners. Nonetheless, while related, each country case has some distinctive characteristics and can be treated as a separate instance of institutional inter-action. As such, these cases can be compared and exhibit instructive similarities and contrasts.

The cases differ with respect to the proximate source of vulnerability, relative financial contributions of the institutions, areas of substantive agree-ment and disagreement among them, relationship to the preferences of the leading creditor states, and relative influence of the institutions. Table 2.1 provides a capsule preview of the seven cases and some of their basic features. The case of Greece 2010 originated in the mismanagement of the government fiscal accounts and was sparked by revelations about the true size of the deficit, whereas most of the subsequent cases had their origins in the over-extension of the banking sector. The IMF contributed roughly one-third of the financing in the early cases but a much smaller proportion in the later programs. European institutions entered the crisis relatively unprepared, but greatly built their capacity for designing and monitoring programs and mobilizing financial resources between the first case and the last.

A plausible hypothesis might suggest, then, that the relative influence of the IMF would decline over time. Indeed, given the strife among the institutions of the troika, an outside observer might have expected European officials to reassert their original inclination during winter 2010 and eject the IMF entirely. The cases thus track the debate about the institutional mix and the design of each program—particularly with respect to the balance between fiscal austerity, "bailing-in" private creditors, and restructuring debt to official creditors. As we shall see, however, the cases do *not* confirm the expectation of diminishing influence, much less ejection, of the IMF. European creditors consistently opted to keep the IMF in the institutional mix and the Fund became more assertive over time on key parameters of the programs.

The cases also track the posture of some of the key member states of the euro area and the IMF. Among the members of the monetary union, the countries whose government credit was rated triple-A served as the financial anchor of the rescues. Germany was the most critical, although its importance, as we shall see, depended on the cohesion of the group of creditor countries in the northern tier. Among the creditor coalition, Berlin's posture is most closely followed in these case studies. The involvement of the IMF in the country programs also hinged on the posture of the large non-European members, the United States being pivotal. Washington's posture on the euro crisis and country programs is thus covered as well.

Table 2.1. Overview of Country Program Cases, 2010–2015

	Principal Causes	Loan Amount	Bail-In or Debt Restructuring	IMF Inclusion Contested	Institutional Mix	Program Success
Greece 2010	Fiscal and Structural	€110 billion	No	Yes	Troika	No
Ireland 2010	Banking	€62.5 billion	No	No	Troika	Yes
Portugal 2011	Structural and Fiscal	€78 billion	No	Yes	Troika	Yes
Greece 2012	Banking and Structural	€130 billion	Yes	Yes	Troika	No
Spain 2012	Banking	€100 billion	Limited	Yes, but agreement on limited role	Commission, ECB; IMF monitoring	Yes
Cyprus 2013	Banking	€10 billion	Yes	Yes	Troika, ESM	Yes
Greece 2015	Structural and Fiscal	€86 billion	TBD	Yes	Commission, ECB, ESM; IMF financing TBD	Unknown

Note: TBD = to be determined.
Source: Author's assessment.

The outcome of each country case is tracked in terms of the role that is assigned to the IMF, substantive agreement and disagreement with the European institutions, design and success of the program, and the overall relationship among the institutions. Matching the causes (independent variables) to these outcomes (dependent variables) across the cases, the analysis exploits the variation in outcomes to draw lessons about the (a) choice of the institutional mix, (b) consequences of the choice, and (c) explanations for the pattern of cooperation and competition that emerged among the institutions. These findings inform conclusions about the strategies of states in the presence of multiple, overlapping institutions, state control of institutions, interinstitutional conflict and coordination, and the design of the troika and its institutions in the future.

MAIN ARGUMENTS

This book argues, to begin with, that the institutional "incompleteness" of the monetary union led the euro area to involve the IMF in crisis programs—but incompleteness of a sort that differs from official rationales and conventional explanations. European leaders' rationales for involving the Fund in the programs for crisis countries emphasized the institution's economic and financial expertise, experience in program lending, financial resources, and political cover for austerity. As the crisis evolved, however, member states filled several of these gaps in the European architecture yet *still* chose to include the IMF in new programs. Fundamentally, the book concludes, the *divergence of preferences* among the euro-area member states and the making of decisions on financial assistance by *unanimity* drove Europe to the IMF. The unwillingness of creditor states to rely solely on the European Commission in this role, out of fear that it would not reflect their preferences in program design, stemmed in turn from these factors.

The choice of the troika as the institutional vehicle to address the sovereign debt and banking crises of the euro area was a collective decision by the governments of the euro area. But the choice was largely determined by the preferences of the coalition of northern creditors, foremost among which was Germany. Germany dominated the outcome not because it was the largest country in the euro area, but primarily because financial rescues required unanimous consent of the euro-area member states and German domestic institutions effectively required that these resources be transferred parsimoniously, with strict conditionality, and in conjunction with the ECB and IMF.

Creditor governments wanted the IMF to be part of the institutional mix because its involvement was critical to securing *domestic political support* for financial assistance to the crisis-stricken countries. Greece, Ireland, Portugal,

Spain, and Cyprus needed substantial adjustment of domestic policies and the Fund had a long-standing reputation for being tough in this respect. Inclusion of the Fund helped to cover governments' right flank in the domestic politics of several creditor countries, but its role was particularly important in Germany, where the governing coalition feared erosion of electoral support owing to the euro crisis. The configuration of domestic and European institutions—not primarily Berlin's financial clout—made Germany the pivotal country.

These cases also illustrate the institutional strategies of key states. Germany and other European creditors were well aware that the IMF would bring an approach and perspective that differed from the European Commission and ECB. If its approach had been more or less the same as those of the European institutions, the Fund would have added little value to the institutional mix from their standpoint. Conflicts among the institutions could easily be, and were, anticipated.

However—and this is an essential point—Germany held positions of influence within all of the institutions in the mix. With the other key states in Europe and the G7, the United States in particular, German authorities were well positioned to arbitrate deadlocks that arose among the members of the troika. Indeed, the mix *required* the intervention of these key creditors at several points to resolve conflicts and this in turn ensured that these states would retain substantial *control* over outcomes.

This book argues, in the language of the institutionalist literature, that *regime complexity is the consequence of a strategy of key states to manage agency drift.* By keeping the Fund in the institutional mix, Berlin prevented the European Commission from drifting outside the set of solutions that were acceptable in Germany. The regime complex was *tangled by design*, in effect, and this design served the northern creditor states well. The presence of multiple, overlapping institutions in the regime for crisis finance in Europe was their deliberate choice, not a given feature of the issue environment that they were compelled to accept.

The realization that complexity arises from state strategies to control agency drift helps to explain a number of puzzles associated with the euro crisis. First, it helps to explain why Germany would tolerate, indeed insist on including, an institution that advocated substantive positions to which it was sometimes opposed. Berlin was in the catbird seat: the IMF could expound at length on the need for debt restructuring, for example, but it was ultimately the German government along with other creditor governments that decided whether, when, and under what terms debt relief would be granted to Greece under the third program.

Second, this conceptualization helps to explain why the troika remains the preferred institutional form for crisis finance among euro-area member states despite conflict among the institutions. To many, such conflict was an indication that the troika was an unstable institutional arrangement, a harbinger of its decay. But interinstitutional conflict is a consequence of state strategy—in fact, it is integral to the use of one institution to check others. Without it, mediation by states would not be necessary and their control would be attenuated.

Finally, states' ability to control institutions relies on leaving cooperation among them incomplete at their formative stages, in advance of crisis episodes. Thorough, effective, ex ante cooperation among institutions would *dis*intermediate key states that are accustomed to holding sway within the institutions. States are not likely to commit resources and grant authority for interinstitutional cooperation that later weakens their influence in the crunch, ex post. Regime complexes are therefore likely to remain messy.

Chronic under-investment in ex ante cooperation among institutions in a complex places a premium on the informal mechanisms by which states coordinate them. This book observes that informal influence and back-channel mediation apply not only within organizations but also to cooperation among institutions within a complex. Given the differences in the formal mandates and the inadequacy of ex ante cooperation, deadlock among the institutions is likely when they are thrown together in a crisis. Because it usually involves brokering, cajoling, or strong-arming the staff and managing directors in ways that are not specified in the institutional charter, to put it mildly, mediation by influential member states is necessarily informal.

So far, we have discussed mainly the politics of the regime complex in Europe. What about the countries outside Europe? The use of the Fund in programs for the euro area countries also depended on the preferences and strategies of non-European countries, of which the United States remained the single most important. U.S. government officials sought to influence European decisions in the euro crisis at several points, especially during 2010–12. From their perspective, the IMF was one of several channels by which they could hope to bring stability to the euro area. Determined to prevent spillover from the crisis through financial markets, the U.S. Treasury endorsed the involvement of the IMF first in Greece and then most of the subsequent country programs. But, Treasury officials also wanted to ensure that Europe itself bore the lion's share of the cost of the rescues and did not want to let European governments "off the hook" by resorting to the Fund before European commitments of large-scale financing were secured.

As the troika evolved through the crisis, cooperation was increasingly mixed with competition. On economic analysis, surveillance and assessment of euro area institutional reforms, the institutions engaged in intense debate both in public and behind the scenes. How the institutions could cooperate in one realm while competing in the other is explained by the nature of the spillovers. Competition among the institutions in providing financial assistance could take the form of underfunding programs or relaxing the policy adjustments required of the borrowers—distinctly negative consequences. Competition in economic analysis and surveillance, by contrast, has positive consequences for member states.

The members of the euro area would do well to create the functional equivalent of a European Monetary Fund. They possess all of the expertise and financial resources necessary for a fully effective sovereign rescue fund. Such a fund could also provide the fiscal backstop for the banking union and should increasingly evolve in this direction over time. As a technical matter, European officials could then design, finance, and monitor financial rescue programs without the help of the IMF—contributing to the completion of the architecture of the monetary union while sparing both Europe and the IMF conflicts between the global and regional institutions. Such an outcome would be "win, win" for both Europe and the rest of the world.

The study finds, however, that the euro area's choice to deploy the IMF for these programs did not stem from a need for its technical expertise or financial resources, fundamentally. It follows that developing these capacities further would probably not be sufficient to eliminate reliance on the Fund in the "next crisis." Jettisoning the Fund from financial rescues in the euro area would require a convergence of preferences among euro area states and a decisive shift away from intergovernmentalism and decision-making by unanimity toward the Community method and majority voting. It would require, in other words, a quantum shift in the governance of the euro area toward a more cohesive political union. While this is not by any means impossible, the recent crisis has soured national electorates toward an "ever closer union." Even if accomplished eventually, therefore, this shift is not likely to arrive before the next financial crisis in the euro area.

The conclusions of this study carry lessons for several communities: scholars of regime complexity, contributors to the discourse on global governance, practitioners of international crisis finance, and stalwart proponents of European integration. With respect to scholarship on regime complexity and global governance, first, the book's argument about state strategy and the control of institutions is novel, a counterpoint to the notion that overlapping institutions restrict states' room for maneuver in international economic relations. Moreover, the study extends scholarship on complexity and institutional interaction to a new issue area, crisis finance, in the process strengthening the field's ability to compare complexes that are relatively cohesive to those that are fragmented. It brings the neglect of international finance by scholars interested in complexity to an end.

Second, the study bears on the discourse in Europe and the euro area over the construction of a more robust architecture for the monetary union, one that would be immune from sovereign debt crises. By identifying the underlying reasons that Europe has called upon the IMF, separating them from the stated rationales, this book serves as a warning to those who might exclude the Fund before the regional architecture is completed. At the same time, the study highlights the tensions within the IMF that are created by its participation in programs in the euro area.

Third, the study holds lessons for the broad international discourse on global economic governance and the relationship between global and regional institutions. This discourse needs a better conceptual toolkit by which to examine relationships among multiple institutions operating in the same issue area and the book, building on previous studies, supplements those tools. Moreover, the intimate connection between the shape of the regional architecture and the role of the global institutions that is emphasized here generalizes to regions beyond Europe.

Finally, this study highlights the importance of informal mechanisms in lubricating the institutional machinery of regime complexes. One important implication is that reforms of global governance must consider these mechanisms in tandem with changes in the formal structures of institutions. Consider, for example, the movement to accommodate emerging-market countries in global institutions. The convention under which the managing director of the IMF has always been a European, while anachronistic, greatly facilitated informal coordination between the Fund and the European institutions. Appointing a non-European to lead the Fund might strengthen the Fund's relationship with institutions in Asia, Africa, or Latin America, but new channels would have to be created in order to avoid the collapse of cooperation with European institutions.

We now turn to introducing in more detail the institutions that played central roles in formulating the financial rescue programs during the euro crisis.

3

Dramatis Institutiones

The regime complex for crisis finance in the euro area included the troika—the IMF, European Commission, and the ECB—but was larger than these three institutions alone. It also included the European Council, Council of the European Union, and Eurogroup. The member states of the euro area acted largely, though not exclusively, through the council system, which placed these bodies at the center of the mix of institutions that were brought to bear on the design and execution of the country programs.[1]

We now review the institutions of this drama as the prelude to examining in subsequent chapters the dilemmas that confronted them over the course of the crisis. This chapter presents some of the basic facts about the origins, membership, and organization of the institutions for readers who would benefit from a brief review. Each section then delves more deeply into their governance, rules, and principles to understand the capabilities of these institutions and the constraints upon them. Each institution faced a set of strategic challenges that shaped their approach to the negotiations over country programs.

The institutional landscape of the euro area was not by any means static; it evolved substantially over the course of the crisis. European states created new financial funds, notably the European Stability Mechanism (ESM) in 2012, and launched the Single Supervisory Mechanism (SSM) in 2014. The ECB, in which the SSM was located, also expanded its set of lending facilities progressively over the course of the crisis. This chapter describes that landscape as it lay at the outset of the crisis; we introduce the new institutions as they emerged later in the subsequent chapters.

EUROPEAN COUNCIL AND EUROGROUP

The member states express their positions and develop a common approach through the system of councils of the European Union. Comprised of heads of

---

[1] Member states, finance ministries, and other national agencies fall outside our definition of the complex. Their roles are reviewed in the case treatments of the chapters that follow.

government of the full EU membership, the European Council sits at the pinnacle of this system. "The European Council," to quote Uwe Puetter, "has emerged as the centre of political gravity of economic governance."[2] Decisions taken there—or sometimes deferred there for too long—shaped Europe's collective response to the crisis, determined the role of the IMF and European Commission, and set many of the parameters within which the ECB would make its decisions. Understanding the operation of the troika thus requires close attention to the European Council.

As keen observers of European integration know, however, the structure of the council system is somewhat intricate.[3] The European Council, which is chaired by a president who is elected by the members, is related to but distinct from the Council of the European Union, whose presidency rotates on a six-month basis among the member states. The Council for Economic and Financial Affairs (Ecofin Council, or simply Ecofin) is one of ten different substantive configurations in which the Council of the European Union meets. Ecofin is comprised of the ministers of economics and finance from all of the EU member states.

Since the introduction of the monetary union, these institutions have straddled the divide between those countries that have adopted the euro and those that have not. The Eurogroup convenes the finance ministers of the euro area alone, a subset of the Ecofin Council.[4] The two bodies usually meet back-to-back once each month, but were also convened separately and irregularly during the crisis. The president of the Eurogroup—Jean-Claude Juncker and

---

[2] Uwe Puetter, "Europe's Deliberative Intergovernmentalism: The Role of the Council and European Council in EU Economic Governance," *Journal of European Public Policy* 19 (2012) (no. 2): 161–78.

[3] An overview of work on the Council is provided by Jeffrey Lewis, "Council of Ministers and European Council," in *The Oxford Handbook of the European Union*, eds Erik Jones, Anand Menon, and Stephen Weatherill (Oxford: Oxford University Press, 2012), pp. 321–35. Contributions that are especially germane to institutional reform over the course of the euro crisis include, but are by no means limited to, Uwe Puetter, "Intervening From Outside: The Role of EU Finance Ministers in the Constitutional Politics," *Journal of European Public Policy* 14 (2007) (8): 1293–310; Puetter, *The European Council: New Intergovernmentalism and Institutional Change* (Oxford: Oxford University Press, 2014); Marion Salines, Gabriel Glöckler, and Zbigniew Truchlewski, "Existential Crisis, Incremental Response: The Eurozone's Dual Institutional Evolution 2007–2011," *Journal of European Public Policy* 19 (5) (2012): 665–81; Desmond Dinan, "Governance and Institutions: Impact of the Escalating Crisis," *Journal of Common Market Studies* 50 (2012): 85–98; Nicolas Jabko, "Which Economic Governance for the European Union?," *Swedish Institute for European Policy Studies, Report 2* (2011); Dermot Hodson, "The EU Economy: The Eurozone in 2010," *Journal of Common Market Studies* 49 (2011): 231–49; Matthias Matthijs and Mark Blyth, eds, *The Future of the Euro* (New York: Oxford University Press, 2014).

[4] See, for example, Uwe Puetter, *The Eurogroup: How a Secretive Circle of Finance Ministers Shape European Economic Governance*, European Policy Research Unit Series (Manchester: Manchester University Press, 2006).

then, after January 2013, Jeroen Dijsselbloem—has a particularly important and visible role in this structure.

Economic and Financial Committee (EFC) brings deputy ministers together with deputy central bank governors to analyze initiatives and prepare higher-level meetings. The EFC is chaired by a president and can meet in two different configurations, one with and the other without the deputies from national central banks. The euro-area member states alone, plus the Commission and the ECB without the national central banks meet in the Eurogroup Working Group (EWG)—the crucible in which the Eurogroup meetings were prepared during the crisis. The president of the EWG, attached to the secretariat of the Council of the EU in Brussels, is elected for two years.[5] Thomas Wieser, who currently serves in this position, is also president of the EFC.

Even this elaborate council edifice proved over the course of the euro crisis to have a missing piece: a forum uniquely for the heads of government of the euro area. The Euro summit was thus inaugurated in October 2008 and formalized with the Treaty on Stability, Coordination and Governance in 2012 (Article 12). It meets twice each year, at a minimum. But the Stability treaty falls outside the regular EU legal and institutional framework and these meetings are held on an intergovernmental basis. The European Council and Eurogroup had also originated outside the "Community method"—the regular legislative process prescribed by the treaty involving the initiative of the Commission and approval of the Council and the European Parliament—and were only subsequently inducted into the formal EU structure. Whether the euro-area summits follow a similar pattern remains to be seen.

Insofar as these councils are part of the EU institutional framework, their roles and rules are specified in the treaties. The decision rules, and in particular whether adoption requires unanimity or qualified majority, are the most important of these. A qualified majority is at least fifty-five percent of the weighted votes of the member states represented in the Council comprising at least sixty-five percent of the population of the EU.[6] But *unanimity* applies to council forums that operate in an intergovernmental mode.

Rules and Principles

The Maastricht treaty famously contained a "no-bailout clause," now codified as Article 125 of the TFEU. The clause is addressed to the Union as a whole

---

[5] "Council Decision of 26 April 2012 on a Revision of the Statutes of the Economic and Financial Committee," *Official Journal of the European Union*, L 121/22–24, 8 May 2012 (2012/245/EU).

[6] Treaty on the Functioning of the European Union (hereafter, TFEU), Article 238. A higher threshold of seventy-two percent of the weighted votes applies to questions on which the Council does not act on a recommendation from the Commission.

and thus all of its institutions, and was the first legal hurdle that the Council and European Commission confronted in the early months of the crisis. The clause had been an effort on the part of the likely creditors in the union, led again by Germany, to lash themselves to the mast—precommit to *not* providing a bailout in order to impose discipline on both them and their private lenders ex ante. It is worth quoting:

> The Union shall not be liable for or assume the commitments of central governments, regional, local or other public authorities, other bodies governed by public law, or public undertakings of any Member State, without prejudice to mutual financial guarantees for the joint execution of a specific project. A Member State shall not be liable for or assume the commitments of central governments, regional, local or other public authorities, other bodies governed by public law, or public undertakings of another Member State, without prejudice to mutual financial guarantees for the joint execution of a specific project.

But the credibility of this clause had been questioned even from the beginning, for three good reasons. First, when faced with the prospect of systemic disruption, these countries, like the international community generally, had consistently chosen to extend financing in prior decades rather than withhold it. Second, another article of the treaty provided specifically for financial assistance to a member that is "in difficulties or is seriously threatened with severe difficulties caused by natural disasters or exceptional occurrences beyond its control."[7] Third, all of the member states already participated in a multilateral facility to provide assistance to sovereigns in a crisis—the IMF—and the Maastricht treaty left their access to its lending arrangements intact. This was a glaring contradiction, as Pisani-Ferry points out.[8] Few analysts appreciated the contradiction at the time because most believed, wrongly, that balance-of-payments problems would not arise within the monetary union.[9] European policymakers were, nonetheless, compelled to design financial rescues in such a way as to avoid technical infringement of the clause.

Early in the Greek crisis, at the behest of the German government, the euro-area summit adopted the doctrine of ultima ratio. This doctrine was understood to mean that financial assistance would be given to a member state only as a last resort if necessary for the survival of the euro area. The threshold was set high in order to justify setting aside the no-bailout clause. The doctrine was not an affirmation that the euro area would play the role of a lender of last

---

[7] TFEU, Article 122, paragraph 2.

[8] Jean Pisani-Ferry, *The Euro Crisis and Its Aftermath*, p. 81.

[9] A leading exception was Jacques J. Polak, "The IMF and Its EMU Members," in *EMU and the International Monetary System*, eds Paul R. Masson, Thomas H. Krueger, and Bart G. Turtelboom (Washington, D.C.: International Monetary Fund, 1997), pp. 491–511. Jean Pisani-Ferry, André Sapir, and Guntram Wolff, "An Evaluation of IMF Surveillance of the Euro Area," *Bruegel Blueprint* 14 (Brussels, 2011) emphasizes the analytical mistake.

resort in the sense of Bagehot—quite the contrary. Euro-area financial assistance would come only after all other avenues became unworkable. The Euro
summit of March 25, 2010, defined the term simply as "meaning in particular
that market financing is insufficient." But, if official financing is not available
until after a sovereign loses market access, it is little use in calming markets.

Strategic Challenges

The European Council and Eurogroup confronted two principal strategic
challenges: Conflicting preferences over economic policy among the euro-
area member states and delegating sovereignty to European institutions.
Member states have had profound differences over macroeconomic policy
virtually since the beginning of European integration. These differences were
confronted during the convergence process leading to the creation of the euro
but were not by any means resolved. While the liquidity bubble of 2003–7
suppressed them temporarily, the global financial crisis brought them to the
fore once again. These differences posed serious obstacles to decisions on
adjustment and financing that were needed to fight the crisis effectively.

The member states struggled over how much authority to reserve for
themselves and to delegate to the European Union. The monetary union
had transferred sovereignty over monetary policy completely to the level of
the union, but ultimate authority on other economic policies remained
decentralized even while being subject to common rules as in the fiscal
arena. Members had delegated the minimum necessary to achieve common
goals. But that minimum was a judgment call that had been made under "fair
weather" conditions. The crisis demanded a new round of sovereignty pooling
and delegation to the European institutions in order to mobilize resources,
enforce rules, and stabilize the monetary union.

Rather than centralize further authority in European institutions, however,
member states preferred to create arrangements outside the Community
method. Most of the funds that were mobilized in the crisis would be chan-
neled through new facilities that were organized on an intergovernmental
basis. That choice was driven in large measure by dissatisfaction on the part of
some key member states with the role of the European Commission.

EUROPEAN COMMISSION

Created with the Treaty of Rome, the European Commission holds the right to
initiate EU legislation and enforces the EU treaties, directives, and regulations.
Its president leads twenty-eight commissioners, one chosen from each of the

member states. The Commission, as they are referred to collectively, is tasked with serving the interests of the European Union as a whole. It embodies the idea of supranationalism and is integral to the Community method. Institutionally, and by personal conviction of most of the commissioners, it is committed to advancing European integration. The Commission is both a technical and political body, habituated to navigating the political terrain among member states in an effort to gather coalitions to support integration initiatives.[10]

The Commission has a long history of engagement with member states across a broad range of the issues that related to the euro crisis: fiscal policy, banking, structural reform, labor market institutions, competition policy, financial assistance, and regional assistance. By contrast, it has no authority in monetary policy, which is the ECB's domain. At the time of the global financial crisis it had no authority to monitor internal imbalances within the monetary union, no financial instrument with which to rescue members of the euro area, and only historical experience with balance-of-payments lending programs. The Commission nevertheless knew more than its troika partners about the structural, fiscal, and political environment of program countries.

The Commission can be said to have one foot inside and one foot outside the monetary union. Its responsibility for economic surveillance and the analysis and enforcement of the fiscal rules place it inside the monetary union. But the ECB is the guardian of the euro, has independent responsibility for monetary policy, and now conducts supervision of systemically important banking institutions. Officials of the Commission attend meetings of the ECB Governing Council, Eurogroup, European Council, and so forth. But the role of the Commission within the euro area was negotiated de novo with each new project, such as reform of fiscal rules and banking union, as was the case with coordinated bilateral assistance to Greece in 2010.

The Commission remains a creature of the European Union in the first instance and, like other European institutions, awkwardly straddles the gap between the non-euro member states and euro area. Straddling became increasingly delicate over the course of the crisis as the members of the euro area sought to deepen the institutions of the monetary union—through tightening fiscal rules and creating the ESM and the banking union—but from which some non-euro countries such as the United Kingdom and Sweden opted out.

---

[10] A useful overview of the scholarly work on the institution is provided by Susanne K. Schmidt and Arndt Wonka, "European Commission," in *The Oxford Handbook of the European Union*, eds Jones, Menon, and Weatherill, pp. 336–49. James A. Caporaso and Martin Rhodes, eds, *Political and Economic Dynamics of the Eurozone Crisis* (Oxford: Oxford University Press, 2016) locate the Commission within the larger institutional edifice of the European Union.

The key officials within the Commission during the most acute phase of the financial crisis were President José Manuel Barroso and Vice President and Commissioner for Economic and Monetary Affairs and the Euro Olli Rehn. The College of Commissioners did not take a position on the euro-area programs as a group and largely deferred to these two officials on crisis measures. Exceptions tended to include Commissioner for Internal Market (DG Markt) Michel Barnier and Commissioner for Competition Joaquín Almunia, who preceded Olli Rehn as Commissioner for Economic and Financial Affairs. The Directorate-General for Economic and Financial Affairs (DG Ecfin) provided macroeconomic analysis while the Directorates-General under Barnier and Almunia contributed analysis of banking-sector restructuring and structural policies to the design of country financial rescues. Measured by employment and budget, the Commission is the largest of the bureaucracies in the regime complex. But its resources were dispersed across its many areas of responsibility and the Commission had to reallocate them toward DG Ecfin and DG Markt after the crisis struck.

Rules and Principles

Enforcement of the fiscal rules of the Stability and Growth Pact (SGP) falls to the Commission, which wields the Excessive Deficit Procedure (EDP).[11] Under the EDP, the Commission can cite a member for running deficits above the three percent limit that was originally specified in the Maastricht treaty and, with the concurrence of a qualified majority of the Council, impose sanctions. This rule had been criticized from the beginning as likely to be procyclical in its application. Faced with its first major test in 2003, it was notoriously vitiated by Germany, previously the champion of the SGP, plus France and Portugal—which effectively blocked action in the Council to impose sanctions. The SGP went through a series of reforms shortly thereafter, but these reforms did not equip the Commission with the data-gathering and surveillance capabilities needed to preempt transgressions. Nor did they repair the distrust between the Commission and key member states over enforcement of the fiscal rules that had arisen over the 2003 incident.[12]

During the euro crisis, member states renovated the fiscal rules yet again. They filled many of the holes in the pre-crisis regime, including by providing

---

[11] DG Ecfin posts a useful and succinct overview of these rules at <http://ec.europa.eu/economy_finance/economic_governance/sgp/index_en.htm>. The political economy of the SGP from inception through the global financial crisis is examined in Martin Heipertz and Amy Verdun, *Ruling Europe: The Politics of the Stability and Growth Pact* (Cambridge: Cambridge University Press, 2010).

[12] President of the Commission at the time, Romano Prodi, called the SGP "stupid" for its procyclical effects. "Farewell to the Stupidity Pact?," *Economist*, October 22, 2002.

for review of national budgets by the Commission and the Council prior to their adoption. The new regime also tightened the fiscal requirements for euro-area member states, a provision known as the "Fiscal Compact," but did so on an intergovernmental basis outside the Community method. The reforms thus layered a new set of rules on top of what had already become a convoluted body of obligations that were enforced variously by European institutions and national agencies.[13]

Suffice it to say, for the moment, that the latest round of reforms had two important effects on the approach to country crises on the part of the Commission. First, they strengthened the EDP by having the Commission's recommendation to sanction a member stand unless reversed by a qualified majority in the Council. Second, when designing rescue programs, the Commission took a keen interest in observance of the SGP and its three percent rule with respect to deficits in particular. At the same time, the Commission sought to soften the procyclical effect of the rule by using flexibility that had been introduced into the pact.[14]

The Commission also administers competition policy and regulates assistance to firms from member states, "state aids." Financial assistance to firms should not distort the competitive landscape and this includes member states' capital injections into private banks. Those limitations conflicted with stabilizing the financial system at several points during the crisis and the conflict had to be reconciled. The Directorate-General for Competition (DG Comp) issued guidelines on how such assistance could be given and reviewed the bank restructuring elements of country programs.[15]

Addressed to the Union as a whole, the no-bailout clause applies to the European Commission as it does to the Council. This clause limited the options available to the Commission in the early months of the crisis by, among other things, rendering euro-area member states ineligible for its Balance-of-Payments facility. The Commission would attempt to create a robust facility for the euro-area countries that was anchored in the Community method.

[13] These reforms are reviewed by, among others: Jean Pisani-Ferry, André Sapir, and Guntram B. Wolff, "The Messy Rebuilding of Europe," *Bruegel Policy Brief* 2012/01 (Brussels, March 2012); Marco Buti and Nicolas Carnot, "The EMU Debt Crisis: Early Lessons and Reforms," *Journal of Common Market Studies* 50 (2012) (6): 899–911; James D. Savage and Amy Verdun, "Strengthening the European Commission's Budgetary and Economic Surveillance Capacity since Greece and the Euro Area Crisis: A Study of Five Directorates-General," *Journal of European Public Policy* 23 (2016; 1): 101–18.

[14] This balancing act and the important role of Eurostat and its accounting conventions are described in Deborah Mabbett and Waltraud Schelkle, "Searching under the Lamp-Post: The Evolution of Fiscal Surveillance," in *The Political and Economic Dynamics of the Eurozone Crisis*, eds Caporaso and Rhodes.

[15] "State Aid Temporary Rules Established in Response to the Economic and Financial Crisis," <http://ec.europa.eu/competition/state_aid/legislation/temporary.html>.

In the event, that facility, the European Financial Stabilisation Mechanism (EFSM), while significant, was relatively small.

For member states that did not share the common currency, and thus qualified for the Balance-of-Payments facility, another very specific EU rule applied. Under the terms of the Balance-of-Payments facility, when such members seek international support they must "first consult the Commission and the other Member States" through the Economic and Financial Committee to "examine, among other things, the possibilities available" through the Community.[16] The Commissioner for Economic and Financial Affairs would carpet crisis-stricken finance ministers repeatedly for ignoring this obligation. But it is a procedural requirement to filter requests for IMF assistance through the European machinery that had practical consequences.

Strategic Challenges

The Commission was thus beset by several strategic challenges during the approach to the euro crisis. First, the Commission was engaged in a continuing struggle with the member states over their adherence to rules and protocols to which they had previously agreed. This was particularly true with respect to fiscal policy, as exemplified by conflict over the enforcement of the SGP, and structural reform. Second, the Commission fought a rearguard action against efforts by some member states to resolve matters of dispute through intergovernmental arrangements, outside the Community method. But when it lost that battle, it acted as the agent for intergovernmental arrangements in negotiating with borrowers over drawings on the euro-area financial facilities, for example. The Commission thus wore two "hats" in the crisis—one as agent for member states and the other as a European institution—and this arrangement gave rise to further complications. Finally, the Commission struggled to prevent a widening of the gap between the states that had adopted the euro and those that had not, this being a central long-term threat to the coherence of European Union.

EUROPEAN CENTRAL BANK

As the issuer of the euro, the ECB is the supranational institution for the monetary union per se. The Maastricht treaty laid down price stability as the ECB's primary objective and supporting the "general economic policies in

---

[16] Council Regulation 332/2002, *Official Journal of the European Communities*, February 22, 2002, L 53/1–3. At the time of the regulation, the facility was called "Medium-Term Financial Assistance."

the Union" and its objectives, such as "full employment" and "balanced economic growth," as a secondary objective. We should add, in light of the euro crisis, that preventing the collapse of the monetary union is a necessary prerequisite for achieving these objectives and an overriding institutional imperative.[17]

Technically, the ECB is the central bureaucracy that sits in Frankfurt at the center of the European System of Central Banks, which comprises all of the national central banks of the European Union. But the single monetary policy for the euro is administered by the ECB together with the national central banks of the countries that have adopted the euro—the Eurosystem. In deference to broad usage, this book will use the acronym "ECB" to refer to "Eurosystem." But when the distinction is important to the discussion, the two will be designated separately here.

The Executive Board, comprised of six members, sits atop the ECB and is chaired by its president. Monetary policy and other important decisions are made by them plus the governors of the national central banks in the Eurosystem; the body is collectively named the Governing Council. The president generally prefers to make decisions by consensus, but the formal decision rule is by simple majority of the members, and voting became increasingly common over the course of the euro crisis.

Rules and Principles

The most important principles of the ECB are its independence and mandate for price stability, both enshrined in the EU treaties.[18] The ECB's monetary policy framework guides its decision-making on interest rates and operations. Its mandate for price stability—which the Governing Council interprets to be below but close to two percent inflation as measured by the harmonized index of consumer prices (HICP) over the medium term—applies to the euro area as a whole irrespective of over- or under-shooting in individual member states.[19]

The prohibition on "monetary financing" comes next in the hierarchy of rules. This was also established in the Maastricht treaty, an effort on the part of stability-oriented countries to bolster the central bank against "fiscal

---

[17] The origins of the ECB are discussed in: Harold James, *Making the European Monetary Union* (Cambridge, MA: Harvard University Press, 2012), especially pp. 265–400 and appendices; Lorenzo Bini Smaghi, *Austerity: European Democracies against the Wall* (Brussels: CEPS, 2013); Tommaso Padoa-Schioppa, *The Euro and Its Central Bank: Getting United after the Union* (Cambridge, MA: MIT Press, 2004); Jakob de Haan, Sylvester C. W. Eijffinger, and Sandra Waller, *The European Central Bank: Credibility, Transparency, and Centralization* (Cambridge, MA: MIT Press, 2005).

[18] Articles 130 and 127, respectively, of the TFEU, and discussed at length in the previously cited literature on the ECB. See also, the ECB's website <http://www.ecb.europa.eu>.

[19] ECB, "The Definition of Price Stability," at <https://www.ecb.europa.eu/mopo/strategy/pricestab/html/index.en.html>.

dominance." Central bank financing of governments can be abused and lead to excessively expansionary monetary policy. To preempt this possibility, Article 123 of the treaties states:

> 1. Overdraft facilities or any other type of credit facility with the European Central Bank or with the central banks of the Member States (hereinafter referred to as "national central banks") in favour of Union institutions, bodies, offices or agencies, central governments, regional, local or other public authorities, other bodies governed by public law, or public undertakings of Member States shall be prohibited, as shall the purchase directly from them by the European Central Bank or national central banks of debt instruments.

> 2. Paragraph 1 shall not apply to publicly owned credit institutions which, in the context of the supply of reserves by central banks, shall be given the same treatment by national central banks and the European Central Bank as private credit institutions.

This provision was cited by the ECB numerous times over the course of the euro crisis when denying requests that it play a more active role in sovereign rescues. It was also cited by critics who argued conversely that the ECB played *too* active a role, serving as the basis for a challenge in German courts and the Court of Justice of the European Union (CJEU) to the creation of the facility that brought to an end the acute phase of the crisis.[20] ECB officials had to anticipate such challenges when designing programs and defining their participation in the troika.

In addition to those three rules, which inhered in the legal framework, the ECB acted within several other principles and constraints. The ECB places a high priority on the unitary character of its monetary union. The "singleness" of monetary policy is tightly connected to the integration of banking and financial markets in the euro area. Disintegration of these markets can break the transmission of central bank operations into monetary conditions in member states, effectively fragmenting monetary policy.

The ECB provides liquidity to banks, solvent banks to be precise, on good collateral. The central bank developed an elaborate set of rules that defined the eligibility of financial assets for refinancing in Eurosystem operations. As the credit ratings on these assets declined over the course of the crisis, however, the ECB eased these eligibility requirements and in some cases suspended them altogether.[21] When it came to country programs, on the

---

[20] German Federal Constitutional Court (GFCC), "Principal Proceedings ESM/ECB," press release 9/2014, Karlsruhe, Germany, 7 February 2014; Case C-62/14 *Gauweiler and Others* v. *Deutscher Bundestag* [2015] ECLI:EU:C:2015:400.

[21] ECB, *The Implementation of Monetary Policy in the Euro Area* (Frankfurt: ECB, February 2011). This document has been updated by ECB, "Guideline on the Implementation of the Eurosystem Monetary Policy Framework," Frankfurt, December 19, 2014 (ECB/2014/60), available at <https://www.ecb.europa.eu/ecb/legal/pdf/oj_jol_2015_091_r_0002_en_txt.pdf>.

other hand, the ECB ruled that governments had to be judged in compliance with program conditionality in order for their bonds to be eligible for refinancing operations—a decision that represented solidarity with the other institutions in the troika.

When banks lost access to ECB financing, they could nonetheless look to their national central banks for Emergency Liquidity Assistance (ELA). Any losses suffered by the national central bank on ELA operations would be covered by it and ultimately the national government; such losses would not be sustained by the Eurosystem. Nonetheless, the Governing Council monitored ELA closely and set ceilings on issuance by, for example, the Central Bank of Ireland and Bank of Greece.

At the outset of the crisis, the ECB relied on the national regulators to supervise and enforce prudential standards on private banks. National regulators made the initial determination as to whether a bank was solvent and thus eligible for ELA. In November 2014, the ECB became the supervisor of the systemically important banks in Europe—about 130 institutions with eighty-five percent of bank assets in the euro area—with authority to take on supervision of smaller banks at its discretion. The ECB staff thus expanded substantially as it took on this responsibility and its enlarged role in banking supervision affects its place in the division of labor among the institutions in the late phases of the crisis.

Strategic Challenges

Among the world's central banks, the ECB confronted a particularly complex set of political and institutional challenges. Its currency area was fragmented politically like no other among seventeen member states, each of which retained ultimate sovereignty over fiscal policy. The connection between the fiscal plight of the sovereign and the soundness of its banks ultimately fragmented the euro area financially. Financial fragmentation in turn threatened not only economic growth but also the ability of the ECB to manage monetary conditions in the currency union. Under the legal provisions of the European treaties, the ECB is more independent than its peers. But no governor of the Federal Reserve would want to trade places with their counterpart on the ECB's Executive Board.

Since the early debates over the design of the monetary union, central bankers have been concerned about being effectively hamstrung by the policies of member governments and financial conditions in the euro area. They have been concerned in particular that these conditions would compel the ECB to run more expansionary monetary policy than warranted by its primary objective of price stability—notwithstanding their formal insulation from any instructions or coercion on the part of governments. The ECB feared, in other words, fiscal dominance. The specter of fiscal dominance was made more severe by the political decentralization of the euro area—no person or body could effectively cut a deal coordinating fiscal adjustments for a shift in monetary policy.[22]

As a consequence of the political fragmentation of the euro area, the ECB accepted the role of a true lender of last resort more reticently and partially than the Federal Reserve. It took great pains to distinguish between providing liquidity to banks on the one hand and financing sovereign governments on the other, even though these were tightly linked and the linkage tightened as the crisis progressed. When the ECB acceded to *indirect* financing of sovereigns, it conditioned its operations on economic adjustment and euro-area governments' collectively committing fiscal resources to stabilization.

From the beginning to the end of the euro crisis, the ECB was thus engaged in strategic interaction with the governments of the euro area. The central bank sought to ride the crisis to extract meaningful measures from governments. Governments for their part naturally attempted to do the same thing, hoping to extract more accommodative monetary policy from the ECB and permissive liquidity provision for crisis countries. Both sides would have been better off with coordination ex ante; but that was not possible owing to the political fragmentation of the euro area and to the divergence of preferences among creditors and debtors. The result was a high-stakes standoff that a number of analysts have compared to a game of "Chicken," in which each side hoped to use the crisis to force the opponent to concede.[23]

INTERNATIONAL MONETARY FUND

The IMF, founded at the Bretton Woods conference of July 1944, predates the European institutions. Its membership, about 180 countries at the time of the

---

[22] The structure of the interaction between monetary and fiscal authorities was famously modeled by Thomas J. Sargent and Neil Wallace, "Some Unpleasant Monetarist Arithmetic," *Federal Reserve Bank of Minneapolis Quarterly Review*, vol. 5, no. 3 (Fall): 1–18. They described two situations subsequently labeled "fiscal dominance" and "monetary dominance." For an overview of the academic discussion of the fiscal threat to the euro prior to the monetary union, see, among others, Michael Artis and Bernhard Winkler, "The Stability Pact: Safeguarding the Credibility of the European Central Bank," *National Institute Economic Review* 163: 87–98.

[23] Willem Buiter, "Games of Chicken between the Monetary and Fiscal Authority: Who will Control the Deep Pockets of the Central Bank?," Citi Economics, *Global Economics View*, July 2010; Lorenzo Bini Smaghi, *Austerity: European Democracies against the Wall* (Brussels: CEPS, 2013); C. Randall Henning, "The ECB as a Strategic Actor: Central Banking in a Politically Fragmented Monetary Union," in *The Political and Economic Dynamics of the Eurozone Crisis*, eds James A. Caporaso and Martin Rhodes (Oxford: Oxford University Press, 2016), pp. 167–99.

euro crisis, is nearly universal.[24] The "Fund," as it is commonly called, was created by contributions from its members and originally intended to serve as a revolving pool of reserves on which all of them could draw to defend their pegged exchange rates and finance temporary current account deficits. After upheavals in the international monetary system during the 1960s and 1970s, the Fund was effectively repurposed for surveillance of the economic policies of members and responding to financial crises. Its service in these roles has been famously controversial for the terms on which it has lent to crisis-stricken countries. The institution insists on economic policy reforms—"policy conditionality"—as a quid pro quo for financing in order to restore confidence, attract capital back to the country in question, and secure balance-of-payments adjustment. Conditionality requires painful austerity, even in cases where a country might be sideswiped by a crisis owing to faults not of its own making but of its economic partners. Among official financial institutions, the Fund pioneered this lending model.

The governance of the Fund reflects its character as a contribution-based institution. Voting roughly matches the share of a country's contributions, "quotas," an arrangement that gives substantial weight to the large creditor countries in the Board of Governors, the senior governing body composed of the finance ministers of all the members. The Executive Board sits in Washington, D.C., and meets several times each week to approve loans to countries, review their economic policies, and otherwise decide the policies of the Fund. Large decisions (such as changes to the Articles of Agreement) require the approval of eighty-five percent majorities, enough to give the United States and any other group that can amass fifteen percent voting power a veto. But lending decisions are almost never decided by votes within the Executive Board and much of the analysis of Fund governance is rightly criticized for giving excessive emphasis on voting weights.

The decade prior to the global financial crisis raised questions about the IMF's relevance on two counts. First, in the wake of the Asian financial crisis

---

[24] Space does not allow referencing the full literature on the IMF. Recent books nonetheless include: the Fund's own history by James Boughton, *Tearing Down Walls: The International Monetary Fund 1990–1999* (Washington, D.C.: IMF, 2013); Mark S. Copelovitch, *The International Monetary Fund in the Global Economy* (Cambridge: Cambridge University Press, 2010); Benn Steil, *The Battle of Bretton Woods: John Maynard Keynes, Harry Dexter White, and the Making of a New World Order* (Princeton, NJ: Princeton University Press, 2013); Onno de Beaufort Wijnholds, *Fighting Financial Fires: An IMF Insider Account* (London: Palgrave Macmillan, 2011); Randall Stone, *Controlling Institutions: International Organizations and the Global Economy* (Cambridge: Cambridge University Press, 2011); Jeffrey M. Chwieroth, *Capital Ideas: The IMF and the Rise of Financial Liberalization* (Princeton, NJ: Princeton University Press, 2009); Grigore Pop-Eleches, *From Economic Crisis to Reform: IMF Programs in Latin America and Eastern Europe* (Princeton, NJ: Princeton University Press, 2009); Erica R. Gould, *Money Talks: The International Monetary Fund, Conditionality, and Supplementary Financiers* (Stanford, CA: Stanford University Press, 2006).

of 1997–8, countries in that region were determined to avoid ever having to turn to the Fund again. Many East Asian countries valued their currencies competitively—many would say at undervalued exchange rates—ran large trade surpluses, and accumulated unprecedented quantities of foreign exchange reserves. They also created regional financial facilities as self-help mechanisms that they expected would, at a minimum, strengthen their hand vis-à-vis the Fund in future crises and, more ambitiously, perhaps serve as the foundation on which to build an institution that could eventually replace it—an Asian Monetary Fund. Second, during the liquidity boom in the mid-2000s the IMF's operating budget came under severe pressure owing to a shortage of borrowers.

The Fund responded to these challenges, first, by launching a charm offensive in East Asia, which included substantial reforms to the lending windows and conditionality guidelines that addressed the post-crisis critique of the programs in that region. Among them was a paring back of conditions related to structural policies, such as labor and product market regulation, to areas that were "macro-critical." Second, Managing Directors Rodrigo de Rato and Dominique Strauss-Kahn engineered the departure of about 380 professional staff (out of a total professional staff of 1950 people in early 2008, not including 636 staff at other levels), and a reform of the institution's income model.[25] When the global financial crisis broke in 2008, many breathed a sigh of relief that the purpose of the Fund had thus been renewed—it was "back in business."

The size of the Fund (its total quotas) was about $355 billion (SDR 238 billion) at the outset of the euro crisis. This implied a forward-lending capacity of slightly less than $240 billion as of January 2010. But the G20 summit in London in April 2009 decided that the resources ultimately at the disposal of the institution should be tripled as a response to the reverberations from the 2008–9 crisis. This was accomplished by expanding the IMF's ability to borrow to $500 billion and authorizing it to issue 250 billion Special Drawing Rights (SDR).[26] (Eventually, in early 2016, well after the acute phase of the euro crisis, the quotas of the Fund were doubled while its ability to borrow was rolled back by an equivalent amount.[27]) These measures simply offset, however, a long, secular decline in the size of the Fund relative to the world economy and international capital flows over previous decades. The size of the Fund constrained the size of the loans that it could marshal on behalf of members and—because the amount of financing is inversely proportional to

[25] IMF, *Annual Report for 2008*, ch. 5, pp. 70–2.
[26] See, for example, C. Randall Henning, "U.S. Interests and the International Monetary Fund," Peterson Institute Policy Brief No. 9–12, June 2009.
[27] IMF, "Historic Quota and Governance Reforms Become Effective," press release no. 16/25, Washington, D.C., January 27, 2016.

the duration of the adjustment of the balance of payments—heightened demands upon borrowing members for austerity.

The technical proficiency and relative autonomy of the staff and management of the IMF are closely related to its success as an institution. While the Executive Board ultimately decides on country programs and sets the parameters for Fund policies, the staff conducts its analysis, issues its economic projections, and surveys the policies of member countries with considerable independence. Staff negotiates with borrowing countries over the terms of financial support, including conditionality, with considerable autonomy as well. The Managing Director, supported by four deputies, is responsible for these operations and chairs the Executive Board.

The managing director of the IMF has always been European, by virtue of an informal arrangement, called "the convention," under which European governments accept an American as President of the World Bank.[28] The regional identity of the managing director is the most salient manifestation of European influence within the Fund. Although the United States holds the largest individual voting share, the combined European share is about twice as large. Europeans dominate the Executive Board numerically and are heavily represented among Fund staff. Such a position in the governing structure of the institution is anachronistic, the legacy of a period when Europe was a much larger share of the world economy than it is now. Shifting quotas and voting share to faster-growing regions of the world has been a long-term project since at least the creation of the euro. Notwithstanding some important steps in this direction, faster progress has been retarded by resistance both within Europe and the U.S. Congress. Europe's position served it well, however, when the euro crisis struck in 2010.

Rules and Principles

First, the eligibility for membership in the IMF is restricted to "countries," as recognized by the international community. While regional groups may represent themselves jointly in the Fund and the Fund can conduct surveillance of such groups, the regions themselves, their financial facilities, and other regional institutions cannot be members per se. This long-standing feature of the Articles of Agreement configures the Fund's relationship to regions. To be specific, without a change in the Articles, the euro area as a whole could not be a member of the Fund or borrow from it.

When providing financial assistance, the IMF's main focus is on its member, rather than the other institutions in which the country might also be a member.

---

[28] Miles Kahler, *Leadership Selection in the Multilaterals* (Washington, D.C.: Peterson Institute, 2001).

The Fund must take the interest of third countries into consideration—maintaining international financial stability is its central mandate—but it has no legal obligation to the region as a whole. The member might have obligations to the European Union, such as with respect to fiscal deficits or competition policy, but these obligations are not rules of the Fund. Controversially, the Fund might arguably be obliged to challenge them when its analysis indicates that they do not serve the economic stabilization of its member. The IMF might be agnostic on a country's membership in the monetary union, more fundamentally, whereas the European institutions have a vital interest in the cohesion of the euro area.

Second, the IMF has a lending framework that establishes rules for access to financing and provides for exceptions to access limits.[29] The Fund revised its lending policies after the Argentine program and default in 2002. It was also reacting to the Asian financial crisis of 1997–8, a capital account crisis that saw the size of loans balloon. The Fund decided that, as a general matter, access to IMF lending would be restricted to several multiples of a country's quota. Exceptions could be granted, provided that four criteria were met, one of which was that the country's debt could be fairly judged to be sustainable.

Third, avoidance of lending into an unsustainable situation is a fundamental principle. This is true not only for the IMF but for all crisis lenders. Recognition of this principle dates back to at least Walter Bagehot's rules for a lender of last resort in *Lombard Street* (1873). Lending under such circumstances piles debt on top of unsustainable debt, facilitates the escape of other creditors, and imposes losses on the official rescuer. Accordingly, the Fund has established a process by which debt sustainability is analyzed. When debt does not appear to be sustainable, the Fund should not lend until it is restructured and the country is thereby made viable.[30] As the euro crisis would show, nonetheless, there are circumstances in which the debt sustainability criterion will be waived.

Fourth, to support adjustment programs and protect against losses, the Fund maintains a policy on financing assurances.[31] A program must be fully financed; that is, the gap between the country's international borrowing needs and anticipated capital inflows must be filled. When the resources available through the IMF do not fill that gap, other official creditors or private lenders

---

[29] IMF, "The Fund's Evolving Approach in Sovereign Debt Crises," *The Fund's Lending Framework and Sovereign Debt—Annexes* (Washington, D.C.: IMF, June 2014), pp. 4–23; IMF, *Sovereign Debt Restructuring* (Washington, D.C.: IMF, April 26, 2013), pp. 7–9.

[30] As discussed in Chapter 11, this principle was reasserted by a decision of the Executive Board in January 2016, based on staff analysis, IMF, "The Fund's Lending Framework and Sovereign Debt—Further Considerations," Washington, D.C., April 9, 2015.

[31] IMF, *Sovereign Debt Restructuring*, "Annex I: Fund Policies on Financing Assurances and External Arrears," pp. 43–5.

must do so before the Fund can finalize the program. The Fund can act on the basis of "good prospects" that the gap over the life of the program will be filled. But, on a twelve-month rolling basis, "firm commitments" on the part of other creditors must be in place before the IMF can disburse. This rule would have special relevance to the euro crisis, where programs would become very large.

Finally, the Fund holds the status of preferred creditor. This means that it has priority over other creditors in repayment from a troubled borrower. This status is not enshrined in the Articles of Agreement or any other formal international agreement. The Fund is nonetheless accorded this treatment in all cases of debt restructuring in practice. Preferred creditor status is fundamental to the role of the Fund as a global crisis lender and to the willingness of members to place their resources at its disposal, for deployment in what might otherwise be a risky loan portfolio. The Fund is active in defending this status, but its preferential status was questioned during the euro crisis.[32]

Strategic Challenges

Although the global financial crisis put the Fund back in business, the euro crisis presented the institution with new challenges. The institution confronted the strategic problem of bridging the preferences of different regions over the design of country programs and conditionality—differences among Europe, East Asia, and increasingly the large emerging market countries. Programs for member states of the euro area required larger loans and deeper structural reforms than in the case of "stand-alone" borrowers because the exchange rate was not available as a tool of adjustment. Although the IMF had dealt with other monetary unions, none of them had experienced problems of the severity of Europe's sovereign debt crisis. The generosity of the size of these loans relative to those offered during previous crises created conflicts with governments in other regions, East Asia in particular.

A second important challenge related to lending into situations in which debt sustainability is questionable. The Fund faces pressure from its members to lend to some countries even in cases where debt does not appear to be sustainable—because a broad subset of the membership fears contagion from a default or restructuring and prefers to use the IMF as the vehicle for assistance rather than taking the risk directly onto government balance sheets. The problem was posed in stark relief by the case of Argentina in 2001–2, which defaulted to creditors even after taking two IMF programs. To extricate

[32] Susan Schadler, "The IMF's Preferred Creditor Status: Does It Still make Sense after the Euro Crisis?," *CIGI Policy Brief* No. 37, March 2014. See also Rutsel S. J. Martha, "Preferred Creditor Status under International Law: The Case of the International Monetary Fund," *The International and Comparative Law Quarterly*, Vol. 39, No. 4 (Oct., 1990), pp. 801–26.

itself from this predicament, in large measure, the Fund staff proposed the Sovereign Debt Restructuring Mechanism (SDRM) in 2001, but this was not adopted. The euro crisis would again pose this dilemma to the Fund, its staff, and members.

DIVERGENCE

The regime complex for the euro crisis, in sum, embraced a set of institutions that were heterogeneous. Their membership, resources, mandate, and rules configured their approaches to fighting crises and differences in these characteristics caused their approaches to diverge. The divergence was reflected in institutional preferences for the design of programs: the amount of financing, duration of loans, speed of adjustment, conditionality, debt restructuring, and the contributions of private creditors.

Acting through the European Council and Eurogroup, for example, member states of the euro area could accept open-ended programs in which the sustainability of debt was ambiguous and the country was not expected to regain market access for an extended period. The IMF, by contrast, required a fully funded program that provided financing to carry the borrower through the adjustment process and restore its access to the market, which should take place over the medium term. To be successful, the IMF's approach required in turn that debt be sustainable and recognized as such by private creditors. The European institutions and the IMF differed over the priority to be given to the formal EU rules, with the IMF questioning some of the rules when it thought they weakened programs. The European institutions complained that the IMF did not take spillover effects on the rest of the euro area into account when designing programs, while the IMF advocated common fiscal commitments and greater burden-sharing on the part of the European partners. Whereas the IMF urged the ECB to expand unconventional monetary policy, Frankfurt was sensitive to the exposure that such operations implied for its balance sheet.

The divergence among the institutions did not mean that they could not work together on crisis programs. Each could instead contribute to the extent and in the manner that was acceptable under its mandate. But the divergence was bound to create conflicts. Fashioning joint programs required agreement on the analysis of program conditionality and coordination of the institutions. These institutions had not worked extensively together prior to the global financial crisis, however, and the arrangements for bringing them together were underdeveloped. The institutions would thus become deadlocked on important elements of the programs, and it would fall to key states to mediate the impasse.

4

Euro Crisis in a Nutshell

Whereas the previous chapter introduced the formal institutions that were charged with responsibility for developing the financial rescues, the present chapter provides an overview of the origins and evolution of the euro crisis. It reviews the economics of the crisis and the financial dynamics that unfolded first over the course of the acute phase, 2010–13, and then over the following two years, during which the crisis was resolved except in the case of Greece. This chapter addresses the management of the euro area as a whole, as the backdrop to the discussion in subsequent chapters of the development of the individual programs for crisis-stricken countries. With the stage thus set, the chapter examines the early programs for countries in Central and Eastern Europe—precursors to the euro crisis. The IMF and European Commission began to work out the terms of their collaboration in the region in those early programs.

ORIGINS AND DIAGNOSIS

The essential financial problem within Europe can be usefully compared to that of the United States during the decade of the 2000s. Both the United States and Europe experienced liquidity-driven booms during which savings were misdirected into real estate and financial investments and on which subsequent losses proved to be massive. Investment flowed from one region to another on a continental scale during these years. The over-investment in real estate in Spain and Ireland, for example, broadly resembled that in Florida and Nevada.

But the responses of the two regions differed substantially as a consequence of the fundamental differences in their political and institutional structures.

[1] Paul Krugman, "The Road to Economic Crisis is Paved with Euros," *New York Times*, January 12, 2011; Paul de Grauwe, "The Governance of a Fragile Eurozone," *CEPS Working Paper* No. 346, Brussels, May 2011.

The United States benefited from a strong central response in the form of federal government rescues of the banking system through Troubled Asset Relief Program (TARP) support for aggregate demand through the fiscal stimulus of 2009–10, and unconventional monetary policy on the part of the Federal Reserve. Although European governments also stimulated their economies early in the global financial crisis and the ECB adopted nonstandard monetary policies, the initial fiscal impulse varied by country and was quickly reversed and the ECB's measures lagged substantially behind those of the Federal Reserve. Critically, Europe lacked the region-wide mechanisms for stabilizing the banking system that served the United States well, deposit insurance, relatively uniform regulation, bank recapitalization, and federal assumption of the associated costs. The euro area lacked, in other words, a "banking union."

The political fragmentation of Europe and the absence of the banking union—which left member states in the role of "first responders" to banking problems—ensured that the resolution of the crisis would become a first-order distributional struggle. Whereas the primary political conflict in the United States centered on the relationship between the banking system and taxpayers, the political conflict within the euro area was among the member states, those that had been prudent and those that had been spendthrift. The same functional problem as in the United States—absorbing the losses from the bubble years, repairing the banking system, and restarting growth—was all too often framed as a member-state fiscal problem in the euro area.

Greece was a genuine case of fiscal mismanagement and misreporting, but exceptional in this way. The exception was important because Greece was the first member of the euro area to experience the crisis and thus established the frame of reference for the public discourse in the creditor countries over extending financial assistance. The Greek case played to the worst fears on the part of the creditors (particularly Germany, the Netherlands, Finland, Austria, and Luxembourg) of being exploited by the countries of the southern tier through the European Union in general and the monetary union in particular. That frame of reference was applied to the countries that were subsequently stricken by the crisis, even when the origin lay instead in the banking system, and shaped the response on the part of the creditors.[2]

The prevalence of the diagnosis of the euro crisis as a fiscal crisis rather than a crisis of a continent-wide banking and financial system focused the original response on the fiscal arrangements within the member states, and the associated structural problems. This diagnosis was at best incomplete, in some cases seriously misleading, as the fiscal problems of many member states

---

[2] See, also, Jean Pisani-Ferry, *The Euro Crisis and Its Aftermath* (Oxford: Oxford University Press, 2014); Lorenzo Bini Smaghi, *Austerity: European Democracies against the Wall* (Brussels: Centre for European Policy Studies, 2013), pp. 44–8.

derived largely if not wholly from their need to rescue their banking systems. The sovereign governments and their banks were embraced in a "doom loop"—the mutual dependence of sovereigns and banks dragged the two down together—and it took more than two years for officials of the euro area to arrive at the collective realization that breaking this connection was essential to resolving the crisis. Structural policies such as labor markets, product regulation, and government ownership of enterprises underlay a divergence in cost competitiveness among countries, as some advocates of deep-rooted reforms stressed, but the payoff to reform in terms of growth was beyond the time horizon of debt sustainability in some cases.[3] At the outset of the crisis, the diagnosis quickly became a bone of contention among advocates of alternative strategies for responding to it.

FINANCIAL CONDITIONS

A series of figures serves as common measures of financial distress over the course of the euro crisis. Figures 4.1a and 4.1b display the differences between the interest rates on government bonds for euro-area countries compared to

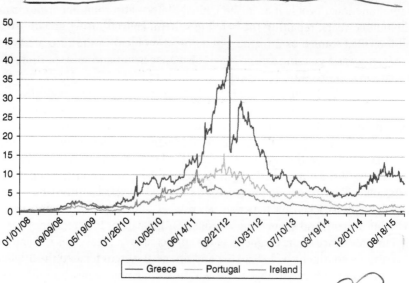

Figure 4.1a. Sovereign 10-Year Bond Spreads over German Bunds.
Source: Bloomberg.

---

[3] See, for example, Erik Jones, "Competitiveness and the European Financial Crisis" in Caporaso and Rhodes, *Political and Economic Dynamics of the Eurozone Crisis*, pp. 79–99. Jones attributes the crisis primarily to financial causes rather than a loss of competitiveness.

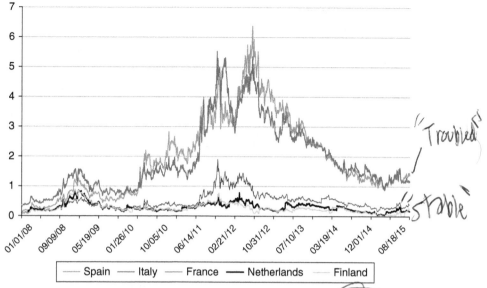

Figure 4.1b. Sovereign 10-Year Bond Spreads over German Bunds.
Source: Bloomberg.

the German ten-year government bond. This "spread" had become trivial during the boom years of the middle of the decade of the 2000s, but began to widen for Greece, Ireland, and Portugal over the course of 2009. The increases in these spreads mark the beginning of the acute phases of the crises for these countries and their resort to official financing—private financing having become too expensive for their debt to be sustainable—in spring 2010 for Greece, November 2010 for Ireland, and spring 2011 for Portugal. The peaks in the spreads for Spain and Italy mark the most acute phases of the generalized crisis—autumn 2011 and summer 2012—when interest rates were well above the growth of nominal income, which, if they had persisted, would have required a debt restructuring for these countries. Note that the yields on French, Dutch, and Finnish (as well as Austrian and Luxembourg) bonds generally stay within one percent of German yields, implying a clear differentiation between the stable and troubled countries.

Figure 4.2a displays the spreads on credit default swaps (CDS) on sovereign bonds, a measure of probability of default as perceived by investors. Greece is in a risk category of its own and not shown here owing to scaling. Portugal and Ireland come next, with Ireland peaking at 1191 basis points in July 2011 and Portugal rising above 1000 on a sustained basis. A rate of 1000 basis points represents an estimated probability of default over five years of about fifty-eight percent. The rates for Spain and Italy show a substantial probability of default at their peaks. Germany remains unscathed throughout the crisis.

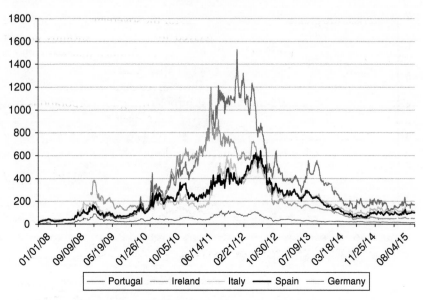

Figure 4.2a. CDS Spreads for Sovereign Bonds (5-year).
Source: Bloomberg.

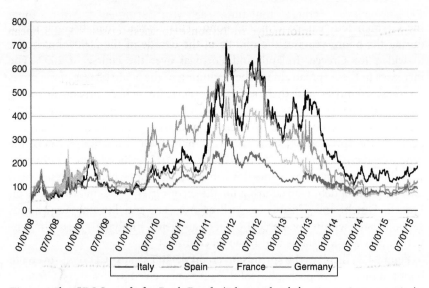

Figure 4.2b. CDS Spreads for Bank Bonds (5 largest banks' average, 5-year, senior).
Source: Bloomberg.

Differences in the creditworthiness of the sovereign governments were reflected in differences in the riskiness of bonds issued by the banks behind which they stood. Figure 4.2b displays the CDS rates on bank bonds. The perceived risks are greater for the banks than for the sovereign in the four large countries, and German banks are perceived to have a significantly greater probability of default than the German government, though that was considerably smaller than French, Italian, and Spanish banks. These risks were eventually incorporated into the cost of funding for banks, differences which were, in turn, incorporated into the cost of borrowing for corporations and small- and medium-sized enterprises (SMEs). A well-integrated financial system facilitates the arbitrage of differences in the cost of borrowing across the euro area. The emergence of substantial differentials, between Italy and Germany, for example, marked an alarming degree of financial fragmentation of the euro area.

EUROPEAN GOVERNMENTS RESPOND

European policymakers responded to the crisis through decisions of summit meetings, the creation of new forums, and the establishment of financial facilities for the benefit of euro-area member states. The global financial crisis and then the euro crisis demanded more frequent meetings of the leaders. EU summits had gathered four times each year during 2004–7, three times formally and once informally. In response to these crises, the European Council and Euro summit met formally or informally seven or eight times each year during 2008–13, counting back-to-back meetings of these groups as single meetings.[5] (Table 4.1 lists these meetings and their main topics.) Their attention was required to overcome disagreements within the Eurogroup, in which the principal negotiations over the response to the crisis took place and which discharged particular tasks assigned to them by the leaders.

The pattern of new forums for leaders and heightened frequency of meetings paralleled developments at the global level, where the G20 summits were inaugurated in November 2008 in Washington, D.C., met biannually in 2009 and 2010, and annually thereafter. Europeans leaders devoted significant time in their meetings to preparing for the G20 summits, where they sought, among other things, to bolster the financial capacity of the IMF and involve it in programs for crisis-stricken members, while they also sought to limit interference on the part of non-Europeans in the euro area's response to the crisis. A number of the G20 summits, as well as a couple of the G8 summits,

---

[4] On the genesis and inauguration of the Euro summit, see, "History of the Euro Summit," <http://www.consilium.europa.eu/en/european-council/euro-summit/>; "Speech by Mr. Nicolas Sarkozy, President of the Republic, before the European Parliament," Strasbourg, October 21, 2008, at <http://www.ambafrance-in.org/21-10-2008-European-Parliament>.

[5] There was one back-to-back meeting of the European Council and Euro Summit in 2010 and 2013 and three such meetings in 2011 and 2012.

Table 4.1. European Council and Euro-Area Summit Meetings, 2008–2015

Year	Date	Council President*	Type of Summit	Main Theme(s)
2008	March 13–14	Slovenia	Regular EU	Energy and climate change policy
	June 19–20		Regular EU	Food prices
	July 13–14	France	Extraordinary EU	Barcelona process for the Mediterranean
	September 1		Extraordinary EU	Georgia–Russian relations
	October 12		Euro summit	Agreement on concerted action for the financial system
	October 15–16		Regular EU	Adoption of measures to stabilize the financial system; energy and climate
	November 7		Informal EU	Preparation for G20 summit on global financial crisis
	December 11–12		Regular EU	European Recovery Programme and upcoming Copenhagen climate summit
2009	March 1	Czech Republic	Informal EU	Maintaining stimulus; ensure financial stability in Eastern Europe
	March 19–20		Regular EU	National stimuli; Single Market; de Larosière Report; London G20 summit
	June 18–19		Regular EU	Irish demands on the Lisbon treaty; EU financial regulation
	September 17	Sweden	Informal EU	Upcoming Pittsburgh G20 summit
	October 29–30		Regular EU	Lisbon treaty; crisis exit strategy
	November 19		Informal EU	Selection of the president of the European Council
	December 10–11	Herman Van Rompuy	Regular EU	Lisbon treaty; crisis exit strategy
2010	February 11		Extraordinary EU	Early Greek adjustment package
	March 25–6		Regular EU	EU 2020 (jobs and growth); competitiveness; G20 preparation; climate change
			Euro summit	Assistance package for Greece
	May 7		Euro summit	Approval of Greek package; launch construction of EFSF and EFSM
	June 17		Regular EU	Greek package; consolidation and reform of SGP
	September 16		Regular EU	EU external policy; task force report on economic governance
	October 28–9		Regular EU	Agreement to create a permanent facility (ESM) by mid-2013 at the latest
	December 16–17		Regular EU	Agreement to amend the treaty in order to create the ESM
2011	February 4		Regular EU	Energy and innovation
	March 11		Euro summit	Reform of the EFSF; details of the functioning of the ESM

	March 11		Extraordinary EU	Arab Spring and Libya
	March 24–5		Regular EU	Reform of stability programs of euro and non-euro members
	June 23–4		Regular EU	Greece and PSI; amendment of EFSF and ESM; first European semester
	July 21		Euro summit	Second Greek program, PSI; new instruments for EFSF and ESM (direct "recap")
	October 23		Regular EU	European semester, acceleration of structural reforms
	October 23–6		Euro summit	Greek PSI; Spain and Italy; Euro Plus Pact; "IMF practices" for PSI
	October 26		Informal EU	
	December 8–9		Regular EU	Adoption of the Fiscal Compact; acceleration of the entry into force of ESM
	December 9		Euro summit	
2012	January 30	Herman Van Rompuy	Informal EU	Reforms in Greece, Portugal, Ireland, Spain, and Italy
	January 30		Euro summit	Finalization of the Treaty on Stability, Coordination, and Governance and ESM treaty
	March 1–2		Regular EU	Preparation of the G20; country-specific recommendations for reform
	March 2		Euro summit	Signing of the Treaty on Stability, Coordination, and Governance (TSCG)
	May 23		Informal EU	Greece should stay in the euro area; use of structural funds; youth unemployment
	June 28–9		Regular EU	Compact for Growth and Jobs; report "Towards a Genuine Economic and Monetary Union"
	June 28–9		Euro summit	Banking union; supervision by the ECB; direct recapitalization by ESM, Spain
	October 18–19		Regular EU	Reviewing the implementation of the Compact for Growth and Jobs
	November 22–3		Regular EU	Mandate to Council President on Multiannual Financial Framework, 2014–20
	December 13–14		Regular EU	Agreement on Single Supervisory Mechanism at ECB; Roadmap for completing EMU
2013	February 7–8		European Council	Multiannual Financial Framework of the Union
	March 14–15		Regular EU	European semester, Foreign Affairs
	March 14		Euro summit	Economic situation; rules of the Euro summits

(continued)

Table 4.1. Continued

Year	Date	Council President*	Type of Summit	Main Theme(s)
	May 22		Regular EU	Tax fraud and evasion; deepening of the EMU
	June 27–8		Regular EU	Youth unemployment, banking union, welcoming Croatia, 28th member state
	October 24–5		Regular EU	Digital economy; innovation; services
	December 19–20		Regular EU	Defense
2014	March 6		Extraordinary EU	Ukraine
	March 20–1		Regular EU	Ukraine
	May 27		Informal EU	European elections; Ukraine
	June 26–7		Regular EU	EU elections
	July 16		Special EU	EU elections; Ukraine
	August 30		Special EU	Ukraine; Gaza; Iraq
	October 23–4		Regular EU	Climate and energy
	October 24		Euro summit	2030 Climate and Energy Framework; Ebola; €300 billion investment program
	December 18	Donald Tusk	Regular EU	Investment and Eastern borders
2015	February 12		Informal EU	Ukraine; terrorism; EMU
	March 19–20		Regular EU	Energy; Libya; Ukraine; Russia
	April 23		Special EU	Migration
	June 22		Euro summit	Greece
	June 25–6		Regular EU	Greece; migration; UK referendum
	July 7		Euro summit	Greece
	July 12		Euro summit	Greece
	September 23		Extraordinary EU	Migration policy and the Syrian refugee crisis
	October 15–16		Regular EU	Migration, EMU, and referendum in the UK
	December 17–18		Regular EU	Migration, euro-area reform, UK plans for referendum, Syria and the fight against terrorism

Source: <http://www.european-council.europa.eu/home-page.aspx?lang=en>.
* The chairmanship of the European Council shifted from a rotating presidency to a president who is elected to a two-and-a-half-year term at the beginning of December 2009.

nonetheless served as important occasions for the non-Europeans to signal their concerns about the management of the crisis and even mediate disagreements among the Europeans.

The most important European meetings corresponded to the key challenges of the crisis. The summits of March 2010 and May 2010 took the critical decisions on the Greek program and the bilateral loan facility. A bilateral meeting between Chancellor Merkel and French President Nicolas Sarkozy in

October 2010, on the margin of the G8 summit in Deauville, decided that bailing in the private sector would become an essential element of any future rescue package. The announcement of this doctrine contributed to a sell-off in Irish and Portuguese government bonds, driving those countries into financing programs, and increased the bond rates for the large southern countries as well, and was thus a serious mistake. The doctrine was effectively suspended as a general approach (to be revived more than two years later for the Cyprus program). Highlighting ambiguity with which private claims on sovereigns would be treated, the summit of June 2011 launched an important review of the Greek program that initiated a debt restructuring, a process reinforced by the Cannes G20 summit hosted by President Sarkozy in October 2011. With the bond yield and CDS spreads rising toward unsustainable levels for Spain and Italy (see Figures 4.1 and 4.2), the October 2011 summit also called upon Spain and Italy to take tough measures.[6]

At the end of January 2012, the leaders of the euro-area member states finalized the treaties on the Fiscal Compact, which tightened rules on fiscal deficits and debt, and on the permanent financial facility, the ESM. Under renewed financial market pressure, the June 2012 summit addressed a new program for the Spanish banking system and, importantly, launched negotiations over the banking union. The June 2013 summit followed through by agreeing to some of the essential features of a mechanism for resolving insolvent banks. The summit meetings thus configured the basic parameters within which the institutions of the troika developed the rescue programs for euro-area countries.

The period from early 2010 through the first half of 2014 covered the life cycle of the crisis programs for Ireland, Spain, and Portugal—from negotiations, agreements, and the initial disbursements through the final disbursements, culminating in the resumption of their governments' access to capital markets. Cyprus, which began a program in spring 2013, regained market access and graduated three years later. Greece, which accessed markets tentatively in 2014, lost it again in 2015 and European leaders negotiated at great length in all-night summits over a solution that might keep the country in the euro area. When Greece no longer requires such assistance, either inside the euro area or outside it, the sovereign debt crisis will recede into the past. But we cannot yet say when that moment might come.

European authorities responded with a series of incremental changes in the institutional arrangements for responding to the financial crises within the euro area. Renovating their common financial facilities quickly became urgent in 2010. The Balance-of-Payments facility that was used for the programs in Central and Eastern Europe was not available for members of the monetary

[6] An episode vividly recounted by Alan Crawford and Tony Czuczka, *Angela Merkel: A Chancellorship Forged in Crisis* (West Sussex: Wiley and Bloomberg, 2013), pp. 7–21.

union. This left European officials in a quandary when the crisis struck Greece and they debated a wide range of responses, including the creation of a European Monetary Fund. As we discuss in the next chapter, they extended loans to Athens on a bilateral basis and created two new facilities for any further contingencies—the European Financial Stabilisation Mechanism (EFSM), for which all of the member states of the European Union were eligible, and the temporary European Financial Stability Facility (EFSF), for the euro-area members alone—together amounting to €500 billion.

EUROPEAN CENTRAL BANK RESPONDS

Meanwhile, the European Central Bank was also responding to the crisis, and doing so more effectively than the collection of euro-area governments. Figures 4.3 and 4.4 offer two windows onto the monetary policy response. The first shows the reductions in the interest rate over the course of the crisis to very low rates. These rates were not as low as those of the Federal Reserve, Bank of Japan, or Bank of England, which generated increasing debate over time that they should be lowered further. Note also that the ECB did not

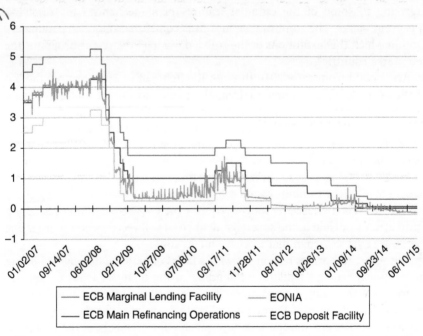

Figure 4.3. ECB Policy Rates and Interbank Rate, January 2007–September 2015.

Note: EONIA is Euro Overnight Index Average.

Source: European Central Bank.

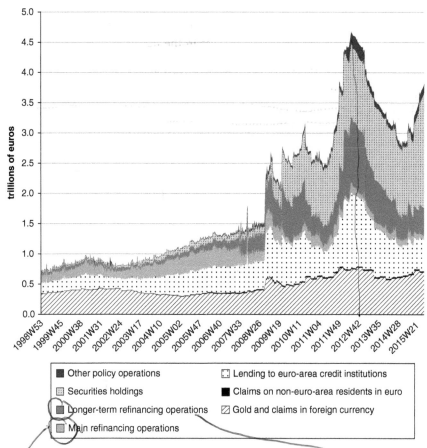

Figure 4.4. ECB Balance Sheet, December 1998–September 2015.

Note: "*Gold and claims in foreign currency*" aggregates the categories of "Gold and gold receivables," "Claims on non-euro-area residents denominated in foreign currency," and "Claims on euro-area residents denominated in foreign currency."

"*Securities holdings*" aggregates "Securities of euro-area residents denominated in euro," "Securities held for monetary policy purposes," and "Other securities."

"*Other policy operations*" aggregates "Fine-tuning reverse operations," "Structural reverse operations," "Marginal lending facility," "Credits related to marginal calls," and "Other claims on euro-area credit institutions denominated in euro."

Source: European Central Bank.

i rates↑

reduce interest rates steadily over the course of the crisis. It raised them in two quarter-point increments in the middle of 2011—a serious mistake—and then lowered them again as the crisis worsened.

Figure 4.4 shows the quadrupling of the size of the balance sheet to €4.5 trillion in mid-2012 and the change in its composition over time. Main refinancing operations, which had been the central bank's preferred mechanism for regulating liquidity in the banking system, took a back seat to direct lending to the banks and long-term refinancing operations (LTROs) with extended maturities. In doing so, the ECB effectively took over the function of intermediating funds within the banking system as banks lost confidence in one another. The ECB also bought more than €1 trillion in securities, most of which were government bonds.

The increase in government bond holdings reflected an innovative and controversial direction for the ECB. In May 2010, the Governing Council of the central bank adopted the Securities Market Programme (SMP). Prohibited by the Maastricht treaty from financing member-state governments directly, President of the ECB Jean-Claude Trichet, explained that the SMP was being introduced to combat the financial fragmentation of the euro area and thus to re-establish the effectiveness of monetary policy.

The ECB placed limits on unconventional monetary policies. It rejected proposals that it provide liquidity directly to the EFSF and ESM by granting these facilities a banking license and thereby making them eligible for refinancing operations,[7] for example, on the grounds that doing so would finance governments indirectly. Nonetheless, at the most acute moment in the crisis, July 2012, President Mario Draghi stated that he, too, would do whatever it took, within the mandate of the ECB, to defend the euro and in September announced the introduction of a program of Outright Monetary Transactions (OMT), which replaced the SMP.[8] The announcement of OMT calmed the markets, much to the relief of countries under stress, but it had taken an existential threat to the euro to bring the ECB to this point.

Governments of the euro area and the ECB were locked in a strategic game in which each withheld measures that could help to resolve the crisis in order to force the other to make its move. Barred from coercing the ECB directly, the creditor governments hoped the crisis would pressure the ECB to ease credit conditions and buy government bonds outright. The ECB, for its part, pressed governments to undertake more fiscal adjustment and structural reform, to be sure. But the central bank also pressed the creditor governments, led by Germany, to develop robust European financial facilities, banking union, a fiscal backstop for it and, more broadly, greater mutualization of fiscal policy. The ECB withheld unconventional monetary programs until governments undertook at least some of these commitments.[9] Political fragmentation of the monetary union prevented coordination between the two sides. Rather

---

[7] Daniel Gros and Thomas Mayer, "August 2011: What to Do When the Euro Crisis Reaches the Core," *CEPS Commentary*, August 18, 2011.

[8] Mario Draghi, Speech to the Global Investment Conference, London, July 26, 2012, at <http://www.ecb.europa.eu/press/key/date/2012/html/sp120726.en.html>; Technical Features of Outright Monetary Transactions, ECB (September 2012) at <http://www.ecb.europa.eu/press/pr/date/2012/html/pr120906_1.en.html>.

[9] C. Randall Henning, "The ECB as a Strategic Actor," in *The Political and Economic Dynamics of the Eurozone Crisis*, eds James A. Caporaso and Martin Rhodes.

than nip the crisis in the bud, therefore, the euro-area member states and institutions collectively let the crisis worsen for two-and-a-half years after the onset of the Greek debacle.

MUDDLING THROUGH AND ARCHITECTURAL REFORM

European negotiations thus resembled the meandering advance of the medieval Echternach Procession.[10] When capital market conditions became acute, euro-area leaders became worried about the integrity of the monetary union and offered potentially costly concessions (in the form of financial assistance, bank recapitalization, or banking union). When market conditions eased, however, governments would "slow walk" their negotiations and qualify or even revoke commitments that they had previously made—until another round of the crisis prompted them to move forward again. This pattern of two steps forward, one step back was the product of strategic bargaining that was avoided, or at least much more successfully constrained, within the federal institutions of the United States and even the individual European countries themselves.[11]

German Chancellor Angela Merkel, her fellow European leaders, the president of the Eurogroup and the president of the ECB would vow to do whatever it took to defend the euro. But, decision-making during the crisis had made clear that collective action was subject to effective individual vetoes on the part of at least the large countries, effectively speaking, and national politics were uncertain in both the borrowing and creditor countries within the euro area—all the more so owing to rising unemployment and increasing popularity of Euroskeptic parties. While European leaders seemed genuinely self-interested in keeping the euro area together, and capable of acting together when their backs were to the wall, it was not at all clear that their progress in building euro-area institutions outpaced deteriorating economic developments. During the first half of the decade of the 2010, these leaders muddled through the crisis.[12]

Six years after the first tremors of the global financial crisis and four years after the onset of the acute phase of the European sovereign debt crisis, the

---

[10] Taking place each year on Pentecost Tuesday in Echternach, Luxembourg, the "hopping procession" is celebrated for its particularly circuitous progression.

[11] See, among a number of others, C. Randall Henning and Martin Kessler, *Fiscal Federalism: U.S. History for Architects of Europe's Fiscal Union* (Brussels: Bruegel, 2012).

[12] The phrase "muddle through" is borrowed from Benjamin J. Cohen, "The Future of the Euro: Let's Get Real," *Review of International Political Economy* 19:4 (October 2012): 689–700.

euro area was in the midst of the second dip of a double-dip recession and few sources of growth appeared on the horizon. In the first quarter of 2013, real output for the euro area as a whole was 3.6 percent below its peak at the beginning of 2008 and would not return to that peak until early 2016.[13] Unemployment had risen from 7.3 percent to over twelve percent and would remain above ten percent, more than double the rate in the United States, through mid-2016.[14]

These figures masked large differences among member countries of the monetary union. Germany had also experienced a recession but had been growing quickly as the euro crisis was unfolding. Its economy remained slightly larger at the end of 2013 than its peak in 2008. The Italian economy was in recession, having shrunk by 8.3 percent since the peak in 2008. Such was its long-term growth challenge that real output was smaller in 2013 than in 2000. Spain, which had grown rapidly during the boom years, was in recession in 2013, with its economy about five percent smaller than the peak in 2008. The economy of Greece had shrunk by roughly a quarter from its peak in 2008.[15] That of Cyprus shrank by more than ten percent. In April 2013, the unemployment rate in Italy was 12.0 percent, Ireland 13.5 percent, Portugal 17.0 percent, Spain 26.3 percent, and Greece 27.5 percent.[16]

Six years after the beginning of the global financial crisis, many of the losses that had been suffered by the European banking system had not been acknowledged and remained to be written off. The scale of these losses was not fully known and in fact evolved with changing economic circumstances. IMF Managing Director Christine Lagarde stated in August 2011 that the euro area would have to write off €200 billion in losses.[17] This could be regarded as a permissive lower bound. *Financial Times* columnist Wolfgang Munchau casually estimated them at ten percent of total European bank assets, €2.6 trillion,[18] but conceded that the lower numbers were more realistic. Several members of the IMF staff estimated that non-performing loans in the euro area amounted to €932 billion (9.2 percent of GDP) at the end of 2014, having

[13] ECB Statistical Data Warehouse, GDP at market price—Chain-linked volumes, euro (series RTD.Q.SO.S.G_GDPM_TO_C.C.), at <http://sdw.ecb.europa.eu>.

[14] ECB, Statistical Data Warehouse, Euro Area 17 standardized unemployment rate, seasonally adjusted (series STS.M.16.S.UNEH.RT T000.4.000) at <http://sdw.ecb.europa.eu>.

[15] Calculated by the author using ESA95 National Accounts data (series MNA.A.N.IT.W2.S1. S1.B.B1GQ._Z._Z._Z.EUR.LR.N) at <http://sdw.ecb.europa.eu/browse.do?node=9484571>.

[16] ECB, Statistical Data Warehouse, Standardized Unemployment (series STS.M.I6.S. UNEH. RTT000.4.000) at <http://sdw.ecb.europa.eu>. By May 2016, the rates would fall only slightly in Italy to 11.5 percent and Greece 24.1 percent, more significantly in Spain to 19.8 percent and Portugal 11.6 percent, and substantially in Ireland to 7.8 percent.

[17] Christine Lagarde, speech at Kansas City Federal Reserve conference, Jackson Hole, August 27, 2011. At <http://www.imf.org/external/np/speeches/2011/082711.htm>.

[18] Wolfgang Munchau, "Europe is Ignoring the Scale of Bank Losses," *Financial Times*, June 23, 2013.

doubled since 2008.[19] Whatever the exact size, allocating these losses among the shareholders, private creditors, and European governments was a monumentally difficult political problem.

Progress in this domain was the object of the project on banking union. The European Council granted the ECB the authority to supervise the largest banks of the euro area, about 130 of them with assets about eighty-five percent of total bank assets in the euro area. European banks underwent an asset quality review and stress test prior to the ECB's taking on this role in November 2014. A combination of government intervention, bank share issues, and asset shedding appeared to fill most of the capital shortfall in the banking systems in euro-area countries. A new regime for recapitalizing and resolving banks was also adopted in 2014 and implemented over the course of the two years that followed.[20]

By the middle of the decade, the euro area had done much to repair the damage caused by the crisis in terms of both economic policy measures and strengthening of the institutional architecture of the euro area. Progress toward banking union had paved the way for the ECB to announce OMT,[21] which, even though it was not activated, contributed mightily to bringing the acute phase of the crisis to an end by early 2014. Aggregate demand nonetheless remained weak, with creditor states unwilling to use fiscal policy actively and with banks deleveraging to meet capital requirements. After attenuated deliberations, which pitted the German Bundesbank and a few like-minded national central banks against a majority of the others and the Executive Board, the Governing Council of the ECB finally announced its first program that could be genuinely described as quantitative easing in January 2015.

The European Union and euro area agreed upon a series of reforms to the architecture of the monetary union. These ranged across the areas of fiscal policy, debt management, financial facilities, public investment, the instruments of the ECB and its activism, in addition to banking union. The first half of the 2010s was by far the most innovative period in EU institutional development since the establishment of the monetary union. Given the political activity associated with concluding these agreements, the list of accomplishments was impressive.

[19] Shekhar Aiyar et al., "A Strategy for Resolving Europe's Problem Loans," *IMF Staff Discussion Note* (Washington, D.C.: IMF, September 2015), p. 6. These authors wrote in their personal capacity.
[20] General treatments of banking union can be found in Nicolas Véron, *Europe's Radical Banking Union*, Bruegel Essay and Lecture Series (Brussels, 2015); Danny Busch and Guido Ferrarini, eds, *European Banking Union* (Oxford: Oxford University Press, 2015); and Rishi Goyal, et al., "A Banking Union for the Euro Area," IMF Staff Discussion Paper, February 13, 2013.
[21] Véron, *Europe's Radical Banking Union*, makes this point.

But the member states of the monetary union shied away from a genuine shift in the political paradigm. The connection between banks and their national sovereigns was only loosened, not broken, and the extent to which the new architecture for banking would reverse the financial fragmentation of the monetary union remained to be seen. Weak growth and the threat of deflation persisted and these macroeconomic conditions made the domestic politics of European integration fraught. Euroskepticism, in turn, raised serious questions about the strength of democratic support for further changes in the institutional architecture that would be necessary to prevent a recurrence of crises at some point in the future.

These late phases of the crisis get ahead of our story, however. The crises in Central and Eastern Europe serve as a bridge between this overview of the euro crisis and the discussion in later chapters of the individual country programs.

FORESHOCKS: CENTRAL AND EASTERN EUROPE

Countries on the periphery of the monetary union, several of which had been running substantial current account deficits during the preceding boom, came under severe financial pressures in the autumn of 2008. Between then and the beginning of 2010, nine countries including Iceland succumbed to crises. Hungary was the first member of the European Union to experience the crisis and thus set the pattern for inter-institutional cooperation that was followed in the subsequent programs. While many of these programs were small, those for Hungary, Latvia, and Romania were significant in size.[22]

The status of these three countries—members of the European Union but not of the euro area—configured their options for financial support. Because these countries maintained their own central banks and their own currencies, the ECB's refinancing facilities were not available. But they were eligible for assistance from the EU Balance of Payments facility administered by the European Commission and their cases were discussed in the Ecofin Council. All of them were also members of the IMF and could call upon its resources accordingly.

The European Union and its member states had a vital interest in the economic health of these countries and the success of their programs. Since joining the EU in 2004, they shared the single market and the *acquis communautaire* and were formally obliged to join the monetary union eventually. Financial assistance and the policy conditionality associated with it would have spillover effects on other EU members and longer-term consequences for

---

[22] An overview is provided by Bas B. Bakker and Christoph Klingen, eds, *How Emerging Europe Came through the 2008/09 Crisis: An Account by the Staff of the IMF's European Department* (Washington, D.C.: IMF, 2012), especially p. 79, Table 5.1.

regional integration. The European Commission was thus included in the development of the lending programs for these countries.

Beginning with Hungary in October 2008, the IMF took the lead in designing and negotiating the program and the European Commission worked alongside it. The third leg of the institutional arrangement was not the ECB but the World Bank, which had been involved with Central and Eastern European countries since their transition to market economies. Anders Aslund colorfully described the role of the IMF as "financial savior," the Commission as "rookie," the World Bank as "third fiddle," and the ECB as "Voldemort," for its refusal to provide more generous swap lines.[23] This institutional team was supplemented by the European Investment Bank (EIB) and the European Bank for Reconstruction and Development (EBRD), which, along with the World Bank, contributed to project funding, bank restructuring, and social safety nets. On this occasion, however, and in contrast to previous cases, the IMF had an institutional partner in the Commission with whom it had to make substantial compromises.

Most official accounts emphasize the effectiveness of cooperation among these institutions.[24] At the working level, relations among officials were indeed generally good. Behind the scenes, however, finding a modus vivendi was fraught. The European Commission had not worked with the IMF on a balance-of-payments program in a very long time. The IMF had not previously worked with a regional financial institution similarly on this scale. Despite multiple calls by outsiders to anticipate exactly this sort of problem,[25] guidelines for such cooperation had not been established and the protocols for inter-institutional communication and consultation in such a contingency had not been concluded.

The sequence in which a finance minister must consult these institutions when submitting a request for financial assistance was a critical procedural question. Several ministers appeared to be unaware of their obligation under the Balance of Payments facility regulation to consult their European colleagues prior to going to the IMF.[26] Commissioner Joaquín Almunia objected strenuously when some of them approached the IMF first.

---

[23] Anders Aslund, *The Last Shall Be the First* (Washington, D.C.: Peterson Institute, 2010), pp. 75–83. In 2008, the ECB extended swap agreements to Denmark and Sweden, which were not under pressure, and repurchase agreements to Hungary and Poland, the value of which was questionable.

[24] See, for example, Bakker and Klingen, *How Emerging Europe Came through the 2008/09 Crisis*, p. 78, Box 5.1.

[25] See, for example, Henning, *East Asian Financial Cooperation*; Henning, "Coordinating Regional and Multilateral Financial Institutions." An indicative set of non-binding principles was later agreed by the G20 finance ministers and central bank governors; see, "G20 Principles for Cooperation between the IMF and Regional Financing Arrangements," October 15, 2011.

[26] Council Regulation 332/2002, *Official Journal of the European Communities*, February 22, 2002, L 53/1–3.

The Latvian program revealed profound disagreement and the need for better procedures to reconcile substantive differences. In this case, exchange rate policy was the principal source of disagreement.[27] The debate was broad ranging: most officials within the IMF advocated a substantial devaluation of the Latvian currency, the lat, consistent with advice to many other borrowers. However, Latvia was a member of the Exchange Rate Mechanism II (ERM II), operated a quasi-currency board, and aspired to join the monetary union within a few years. A large majority of domestic borrowing, surprisingly, was denominated in euro or Swiss francs. Devaluation would have forced many borrowers into default, which would have rebounded on Swedish banks, among the other foreign banks that had been operating in the country. The European Commission and other member states thus opposed devaluation, supporting the Latvian government position. IMF Managing Director Dominique Strauss-Kahn and Commissioner Almunia debated the question in a meeting of the G7 finance ministers.[28]

In the end, the European position prevailed and the currency peg to the euro was maintained. But, in the absence of a devaluation to hasten the correction in the current account deficit, the reduction in domestic wages and tightening of fiscal policy had to be correspondingly more severe, the adjustment period longer, and the size of the loan larger. The IMF called upon the European side to contribute the additional financing that was required as a consequence of the decision to keep the peg. Of the €7.5 billion package, the IMF contributed €1.7 billion, twenty-three percent of the total. The Fund's minority share was exceptional by the standard of previous programs, but would become the rule for programs in the euro area.[29]

Agreement on the program did not settle the debate over the currency peg, however. IMF officials continued to believe that Latvia would not escape the crisis without a devaluation and pressed for a "Plan B," which mandated one. They also pressed the Latvian government for further fiscal measures during the first program review, which would unlock a disbursement in summer 2009. But, determined that the exchange rate question not be reopened, the Europeans took a preemptive course of action. The European Council issued a strong statement of support for Latvia at its meeting in June. The European Commission, rather than waiting until the IMF concluded its review, disbursed

---

[27] Anders Aslund, *The Last Shall Be the First: The East European Financial Crisis* (Washington, D.C.: Peterson Institute, 2010), pp. 53–66; Anders Aslund and Valdis Dombrovskis, *How Latvia Came through the Financial Crisis* (Washington, D.C.: Peterson Institute, 2011), pp. 51–64; Olivier J. Blanchard, Mark Griffiths, and Gertrand Gruss, "Boom, Bust, Recovery: Forensics of the Latvia Crisis," *Brookings Papers on Economic Activity* (Fall 2013), pp. 325–88; Paul Krugman, "Latvia is the New Argentina," *New York Times* blog, December 23, 2008; Aslund, "Paul Krugman's Blind Spot," *Foreign Policy* blog, November 8, 2013.

[28] Interviews with European and IMF officials, Washington, D.C., October 2010.

[29] IMF, "Latvia: Request for Stand-By Arrangement," December 19, 2008.

its tranche separately at the beginning of July—effectively daring the Fund not to disburse. The IMF did not release its disbursement until the end of that month.[30]

In the event, Latvia recovered well and even joined the monetary union at the beginning of 2014. Its success was mirrored generally by other program countries in Central and Eastern Europe. But these debates laid bare key substantive differences between the IMF and the Commission, differences that inhered in their institutional positions, and underscored the inadequacy of coordination mechanisms. Many Europeans thus sought a different institutional solution when the crisis spread to countries within the euro area, raising the financial and political stakes by an order of magnitude.

When Central and Eastern Europe confronted crises during 2008, many observers thought that the euro-area countries were insulated from crises. As part of the monetary union, it was argued, these countries could run substantial current account deficits without risking a sudden stop in capital inflows. These observers were very much mistaken.

---

[30] Aslund and Dombrovskis, *How Latvia Came through the Financial Crisis*, pp. 85–8.

5

Greece 2010

The Greek crisis of 2010 was a formative episode, during which European governments chose the mix of institutions that would formulate the rescue program and the institutions established the modalities for cooperation. The decisions made then affected the choices for the institutional mix for the subsequent programs during the euro crisis. This chapter examines the onset of the crisis in Greece and the genesis of the rescue program, the first of three programs for the country over the coming five-year period. Specifically, it addresses the debate over the role of the IMF in the institutional mix and the reasons why the Fund was included. The chapter also examines some of the institutional alternatives to the troika that might have been chosen but were rejected, creation of temporary financial facilities of the euro area, and role of German politics and preferences in the development of the euro's institutional framework.

CONTENTIOUS PATH TO RESCUE

At the end of 2009, a change in government and the drastic revision of statistics on the deficit position and debt triggered Greece's financial crisis. But the fundamental problems, economic and political, had been building up for well over a decade. Prior to joining the European Community as the tenth member in 1981, Greece underwent a transition from military rule to democracy. That transition was accompanied by the development of political parties that effectively colonized the state. Though not an original member of the monetary union, Greece petitioned for entry and was admitted in 2001.[1] Within a few years, however, rumors were swirling about the veracity of Greek

---

[1] For a definitive treatment of the state of the Greek economy and challenges confronting it immediately after entry into the monetary union, see Ralph C. Bryant, Nicholas C. Garganas, and George S. Tavlas, eds, *Greece's Economic Performance and Prospects* (Washington, D.C.: Bank of Greece and Brookings Institution, 2001).

fiscal accounts. While growing satisfactorily during the boom years of the mid-2000s, Greece experienced a steady and dramatic decline in international competitiveness. On the measure of wage increases relative to productivity gains, Greece was a significant outlier among euro-area countries.

In November 2009, Greece held a national election that replaced the conservative New Democracy government of Costas Karamanlis with a Panhellenic Socialist Movement (PASOK) government led by George Papandreou, the third of the Papandreou family to lead his country. Shortly after becoming prime minister, Papandreou telephoned IMF Managing Director Dominique Strauss-Kahn to ask for the IMF's assessment of Greece's economic situation. Strauss-Kahn told him that it was possible that Greece would need a loan program but that, given the experience with joint programs for the three Central European countries, and the fact that Greece was a member of the euro area, Papandreou's European colleagues might have strong views about how such a program should be organized (i.e., not want the Fund involved). Papandreou checked with his European counterparts and phoned back three days later, confirming that they wanted to organize any financial assistance to Greece on a European basis alone. Nor was IMF involvement an "easy sell" in domestic politics, Greece having borrowed from the European Union but not the Fund in 1985 and 1991.

The problem with this option, however, was that the European Union and euro area had no vehicle or program through which to lend to Greece. In fact, the Maastricht treaty specifically forbade members of the euro area from assuming one another's financial obligations (Article 125). Many interpreted this "no bailout" provision as preventing financial assistance to countries in Greece's situation and indeed under almost any circumstances. The logical implication of this strict reading was that any financial support to Greece would have to come from the IMF. The euro area had thus to (a) clarify the legal status of assistance to Greece, and if it were permissible under the treaties, (b) create a financial facility for members of the euro area. Advocates of deeper integration in the euro area sought to use this emergency as a fulcrum against which to leverage a movement to build more robust institutions.

January 2010 Stability Program

The Greek prime minister sought to assuage fears in the financial markets in December, telling reporters that ECB President Jean-Claude Trichet and Luxembourg Prime Minister Jean-Claude Juncker saw "no possibility" of a Greek default. Papandreou also said that there was no possibility of Greece

---

[2] Interview with a former IMF official, Paris, May 22, 2012.

leaving the euro area, according to the report.[3] But there was virtually no progress behind the scenes toward securing financial assistance from the Eurogroup in late 2009 and early 2010. Papandreou and Finance Minister George Papaconstantinou oversaw the introduction of the first of several stabilization packages—effectively reversing PASOK's electoral pledge to stimulate the economy—and might have expected some credit for this in European councils.[4] At the meetings of the Eurogroup and Ecofin in Brussels during January 18–19, Spain, Italy, and France began a discussion among themselves about a prospective program for Greece. Still reeling from the revelation of huge deficits, however, the Dutch and German finance ministers refused to entertain any such proposal.[5] Commissioner Almunia told Papaconstantinou that there was no "Plan B" for the Greek economy—that is, the government's austerity package(s) would have to suffice without financial assistance.[6]

If there were to be an exclusively European solution to the Greek crisis, the European Commission would have to provide the analytical work that defined the extent of the financial requirement, the terms of assistance, and the policy adjustments required of Greece. This task fell mainly to the Commissioner for Economic and Monetary Affairs—a position assumed by Olli Rehn on February 9, 2010—and the Directorate-General for Economic and Financial Affairs (DG Ecfin), headed by Marco Buti, on behalf of the President of the Commission, Barroso. The Commission presented its assessment of the stability program of the Papandreou government in early February. It cited Greece's failure to provide accurate financial statistics, underscored the need to follow through on the fiscal and structural reforms to which the government had committed, and demanded greater specificity on the measures to be introduced and the calendar for adoption.[7] It reiterated the autumn forecasts for the ratio of government debt to GDP, expected to rise to 135.4 percent in 2011. Consistent with the position that there would be no "Plan B," however,

[3] "Papandreou Says ECB, Juncker See No Possibility of Greek Default," *Bloomberg News*, December 11, 2009.

[4] Papaconstantinou has written his own account of first two years of the crisis, which includes treatment of the meetings with European, IMF, and U.S. officials during the gestation of the first program. See George Papaconstaninou, *Game Over: The Inside Story of the Greek Crisis* (Athens: Papadopoulos, 2016).

[5] Carlo Bastasin, *Saving Europe: How National Politics Nearly Destroyed the Euro* (Washington, D.C.: Brookings Institution Press, 2012), p. 154. Simeon Djankov emphasizes the sense of betrayal on the part of Greece's partners over the falsification of fiscal statistics. See Djankov, *Inside the Euro Crisis* (Washington, D.C.: Peterson Institute, 2014), ch. 4.

[6] Interview with a former senior Greek official, Athens, July 18, 2012. Commissioner Almunia declared this position publicly at the end of the month. Angela Monaghan, "Joaquin Almunia: We don't need a Greek bail-out because the country won't default," *Daily Telegraph*, January 29, 2010.

[7] European Commission, "Commission Assesses Stability Programme of Greece," Document No. IP/10/116, Brussels, Belgium, February 3, 2010.

the assessment raised no concerns about debt sustainability and made no mention of the need for official financing—despite the fact that interest rates had risen to 6.8 percent while the economy was expected to shrink over the next two years.

The Commission no doubt had concerns that it preferred to raise confidentially with the Eurogroup rather than publicly. But senior officials from several of the member states were surprised at the relative complacency of the Commission's assessment of the long-term prospects for Greek financial sustainability. By contrast, the Eurogroup highlighted several of the downside risks at its meeting back-to-back with the Ecofin Council during February 15 and 16. It noted that Greek government finances were at "high risk in relation to their long-term sustainability."[8] In Berlin, the Chancellor's Office and the Finance Ministry, in particular, were surprised at the discrepancy between the Commission report and market developments, and this entered their calculus on the institutional mix for the rescue.

Opposition to the IMF

Although the IMF was eventually included in the Greek program, this outcome could not by any means have been taken for granted. The starting point of European officials was, in fact, quite the opposite, to organize the rescue on an exclusively European basis. Heads of government and finance ministers met several times in different configurations (the Eurogroup, Ecofin Council, European Council, and Euro summit) to consider precisely such a solution to the Greek crisis.

Advocates of European integration understandably sought to use the Greek crisis as an opportunity to strengthen the governance and cohesion of the monetary union. Involvement of the IMF, they worried, could undercut momentum toward deeper integration. The European Commission and the ECB had a fairly clear institutional interest in excluding the IMF, which did not prioritize European rules and commitments such as the budget deficit limits set down in the Maastricht treaty. The Commission's experience with the programs for Hungary and Latvia drove this lesson home. Working with the Fund would require debating such matters, require compromises, and undercut their strategies to use the crisis to strengthen their own roles within the European architecture.

It was thus no surprise that the European Commission opposed the involvement of the IMF in the Greek program. Commission President Barroso consistently advocated a Europe-only solution without the IMF during

[8] Council of the European Union, "Council Opinion on the Updated Stability Programme of Greece, 2010–2013" 6560/10, Brussels, February 16, 2010.

winter 2010.[9] "We don't need to call in the IMF," Commissioner Almunia told the European Parliament on February 9. "We have more than enough instruments in the treaty to tackle a situation like the one we're faced with at the moment in Greece," he added.[10]

Officials at the ECB were similarly opposed to including the IMF. Programs administered by the IMF typically place conditions on the borrower's monetary policy. Doing so for a country within the euro area could potentially create tension between the rescue program and the objective of maintaining price stability for the monetary union as a whole, as well as constrain the independence of the ECB. Anticipation of these frictions gave officials in Frankfurt pause about involving the Fund. More immediately, however, they were concerned about the substantive differences with Fund officials over program design and relieving euro area governments of the financial responsibility to resolve the crisis. The President of the ECB, Jean-Claude Trichet, publicly opposed the inclusion of the IMF in any financial package for Greece. While accepting a role for the Fund in technical assistance, he said, "I do not believe that it would be appropriate to introduce the IMF as a supplier of help through standby arrangements or through any such kind of help."[11]

Trichet had been engaged in an ongoing struggle with euro-area governments for years. He hoped that the crisis would finally force them to address the fundamental fiscal and structural problems about which he had been warning. Participation of the IMF would not only pose bureaucratic friction over program design, he feared, but also weaken the incentives for governments to implement reforms and create their own fund and fiscal backstop for the monetary union.[12]

Jean-Claude Juncker, President of the Eurogroup and Prime Minister of Luxembourg, said in February that it would be "absurd" for the IMF to provide financial assistance to Greece. "The IMF can send technical experts

[9] "IMF Aid for Greece 'Not a Question of Prestige' Says EU's Barroso," France 24 International News, March 22, 2013.

[10] Adam Cohen, "EU Debates IMF Role for Greece," *Wall Street Journal*, February 10, 2010.

[11] Jean-Claude Trichet, President of the ECB, Lucas Papademos, Vice President of the ECB, press conference, Frankfurt, March 4, 2010, <http://www.ecb.int/press/pressconf/2010/html/is100304.en.html>. See also Gerrit Wiesmann and Quentin Peel, "Berlin Shifts Stance on IMF Role in Greece," *Financial Times*, March 16, 2010. In an interview in early April, Trichet would recharacterize his opposition to the Fund: "I was not against the IMF involvement in itself. I was against the involvement of the IMF alone. I have always been in favour of the maximum level of responsibility exerted by the governments of the euro area as is prescribed by the Stability and Growth Pact." He explained that he did not want governments evading their responsibilities by calling upon the IMF. Jean-Claude Trichet, Interview with *Il Sole 24 Ore*, April 9, 2010. But it also must be said that there was never a realistic possibility that the IMF would be Greece's *only* lender.

[12] Interviews with a former ECB official, Paris, May 23, 2012, and July 8, 2015. Lorenzo Bini Smaghi provides a perspective from the ECB in *Austerity: European Democracies against the Wall* (Brussels, Centre for European Policy Studies, 2013).

to Greece because the European Commission doesn't have the human resources to deal properly with that job," Juncker said. "But it's not a matter of having the IMF designing the exit strategy as far as public finances are concerned."[13]

Juncker's comments reflected what was a dominant view if not a consensus among the finance ministers of the Eurogroup. "What's clear is that this is a matter for the Europeans," German Finance Minister Wolfgang Schäuble said in early February. "There is no doubt that Greece is not a question for the International Monetary Fund." Intriguingly, given her subsequent appointment as managing director of the IMF fifteen months later, French Finance Minister Christine Lagarde also rejected calling upon the IMF to help Greece.[14] She reflected in turn the strong position of French President Nicolas Sarkozy.[15] Some observers noted that Sarkozy had a personal political interest in minimizing the role of Dominique Strauss-Kahn, a prospective competitor for the French presidency.[16]

Europe's leaders and senior policymakers of the euro area harbored a very strong disposition against including the Fund and addressing the Greek crisis on their own as a Community. The strength of that consensus was remarkable. Although some officials from the non-euro countries within the European Union, such as Poland, Sweden, and the United Kingdom, favored a role for the Fund, almost no senior official within the euro area publicly advocated IMF financing for Greece during January and February 2010.[17]

Bringing in the IMF

However, this dominant view was not unanimous. One critically important player had not made up her mind on the IMF question and the German government as a whole was still feeling its way forward on the Greek problem, deciding its preferred course of action. In March, German Chancellor Angela

---

[13] "Juncker Says 'Absurd' to Talk of IMF Aid for Greece," *Bloomberg News*, February 16, 2010.

[14] "Grèce: Christine Lagarde dit non au FMI," *Le Figaro*, February 12, 2010. See also Liz Alderman, "France's Lagarde Named New Head of I.M.F.," *New York Times*, June 28, 2011; Tony Barber, "IMF's Role in Rescue Finally Wins Backing of Reluctant States," *Financial Times*, May 4, 2010.

[15] Helene Fouquet, "Sarkozy Opposes IMF Greek Loan, Widens German Rift," *Bloomberg News*, March 19, 2010.

[16] See, for example, Bob Davis and Marcus Walker, "EU Leaders Keep IMF on Sidelines in Greece," *Wall Street Journal*, March 1, 2010.

[17] One exception appears to be Belgian Finance Minister Didier Reynders, see <http://www.theguardian.com/world/2010/feb/10/greece-france-germany-euro>. Dutch Finance Minister Jan Kees de Jager supported the inclusion of the IMF in March. See "Dutch Government Backs IMF Option for Greece," *EUbusiness*, March 19, 2010.

Merkel made two statements that shocked many of her euro-area partners.[18] First, she announced that it should, in principle, to be possible to eject a member state from the monetary union if it repeatedly violates its obligations under the treaties. Second, she declared that the IMF should be a lender to Greece along with the member states of the euro area. The stance placed her very publicly at odds with Finance Minister Wolfgang Schäuble, who was widely known to be a committed European.[19]

During the winter of 2010, the debate in Europe over the solution to the debt problem exhibited extraordinarily unconstrained "blue-sky" thinking.[20] Some analysts openly entertained the idea of a debt restructuring for Greece at the outset. A number of German policymakers were (relatively quietly) sympathetic with "bailing-in" the private sector. The problem, of course, was that the euro area lacked a facility to prevent the Lehman-style contagion that a surprise restructuring of Greek debt would almost inevitably produce.

Daniel Gros and Thomas Mayer proposed the creation of a "European Monetary Fund" that could finance countries in crisis but also facilitate an "organized default" in cases where debt was not sustainable.[21] Schäuble himself proposed the creation of a European Monetary Fund in an article in the *Financial Times*, an idea that quickly won the support of the new European Commissioner for Economic and Monetary Affairs, Olli Rehn.[22] At first, Merkel seemed to support her finance minister, saying, "We want to be able to solve our problems in the future without the IMF." But she also warned that his proposal to create an EMF would require a change in the treaties, which would not be immediately feasible.[23]

In his careful treatment of European decision-making during this period, Carlo Bastasin highlights the first half of February as a particularly acute phase of the behind-the-scenes debate over the mix of regional and multilateral

[18] German Bundestag, "Statement by the Federal Chancellor," 30th Session, 17th Legislative Period, March 17, 2010.

[19] Markus Feldenkirchen, Christian Reiermann, Michael Sauga, and Hans-Jürgen Schlamp, "Berlin Divided on Greece: Merkel Takes on the EU and Her Own Finance Minister," *Spiegel Online International*, March 22, 2010.

[20] For a review of the institutional options at the time, see Daniela Schwarzer and Sebastian Dullien, "Policy Options for Greece—An Evaluation," *Stiftung Wissenschaft und Politik* Working Paper 2010/01, Berlin, March 2010.

[21] Daniel Gros and Thomas Mayer, "How to Deal with Sovereign Default in Europe: Create the European Monetary Fund Now!," *CEPS Policy Brief*, No. 202, Brussels, Centre for European Policy Studies, February 2010, updated May 17, 2010.

[22] Wolfgang Schäuble, "Why Europe's Monetary Union Faces Its Biggest Crisis," *Financial Times*, March 11, 2010; Gerrit Wiesmann and Ralph Atkins, "Schäuble Calls for Tough EMF Sanction," *Financial Times*, March 11, 2010; "Greek Debt Crisis: Proposal for European Monetary Fund Wins EU Support," *Spiegel Online International*, March 8, 2010.

[23] Quentin Peel, Ben Hall, and Tony Barber, "Merkel Warns of Hurdles in EMF Plan," *Financial Times*, March 8, 2010. See also, "EU at Odds Over Treaty Change for EMF," *EurActiv*, March 18, 2010.

institutional solutions.[24] The European Commission drafted a statement of the Eurogroup that would have placed it at the center of an effort to organize "determined and coordinated action and provide support, if needed, to safeguard financial stability in the euro area as a whole." Chancellor Merkel objected to it, however. In order to prepare a common position of the EU summit on February 11, European Council President Herman Van Rompuy convened a small group on the morning of that day which included Juncker, Trichet, Barroso, Merkel, Papandreou, Sarkozy, and Spanish Prime Minister Zapatero. In a spectacular confrontation between the French and German leaders, Sarkozy urged immediate and forceful action. Merkel, however, insisted that the legal basis and conditionality be spelled out in a coherent plan before any financial commitments were announced. The French President opposed involvement of the Fund on the grounds that it would open the monetary union to American influence, but the Chancellor stated that she wanted the IMF directly involved in the operation.[25]

Meanwhile, faced with indecision over the development of a financial response, Greek officials used the threat of going to the IMF to prod their fellow Europeans forward.[26] Prime Minister Papandreou said pointedly that Greece would draw from the IMF if his European colleagues failed to produce a solution at the EU summit in late March 2010.[27] The threat was limited by the fact that the Europeans could, in principle, block Greece's access at the Executive Board. Nonetheless, going directly to the IMF could publicly embarrass the European Council and create procedural complications for the European institutions.

For his part, Dominique Strauss-Kahn maneuvered to insert the IMF in the resolution of the Greek problem, but did not force the IMF upon his erstwhile European colleagues. "We are there to help. I have a mission in place providing technical advice at the request of the Greek government and if they ask me to intervene, we will do it," he told France's RTL radio. "But I totally understand the Europeans who want to try and sort the problem out amongst themselves." He said the Greek situation was serious but did not think the country was on the verge of bankruptcy.[28] Statements that he made to media outlets are reportedly also typical of his private communications with European leaders and finance ministers in February 2010.[29]

[24] Bastasin, *Saving Europe*, pp. 165–9.   [25] Bastasin, *Saving Europe*, p. 168.

[26] Papaconstantinou, *Game Over*, pp. 81–4. The former finance minister also discloses a covert meeting about IMF assistance with Strauss-Kahn and Papandreou in Davos in late January, pp. 69–73.

[27] Aoife White, "Greece: Will Ask for IMF Help If EU Fails," *Seattle Times*, March 18, 2010.

[28] See the interview with Strauss-Kahn at <https://www.youtube.com/watch?v=ghO6cgyJKOk>; "Strauss-Kahn Calls on Europe to Help Greece," *L'Express*, February 4, 2010.

[29] Interviews with a former IMF official, Paris, May 22, 2012; and a former Greek official, Athens, July 18, 2012.

During March 24–5, in Brussels, the EU summit finally agreed on the principles of a financial arrangement for addressing Greece. The facility would not be a common fund, however; instead it would be a set of coordinated bilateral loans. Euro-area member states would contribute in proportion to their shares of the capital key for the ECB and disbursements under these loans would be decided by unanimity. They would be available only as a last resort after a country lost access to the financial markets (ultima ratio) and when necessary to safeguard the stability of the euro area. These loans would be subject to conditionality in a program that was to be assessed by the Commission and the ECB.

As a condition for her acceptance, Chancellor Merkel secured the commitment to involve the IMF. Merkel was supported by most of the other triple-A-rated countries in the euro area in advocating the involvement of the IMF.[30] But German commitment to the Fund was pivotal. As Bastasin points out, the role that was envisaged for the Fund had thus evolved from a marginal provider of expertise in the February Council meeting to a full partner in complementary financing in the March Council statement.[31]

Notably, the EU summit agreement did not put to rest the question of involvement of the Fund; the Commission, ECB and Merkel's own finance minister continued to object and sought to subordinate the Fund to the European institutions in interinstitutional cooperation. From this point forward, nonetheless, the IMF was at the center of the troika arrangements, not just for Greece but for the other programs as well. This position was not secure; the overall troika arrangement did not please many participants and was reconsidered with all but one of the subsequent programs. However, for the remainder of the euro crisis, the involvement of the Fund, while uneasy, and coming sometimes without a financial contribution, proved to be a durable institutional equilibrium.[32]

The First Program

Formal negotiations among the IMF, Commission, and ECB officials—now dubbed the "troika"—with the Greek government began immediately after a Eurogroup meeting on April 11. Servaas Deroose served as the mission chief for the Commission, Poul Thomsen for the IMF, and Klaus Masuch for the ECB.

---

[30] "Europeans Agree Bailout for Greece," *Wall Street Journal*, March 26, 2010, which also lists Spain as a supporter.
[31] Bastasin, *Saving Europe*, pp. 180–2.
[32] Bini Smaghi concludes, "[t]he decision to involve the IMF was the product of European politicians' lack of confidence in Greece, the European Commission and ultimately themselves to manage relations with the Greek government." See *Austerity*, p. 34.

Across the table, they faced Finance Minister Papaconstantinou and the Governor of the Bank of Greece, George Provopoulos, both of whom would sign the memorandum of economic and financial policies for the European institutions and the letter of intent for the IMF. With a debt payment looming, and with the discussions over the previous couple of months having taken place in some detail, the negotiations proceeded quickly, concluding on May 2.

German officials had wanted to limit the headline figure for assistance to Greece by announcing financing only for one year.[33] But the IMF insisted that the program cover three years' worth of Greece's financing needs until the country could, in principle, anticipate reaccessing international capital markets, which nearly tripled the headline figure.[34] The total amount was €110 billion: €80 billion through bilateral loans from the euro-area member states, and €30 billion from the IMF through a regular standby arrangement (SBA). Even this minority share represented roughly thirty times Greece's €1 billion quota in the Fund, the largest (non-concessionary) loan in absolute terms and as a percentage of quota that the IMF has ever made (see Appendix: Financial Rescues for Euro-Area Countries, 2010–2015).[35]

The January Stability Programme agreed with the Commission and European Council had provided for a reduction in the fiscal deficit of four percent in 2010 (from an expected 12.7 percent), three percent in 2011, and the same in 2012 (the "four–three–three program"). The Commission forecast a mere 0.3 percent economic contraction in 2010 followed—miraculously, given the continuing fiscal restriction—by three years of steady growth. By contrast, the new troika program demanded a much larger overall reduction in the budget deficit—eleven percent of GDP, on top of measures that amounted to five percent of GDP in the first half of 2010 under the Stability Programme. The new program forecast a four percent contraction in 2010, followed by a 2.6 percent decline in 2011 and then 1.1 percent growth in 2012. The new growth forecast was hailed by some at the time,[36] but it turned out to be anything but realistic. Rather than contracting by 5.5 percent as predicted for the period 2010–12 as a whole, the Greek economy contracted by seventeen percent and its recession continued into 2013.

It is apparent that Greece's debt was not sustainable, certainly in retrospect. But the not-so-hidden agenda of many policymakers was to buy time to build

---

[33] Merely twelve days before the full program was announced, the Eurogroup would not commit to a figure for three years, using the first-year number of €30 billion for Greece, supplemented by the IMF. "Statement on the Support to Greece by Euro area Members States," Brussels, April 11, 2010.

[34] Bastasin, *Saving Europe*, pp. 187 and 193.

[35] The IMF has approved a Flexible Credit Line for Mexico, which is larger in absolute size, and one for Poland, which is comparable, but neither country has drawn on the facility.

[36] Tony Barber, "IMF's role in rescue finally wins backing of reluctant states," *Financial Times*, May 4, 2010.

European, and multilateral, arrangements to the point where it would be safe to restructure Greece's debt without triggering a "Lehman moment." We return to this matter later, after considering the IMF's participation in this strategy.

IMF ANALYSIS AND DECISION

In approaching their decision as to whether to approve the loan program in May 2010, the staff, managing director, and Executive Board of the IMF faced the fundamental question of whether Greece's debt was sustainable.[37] If it were, then lending over the medium-term until market access was restored under program conditionality was a logical response that accorded with Fund policy. If it were not, then the Fund's participation could not expect to restore market access and the program would (a) simply delay, not prevent, an eventual debt restructuring, (b) substitute official credits for private credits in the meantime, shifting risk onto the public sector, and (c) deepen and prolong Greece's recession.[38] The risk associated with lending into a debt that later might prove to be unsustainable was balanced by a desire to avoid contagion to a larger group of countries in Europe and perhaps beyond, at a time when memories of the Lehman contagion were fresh and markets still jittery.

The question of debt sustainability, how to evaluate it, and how to respond in cases of unsustainability later became major points of contention among the troika institutions. But it was also a major bone of contention *within* each of the institutions, and among member governments, at the outset of the first Greek program. Some of these differences were later laid bare in the IMF's ex post evaluation of the first program, published in May 2013, which foreshadowed intensification of debates among the institutions as the euro crisis evolved.[39]

The program documents prepared by the IMF staff for the Executive Board laid out the case for the IMF contribution to the Greek program. An annex

---

[37] On IMF decision-making in the first Greek program, see also, Susan Schadler, "Unsustainable Debt and the Political Economy of Lending: Constraining the IMF's Role in Sovereign Debt Crises," *CIGI Papers* No. 19 (Waterloo, Ontario: Centre for International Governance Innovation, October 2013); Paul Blustein, "Laid Low: The IMF, the Euro Zone and the First Rescue of Greece," *CIGI Papers* No. 61 (April 2015).

[38] The IMF had made debt restructuring a precondition for lending in Uruguay in 2002 and foreign creditors had been effectively bailed-in for Iceland in 2008, whereas Hungary, Latvia, and Romania received loans in parallel with the Vienna Initiative in which banks maintained their credit lines. IMF, "Greece: Ex Post Evaluation," May 20, 2013.

[39] IMF, "Greece: Ex Post Evaluation," May 20, 2013. See also, Charles Wyplosz and Silvia Sgherri, "The IMF's Role in Greece in the Context of the 2010 Stand-By Arrangement," Background Paper, IEO–IMF, Washington, D.C., July 2016.

presented the debt sustainability analysis, projecting that the government debt-to-GDP ratio would peak at 147 percent in 2013 and then decline to 120 percent in 2020. A fan chart displayed debt scenarios under alternative assumptions, showing, for example, that with three percent more deflation than projected under the program, debt would not diminish for the foreseeable future. The last bullet in the Executive Summary acknowledged, "Risks to the program are high."[40] The view that Greece's debt was not sustainable was common within the private financial sector and academe.[41]

The size of the loan to Greece exceeded by far the normal access limits as a percentage of quota. To justify exceptional access, the Fund staff had to certify that four criteria were met. However, one of them—a "high probability of public debt being sustainable in the medium term"—was simply not realistic in the judgment of the staff. As a consequence, the criterion was modified during the Executive Board meeting that considered the Greek program on May 9, 2010. Thenceforth, the debt sustainability criteria could be waived where there was a "high risk of international systemic spillover effects."[42]

The Greek package—the loan, conditionality, exceptional access, and the procedure for modifying it—was highly controversial within the Executive Board. The Greek loan decision was probably the most hotly contested since the 1995 loan to Mexico. Although they apparently did not oppose the program outright, several of the non-European Executive Directors raised strenuous criticisms. The summary of the Board discussion, which has been made public, gives us a reasonably clear view of the objections.[43]

The most fundamental objections revolved around the risks to debt sustainability and thus to the program. Referring to whether debt was sustainable over the medium term, the staff recognized explicitly that it was "difficult to state categorically that this is the case with a high probability." To many Executive Directors, this was a considerable understatement. Those from India, Brazil, Argentina, Russia, and Switzerland complained that the program contained no debt restructuring or private sector involvement. These Executive Directors

[40] IMF, "Greece: Staff Report on Request for Stand-By Arrangement," IMF *Country Report* No. 10/110, May 2010.

[41] The IMF counts at least fifteen economists who, writing separately, expressed this conclusion in 2010. See "Greece: Ex Post Evaluation," p. 28, n. 17.

[42] IMF, "Greece: Ex Post Evaluation," p. 29. The procedure by which this exemption was introduced has been roundly criticized. See, among others, Independent Evaluation Office, "The IMF and the Crises in Greece, Ireland, and Portugal" (Washington: IEO–IMF, July 8, 2016).

[43] Ian Talley posted an unofficial summary of the minutes of the Executive Board meeting of May 9, 2010 at <http://online.wsj.com/public/resources/documents/Greece-IMF-2010-Bailout-Minutes.pdf>. See also, "History of the IMF and Greece's Bailout," Real Time Economics, *Wall Street Journal*, January 31, 2014. Excerpts from the confidential statements of the Executive Directors were published by Thomas Catan and Ian Talley in the *Wall Street Journal*, October 7, 2013; see also, "IMF Document Excerpts: Disagreements Revealed," *Wall Street Journal*, October 7, 2013. In 2015, the Fund released the official record of the meeting, "The Acting Chair's Summing-Up, Greece—Request for Stand-By Arrangement," May 9, 2010 (BUFF/10/56).

represented large swaths of the membership from Latin America, the Middle East, and Asia.

Brazil's Executive Director Paulo Nogueira Batista, was perhaps the most forceful. "The risks of the program are immense," he declared. "[I]t may be seen not as a rescue of Greece, which will have to undergo a wrenching adjustment, but as a bailout of Greece's private debt holders, mainly European financial institutions." He was joined in this criticism by several of his colleagues, who (in the case of the Swiss and Chinese Executive Directors) also warned that the economic forecasts for Greece were optimistic. The Swiss Director seconded the criticism about the lack of debt restructuring, to the consternation of his fellow Europeans, and proposed a resumption of the 2001–2 discussions about the Sovereign Debt Restructuring Mechanism (SDRM).

The IMF staff offered three points in response to the criticism that debt restructuring was not included in the program. Such an option was complicated, first, by the fact that the overwhelming majority of Greek government bonds did not include collective action clauses (CACs), the bonds were held by a large number of dispersed, anonymous investors, and the opposition of the Greek government itself. Structural reforms were necessary for the success of the program, prompting the Australia Executive Director to respond that the IMF's structural conditions were "macro-critical," but those of the Commission seemed to be a "shopping list."[44]

The Executive Directors from China, Egypt, and Switzerland worried that joint program reviews with the Commission and ECB would expose substantive differences among the institutions. Staff downplayed these concerns, saying that if the Commission did not disburse a given tranche, the Fund could withhold its own disbursement on the grounds of financing assurances (invoking the twelve-month forward financing rule); but this appeared to be "only a theoretical possibility." Four Executive Directors objected to the procedure by which staff snuck the systemic-spillover exemption into the sustainability criterion of the exceptional access policy. Meg Lundsager, the U.S. Executive Director, emphasized that the preferred-creditor status of the Fund made its loan senior to the bilateral loans from the euro-area governments to Greece.

The Executive Directors from Belgium, Denmark, Germany, France, the Netherlands, and Spain presented a joint statement supporting the loan to Greece. They gave priority to securing financial stability in European and international markets to prevent contagion and were willing to countenance uncertainty about debt sustainability and exposure of the Fund in order to calm the markets. Outside and inside the IMF, many European officials argued

[44] Running the risk that the Fund was repeating the mistakes during the Asian financial crisis of 1997–8. IMF, "Board Meeting on Greece's Request for an SBA—May 9, 2010," Office Memorandum, May 10, 2010, p. 3.

that the United States had erred in imposing losses on the private sector by allowing the bankruptcy of Lehman Brothers twenty-one months earlier and that the better course, in light of uncertainty about debt sustainability, was to stabilize the markets presently and address the debt overhang in the fullness of time. Their strategy was, in the vernacular, to "kick the can down the road," which they compared to the U.S. strategy of stabilizing money-center banks during the Latin American debt crisis in the 1980s.[45]

The United States and a number of other non-European countries also supported the loan. Even those Executive Directors who criticized the program nonetheless apparently acquiesced. We have no public reports of any abstentions from this decision.[46] John Lipsky, the First Deputy Managing Director, who chaired the meeting in Strauss-Kahn's absence, could thus declare—without taking a formal vote, which is very rare in the Board—that a majority supported a decision in favor of the program.

The terms of this program spawned a wide-ranging debate among observers about whether the Fund had "sold out" to the European institutions, caved in to their preferences at the cost of candor and realism in the conditions and their projected impact on the Greek economy. This debate intensified as the program went "off track" during the following autumn and winter. The IMF was known to have distinct analytical views and preferences with respect to several issues in the program, including the fiscal path, growth forecasts, speed of deleveraging, bank consolidation, debt sustainability and the ultimate need for restructuring, and private sector involvement in bank reform. Some non-European members of the Fund did not want management risking the credibility of the institution in the eyes of the markets by excessive compromise.

There are a couple reasons why the managing director and staff were inclined to accommodate the euro-area governments, the Commission, and the ECB in spring 2010. First, the Fund had faced fundamental budget reform of its own during 2007–8—a period of relative tranquility in international finance—when it was forced to cut its expenditures, downsize by roughly 400 employees, and renovate its budget model.[47] Management and staff were, from the perspective of bureaucratic purpose, relieved to be "back in business" as an emergency lender with the global financial crisis. Greece demonstrated that the euro area had not rendered the Fund irrelevant even in the world's most highly integrated region.

Second, Fund staff and management came to the "party" late. Whereas, the Commission had been engaged in close discussions with Greek authorities

---

[45] Chris Giles, "Policymakers Can't Kick the Can Down the Road for Ever," *Financial Times*, June 16, 2011.

[46] Some of the non-European Executive Directors would abstain on later decisions with respect to Greece.

[47] See, for example, IMF, "The FY 09–11 Medium-Term Administrative, Restructuring, and Capital Budgets", <https://www.imf.org/external/np/pp/eng/2008/032008.pdf>.

since late 2009, the IMF only sent a technical assistance team to Athens to advise on tax administration and budget reform in January and it was not until mid-April that serious program discussions got underway. So, the Fund staff and management were playing catch-up in technical respects. Some officials within the Fund thought that Greece's debt was not, in fact, sustainable.[48] But this was a matter of internal disagreement, just as it was within the Commission and the ECB. As long as there was agreement among the institutions on what the Papandreou government must do in the first year, some close to the program asked, why fight over fiscal adjustment worth a couple of percent of GDP in the third year when there was a good chance that the program would be renegotiated in the meantime?[49]

Third, a number of observers point to the national identity and the personal interest of the managing director, suggesting that Strauss-Kahn might have been willing to overlook risks to the program in order to assist the euro area as a whole. This suggestion is offered both by people who inveigh against the European bias of the IMF in general and by those who suspect that Strauss-Kahn's ambition to become president of France led him to soften the Fund's insistence on debt realism. At the time of the first Greek program, ultimately, Strauss-Kahn believed that lending to Greece was necessary to avoid contagion and debt restructuring could be addressed subsequently.[50]

In proposing the program to the Executive Board, fourth, Strauss-Kahn's position coincided with the immediate concerns of the large number of member states outside Europe, whose financial markets were potentially vulnerable to contagion. Whatever his political ambitions, the most influential countries within the Fund accepted the program in the hopes of protecting financial stability globally and within their own economies. The Greek program would not have passed without support from the United States and most other countries. Their posture, not the machinations of a managing director, was the fundamental reason why the IMF deferred to European governments on the question of debt sustainability for Greece in May 2010.

In the event, many of the criticisms of the Greek program proved to be prescient. The troika's forecast that the severe fiscal contraction could accommodate a resumption of growth in 2012 proved to be wildly optimistic. The Greek government did not implement many structural reforms or privatization on a timely basis; the expected €50 billion in privatization revenue proved

[48] Blustein offers a nice discussion of the debate among the departments of the Fund on this matter. See Blustein, *Laid Low* (April 2015).

[49] Interview, Washington, D.C., February 20, 2013.

[50] Strauss-Kahn presented his own view in a web posting on June 27, 2015, at <http://fr.slideshare.net/DominiqueStraussKahn/150627-tweet-greece>. Blustein, in *Laid Low*, reveals that Strauss-Kahn and a handful of people at the Fund consulted with the finance ministries of France and Germany about debt restructuring well before, during, and even immediately after the May 2010 decision.

to be a fantasy. Greek politics could not support an adjustment program of this magnitude and the Papandreou government fell in late 2011, followed by a period of political uncertainty. Greece's debt proved not to be sustainable and was restructured twice during 2011–12. The program allowed Greece to remain within the euro area and limited contagion outside Europe, the IMF later pointed out. But, in terms of restoring growth and market confidence, the basis on which it was originally advanced and defended, the program was a spectacular failure.[51]

COMMON FACILITIES

The euro-area member states funded the Greek program not by a common financial facility but by a series of bilateral loans. This institutional arrangement did not command confidence in the markets, which worried about the "next Greece." Euro-area governments realized that they needed to create a common fund in order to stem contagion. In rapid succession after the decisions on the Greek program, they announced the launch of negotiations to this end, while the ECB announced a new program to purchase government bonds.

EFSM and EFSF

European capitals eventually agreed to establish two new facilities. The first fund copied the Balance of Payments facility, which was operated by the Commission under the Community method for countries outside the euro area, and was named the European Financial Stabilisation Mechanism (EFSM). It could provide a total of up to €60 billion to members of the European Union, including, of course, those euro-area countries that were ineligible for the Balance-of-Payments facility. The second fund was advertised as providing up to €440 billion for members of the euro area only and was named the European Financial Stability Facility (EFSF). The EFSF was to be temporary, bridging the period until a large permanent mechanism could be agreed by treaty and eventually domiciled in Luxembourg. Together, the EFSM and the EFSF were supposed to mobilize up to €500 billion beyond what member states had already been pledged to Greece. (The evolution of European financial facilities is treated in greater detail in Chapter 9 and an overview is provided in Table 9.1.)

Lending from the EFSF was expected to be closely tied to IMF programs. For its part, the IMF was expected to make €250 billion available for euro-area

---

[51] The Fund itself pronounced the record "mixed." IMF, "Greece: Ex Post Evaluation," p. 11. Some European assessments, discussed in Chapter 9 of this volume, are more favorable.

contingencies. This figure was announced by Spanish Finance Minister Elena Salgado, who chaired the Ecofin meeting of May 8–10, 2010, where the EFSF's terms of reference were agreed.[52] However, there had been no prior discussion in the IMF Executive Board that committed these funds to the euro area and Salgado was, of course, in no position to commit the IMF. Nor was it possible even in principle to commit the Fund in this way, since its lending would go to individual countries rather than the euro area as a group. First Deputy Managing Director John Lipsky said that the €250 billion was "hypothetical," stressing that the IMF was not negotiating with other members. But both the Europeans and Fund officials wanted a big headline number to project solidarity and impress the markets.[53] Dominique Strauss-Kahn did not object but rather affirmed that the EU and IMF would provide assistance in a ratio of roughly two to one (although this ratio described neither the Greek program nor those in Central and Eastern Europe, exactly).[54] Europeans were thus able to argue that more than $1 trillion was being made available for euro-area contingencies, an amount that roughly equaled the combined government debt of Greece, Ireland, Portugal, and Spain.

Securities Market Programme

During the negotiation of the first Greek package, and as bond spreads were widening for several countries, there was pressure on the ECB to act decisively in the secondary market for government bonds. The Federal Reserve and Bank of England had bought government bonds outright (as opposed to holding them temporarily as part of refinancing operations) in very large quantities during the global financial crisis. Similar action by the ECB could ease government funding constraints and, because the ECB was not purchasing bonds directly from governments in the primary market, would not run afoul of the treaty prohibition against "monetary financing." The ECB insisted that the governments take collective responsibility for long-term financing and thus refused to act before the Eurogroup approved the program with Greece.

Once it did so, however, the ECB quickly announced the launch of its new Securities Market Programme (SMP) on Monday, May 10, 2010.[55] On the

---

[52] Council of the European Union, Extraordinary Ecofin Council meeting, press release 9596/10, Brussels, May 10, 2010.

[53] Ian Talley, "EUR250 Billion IMF Contribution To Europe Hypothetical-IMF's Lipsky," *Dow Jones*, May 11, 2010.

[54] "IMF's Strauss-Kahn: ECB Move Very, Very Significant," *Dow Jones*, May 10, 2010. The ratio for the first Greek program was eight to three.

[55] The measures also included fixed-rate tender with full allotment in three-month refinancing operations, a six-month longer-term refinancing operation, and reactivation of the swap facility with the Federal Reserve. ECB, "ECB Decides on Measures to Address Severe Tensions in

same day, national central banks within the Eurosystem announced the purchase of Greek, Irish, and Portuguese sovereign bonds. These purchases had the intended effect of reducing the yield spread on these bonds over the German government bond rate during the following several weeks. Over the course of the next two years, the ECB would buy and hold more than €220 billion in bonds of distressed countries, with powerful and country-specific effects on the markets.

The introduction of SMP was important for several additional reasons as well. First the ECB became a large holder of government bonds outright and its balance sheet thus became exposed to losses. Second, the ECB began operating a program that affected the viability of troika programs without being integrated into them or coming under the purview of the troika agreements. Finally, by adopting the SMP, the ECB crossed the threshold into the realm of the overtly political.

GERMAN PREFERENCES AND STRATEGY

German policymakers had several reasons to include the IMF in the Greek and subsequent programs. These reasons highlight the German strategy in fighting the crisis and the role of domestic politics in the choice of the institutional mix. We review them here and return to this list after considering the choices made in subsequent country programs in later chapters to sort the motives of officials from enduring explanations of the IMF's involvement.

The reason most cited by German officials is the IMF's expertise in designing, negotiating, implementing, and monitoring programs.[56] Such "program technology" is highly specialized and the Fund staff has a long track record in this area. This capacity gave the Fund credibility in the financial markets, which German officials also valued, along with its financial resources. But these were not the only or even the most important reasons necessarily for including the IMF.

For the German government, the attractiveness of including the IMF in the solution to the Greek crisis derived from Germany's position as a creditor and

Financial Markets," Frankfurt, May 10, 2010, <https://www.ecb.europa.eu/press/pr/date/2010/html/pr100510.en.html>. The ECB would not announce in advance the quantity of bonds that it expected to purchase or the interest rate that it would target with the operations; instead it would announce total purchases (not disaggregated by country) after the fact.

[56] The treatment of German strategy in this section is based on a series of interviews with German officials, former officials, and close observers that were conducted by the author in Berlin and Frankfurt during September 28–30, 2011; January 31–February 3, 2012; December 10–12, 2012; June 11–12, 2013; and July 13–16, 2015, as well as in Washington, D.C., and Brussels on other occasions.

the domestic politics of shouldering the cost of financing the weaker countries in the euro area. The government expected substantial domestic criticism for bailing out Greece and support for Greece would have to be approved by the German Bundestag. The IMF had a reputation of applying strict conditionality and was known to lend into fully funded programs with debt sustainability. Its imprimatur provided a greater measure of reassurance to the Bundestag and German taxpayers that adjustment would be secured and the loan repaid. The Fund's participation provided the Chancellor's Office and Ministry of Finance with domestic political cover.

The Federal Constitutional Court based in Karlsruhe was a significant constraint on government policy. German academics and politicians brought several cases to the Court on the grounds that European arrangements exceeded the scope of government powers under the Basic Law and the European treaties. These had included, or could quite predictably include, cases brought on the grounds of the no-bailout clause,[57] the prohibition against monetary financing in the ECB statute,[58] and the limits on authorities that could be devolved to European institutions. The Court was known to harbor reservations about the transfer of competence to European authorities and the conviction that such transfers should be made only with clear democratic consent. Although it deferred to decisions made by the government in the crisis, for example, the Court later required that loans be subject to votes in the Bundestag even though that body had already approved the EFSF.[59] These votes raised the domestic political costs of programs for the government and thus the value of IMF cover.

The German Chancellor's sponsorship of the IMF, while that of a single, important official, was grounded in a clear conception of the legal constraints and opposition from within her own coalition. Some, including this author, lament the narrowness of that conception and its emphasis on the costs as compared to the benefits to Germany from its membership in the monetary union. But a more balanced "European" approach would have required a comprehensive national debate in Germany during the winter and spring of 2010 that was not possible under the circumstances. For better or worse, Merkel's politics were more realistic about what could be accomplished in the short term than Schäuble's. The Fund's role in the euro crisis thus rested on a solid foundation in the politics of the European Union's most influential member state.

German officials hoped that IMF participation would also provide protection against the political backlash within Greece against austerity. They

---

[57] Article 125 of the Treaty on the Functioning of the European Union (TFEU).
[58] Article 21, TFEU.
[59] See, among other rulings, GFCC, Judgment of the Second Senate of 07 September 2011–2 BvR 987/10–paras. (129, 124), <http://www.bverfg.de/e/rs20110907_2bvr098710en.html>.

expected to become the target of verbal attacks by the opponents of austerity—
and this was certainly the case not only in Greece but also in subsequent
program countries. What is more, political backlash could be directed not
simply at Germany but also at the European institutions and European
integration. As Pisani-Ferry and Sapir noted in an important article in the
Financial Times, the IMF would be less vulnerable than the Commission to
anger in program countries. "[A]t core the matter is really political," they
wrote.[60] We must add that the problem is compounded by the need for
unanimous ratification of amendments to the European treaties, which is
conducted by referendum in some member states. Austerity, recession, and
unemployment create massive hurdles in program countries for ratification of
treaty changes that were required to advance new European projects—and
astute policymakers knew that quantum institutional change would be necessary to complete the architecture of the euro area.

Finally, many German officials simply did not trust the European Commission to carry out the programs under strict conditionality. German officials
blamed the Commission for being too soft on Greece during its application to
join the euro area in 2000.[61] They were chastened by the deterioration in
market confidence after the Commission's relatively complacent assessment of
the Stability Programme in early February and they worried that President
Barroso would not be a firm steward of conditionality. But their distrust was
fundamentally institutional rather than personal. The Commission is both a
political and a technocratic institution and is often tempted to trade one
mandate off against the other. To the extent that the Commission is political,
seeking to build support for policy initiatives and institutional change, it
necessarily addresses the preferences of potential majorities of member states.
German policymakers could not count on the Commission to back their
position when they were outliers—as they expected to be on the mutualization
of the cost of sovereign debt rescues.

Officials in Berlin thought that they could count on the IMF to be strict with
respect to fiscal policy and support aggressive structural reform. They also
expected the IMF to bring the lessons of debt restructuring in other country

---

[60] Jean Pisani-Ferry and André Sapir, "The Best Course for Greece is to Call in the Fund,"
Financial Times, February 1, 2010.
[61] Chancellor Merkel hinted at this during her press conference with Dominique Strauss-
Kahn in Berlin on April 28, 2010 (<https://www.imf.org/external/np/tr/2010/tr042810.htm>):

I would like to thank the IMF again. I think it is good and important that the IMF is
involved in these negotiations. In the year 2000, the issue was whether Greece could or
could not join the euro zone. It turns out that the decision made then was not examined
thoroughly enough. I think it is right for the European Commission, the European Central
Bank, and the IMF with their combined experience to be leading these program negotiations together. I have total confidence in these negotiations and I think they can be
successfully completed.

cases to the Greek problem, and they were actively considering private-sector bail-in as a way to limit the cost of crises for the national budget and to prevent moral hazard. If the European Commission and the IMF deadlocked on one of these important matters, the ECB might break the tie and would probably, though not necessarily always, do so in line with German preferences. As the crisis evolved over the following years, the German chancellor and finance ministry would quarrel with the Fund, sometimes intensely. But, Berlin remained faithful to the institution throughout the euro crisis nonetheless.

Fundamentally, German preferences were rooted in the position of the German economy in the European and global economies. As an industrially competitive, high-savings, high-export and current-account-surplus economy, Germany had an abiding fear that it would be asked to bear the costs of the mistakes of other members of the euro area and their unwillingness to undertake necessary fiscal and structural adjustment. (Greek deception on fiscal statistics played directly into these fears.) German government policy has avoided commitments that would require stimulating its economy, adjusting away external surpluses, or collectivizing costs and has instead sought to keep the burden of adjustment on deficit countries. Some German economists and many foreign ones have argued that German interest lies instead in more symmetrical adjustment and cost sharing. But the positions that Berlin has taken with respect to fiscal rules, the excessive imbalances procedure, debt redemption funds and Eurobonds, and adjustment obligations in the G20, reflect the fundamental "stability culture" that has characterized German policies in international economic debates since at least the 1960s.[62] The consistency and predictability of this posture—notwithstanding the economic transformations of the second half of the twentieth century, European integration, the end of the Cold War, and German unification—is remarkable.

In calling in the IMF, and keeping it in as the crisis wore on, Chancellor Merkel was not acting single-handedly. Germany would not necessarily have prevailed on the question of IMF inclusion had it been isolated. Germany had support from those countries that had been the most conservative in their government finances and wished to ensure adjustment on the part of borrowers, which generally included the Netherlands, Luxembourg, Austria, and Finland.[63] As the crisis evolved, these countries became concerned that the accumulation of contingent liabilities in the course of the rescues would weigh on their own triple-A credit ratings; indeed, France lost that rating in 2012. Support for including the IMF also came from less affluent, relatively

---

[62] See, among many others, C. Randall Henning, *Currencies and Politics in the United States, Germany and Japan* (Washington, D.C.: Peterson Institute, 1994).

[63] See, for example, Tony Barber, "IMF's Role in Rescue Finally Wins Backing of Reluctant States," *Financial Times*, May 4, 2010. Italy also backed the inclusion of the IMF in May 2010.

new members of the monetary union, such as Slovakia and, after it adopted the euro, Estonia. Nonetheless, German support was pivotal for the inclusion of the IMF.

WHY NOT THE WORLD BANK?

The World Bank and its financial arms regularly participated in the programs that had been led by the IMF and the European Commission in Central and Eastern Europe. The IMF and World Bank had had decades of experience working together in developing countries, during which they were occasionally in conflict over the design and funding of adjustment programs. Their cooperation extended to the transition economies after the end of the Cold War. Once the ten Central and Eastern European countries joined the European Union in 2004, though, the economic policies of the new members fell under the ambit of the European treaties. Economic surveillance and any adjustment programs also fell under the aegis of the European Commission.

The programs for Hungary, Latvia, and Romania in the wake of the global financial crisis thus combined lending from the European Balance-of-Payments facility, the IMF and, always in smaller amounts, the World Bank.[64] Within this mix of institutions, the Bank thus specialized in long-term development projects and structural reforms in these economies and issued longer-term loans to match them. When the crisis migrated from Eastern Europe to the euro area, however, the World Bank was replaced by the European Central Bank in the troika.

One might legitimately ask whether the World Bank should have been included in the program for Greece. After all, Greece needed not just financing and macroeconomic adjustment, but also a series of structural reforms of a microeconomic, deregulatory nature, including in the fields of healthcare, agriculture, privatization, budget and tax administration, which could better prepare Greece to absorb structural and cohesion funds from the European Union. The World Bank had recent experience with all of these problems in other countries of the European Union. This led Agustin Carstens to suggest, when he was a candidate to succeed Dominique Strauss-Kahn as managing director of the IMF, that the World Bank should be involved in the Greek program.[65]

---

[64] The other Central and Eastern European countries that received official financial assistance include Ukraine, Serbia, Kosovo, Bosnia, and Moldova. Poland received a Flexible Credit Line. Iceland also received assistance. For a partial list of programs, see IMF, "Factsheet: IMF and Europe," at <https://www.imf.org/external/np/exr/facts/europe.htm>.

[65] Bob Davis and Owen Fletcher, "World Bank Can Help, Says IMF Candidate," *Wall Street Journal*, June 17, 2011.

However, under President Robert Zoellick, the management of the World Bank took a dim view of the Bank's involvement in Greece, as well as the other program countries in the euro area. The reasons for this were several. These countries were "rich" relative to those in which the World Bank was more active and in which the Bank had the strongest mandate. The Bank had to focus on its main purposes, poverty reduction and development. European governments and the European Union had the wherewithal to take care of their own, if they chose to do so. Participation in these programs would have associated the Bank with their austerity and the hardship associated with adjustment—exposing the Bank to scapegoating and possibly undercutting political support for the institution. Senior officials were conscious that political support in the creditor countries would be needed to secure the capital increase they were seeking. Doing so would be greatly complicated by the Bank's involvement in controversial adjustment programs. Nor does it appear, we should add, that in 2010 Greek officials solicited Bank involvement in their program.

This strategy proved successful for the institution in at least one important respect. The World Bank secured a major capital increase, its first in twenty years, during this period.[67] The IMF received a tripling of resources in 2009 and further bilateral loan commitments from members in 2011 as well. But, congressional approval of a quota increase and redistribution that was agreed in 2010 was delayed for years owing in large measure to questions about the IMF's involvement in the euro crisis.

The European Commission instead took on the lion's share of the task of surveying and building the administrative capacity in Greek ministries that was required for following through on the commitments in the program. The Commission created a team of officials that numbered about seventy-five, roughly one-third of whom were based in Athens, referred to as the Task Force for Greece. (A similar, much smaller task force was created for Portugal.) The Task Force specialized in structural reforms ranging from the absorption of cohesion project financing to taxation and anti-corruption.[68] Eventually, in 2013, under President Jim Yong Kim, the World Bank began providing a modest amount of technical assistance on investment licensing and improvement of the business environment in conjunction with the Task Force and other international organizations.[69]

---

[66] Interview with a former senior World Bank official, Washington, D.C., June 20, 2013.

[67] See, among others, Martin A. Weiss, "Multilateral Development Banks: General Capital Increases," Washington, D.C., Congressional Research Service, January 27, 2012.

[68] See, for example, the fourth progress report of the Task Force: European Commission, "Task Force for Greece: Progress on Technical Assistance," Brussels, April 29, 2013.

[69] See World Bank, "Teleconference with World Bank Group President Jim Yong Kim," Washington, D.C., April 12, 2013; Agence France-Presse, "World Bank in talks to help Greece, Portugal," November 6, 2012.

But the most fundamental reason for not including the World Bank at
the outset and limiting its involvement since then is not the preferences of
management but domestic politics. While the World Bank had attached
conditions to its structural adjustment lending, it hardly had the tough reputation of the IMF. The Bank could not have provided political cover for creditor
governments in national parliaments or protection from the political backlash
against austerity in program countries. Although it possessed capabilities that
Greece could have very much used early in its program, the World Bank was
next to useless in European politics.

KEY OBSERVATIONS

The first Greek program was a moment of truth, when European officials
debated the role of the IMF and then decided to include it in the rescue.
Common explanations for this choice include the expertise, credibility, and
financial contribution of the Fund as well as its usefulness in deflecting
criticism of austerity away from creditor states and their concerns about the
European Commission. These explanations leave the inclusion of the IMF
over-determined and subsequent cases winnow down the list substantially.

The principal alternative, a Europe-only rescue of Greece, had a high bar in
terms of consensus among euro-area member states on financial arrangements—
agreement that was distinctly lacking. The stark contrast between the initial
preference of most European officials for a European solution, which was
widely shared, and the ultimate decision to include the Fund, testifies to the
enduring usefulness of the multilateral institution in the face of deep divisions
within the region. The IMF in effect helped to complete the monetary union
and give the member states the breathing room in which to repair its
architecture.

This case also shows how creditor states shaped the institutional configuration of the crisis response. The position of the German government, in
particular, on the matter was pivotal; involvement of the IMF served Chancellor Merkel's economic and political strategies well. Although other creditor
governments supported her, the Chancellor more than any other single
European official was responsible for the inclusion of the Fund.

We cannot know with certainty how the Greek program would have
evolved if Europe had chosen to go it alone, but euro-area governments
certainly would have been forced to confront the difficult choices about the
fiscal path, financing gap, and debt sustainability earlier. Financial markets
would quite likely have forced a decision before the governments of the euro
area were politically and institutionally equipped to provide financing to
Greece. Without the participation of the Fund, domestic political support

for the rescue in countries such as Germany could well have been out of reach. An exit by Greece from the monetary union in 2010 would have been much more likely as a consequence.

Greece's membership in the monetary union, nonetheless, remained something of an open question. The country would become engaged in what seemed to be a nearly continuous renegotiation of its program and its debt in the coming years. We examine the second and third programs for Greece in Chapters 10 and 11. Before doing so, we turn to the other cases, beginning with Ireland and Portugal.

6

The Troika, Ireland, and Portugal

Contrary to the hopes of many, the Greek program did not stem the crisis. Within six months, the crisis metastasized to Ireland and several countries in the southern tier, infecting the whole of the monetary area. Four additional countries were forced to accept programs, a couple of others narrowly escaped, ejection from the monetary union briefly became a distinct possibility, and the euro area became financially fragmented, impairing the transmission of monetary policy and pushing the union as a whole into a recession during 2012–13.

Once chosen for inclusion in the Greek program, the IMF remained in the programs that followed. Its role and assertiveness evolved over the course of the crisis, setting up a debate among the members of the troika over the design of national country programs as well as, more broadly, policies and reforms of the euro area as a union. This evolution reflected in large measure changes in the stance of the United States and the large emerging market countries on the euro crisis and the use of the IMF to address it.

This chapter examines the dynamic among the institutions of the regime complex for crisis finance—commonly known as the troika, although that term has been and remains a somewhat misleading descriptor—their division of labor, conflicts, and modus vivendi. It then reviews the cases of Ireland and Portugal in the sequence in which they succumbed to crises. These case treatments pay particular attention to the deliberations about whether to include the Fund, substantive arguments over the design of programs, and strategies for exiting from the programs. The final section distills some of the key observations, including with respect to the enduring attractiveness of having the IMF in the institutional mix.

COMPLEX AND CONFLICT

The term troika came to describe the cooperation among the European Commission, European Central Bank, and the International Monetary Fund in providing conditional financial assistance to countries in the euro area. The term is used in two different ways: to refer to the three institutions collectively in their work on the crisis and far more narrowly, to the specific teams of officials sent on missions to country capitals to negotiate, review, and sometimes renegotiate the programs. Common usage usually does not distinguish carefully between the broad and narrow meanings. This book examines the operation of the troika at both levels.

We also place the operation of the troika within the broader context of the regime complex for crisis finance in the euro area, which is presented in Figure 6.1. (The figure is a conceptual representation, rather than the physical arrangement of meetings.) Note three things about the portrayal of the complex here. First, the table around which program negotiations take place is multisided. Many debates about the troika—such as over the side on which the central bank should sit—assume the table has two sides; but that is an oversimplification of the program negotiations. Second, new institutional actors, the ESM and SSM, join the negotiations in the later phases of the crisis. Third, the member states inside and outside the euro area, in essence, stand behind the institutions and observe the negotiations. They weigh in on the programs through multiple channels, informal and formal, including the Eurogroup and Euro summits.

When a program country requests financial assistance, each institution constitutes its team. The IMF brings officials from the European Department as well as from the departments covering Fiscal Affairs, Monetary and Capital Markets, Statistics, and Legal Affairs. The European Commission's team is led by an official from the Directorate-General for Economic and Financial Affairs (DG Ecfin) and includes officials from the other Directorates-General, not the least of which are DG Internal Market and DG Competition. The European Central Bank similarly brings officials from the Directorates-General for Economics, Market Operations, Financial Stability, and Legal Services. Troika missions to Greece were the largest, with thirty to forty officials in total, while those to Ireland and Portugal were substantially smaller. (Table 6.1 identifies the troika mission chiefs for the five countries with programs.) The mix of expertise varies depending on whether the country confronts primarily banking, structural, or fiscal problems. While it is the governing bodies of these institutions that ultimately approve, it is these working-level officials that do the heavy lifting in designing rescue programs.

The three institutions established a rough division of labor that corresponded to their comparative advantage. The IMF tended to lead on the macroeconomic analysis, the Commission on structural reform, and the ECB on repairing the balance sheet of the banking system.[1] But each institution also had vital interest, expertise, and strong preferences on matters outside their

---

[1] As described, for example, by Fund staff during its presentation of the first Greek program to the Executive Board. See IMF, "Summary of Discussion in the Executive Board," May 9, 2010.

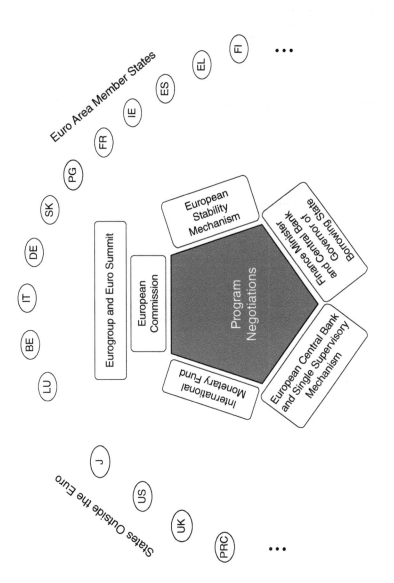

Figure 6.1. The Regime Complex for Euro Crisis Programs and Member States.

Note: The ESM and SSM joined program talks in 2013 and 2015 respectively.

Table 6.1. Troika Mission Chiefs

		Greece	Ireland	Portugal	Cyprus	Spain
IMF	Original	Poul Thomsen	Ajai Chopra	Poul Thomsen	Delia Velculescu	James Daniel
	Succeeded by	Rishi Goyal (August 2014)	Craig Beaumont (July 2013)	Abebe Aemro Selassie (June 2012)	Mark Lewis (November 2014)	
	Succeeded by	Delia Velculescu (July 2015)		Subir Lall (July 2013)	Rachel van Elkan (September 2015)	
EC	Original	Servaas Deroose	István Székely	Jürgen Kröger	Maarten Verwey	Servaas Deroose
	Succeeded by	Matthias Mors (July 2011)		John Berrigan (July 2013)	Jakob W. Friis (December 2014)	
	Succeeded by	Declan Costello (May 2014)		Carlos Martinez Mongay (July 2014)		
ECB	Original	Klaus Masuch	Klaus Masuch	Rasmus Rüffer	Isabel von Köppen-Mertes	Massimo Rostagno
	Succeeded by	Rasmus Rüffer (by July 2015)	Diego Rodriguez-Palenzuela (April 2012)	Isabel Vansteenkiste (February 2014)		

Source: Various publications of the IMF, European Commission, and ECB, media sources, and the author's email communication with the institutions.

main areas. The three issue areas were substantively interdependent—structural and banking reform had to be consistent with the fiscal targets, for example—and no agreement on individual elements was complete until all three institutions, and the national government concerned, agreed on the package as a whole.

The borrowing country, usually its minister of finance and governor of its central bank, signs a Letter of Intent with the IMF and a Memorandum on Economic and Financial Policies. For the European portion of the financial package, the borrower signs a Memorandum of Understanding (MOU), which is longer and more specific with respect to structural measures but which has been negotiated jointly with, and is in principle consistent with, the rest of the policy conditions in the package. Thus, each program is technically two coordinated parallel agreements between the member country, on the one hand, and the Commission/ECB and IMF, on the other. Although as a legal matter the IMF and European lenders could disburse financial assistance independently, uncoordinated disbursements would undercut creditors' leverage over borrowers' reforms. So these institutions usually coordinated disbursements effectively—doing so being a principal purpose of the troika arrangement.

Perhaps predictably, the troika institutions confronted a number of substantive differences in the design of the program. As one participant acknowledged, "Sometimes the debate within the troika is greater than between them and the program country."[2] These differences began with the negotiations in spring 2010 and continued virtually throughout the euro crisis. The members of the troika were careful to disguise their differences to outsiders, at least while they were negotiating with the government officials of program countries. These differences were nonetheless substantial, which is not surprising given the different mandates, memberships, and missions of the institutions. What could not be taken for granted, and is interesting from the standpoint of this study, is whether and how those differences were resolved.

Substantive conflicts arose in five areas in particular: financing (the size, maturity, and interest rate of official loans); the speed of fiscal adjustment; pace of deleveraging and reform of the banking system; structural reforms; and private sector involvement.[3] Several of these differences manifested during the negotiations over the first Greek program; some of them emerged during the subsequent programs. We will consider each in turn. (Debt sustainability later became an area of particularly severe conflict, which we address in depth in the later chapters of the book.)

---

[2] Quoting an interview with an official of the European Commission, Brussels, October 6, 2011, an assessment that was widely shared.

[3] The treatment of institutional positions outlined here is compiled largely from an extended series of interviews conducted by the author between 2011 and 2015 with officials of each of the institutions and covering the seven country programs.

Program Financing

The most basic questions in the design of these rescue packages were the overall amount of financing, the period that it would cover for the borrower, and the relative contributions of the European facilities and the IMF. European governments initially proposed that the first Greek program be limited in coverage to one year, which would have limited the headline amount but would have also required a second, follow-on program. IMF procedures required that the program cover the period needed for the country to undertake adjustment and return to the capital markets for private financing—which required in turn the announcement of larger programs. The IMF's approach was generally followed.

Pronouncements in April 2010 by Dominique Strauss-Kahn and Elena Salgado, the chair of the Ecofin Council, established the expectation that the contributions of the European facilities and IMF would be split on a two-to-one basis respectively. The contribution ratio for the IMF tended to decline over the course of the euro crisis, falling to ten percent in the case of the Cyprus package in spring 2013 (not including Cyprus's own contributions to the deal). When the IMF and European authorities could not agree on renegotiated programs for Greece that would cover the forecasted financing gap, the Fund extracted the commitment that European authorities (not the IMF) would come up with the difference when the moment of truth arrived.

European governments initially lent at interest rates that were intended to reduce moral hazard and encourage borrowers to return to private markets—Bagehot's "penalty" rate. At the outset of the crisis, this rate was significantly higher than the IMF's lending rate, which was keyed principally to the cost of funds for governments whose currencies had weights in the SDR. Initially, the Eurogroup and the IMF wished to limit maturities to five years, the period over which countries might be expected to replace their official borrowings from private sources. In the event, high interest rates on European financing and medium-term maturities proved to be unrealistic for the highly indebted program countries and these terms were eased considerably over the course of the crisis.

The ECB's operations were financially closely related to euro area and IMF financing but were technically and operationally independent of the troika program. This applies to regular liquidity operations, nonstandard refinancing operations, and extraordinary bond purchases. When countries exhausted the ECB's willingness to provide liquidity to their banking systems, the central bank would push them toward a longer-term, risk-bearing troika program. Thus, within the troika, the ECB tended to argue for government financing to replace its own liquidity, while the IMF and euro-area governments preferred that the ECB provide generous liquidity in order to limit the overall size of the program.

Fiscal Adjustment

All three institutions favored drastic reductions in the central government budget deficits of program countries. This was required to enable governments to reaccess the capital markets, after all, and was a natural response to the Papandreou government's bombshell revelations on the size of the deficit for 2009. Budget-deficit reduction also accorded with the primal institutional predispositions of the ECB, Commission, and the IMF. The IMF, after all, had been chided for standing for "It's Mostly Fiscal" for giving primacy to budget-deficit reduction in programs that addressed previous crises. The Commission was charged with overseeing and enforcing the fiscal rules of the Stability and Growth Pact.

But the three institutions nonetheless had starkly different assessments of the impact of fiscal austerity on growth and employment; they thus differed on the extent of the adjustment and the time path over which it should be required of borrowers. Of the three, the ECB was typically the most hawkish, arguing that restoring market confidence and preempting austerity fatigue favored frontloading painful spending cuts and tax increases. The Commission, which privately acknowledged the tension between growth and austerity, tended to be located between its two troika partners. The IMF took the most permissive stance, privileging minimization of the negative impact on growth over the return to compliance with the three-percent limit of the Stability and Growth Pact (SGP), earning criticism that it dismissed European rules.

The debate centered largely on the size of the fiscal multiplier, the extent to which output would respond to a change in the deficit. If the multiplier were less than one, a reduction in the deficit would help to reduce the ratio of debt to GDP. If, on the other hand, the multiplier were greater than one, a reduction in the deficit would reduce output even more, leading to an increase in the debt ratio with disturbing implications for debt sustainability.

Institutions' judgments about the impact of fiscal austerity on growth—the multiplier—evolved over time. The first Greek program assumed a very low multiplier of around 0.5; it became clear within months that this was far too optimistic. The IMF was first to revise its estimates of the multiplier upward and went public on the question with a series of papers, the most frequently cited being one by Olivier Blanchard and Daniel Leigh that first appeared in 2012.[4] The European Commission countered with dueling analyses in reports

---

[4] Olivier Blanchard and Daniel Leigh, "Growth Forecast Errors and Fiscal Multipliers," IMF Working Paper 13/1, Washington, D.C., January 2013; IMF, "As Downside Risks Rise, Fiscal Policy Has to Walk a Narrow Path," *Fiscal Monitor Update*, January 24, 2012. Mark Blyth reviews IMF studies that debunk the notion that fiscal contraction can be expansionary in *Austerity: The History of A Dangerous Idea* (New York/London: Oxford University Press, 2013), especially pp. 205–16.

from DG Ecfin,[5] as did the ECB, as the debate played out openly during the second half of the crisis.[6] These differences had to be resolved when programs, such as the Greek arrangement, had to be renegotiated.

Bank Deleveraging and Recapitalization

Having been backed into providing liquidity to banks in crisis-stricken countries, the ECB was anxious to stabilize the banking system by recapitalization and deleveraging. Recapitalization was desirable; but if that were not possible by means of injections of capital by private investors or euro-area governments, quick deleveraging was necessary. The ECB initially favored faster recapitalization and deleveraging than the Fund and Commission. The Fund favored rapid recapitalization but feared the destabilizing effects of deleveraging on the economy. The Commission had similar concerns but also administered the competition rules on state aid to the banking system. Responsible for enforcement, but not primarily for financial stability, DG Competition had to sign off on capital infusions and bank restructuring before these reforms could be implemented. During acute phases of the crisis, "waiting on DG Comp" was sometimes agonizing for national authorities and the troika partners.

Private-Sector Involvement

As the deliberations over the first Greek program show, the contribution of private-sector creditors was a flashpoint in the euro crisis from the beginning. None of the institutions of the troika, nor many of the member governments of the euro area, were internally unified on this matter. But the ECB took particular exception to the "Merkozy" Deauville declaration. President Trichet, in particular, argued that it was completely contradictory to expect private investors to remain committed to government bonds in some countries of the periphery while losses were being imposed upon them in others. Agreeing that telegraphing "haircuts" in advance set up an insurmountable "time-consistency" problem, to put it technically, several departments of the IMF and many members of the Executive Board favored a more aggressive approach to writing down private claims prior to official injections.

---

[5] See, for example, Macro Buti and Nicolas Carnot, "The Debate on Fiscal Policy in Europe: Beyond the Austerity Myth," *ECFIN Economic Brief* No. 20 (Brussels, European Commission, March 2013).

[6] Alan Beattie, "Troika a Barrier to IMF New Fiscal Faith," *Financial Times*, October 12, 2012; Marc Jones and Huw Jones, "IMF, ECB Square Off in Europe Austerity Debate," *Reuters*, April 25, 2013.

Recall that the ECB participated in these negotiations formally "in liaison with" the Commission, a phrase that ECB officials repeated often to underscore the notion that Brussels, not Frankfurt, was responsible for conditionality. At the same time, the ECB conducted bank-refinancing operations and bond purchases that had far-reaching effects on the success of the program but over which the ECB maintained complete discretion. This created, in the words of one well-placed insider, a profound "conflict of interest." One particular form of this conflict arose in prioritizing the protection of its balance sheet over other objectives.[7] This created hurdles to writing down claims on both banks and sovereigns over the course of the crisis.

At the close of the acute phase of the euro crisis in 2013, the long-term debt sustainability of countries such as Greece and Portugal had not been resolved. Debt restructuring in the form of "official sector involvement" was debated fiercely. The member governments of the euro area were very sensitive to the particular form in which official debt would be restructured, however. They granted relief in the form of interest-rate reduction and maturity extension, but strongly resisted writing down the principal. European institutions were generally sympathetic to the governments' position, but as the euro crisis evolved the IMF became increasingly insistent on restructuring and skeptical that writing off principal could be avoided.

Structural Reform

Rebalancing the current account and raising long-term growth in program countries required various degrees of structural adjustment. Such adjustment involved reforms in the labor and product markets and privatization of government-owned firms and assets, a heterogeneous mix. On these, the neoliberal institutions of the troika generally agreed as a matter of principle. Whether these reforms would depress growth in the short term and how much growth they might generate in the longer term were points on which they disagreed. They also disagreed on the financial and political realism of privatization, the estimated revenues from which were particularly delusional in the first Greek program. Structural matters were generally the Commission's forté.

In the context of the monetary union, in which nominal exchange rate devaluations were not possible, reducing domestic wages and prices and/or increasing productivity was the only path to restoring competitiveness. The tactic took the label "internal devaluation." Though governments controlled public-sector wages, their influence over private wage settlements was at best

[7] See, for example, Silvia Merler, Jean Pisani-Ferry, and Guntram B. Wolff, "The Role of the ECB in Financial Assistance: Some Early Observations," European Parliament, Directorate-General for Internal Policies, Department A: Economic and Scientific Policy, Brussels, June 2012.

indirect. But program conditionality sometimes provided for a reduction in employer social security contributions that reduced labor costs, while replacing the revenue in areas that did not have competitiveness implications. The IMF was particularly fond of this variant of internal devaluation, dubbed "fiscal devaluation" in the Portuguese program.[8]

IRELAND

That the crisis would spread beyond Greece was not a foregone conclusion during the summer and early fall of 2010. However, the German government led an effort to force private banks and other investors to accept losses on their bond holdings in future crises as a stipulation for funding large financial facilities with public money. Chancellor Merkel and President Sarkozy agreed on this during a walk on the beach at Deauville on the Normandy coast, in October.[9] Their announcement backfired spectacularly. Private investors reassessed the risk of their bond portfolios and the interest rates on the bonds of the governments of Ireland and the countries of the southern tier rose perilously. Consternation in the market was aggravated by decision-making within the Eurogroup, which was slow and uncertain owing to the requirement of unanimity and parliamentary ratification in some countries. Ireland was the first casualty of the Deauville declaration.

Ireland's position within the monetary union had been the subject of considerable academic speculation from the advent of the euro. The country entered the new currency area at an undervalued exchange rate and the euro-area-wide interest rate seemed below that consistent with balanced growth and price stability in Ireland. Ireland experienced a sustained boom and eventually a pronounced bubble in the real estate market, fueled in substantial measure by capital inflows through the banking system. Ireland became a prime example of a country whose banking system had outgrown the national fiscal resources that could be called upon to back it in a crisis—"too big to save."[10]

---

[8] IMF, "Portugal: Request for a Three-Year Arrangement under the Extended Fund Facility," *Country Report* No. 11/127, June 2011; European Commission, DG Ecfin, *The Economic Adjustment Programme for Portugal*, European Economy, Occasional Papers 79, June 2011.

[9] "Franco–German Declaration, Statement for the France–Germany–Russia Summit," Deauville, France, October 18, 2010; German Bundestag, "Statement by the Federal Chancellor with Regard to the European Council on October 28/29, 2010 in Brussels and the G20 Summit on November 11/12, 2010 in Seoul," 67th Session, 17th Legislative Period, October 27, 2010.

[10] Useful overviews of the origins of the Irish crisis include Patrick Honohan, "What Went Wrong in Ireland?," prepared for the World Bank, May, Manuscript, 2009; Klaus Regling and Max Watson, *A Preliminary Report on the Sources of the Ireland's Banking Crisis* (Dublin: Government Publications Office, 2010); Simon Carswell, *Anglo Republic: Inside the Bank That Broke Ireland* (Dublin: Penguin Ireland, 2011); Philip R. Lane, "The Irish Crisis," *CEPR*

The case of Ireland contrasted with that of Greece in several important respects. First, Ireland's economic growth had surpassed all of the other member states in the European Union during the three decades prior to the crisis. Its economy was open and competitive, integrated not simply with the United Kingdom and the European continent, but the transatlantic economy as well. Ireland had been strikingly successful in attracting foreign direct investment (FDI) from multinational firms and building an industrial export base in, for example, the information technology and pharmaceutical sectors. For this success, Ireland had won the moniker the "Celtic Tiger" and its export base provided a platform for eventually rebounding from the crisis. Second, whereas the Greek crisis inhered in the government fiscal deficit, the Irish crisis inhered in the banking system. Third, whereas the government of Greece had misreported its fiscal accounts and then failed to implement the policy adjustments that were stipulated in its troika program, the government of Ireland adhered faithfully to its program. Ireland became the "poster child" for reliable implementation of austerity and bank restructuring under the agreements.

Path to the Program

Crises in the UK and Icelandic banking systems during 2007 and 2008 highlighted the vulnerability of Ireland's banks. Then the Lehman Brothers bankruptcy of mid-September 2008 caused a seizing up of the wholesale interbank funding markets in Europe as well as the United States and forced Irish banks to seek government assistance. The Irish government responded on September 30 by guaranteeing the liabilities of the six largest banks. The guarantee was temporary, lasting for two years, and extended to all deposits, covered bonds, senior debt, and dated subordinated debt—which would eventually amount to €440 billion, though government leaders might not have known it at the time. The decision was fateful, exposing the Irish government, its economy of €180 billion (in 2008), and population of 4.3 million to large losses indeed. The financial fate of the sovereign was locked inexorably to that of Irish banks from that point forward. Michael Noonan, finance minister in the subsequent government, later described it as "the blackest day in Ireland since the Civil War broke out."[11]

Discussion Paper No. DP8287, March 2011; Zsolt Darvas, "A Tale of Three Countries: Recovery After Banking Crises," *Bruegel Policy Contribution* No. 2011/19, Brussels, December 2011; Bastasin, *Saving Europe*, especially chapters 15–17; Donal Donovan and Antoin E. Murphy, *The Fall of the Celtic Tiger: Ireland and the Euro Debt Crisis* (Oxford: Oxford University Press, 2013). The most detailed treatment is by the Joint Committee of Inquiry into the Banking Crisis, Houses of the Oireachtas, *Report* (Dublin, January 2016).

[11] The decision is the subject of minutely detailed retrospectives in the Irish press and discourse. See, for example, Hugh O'Connell, "30 Days in September: An Oral History of the

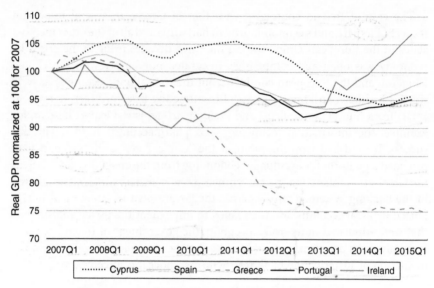

Figure 6.2. Real GDP of Program Countries, 2007–2015.

Given the global crisis and the instability of the banking system, the Irish economy contracted by 2.2 percent in 2008, 6.4 percent in 2009, and would contract further still in 2010. (Figure 6.2) The fiscal position, which had been in substantial surplus as recently as 2006 and was balanced in 2007, shifted to a deficit of 7.3 percent of GDP in 2008 and was projected to increase somewhat further in 2009. In response, the government introduced a stability program to bring the deficit gradually back within the three percent threshold of the SGP by 2011.[12]

The government's strategy, while risky, did not appear to be obviously misguided in late 2008; a full-blown sovereign debt crisis was not inevitable even after the extension of the guarantees. Irish government debt had been extraordinarily low before the banking crisis, twenty-five percent of GDP in 2007. Government bond spreads above German bunds rose only modestly to between two and three percent in early 2009 and then declined until the Greek crisis in spring 2010. However, the Deauville announcement raised the spread to over 6.5 percent by mid-November 2010 (see Figure 4.1b), which

Bank Guarantee," *TheJournal.ie*; *EU Observer*, "Lessons for Ireland's Failed Bank Guarantee," October 1, 2013; Simon Carswell, "The Big Gamble: The Inside Story of the Irish Bank Guarantee," *Irish Times*, September 25, 2010. Donovan and Murphy, *The Fall of the Celtic Tiger*, concludes that the government had no better alternative.

[12] In the event, the deficit would register 11.3 percent in 2009, 10.6 percent in 2010, and 8.9 percent in 2011—excluding the government's capital infusion into the banking system, which roughly *tripled* the number for 2011. IMF, "Twelfth Review under the Extended Arrangement," December 2013, table 1, p. 40.

if sustained for long would render Irish government debt unsustainable. At that point, November 2010, the government of Ireland formally approached the Eurogroup and then the IMF for a program, which was negotiated in relatively short order.

The troika made €85 billion available to Ireland, including €17.5 from Ireland's own National Pension Reserve Fund.[13] Of this, the IMF contributed €22.5 billion and the Europeans €22.5 billion through the EFSM and €17.7 billion through the EFSF (increasing somewhat the relative IMF contribution compared to the first Greek package).[14] These loans had a maturity of seven and a half years and an interest rate of 5.7 and 6.0 percent in the case of the European funds and a repayment period lasting between four and a half and ten years and an interest rate averaging 3.85 percent in the case of the IMF (see Appendix: Financial Rescues for Euro-Area Countries, 2010–2015).[15] The maturity and interest rate were important as they related to the sustainability of debt, to which the Greek episode had sensitized the markets, and were the focus of considerable interest in the Irish domestic debate over the program.[16]

Restructuring and recapitalizing the Irish banking sector was the immediate priority and prime objective of the program. But Ireland was also called upon to reduce the fiscal imbalance by €15 billion over the term of the program, which amounted to about ten percent of GDP, €6 billion of which was frontloaded in the first year—this at a moment when Ireland had already experienced, and remained in, a deep recession. The rationale of the troika was that the small and open Irish economy could recover through exports, and indeed in the event these largely offset the severe contraction in domestic demand. But the prescription nonetheless prompted general debate about whether fiscal austerity was appropriate remedy for a *banking* problem, as opposed to a fiscal problem, and debate within the troika about the fiscal glide path and multipliers.

The Irish government also signed onto a list of structural reforms, which were considerably less important than in the Greek program, the major exception being a €1 reduction in the national minimum wage. Several

---

[13] Plus €3.8 billion from the U.K., €0.6 billion from Sweden, and €0.4 billion from Denmark that could be drawn upon later if needed.

[14] IMF, "Ireland: Request for an Extended Arrangement," *Country Report* No. 10/366, December 2010.

[15] IMF financing was provided through the Extended Fund Facility (EFF) rather than a Stand-by Arrangement (SBA) as in the case of the first Greek program.

[16] The institutions' documents reveal an open debate over whose terms were more favorable to Ireland. See IMF, "IMF Reaches Staff-level Agreement with Ireland on €22.5 billion Extended Fund Facility Arrangement," press release no. 10/462, November 28, 2010; European Commission, Directorate-General for Economic and Financial Affairs, European Economy Occasional Papers 76, "The Economic Adjustment Programme for Ireland," February 2011, box 10, p. 40. By a decision of the Eurogroup, the maturity on the loans to Greece was extended similarly at the time of the Irish program.

euro-area governments sought to make an increase in the Irish corporate tax rate a condition of their assistance. This effort was ill-advised for a number of reasons and was eventually abandoned, but complicated politics of the program and its implementation.[17]

Eurogroup and Bank Exposure

The Eurogroup was again at the center of the design of the Irish program, notwithstanding the fact that its president and members do not sign the troika program documents. By the fall of 2010, the euro-area member states had created the EFSF and activated it for the first time for Ireland. The Eurogroup meeting of November 16 was by all accounts especially chaotic, much to the dismay of the Irish finance minister, and was followed by another meeting the next weekend, on November 21.[18]

The European partners in the euro area were preoccupied largely with their banks' exposure to the large Irish banks. German banks were most exposed with claims on Irish banks of $139 billion, followed by UK banks with claims of $132 billion, followed in turn by France ($44 billion), Belgium ($29 billion), and the Netherlands ($19 billion)—amounting to well over $400 billion for the EU countries as a group.[19] (U.S. banks held claims on Irish banks of $57 billion. These figures compare to claims on the Greek banking system of $57 billion on the part of France, $37 billion on the part of Germany, and $12 billion on the part of the U.K. in mid-2010.)

The Irish program thus served not only to stabilize the Irish economy and banking system but that of Europe as a whole. Irish authorities would argue that, by taking the program and its punishing fiscal contraction, Ireland was being a good team player and, furthermore, that should be acknowledged in various ways—including the terms of financing, pace of fiscal consolidation, and writing down of private claims on the banking sector that had not been covered by the guarantees. The euro area, on which Irish officials were wholly reliant for revising the terms of the program, seemed to give scant political

---

[17] C. Randall Henning, "European Pressure to Increase the Irish Corporate Tax is Deeply Misguided," RealTime Economic Issues Watch, Peterson Institute, Washington, D.C., November 19, 2010.

[18] Statement by the Eurogroup and ECOFIN Ministers, Brussels, November 21, 2010, <http://www.eurozone.europa.eu/media/368556/eg_and_ecofin_statement_ireland_21_nov_2010.pdf>; Statement by the Eurogroup—Ireland, Brussels, November 16, 2010, <http://www.consilium.europa.eu/uedocs/cms_data/docs/pressdata/en/ecofin/117743.pdf>.

[19] Jacob F. Kirkegaard, "The To-Do List in Ireland," RealTime Economic Issues Watch, Peterson Institute, November 19, 2010; BIS Consolidated Banking Statistics, Table 9d. The figures are for June 2010.

credit to Ireland on this account.[20] Ireland might have chosen a more confrontational path, deviating from its program and threatening contagion to the rest of the monetary union, which some Greek officials did explicitly on a number of occasions over the crisis. But Irish officials decided that a cooperative path was their best course and this decision survived the change of government in February 2011.

Prominence of the ECB

One critical consequence of the origin of Ireland's crisis being in the banking sector was that the ECB played a larger role than in the first Greek program. This was for several reasons. Stabilization of the banking sector depended on continued access to refinancing facilities for which the ECB determined the eligibility of collateral and banks. Irish banks' access to these facilities depended on a determination that the banks were solvent and then the ECB's easing the rules that defined which assets were eligible as collateral. The ECB's Governing Council supervised and determined the limits on the amount of Emergency Liquidity Assistance (ELA) that could be granted by the Central Bank of Ireland. Moreover, through the Securities Market Programme (SMP), the ECB bought and held a substantial amount of Irish government bonds.

Ireland had been effectively caught in the middle of the dispute over how to handle potentially unsustainable debt. The "Merkozy" declaration at Deauville and the insistence thereafter on private sector involvement raised the risk premium on Irish bonds and brought the viability of government backing for the Irish banking system into question. Irish banks had become increasingly dependent on the ECB for financing, as banks in Europe declined to roll over their loans. By October 2010, the ECB provided €130 billion in refinancing operations to the Irish banking system. The roughly €5 billion in SMP purchases reported by the ECB in the fourth quarter of 2010 was largely an effort to contain the rise in the yield on Irish sovereign bonds.[21] Irish banks were also increasingly dependent on ELA, which they had started drawing in September and October 2008.

[20] See, for example, the letter from the former Prime Minister John Bruton (1994–7) to Commission President Barroso of January 2011, quoted in Alan Ahearne, "The Political–Economic Context in Ireland," in *Resolving the European Debt Crisis*, eds William R. Cline and Guntram Wolff (Washington, D.C.: Peterson Institute, March 2012), p. 43, n. 16.

[21] Fabian Eser and Bernd Schwaab, "Assessing Asset Purchases within the ECB's Securities Markets Programme," *ECB Working Paper Series* No. 1587, September 2013, Figure 2, p. 12. Although ECB data on SMP purchases does not break out individual countries, Jean-Claude Trichet has acknowledged these purchases included Irish government bonds. See, for example, Joint Committee of Inquiry into the Banking Crisis, Lecture by Jean-Claude Trichet, Institute of International and European Affairs, Dublin, April 30, 2015.

The ECB was deeply concerned about the exposure that it was accumulating. It was on a slippery slope, lending increasing amounts to Irish banks through regular and unconventional windows that were ostensibly short-term but in reality medium- and long-term exposure. Moreover, the main Irish banks could be deemed solvent only as long as their government fiscal backstop was sound. But the Irish government maintained access to the capital markets owing largely to the ECB's purchases through the SMP. The banks' solvency became increasingly untenable and with it their access to refinancing facilities. The Irish situation had morphed from a bank liquidity issue to a sovereign debt problem and the ECB wanted the euro-area governments to take the financial exposure associated with the rescue and the political responsibility associated with policy adjustments. Ireland was thus another case in a strategic game between the ECB and the national governments of the monetary union that played out during the crisis.[22]

It is now clear, though the exact sequence of events was murky at the time, that it was the ECB that effectively delivered Ireland to the troika. In a series of letters, email messages, and telephone conversations between late October through mid-November, ECB President Trichet explained to Finance Minister Brian Lenihan and other Irish officials that the situation was untenable and urged the government to take a troika program.[23] In this correspondence, Trichet conditioned Irish banks' access to central bank liquidity on the government introducing fiscal and banking measures and threatened to halt further ELA unless the government requested a program. Because such access was essential, Irish officials had little choice but to comply. The ECB stance was the trigger that brought Irish officials into negotiations with their euro-area counterparts on November 15 and at the Eurogroup meeting on November 16,[24] and got them to acknowledge publicly on November 18 that they were seeking a program. This catalytic role of the ECB would become a pattern in the subsequent programs during the crisis.

The ECB weighed in heavily on a second controversial matter: the treatment of senior bank debt. In the course of restructuring and recapitalizing the banks, shareholder equity was completely wiped out and large losses were

[22] Henning, "The ECB as a Strategic Actor."

[23] Letters from M. Jean-Claude Trichet to Mr Brian Lenihan, October 15, 2010 and November 19, 2010; letters from Mr Brian Lenihan to M. Jean-Claude Trichet, November 4, 2010 and November 21, 2010; available at <http://www.ecb.europa.eu/press/html/irish-letters.en.html>. The disclosure of these letters was prompted by an examination by Irish journalists and academics in minute detail. Karl Whelan has published one of the most insightful series of commentaries on the Irish crisis in his *Forbes* blog. See Karl Whelan, "The ECB's Secret Letter to Ireland: Some Questions," August 17, 2012 and Gavin Sheridan, "Those ECB Letters," September 3, 2012; Daniel McConnell, "We Were a War Cabinet and Lenihan Was Leader: Interview with Alan Ahearne," *Irish Independent*, October 9, 2011.

[24] Joint Statement by the Eurogroup, November 16, 2010, Brussels.

imposed on the holders of subordinated bank debt. Senior bank bonds that were not subject to the guarantees amounted to €16 billion as of October 2010, equivalent to the total amount of fiscal adjustment to which Ireland was committed under the program. These accordingly became the focus of a fierce debate within Ireland as the Fianna Fail government fell and elections were called for February 2011. The new governing coalition, comprised of Fine Gael and the Labour Party and headed by Enda Kenny, faced a decision as to whether to redeem or restructure a substantial number of these bonds by their due date, November 2011.[25] Although the bonds that were potentially subject to losses had shrunk to perhaps €3.5–€4 billion, this amount remained equivalent to one year's fiscal deficit reduction and thus pivotal to the politics of program implementation. Irish citizens and taxpayers were making great sacrifices, while senior bondholders were being made whole, and a broad swath of the Irish electorate favored bailing them in.

The ECB was steadfastly opposed to bailing in the senior bondholders, however.[26] President Trichet thought that it was madness to expect private investment in banks and sovereigns when investors were being told they would quite likely be given a substantial "haircut," he made no secret of his disdain. He combatively confronted French President Sarkozy and the other heads of government over this at the European Council meeting in October 2010.[27]

The ECB threatened in November 2010 and March 2011 to revoke access to emergency liquidity if the government imposed losses on the senior bondholders.[28] Ireland continued to depend heavily on the ECB for regular refinancing, SMP purchases, and ELA approval. The magnitude of these operations, and the benefits for Ireland, were far larger than any haircuts that could be imposed on a narrow class of bondholders, however morally compelling such burden-sharing might have been. So, the Irish Treasury paid off the bonds as they came due.

In the event, the Governing Council did not block ELA in the amounts that the Central Bank of Ireland wanted to issue—these amounts posed no problem for the overall stance of monetary policy as they were easily mopped up in countervailing liquidity operations elsewhere in the euro area. But some

---

[25] The domestic politics of this issue are examined in Alan Ahearne, "The Political–Economic Context in Ireland," in *Resolving the European Debt Crisis*, eds William R. Cline and Guntram Wolff (Washington, D.C.: Peterson Institute, March 2012).

[26] Because its position was politically controversial, the ECB posted a set of relevant documents on its website to set the record straight. See <http://www.ecb.europa.eu/press/html/irish-letters.en.html>.

[27] Bastasin, *Saving Europe*, pp. 233–42.

[28] The episode is treated exhaustively by the Joint Committee of Inquiry into the Banking Crisis, *Report*, Chapter 11. See also, its Witness Statement of Michael Noonan, Minister of Finance, Session 64, Dublin, September 10, 2015, pp. 84–90.

individual members of the Governing Council opposed these operations and some officials in Ireland believed those views had weighed substantially on market confidence in fall 2010.[29]

The outstanding ELA on the books of the insolvent Irish banks, combined with the stricture against "monetary financing," gave the ECB an integral role in the resolution of the banking system. Over the course of the crisis, the weakest Irish banks became nearly wholly reliant on the ECB for financing the withdrawal of deposits and repayment of debt. When they ran out of assets that were eligible for refinancing in the Eurosystem, the banks were forced to turn to the Central Bank of Ireland for ELA. When Anglo Irish Bank and the Irish Nationwide Building Society were merged to create the Irish Bank Resolution Corporation (IBRC) in July 2011, these liabilities to the ECB and Central Bank of Ireland were transferred to the new entity. But losses on the corresponding assets that were transferred along with them amounted to about €35 billion. To justify the extension of ELA, which replaced ECB financing over the course of 2011, the government had placed about €30 billion in promissory notes on the balance sheet of the IBRC.[30]

The Irish finance ministry sought to retire both the promissory notes and the ELA backed by them over the course of the program.[31] The ECB objected to any solution that would write down the liabilities that the government issued against ELA on the grounds that this constituted "monetary financing," prohibited by the treaty. After months of negotiation, the Irish government announced in early 2013 that IBRC would be resolved and its promissory notes used to redeem ELA at the Central Bank of Ireland and then exchanged for bonds issued by the National Asset Management Agency that paid a considerably lower interest rate, thus reducing the measured fiscal deficit. This mechanism was clearly designed to circumvent the monetary financing objection, but Mario Draghi and the Governing Council nonetheless acquiesced.[32]

---

[29] Interviews with Irish officials, Dublin, October 3, 4, and 5, 2011.

[30] This convoluted financial arrangement is best explained by Karl Whelan, "ELA, Promissory Notes and All That: The Fiscal Costs of Anglo Irish Bank," *The Economic and Social Review*, Vol. 43, No. 4, Winter 2012.

[31] On the fiscal accounting, See Deborah Mabbett and Waltraud Schelkle, "Searching under the Lamp-Post: The Evolution of Fiscal Surveillance," in *Political and Economic Dynamics of the Eurozone Crisis*, eds James A. Caporaso and Martin Rhodes.

[32] See, for example, Whelan, "Ireland's Promissory Notes Deal," *Forbes*, February 11, 2013; Wolfgang Munchau, "Ireland Shows the Way with Its Debt Deal," *Financial Times*, February 10, 2013; Jacob F. Kirkegaard, "Why the Irish Bank Deal Matters—Especially for Cyprus," RealTime Economic Issues Watch, Peterson Institute, February 12, 2013. Referring to the ECB's position, Draghi declared, "There was not a decision to take. The Governing Council unanimously took note of the Irish operation...," repeating the words "took note" twice thereafter.

Conflict among the Institutions

The choice of the troika as the institutional arrangement for the Irish rescue was more or less a default solution, rolled over from the Greek program. The question of the inclusion of the IMF had been debated and settled in winter and spring 2010. So, in contrast to the intense argument over the Greek program, there was virtually no debate about including the IMF in the Irish program. The same incentives applied in the Irish case as in the Greek case for Germany and the other creditors. Of the five program countries, therefore, the role of the IMF was the least contentious at the beginning of the Irish program.

The most disputed issues over the program within the troika were the treatment of the holders of bank bonds in the bank restructuring, pace of deleveraging, and path of the consolidation of the fiscal deficit. These issues were substantively linked—the greater the bail in of bondholders, the easier the fiscal adjustment, both financially and politically. Having diagnosed Ireland's predicament as a banking rather than a fiscal crisis, the IMF largely sympathized with the government on these questions and pushed the ECB to be more forthcoming.[33] Among the troika programs, the IMF clashed with the ECB the most in the case of Ireland.

The U.S. Secretary of the Treasury, Timothy F. Geithner, sided firmly with the ECB on the matter, apparently concerned for the health of the market in credit default swaps among other things.[34] During a teleconference in November 2010, he and the other G7 finance ministers discussed the merits of imposing losses on the senior bondholders and rejected the measure. Minister Noonan declared, "I can't go against all of the G7."[35]

The European Commission had as its responsibility the oversight and enforcement of the SGP and the competition rules on state aid as they applied to government assistance to private banks in Ireland. As in the other program cases, the Commission favored a return to the three-percent-of-GDP threshold for the general government deficit by the end of the program, 2013. As in the case of Greece, the IMF took the most permissive stance. In the end, the

---

[33] As made abundantly clear in the IMF mission chief's testimony to the subsequent parliamentary inquiry on the crisis. See Joint Committee of Inquiry into the Banking Crisis, Houses of the Oireachtas, Witness Statement of Ajai Chopra, Session 63 (a), Dublin, September 10, 2015. See also Ajai Chopra, "The ECB's Role in the Design and Implementation of Crisis Country Programs: Ireland and Beyond," European Parliament, Directorate-General for Internal Policies (IP/A/ECON/2015–07), Brussels, November 2015.

[34] Joint Committee of Inquiry, *Report*, p. 362. See also, Donovan and Murphy, *The Fall of the Celtic Tiger*, p. 247; Timothy F. Geithner, *Stress Test: Reflections on Financial Crises* (New York: Crown, 2014), pp. 449–50.

[35] Quoting Patrick Honohan's testimony to the Joint Committee of Inquiry, *Report*, p. 362.

three institutions compromised on the consolidation path in the program,[36] requiring a total reduction of €15 billion and return to three percent by 2015.

The IMF was known to be on the "right" side of these issues of high salience in domestic politics. Ajai Chopra, the Fund mission chief in 2011, was treated, in the words of one senior Finance Department official, as a "rock star" in Dublin. (In Athens, by contrast, the Fund was demonized in the press.) That said, Irish officials were not able to take much advantage of the disagreements among the troika institutions on these matters.

The IMF explicitly advocated more robust support from the rest of the euro area for the Irish program.[37] It applauded the June 29, 2012 decision of the European Council to break the sovereign-bank link and to specifically examine Ireland's situation with a view to "further improving the sustainability of the well-performing adjustment program." In December 2012, the Fund specifically advocated ESM direct recapitalization and proposed that, in the meantime, the amortization schedule on the promissory notes be eased, OMT qualification for Ireland be considered, and post-program "financing backstops" be explored.[38] As the discourse among international institutions goes, this was strong language. The experience with the Irish program had converted the IMF into an enthusiastic proponent of banking union and Fund staff pressed euro-area governments and institutions to follow through on the Council's commitment.

Exit from the Program

The easing of credit conditions and risk premia in the wake of the ECB's announcement of the Outright Monetary Transactions program in September 2012 helped Ireland's prospects dramatically. From six percent in June 2012, the Irish government bond spread over German ten-year bunds declined fairly steadily through the remainder of 2012 and 2013 (see Figure 4.1a). By January 2014, the Irish government could issue short-term debt for about the same rate as Germany's government and briefly less than the U.K. Treasury. The IMF projected that Irish government debt ratio would

---

[36] Interviews with officials in the troika institutions and Irish government, Washington, D.C., August 3, 2011, and May 29, 2013; Brussels, February 7, 2012; Frankfurt, September 29 and 30, 2011; and Dublin, October 3 and 5, 2011.

[37] The summary of the Article IV staff report (August 2012) said, "Public debt is high and still growing...risks to economic recovery remain large, with profound implications for debt sustainability...Success hinges on external economic recovery and more European support." See IMF, "Ireland: Article IV and Seventh Review Under the Extended Arrangement," *Country Report* No. 12/264, September 2012.

[38] During the seventh program review. See IMF, "Ireland: Eighth Review Under the Extended Arrangement," *Country Report* No. 12/336, December 2012, Box 2, page 13.

peak at 123.3 percent of GDP in 2013—a far brighter picture than Greece and even Portugal.[39] Ireland also had reasonable prospects of a full return to market access after its last disbursement under the program in December 2013.[40]

But Ireland was also vulnerable to a change in external conditions, critical among which were the growth rate in the rest of the European Union and Britain and a return to "risk-on" mode in the capital markets as a possible consequence of the tapering from quantitative easing on the part of the U.S. Federal Reserve or the upcoming assessment of banks prior to the transfer of supervision to the ECB in November 2014. For this reason, the Irish government explored the possibility of securing a precautionary facility to bridge its exit from the program—a loan commitment on which it could draw in case market conditions made issuance of government bonds infeasible. That could take the form of an Enhanced Conditions Credit Line (ECCL) from the ESM and a Precautionary and Liquidity Line (PLL) or a precautionary SBA from the IMF. The Irish government even hoped at one point that qualification for an ECCL might enable it to access the ECB's Outright Monetary Transactions.

The IMF and the ECB strongly favored the opening of a precautionary credit line during Ireland's exit from the regular program. Ireland's partners in the euro area discouraged these applications equally strongly, however, effectively blocking access. These deliberations unfolded as Germany was preparing for national elections in late September 2013 and the governing conservatives and SPD were negotiating at length the new grand coalition under Chancellor Merkel that would follow. The costs of the euro crisis had been a sensitive issue in the election and neither side of the emerging coalition wished exposure on the issue.[41] Even a precautionary program would have to be approved by the Bundestag and the German government did not want to present the case. Euro-area governments wanted to have a "success story" in order to argue that they had put the crisis behind them. So, Ireland did not formally request a precautionary program.

After the conclusion of the program, the Irish parliament conducted a comprehensive inquiry into the banking crisis to which participants from

---

[39] IMF, "Ireland: Twelfth Review," *Country Report* No. 13/336, Washington, D.C., December 19.

[40] It also had a substantial cash buffer that could carry it through much of 2015 if that were necessary. Statement by the Eurogroup on Ireland, November 14, 2013 at <http://www.eurozone.europa.eu/newsroom/news/2013/11/statement-by-the-eurogroup-on-ireland/> and Joe Brennan and Donal Griffin, "Irish to Exit Bailout Program without Precautionary Credit Line," *Bloomberg*, November 14, 2013.

[41] The SPD would have tied precautionary support for Ireland to the Irish corporate and EU financial transactions tax. See Eoin Burke-Kennedy, "EU Support for Ireland becomes Sticking Point in German Coalition Talks," *Irish Times*, October 10, 2013; Stefan Wagstyl, "Germany's SPD hints at greater solidarity with troubled EU states," *Financial Times*, December 12, 2013.

each of the institutions gave evidence.[42] The IMF and the European Commission also presented ex post evaluations of the Irish program in 2015.[43] These reports revealed disagreements among the institutions that had been held in confidence during the program. European institutions defended the decision not to bail in senior bondholders, but the IMF now openly criticized it. More broadly, the IMF wrote, "the Fund's objectives (focused on supporting its member country) may not necessarily always be aligned with those of the EC and ECB (generally focused more on EU and euro area wide concerns)." "[S]tronger upfront commitments in addition to financing assurances would have strengthened program planning and implementation," and, the report suggested, would be necessary to justify exceptional access in programs in the monetary union in the future.[44]

Ownership and resolute implementation by the Irish government, and the relatively successful economic outcome, spared the troika from sharper disagreements. Other programs would place greater stress on cooperation among these institutions.

PORTUGAL

Portugal's economic challenges were more fundamentally structural than the previous two program countries. It had entered the euro area at an overvalued exchange rate and its economic growth suffered as a consequence. Whereas Greece's fiscal problem derived from overspending, Portugal's fiscal deficits stemmed largely from sluggish growth since the inception of the monetary union and the 2008–9 financial crisis. Portugal's banking system was more highly leveraged and more dependent on wholesale funding than Greece's. In contrast to Ireland, where the banks dragged down the sovereign, the Portuguese sovereign, whose debt was ninety-four percent of GDP, dragged down the banks by raising their cost of borrowing during 2010–11.

Two further environmental conditions worked against Portuguese access to private capital markets: Ireland's turn to the troika and Greece's failure to implement key elements of its program. Over the course of winter and spring 2011, the troika members acknowledged that Greece's program had gone badly off track, owing in part to underestimating the fiscal multiplier and in

---

[42] The testimonies of Patrick Honohan (January 15 and March 11, 2015), Marco Buti (February 18, 2015), Jean-Claude Trichet (April 30, 2015), and Ajai Chopra (September 10, 2015) are particularly interesting: <https://inquiries.oireachtas.ie/banking/hearings>.

[43] IMF, "Ireland: Ex Post Evaluation of Exceptional Access under the 2010 Extended Arrangement," January 2015; European Commission, "Ex Post Evaluation of the Economic Adjustment Programme for Ireland (2010–2013)," July 2015.

[44] IMF, "Ireland: Ex Post Evaluation," pp. 37–40.

part to failure to adopt the structural reforms. A debate emerged over whether the ECB should act as a lender of last resort to sovereigns as well as to banks and, in April 2011, the ECB actually raised the intervention rate one-quarter point, the first of two such increases. The Socialist government of José Sócrates was able to hold out until winter 2010–11, when looming refinancing requirements forced Lisbon to turn to official creditors.

On this occasion, however, there was an effort to resist the inclusion of the IMF and conduct the program on a Europe-only basis. Both the Portuguese government and the European institutions had incentives for handling the program themselves. The debate over the role of the Fund was thus repeated on the first anniversary of the decision to include the Fund in the Greek program.

Portugal held the dubious distinction of having been the last developed country to draw from the IMF prior to the global financial crisis. Its 1983 program was within living memory of Lisbon policymakers in 2011 and they wished to avoid a repetition of IMF conditionality. Sócrates invited the Commission and ECB to come to Lisbon to assess Portugal's financial situation in February, but did not involve the IMF. He resigned in late March after the Parliament rejected his austerity plan, paving the way for snap elections in early June 2011.

For their part, the Commission and ECB had accumulated another year of conflict with the IMF since the first Greek program and hoped to avoid these in the Portuguese rescue. Those arguments went beyond the narrow question of program conditionality and design and now extended to broader questions of euro-area-wide policies of the ECB, the size of the financial safety net, and Greek debt restructuring. Commission President Barroso was, after all, Portuguese and probably became personally involved in negotiating the program. Among some creditor-country officials, convinced that Barroso had protected Portugal from criticism during macroeconomic surveillance prior to the crisis, distrust of the Commission ran especially deep in the case of Portugal.[45]

The Commission worked with the Portuguese government for several weeks to develop a program without the IMF. These conversations began in earnest in early February under Sócrates, carried over to the interim government, and specified the adjustment measures in some detail. The government formally announced its request for a rescue loan from the European partners on April 6. It made no mention of the IMF, which said in Washington only that it stood ready to help Portugal if requested. When the program was presented to the European Council meeting of March 24–5, however, Chancellor Merkel had insisted that the IMF be involved.[46] That message was

---

[45] Interviews with government officials, Luxembourg, January 31, 2012; Berlin, February 2 and 3, 2012; and Washington, D.C., March 19, 2014.

[46] Interviews with former officials, Washington, D.C., April 16 and 26, 2012.

reinforced at the Eurogroup meeting on the Portuguese situation of April 8, the same day that Dominique Strauss-Kahn announced that the IMF had received a formal request from Portugal for financial assistance.[47]

National electoral politics had delayed the acceptance of the need for a program and the development of the financial package. The transition to the new government in Portugal was one element. Elections in Finland in mid-April, the approach to which saw the Euroskeptic party True Finns gaining on the national governing coalition in public opinion polls, was another. Neither the Portuguese government nor the Eurogroup wanted to highlight a program that would inflame anti-euro sentiment in Finland and elsewhere.[48] Euro-area governments thus sought to strengthen fiscal rules in the Euro-Plus Pact and reinforce the lending capacity of the European Financial Stability Facility (EFSF). But delaying a formal request until late spring, as in the case of Greece one year earlier, increased the size of the program and as a consequence made the involvement of the IMF more important.

Program Negotiations and Outcome

The troika institutions confronted a number of substantive differences in the design of the program. The fiscal glide path to the three percent deficit target was the first matter of disagreement. The Portuguese government had announced its intention to achieve this goal by 2012. The Lisbon press reported, however, that IMF officials were seeking to extend the date as far as 2015, having learned from their experience in Greece and Ireland. The Commission and ECB, by contrast, pressed to reach the target much earlier.[49]

The Commission stressed the structural elements of the challenges facing Portugal as the basis for raising potential long-term growth and exports. The Commission's emphasis on these factors at the outset caught its counterparts in the troika somewhat by surprise, but the structural conditions were included. The ECB wanted to stabilize the banking system quickly through

[47] IMF, "Statement by IMF Managing Director Dominique Strauss-Kahn on Portugal," April 8, 2011. Paul Blustein reports that Strauss-Kahn tried to withhold IMF participation in the Portuguese program until Germany and the other Europeans agreed to a comprehensive resolution of the euro crisis, but was overruled in a G7 meeting. See Paul Blustein, *Laid Low: Inside the Crisis that Overwhelmed Europe and the IMF* (Waterloo, ON: Centre for International Governance Innovation, 2016), pp. 186–7.

[48] Simeon Djankov, *Inside the Euro Crisis: An Eyewitness Account* (Washington D.C.: Peterson Institute, 2014) makes a persuasive theme of this dynamic over the whole of the euro crisis; chapter on Portugal.

[49] Joao Lima, "IMF Wants Portugal to Reach Deficit Target Later, Negocios Says," *Bloomberg*, May 2, 2011; interviews with troika officials, Frankfurt, September 29–30, 2011; Brussels, October 6, 2011, and February 7, 2012; Washington, D.C., August, 29, 2011, and April 16, 2012, among others.

deleveraging and recapitalization. The Fund favored quick recapitalization but feared that rapid deleveraging would deepen the recession unnecessarily. The institutions discussed explicitly the balance to be struck between the size of the liquidity buffer provided to the banks and the amount of the loan to the Portuguese government, which were linked. The IMF preferred that the ECB provide generous liquidity, which would allow the size of the program to be reduced. The ECB preferred to extend less bank liquidity, and incur less exposure, which would require a larger program, financed, of course, by the governments.

The program, which was approved by the Eurogroup on May 16 and the IMF Executive Board on May 20, had three main planks: fiscal adjustment, financial reform, and structural reform.[50] It envisioned an overall fiscal consolidation of ten percent of GDP, half of which was supposed to be implemented in the first year, and a deficit of three percent in 2013.[51] Two large banks were to be reorganized and all banks were to raise capital to ten percent of assets by 2013. The government was to reduce or eliminate holdings in firms in the transport, energy, communications, and insurance sectors, with the aim of reducing costs to the state and raising revenue. The prominence of the "fiscal devaluation" distinguished this from the programs for Greece and Ireland; it aimed to reduce firms' contributions to pensions, replacing the revenue with a value-added tax (VAT) increase. The success of the program would depend in large part on attracting foreign direct investment, enhancing competitiveness, and shifting the Portuguese economy at least some degree toward the model of the internationally engaged Irish economy.

Portugal's sovereign debt was recalculated to be 106 percent of GDP in 2011 and was predicted to peak in 2013 at 115.3 percent. As in the case of the other programs, however, the debt scenario would later worsen as the recession proved deeper, unemployment higher, and the deficits targets were missed.[52] There was a fundamental tension between debt sustainability and the strategy of enhancing competitiveness by reducing costs through internal devaluation: domestic deflation rendered debt more difficult to service. The escape from this trap—a general problem among the highly indebted countries of the euro area[53]—depended greatly on external growth and financing conditions.

---

[50] IMF, "Transcript of a Conference Call with IMF Mission Chief Poul Thomsen," May 20, 2011.

[51] The European institutions prevailed in the program target, but the actual outcome was even less ambitious that the IMF's preference. Portugal did achieve the three percent target during the program over the following year.

[52] Zsolt Darvas, "The Long Haul: Managing Exit from Financial Assistance," *Bruegel Policy Contribution* No. 2014/03, Brussels, February 20, 2014.

[53] Zsolt Darvas, "The Euro Area's Tightrope Walk: Debt and Competitiveness in Italy and Spain," *Bruegel Policy Contribution* No. 2013/11, Brussels, September 3, 2013.

The IMF staff report on the program addressed the risks to debt sustainability. It justified the large size of the loan relative to quota on the basis of the language inserted into the exceptional access criteria in the course of the approval of the Greek program:[54]

> Debt dynamics may worsen should growth, inflation, or real interest rate outturns be worse than expected, or contingent liabilities (e.g. from SOEs or PPPs) materialize, making it difficult to state categorically there is a high probability that debt is sustainable over the medium term. Fund support at the proposed level is justified given the high risk of international systemic spillover effects.

Total assistance to Portugal amounted to €78 billion, the equivalent of 45.6 percent of GDP. (Portugal's GDP was €171 billion and its population was 10.6 million in 2011.) The IMF contributed one-third of this amount (€26 billion) and Europe contributed two-thirds (€52 billion). The European portion was split evenly between the EFSF and the EFSM. Learning the lessons of the previous programs, financing was provided at longer maturities, the IMF's at nine years through the Extended Fund Facility (EFF) and Europe's at seven and a half years (see Appendix). The Eurogroup funds did not come at a penalty rate, as in the first Greek program, but the rate would nonetheless have to be reduced later.

Implementation

Portugal's political economy of adjustment contrasted with the other program cases. Whereas Greece's domestic political commitment to the program was dubious from the beginning, the commitment of Portugal's government was strong at the outset, similar to Ireland's. But Ireland's economy was externally oriented and its modern industrial base offered a springboard for exports, which Portugal's economy did not match. Portugal thus offers a contrast between political "ownership" of the program and the economic foundation for its success.

The task of implementation fell to the conservative government of Pedro Passos Coelho, who became prime minister after national elections in early June 2011. His government's first test was the design and implementation of the fiscal devaluation. This was controversial, negotiated with the social partners, and ultimately implemented under the management of the Minister of Finance, Vitor Gaspar. But as the recession deepened and unemployment rose, trade unions and the Socialist Party, which had negotiated the program prior to the election, became increasingly opposed. The achievement of the

---

[54] IMF, "Portugal: Request for a Three-Year Arrangement Under the Extended Fund Facility," *Country Report* No. 11/127 (June 2011), p. 22.

three percent target was postponed by one year in September 2012 and then by another year in March 2013.

Opponents of austerity petitioned the Portuguese Constitutional Court in a succession of cases over 2013 and 2014. The Court decided with the government on most of these, but its decisions against the government raised problems that complicated the politics of the budget. Watching the gap grow between public sentiment and the troika, Gaspar resigned in early summer 2013, followed by Paulo Portas, the foreign minister, presenting Prime Minister Coelho with a political crisis. President Aníbal Cavaco Silva declined to call for elections, however, and Coelho instead reorganized his government.[55]

Portuguese national politics thus collided with German politics. During the German election campaign over the summer of 2013, there would be no renegotiation of the Portuguese program or any explicit acknowledgement by the governments that the date for reaching the three percent target must be deferred, which would become the third deferment.[56] In the face of this collision, the troika institutions postponed the eighth program review, which had been scheduled for the summer, and combined it with the ninth review, which they released in November 2013, safely after the German elections as well as elections in Austria.

Exit from the Program

The Portuguese economy contracted by 6.1 percent during 2011–13, less than Ireland's and far less than in Greece's, but again greater than anticipated at the outset of the program. This drop came on the heels of a flat economy in 2008, a 2.5 percent of GDP contraction in 2009, and only a modest, short-lived expansion in 2010 (see Figure 6.2). In February 2014, the IMF could not predict a return to the level of real output of 2007 until about 2020 and unemployment was projected to remain high for the foreseeable future.[57]

Whereas the prospects for Irish debt sustainability appeared favorable, and Greek debt underwent two restructurings, the long-term prospects for Portugal appeared evenly balanced between sustainability and unsustainability at the end of its program in spring 2014. Portuguese government debt had

---

[55] Editorial, "Portugal's Crisis of Politics and Growth," *Financial Times*, July 3, 2013; Peter Wise, "Portugal's Passos Coelho Pledges to Stay as Prime Minister," *Financial Times*, July 2, 2013.

[56] Peter Wise, "Lisbon set to win deficit target extension," *Financial Times*, March 13, 2013.

[57] IMF, "Portugal: Request for a Three-Year Arrangement Under the Extended Fund Facility," p. 26, Table 1; IMF, "Portugal: Eighth and Ninth Reviews Under the Extended Arrangement," *Country Report* No. 13/324, p. 40, Table 1; IMF, "Tenth Review Under The Extended Arrangement," *Country Report* No. 14/56 (February 2014), Table 1.

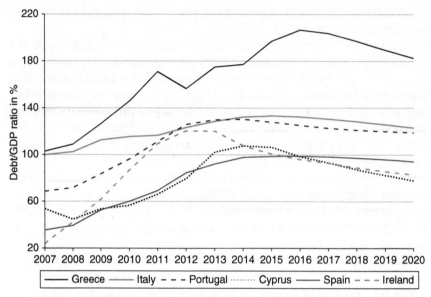

Figure 6.3. Government Debt to GDP Ratio and Projections, 2007–2020.
Source: World Economic Outlook Database, October 2015.

risen to about 127 percent as of 2013 after which the IMF's central scenario anticipated a decline toward 110 percent around 2020. But this scenario was subject to a number of risks. The long-term risk was that structural reform of the Portuguese economy would prove insufficient to raise the potential growth rate to two percent, on which the favorable scenario was premised. Deflation in the euro area, should the ECB fail to prevent it, would undercut sustainability.

In the short term, Portugal needed to borrow a substantial amount on the capital markets over the course of 2014–16. So, the immediate risk in 2014 was that Portugal might succumb to the volatility that harassed emerging markets in the wake of tapering from quantitative easing in the United States. On the threshold of the exit from its program, like Ireland, Portugal faced the question as to whether to seek a precautionary program. It had succeeded in floating a five-year bond issue in January 2014, but it had done so at a higher rate than Ireland. Portugal's higher debt and weaker long-term growth prospects weighed on confidence, placing a premium on securing insurance against an accident.[58]

---

[58] A precautionary exit program was advocated by, among others, André Sapir, Guntram B. Wolff, Carlos de Sousa, and Alessio Terzi, "The Troika and Financial Assistance in the Euro Area: Successes and Failures," Study on the Request of the Economic and Monetary Affairs Committee, European Parliament, February 2014; Zsolt Darvas, André Sapir, and Guntram B. Wolff, "The Long Haul: Managing Exit from Financial Assistance," *Bruegel Policy Contribution*, No. 2014/03, Brussels, February, 2014.

The IMF staff, European Commission, and ECB confidentially recommended a precautionary program for Portugal. But this recommendation again ran up against opposition on the part of the European creditors, especially Germany, who would be called upon to activate the precautionary facilities of the ESM for the first time and justify their use to their national parliaments. Ultimately, buoyed by favorable conditions in the capital markets, Prime Minister Coelho in the April 2014 decided to forgo a precautionary program and opted instead for a "clean" exit.[59]

The IMF review stressed realism in the debt sustainability analysis during its post-program monitoring discussions. The peak for the debt ratio was revised upward and outward to 130 percent in 2014 and the baseline scenario forecasted a decline to 118 percent by 2020 (see Figure 6.3).[60] These numbers were considerably more pessimistic than Lisbon's stability program and the Fund's analysis stressed the fragility of the debt ratio with respect to growth and the primary surplus. The IMF's analysis should be read in the context of the debate between the Fund and the European institutions, which mirrored the debate between the non-European and European member states, over the need for and modalities of debt restructuring with respect to Greece—a debate that took place in parallel with the Portuguese program and which we review in Chapter 10.

KEY OBSERVATIONS

This chapter reviewed the cases of Ireland and Portugal, examining the decision on the role of the IMF, key differences with the European institutions over program design, the resolution of those differences, and the role of precautionary financing during the exit from the program. In the Irish case, the decision to include the IMF was uncontroversial. But this would prove to be the exception rather than the rule; the Fund's inclusion was contested in the Portuguese case and, as we shall see, subsequent cases as well. Creditor governments within the euro area effectively decided the institutional configuration of these financial rescues, with Germany being a leading advocate of the inclusion of the Fund. Concern about the lack of toughness of the European Commission weighed heavily in their considerations. The Fund,

[59] Peter Spiegel and Peter Wise, "Portugal to Exit €78bn Bailout Without Emergency Backstop," *Financial Times*, April 30, 2014.

[60] IMF, "Portugal: Second Post-Program Monitoring Discussions," Country Report no. 15/226, July 16, pp. 30–38; IMF, "Portugal: Tenth Program Review," *Country Report* No. 14/56, February 2014. For the reaction from the Portuguese government in February 2014, see Rita Faria, "Portas responde ao FMI: 'Acredito mais na realidade económica do que algumas instituições'," *Negocios*, February 19, 2014.

for its part, was predisposed to participate in these programs, although its provisos for doing so hardened over time vis-à-vis creditors. The two cases also highlight the essential role of the ECB in first supporting countries' banking systems at the onset of crises, thereby delaying the loss of market confidence, and then revoking such support when dependence on its financing became excessive, thereby pushing the borrower into the arms of the troika. The role of the G7 finance ministers was revealed in the debate over bailing in senior bondholders in the Irish banks; the group opposed doing so, which allowed the ECB to prevail. Finally, the fact that the creditor governments in the euro area overruled the unanimous recommendation of the troika for precautionary programs in both cases vividly illustrates where ability to make that decision ultimately lay.

7

Spain and Italy

While Greece, Ireland, and Portugal posed challenges for the euro area, Spain and Italy posed problems of another magnitude entirely. Spain stretched the limits of the euro area's ability to rescue, while Italy exceeded them. A country such as Greece could, in principle, exit the euro without transforming the monetary union, but the same could not be said for Spain or Italy. It was essential for the coherence of the euro area that these countries avoid a full-fledged crisis. The present chapter considers these two countries, one of which had a program while the other, in the end, did not need one.

CONTRASTS

The two countries, while large in economic size, differed in significant ways. Spain's crisis bore some similarity to the U.S. subprime crisis, with the banking system having intermediated a great deal of finance to the real-estate sector in a boom that proved to be a bubble. Italy's main problem inhered in high public debt, 106 percent of GDP in 2008, under which it had been laboring for decades, coupled with very low growth on average since the advent of the euro. Italy's private sector ran a positive financial balance, whereas Spain's was distinctly negative.

In the context of the tightening link between sovereigns and banks, however, the difference in sectoral financial balances did not much matter. The weakness of Spain's banks raised borrowing costs for the Spanish government and the weakness of Italian government finances raised borrowing costs for Italian banks. Both sovereigns suffered deteriorating bond prices as the crisis metastasized from the small countries to the rest of the euro area over the course of 2011 (see Figure 4.1b), helped by the Deauville mistake, the failure of the first Greek program, and uncertainty surrounding Greek debt restructuring.

Spain was frequently grouped with the three smaller program countries by private analysts of sovereign bonds. Concern about its finances and the yields of its bonds rose significantly in spring 2010 with the first Greek package. Spain had suffered a substantial recession during 2009 and its economy had begun to turn the corner in 2010. The Socialist government of Prime Minister José Luis Zapatero nonetheless introduced austerity measures in early 2010 and, while its deficits were substantial, its debt had been contained and the losses in the banking system had not yet been realized. During 2010 and well into 2011, therefore, one might have concluded that Spain's fundamentals were manageable, that its financial sustainability depended primarily on maintaining market confidence.

To Dominique Strauss-Kahn, Spain thus appeared to be a good candidate for precautionary financing from the IMF. The managing director tried to persuade Zapatero and his minister of the economy, Elena Salgado, to apply for precautionary funds.[1] With access to these, he and the IMF European Department reasoned, the secondary market in Spanish sovereign debt could relax and yields could hold or fall rather than rise. Such was the experience of Poland, Mexico, and Colombia shortly after those countries were approved for their Flexible Credit Lines (FCLs) by the Executive Board.[2] Zapatero rejected the proposal, however, to Strauss-Kahn's regret.

For its part, Italy had pursued relatively conservative fiscal policies during the global financial crisis. Its debt ratio had peaked at 122 percent of GDP in 1994 and had fallen to about 105 percent in 2007. Its government issued the third largest public debt in the world, roughly €2 trillion, behind the United States and Japan. So the government of Silvio Berlusconi had little "fiscal space" to exploit during the 2008–9 crisis.

But Italy also suffered from very weak long-term growth. During the fifteen years after the advent of the euro, the Italian economy had grown barely five percent—the weakest performer of the monetary union. Its challenge was thus reforms in the labor market and the corporate and government sectors to increase potential growth. The political question was whether the crisis could break the deadlock that has long characterized the politics of Italian reform.

EUROPEAN CENTRAL BANK DEMANDS REFORM

As yields rose further in mid-2011, attention gravitated to the Securities Market Programme of the ECB. Could the central bank be persuaded to buy Spanish and Italian government bonds as well as those of the program countries? The ECB for its part did not want to let the two governments off

[1] Interview with a former IMF official, Paris, May 22, 2012.
[2] IMF, "Review of the Flexible Credit Line and Precautionary Credit Line," November 1, 2011, pp. 11–12.

the hook for fundamental reforms; nor did it want to relieve the Eurogroup from the burden of financial support of its euro-area partners.[3]

The president and future president of the ECB, Jean-Claude Trichet and Mario Draghi, jointly signed a letter to Italian Prime Minister Silvio Berlusconi on August 5, 2011. Sweeping in scope, the two central bankers said that a series of measures were "essential" to underpinning the government's "sovereign signature" and "commitment to fiscal sustainability and structural reforms"—measures beyond those to which the Berlusconi government had yet committed. Trichet and Draghi considered essential the acceleration of fiscal consolidation in order to reduce the deficit for 2011, reduce the deficit for 2012 below one percent, and achieve a balanced budget in 2013 rather than in 2014 as was then forecast. An overhaul of public administration should eliminate administrative layers, the provincial layer in particular, and a constitutional reform should tighten fiscal rules—among a number of other measures.[4]

A similar letter, signed by Trichet and Bank of Spain Governor Miguel Ordóñez, was sent to Prime Minister Zapatero. Trichet and Ordóñez said that measures in the labor market, fiscal policy, and product market were essential. The labor market reforms included measures to decentralize wage bargaining, abolish the indexation of wages, moderate wages in the private sector—all within four weeks. The ECB demanded additional measures amounting to 0.5 percent of GDP to achieve the six percent target for the 2011 deficit. Trichet and Ordóñez asked for no additional measures to stabilize the banking sector, which is extraordinary given that Spain would seek access to €100 billion within ten months to recapitalize it.[5]

Although the letters made no explicit link to bond purchases, they effectively laid down the conditions under which the ECB would be willing to deploy the Securities Market Programme (SMP) for Italy and Spain.[6] The ECB began purchases of Italian and Spanish government bonds within days,

---

[3] By contrast, many analysts argued that the ECB should serve as a lender of last resort for sovereigns. See, for example, Paul de Grauwe and Yuemei Ji, "Economic and Monetary Union in Europe," in *Global Economics in Extraordinary Times: Essays in Honor of John Williamson*, eds C. Fred Bergsten and C. Randall Henning (Washington, D.C.: Peterson Institute, 2012), pp. 53–82.

[4] With respect to structural policies, they saw a need for "full liberalization of local public services and of professional services," "reform of the collective wage bargaining system," "review of rules regulating the hiring and dismissal of employees," and "the establishment of an unemployment insurance system." The letter was published by *Corriere della Serra*, September 29, 2011.

[5] The letter is published with his memoirs, Jose Luis Rodriguez Zapatero, *El dilema: 600 días de vertigo* (Editorial Planeta, 2013); excerpts from the letter are translated at <http://openeuropeblog.blogspot.com/2013/11/whats-best-place-to-publish-ecb-letter.html>.

[6] SMP purchases were also premised on collective action on the part of euro-area governments. See ECB, "Statement by the President," press release, Frankfurt, August 7, 2011. See also Paul Carrel, "ECB says will 'actively implement' bond buying," *Financial Times*, August 7, 2011.

having received assurances from both prime ministers.[7] Weekly purchases under the SMP amounted to more than €80 billion through the end of September. The interest rate on Italian ten-year bonds, which had reached 6.5 percent in early August, dropped sharply, as did that on Spanish bonds (see Figure 4.1b).

EURO LEADERS DEMAND REFORM

Prime Minister Berlusconi and Finance Minister Giulio Tremonti, however, failed to follow through on many of the demands in the August letter.[8] Once Berlusconi's backtracking became evident, Merkel, Sarkozy, and the other leaders took over the negotiations with him from the ECB. What we might call the "conditionality baton" thus passed from the central bank to the Eurogroup and Euro summit. At two summits in Brussels in late October and at the G20 summit in Cannes in early November, the leaders pressed Berlusconi forcefully.[9]

Chancellor Merkel and President Sarkozy, in particular, pressed Berlusconi not only to specify precisely the nature and timing of fiscal measures, but also to take a precautionary program from the IMF.[10] Managing Director Christine Lagarde reiterated the offer.[11] She denied doing so afterward,[12] but Berlusconi, one anonymous participant at the meeting, and Zapatero report Berlusconi indeed being asked at Cannes to accept precautionary financing from the Fund.[13] Berlusconi rejected this, however. Meanwhile, German Finance Minister Schäuble, French Finance Minister François Baroin, and Treasury Secretary Geithner insisted that Italian Finance Minister Tremonti allow the IMF to monitor the fiscal and structural reforms that he had promised to the Commission and Eurogroup, which the Italians accepted.[14]

[7] Guy Dinmore and Ralph Atkins, "ECB Letter Shows Pressure on Berlusconi," *Financial Times*, September 29, 2011.

[8] Bastasin, *Saving Europe*, pp. 319–21.

[9] Crawford and Czuczka, *Angela Merkel*, pp. 7–21; Bastasin, *Saving Europe*.

[10] President Obama participated in one of two meetings among these officials prior to the G20 plenary. Bastasin, *Saving Europe*, p. 338.

[11] The IMF had refashioned the Precautionary Credit Line (PCL) as the Precautionary Liquidity Line (PLL) with just such a contingency in mind.

[12] IMF, Transcript of a Press Briefing with Christine Lagarde, November 4, 2011, at <http://www.imf.org/external/np/tr/2011/tr110411.htm>.

[13] See, respectively, Leslie Wroughton and Paul Taylor, "IMF in Exploratory Talks with Italy on Support: Sources," *Reuters*, November 29, 2011; Bastasin, *Saving Europe*, p. 338; "Las Tres Amenazas de Rescate Contra el Expresidente Zapatero," *El Pais*, November 26, 2013. These three sources differ on the amount that was offered—€50 billion, €45 billion, €85 billion respectively.

[14] Bastasin, *Saving Europe*, pp. 336–8.

With the objective of bolstering credibility of the reforms, and thus reducing the bond spread, the IMF was to report quarterly on progress on implementation.[15]

Former Prime Minister Zapatero reports being ambushed by Merkel just before the Cannes summit meeting on November 3 with a proposal for €50 billion in IMF precautionary financing for Spain.[16] Zapatero also rejected this proposal, noting that Spain still had access to the capital markets and had taken the measures agreed with the other euro-area leaders, which distinguished his case from Berlusconi's. His country, he added, was in the middle of an election campaign. Looking him in the eye, Merkel responded in English, "Okay, I understand."[17]

The ECB, for its part, had suspended SMP purchases of Italian bonds for noncompliance in October. The controversy surrounding the Italian adjustment measures before and after Cannes thus drove government bond yields upward and, with them, the Italian Prime Minister into a political crisis. Berlusconi offered his resignation on November 8 and, on November 13, Italy's President Giorgio Napolitano asked Mario Monti to form a new government.[18] The ECB then appears to have resumed purchases of Italian bonds. By contrast, acceptably content with Madrid's reforms, the ECB seems to have continued to purchase Spanish government bonds throughout this period.[19]

With the letters and SMP purchases, the ECB had crossed an important threshold, explicitly demanding deep policy reforms that were the province of elected national parliaments as a condition for support. The ECB was complicit, with the leaders of the other governments in the euro area, in the ousting of Berlusconi and the change of government in Italy. The ECB was thus exposed to political backlash within a key member state and ECB officials were sensitive to this exposure.[20] They accepted it because the alternatives that were available in early August carried even greater risks.[21]

---

[15] "Berlusconi Burlesque," *Economist*, November 4, 2011.

[16] Precautionary financing for both countries had been recommended by several outside observers. See, among others, C. Randall Henning, "IMF Precautionary Finance for the Euro Area: A Bold But Necessary Step," RealTime Economic Issues Watch, Peterson Institute, July 15, 2011.

[17] José Luis Zapatero, *El dilema: 600 días de vertigo*, p. 143. Press summaries of highlights of the book include "Las tres amenazas de rescate contra el expresidente Zapatero," *El Pais*, November 26, 2013; Paul Taylor, "Merkel Tried to Bounce Spain into IMF Bailout: ex-PM," *Reuters*, November 25, 2013.

[18] The governmental crisis and the conflict between Berlusconi and Tremonti, among other elements of this saga, are treated in Erik Jones, "Italy's Sovereign Debt Crisis," *Survival* 54 (no. 1, February–March 2012): 83–110.

[19] The suspension of purchases, though widely accepted, is an educated conjecture. The ECB did not release a country-specific breakdown of weekly transactions. The suspension coincides with the publication of the letter in late September, which Bastasin, *Saving Europe*, reports was deliberately leaked by Berlusconi himself.

[20] Interviews with central bank officials, Frankfurt, September 29–30, 2011.

[21] Strategic interaction among the ECB and euro-area governments is analyzed in C. Randall Henning, "The ECB as a Strategic Actor," in *The Political and Economic Dynamics of the Eurozone Crisis*, eds James A. Caporaso and Martin Rhodes.

But the ECB learned from this experience that imposing conditionality was potentially extremely hazardous to the institution. This lesson colored the ECB's approach to participation in the troika and its public salience as a member of the institutional team. The leadership of the central bank looked more favorably on the inclusion of the IMF as a consequence. By the time the letter to Berlusconi leaked to the public, Trichet had concluded that it had been a mistake to try to exclude the IMF from the first Greek package in winter 2010.[22] ECB officials also resolved to induce the Commission and euro-area governments to take political responsibility for such conditionality in the future.

GOVERNMENT TRANSITIONS

During November 2011, Spain and Greece also experienced important changes in government. In Spain, Zapatero's Socialist Party lost to the Popular Party in national elections on November 20. In Greece, Prime Minister Papandreou resigned, having announced and then retracted a referendum on his program, and was replaced by Lucas Papademos. Mario Monti's replacement of Berlusconi in Rome thus raised to three the number of new leaders on the European political landscape.

Prime Minister Monti served as his own finance minister and, despite an initial visit by Fund officials to discuss modalities in December, just never found a convenient time to host a mission to conduct the monitoring to which his predecessor had agreed. That procedure was quietly shelved, despite the fanfare with which it had been agreed at Cannes, overtaken by the regular Article IV consultation by the Fund in spring 2012. Commission surveillance of Italian public finance was exercised instead through the Macroeconomic Imbalances Procedure and the Excessive Deficit Procedure under the Stability and Growth Pact (SGP) and the European Semester.[23]

Spain and Italy were the primary beneficiaries of the next major move on the part of the ECB. In December 2011 and February 2012, the central bank, now under the leadership of Mario Draghi launched two tranches of Longer-Term Refinancing Operations (LTROs). These were distinguished from regular refinancing operations by providing liquidity to private banks over a thirty-six-month time horizon.[24] They were also very large, together amounting to

---

[22] Interview with an ECB official, Frankfurt, September 29, 2011.

[23] See European Commission, Economic and Financial Affairs, webpage on Policy and Surveillance, "Italy," <http://ec.europa.eu/economy_finance/eu/countries/italy_en.htm>.

[24] See "ECB Announces Measures to Support Bank Lending and Money Market Activity," ECB press release, December 8, 2011; "ECB Announces Details of Refinancing Operations from October 2011 to 10 July 2012," ECB press release, October 6, 2011. The ECB also reduced the

more than €1 trillion. The banks in the southern periphery, Spanish and Italian banks in particular, had suffered larger increases in the cost of inter-bank funding and thus drew on the LTROs disproportionately. The effect of these operations was temporary, however, and the fragmentation of the European banking system became more severe over the course of the first half of 2012.

Meanwhile, the new Spanish Prime Minister, Mariano Rajoy, wrestled with the Euro summit and Commission over fiscal adjustment. The previous government had overshot the six percent target for the deficit in 2011 by 2.5 percent and the economy was now in recession. Rajoy announced an upward revision of the target for 2012 from 4.4 percent to 5.8 percent unilaterally. In the ensuing uproar within European councils, Spain agreed on a 5.3 percent target in the Eurogroup meeting of March 12. Nearly simultaneously, the fiscal rules in the monetary union were being tightened under the Fiscal Compact in the Treaty on Stability, Coordination, and Governance (hereafter simply the "Stability treaty"), signed at the beginning of March.

Later, the Commission revised the targets in Spain's recommendation under the Excessive Deficit Procedure upward to 6.3 percent for 2012 (0.5 percent *above* Rajoy's initial figure), 4.5 percent in 2013, and 2.8 percent in 2014, and these were approved by the Council. This required a fiscal "effort"— that is, new austerity measures—of 2.7 percent, 2.5 percent, and 1.9 percent during these years respectively.[25] The IMF staff differed openly with the Commission on the speed of deficit reduction and argued privately that deficit reduction of this magnitude during a recession, as forecast, was dangerous. This dissent was reported in the Spanish press.[26]

SPAIN'S FINANCIAL SECTOR PROGRAM

Prime Minister Rajoy wanted to avoid a "full program"—one that financed government deficits, as opposed to simply bank recapitalization, with draw-ings from the IMF, as well as European institutions—at all costs. In doing so,

reserve ratio and eased collateral requirements. Mario Draghi, "Introductory statement to the press conference (with Q&A)," *European Central Bank Press Conferences*, December 8, 2011 and January 12, 2012.

[25] European Commission, DG Ecfin, "The Financial Sector Adjustment Programme for Spain," *European Economy*, October 2012, section 7.4.9, p. 52; European Commission, "Recom-mendation for a Council Recommendation Bringing an End to the Excessive Government Deficit in Spain," Brussels, COM (2012) 397 final, July 6, 2012. See also, European Commission, "Macroeconomic Imbalances—Spain," *European Economy* Occasional Papers 103 (July 2012).

[26] "El FMI advierte al Gobierno de que la recession arruninara el plan de ajuste," *El Pais*, January 25, 2012. The IMF's view was presented in muted tones the *World Economic Outlook* update of January 2012, but was repeated in its July 2012 Article IV Report, Box 5.

he hoped to differentiate Spain's plight from the countries that had accepted full troika programs and avoid the associated domestic political costs. So he worked to preempt that outcome by introducing structural measures in the labor market and collective bargaining system, strengthening central control over regional and municipal budgets—measures listed in the ECB's August letter—and establishing a €50 billion provisioning requirement for banks. But his new government delayed presentation of a new budget until the end of March 2012, which raised concerns in the capital markets.[27] He thus could not avoid turning to his European counterparts to finance a restructuring of the Spanish banking system.

During the global financial crisis Spain had been proactive in addressing the banking sector problem. Banks raised their capital ratios and merged into larger banking groups, with a number of weaker savings banks (cajas) being consolidated into BFA-Bankia.[28] The European Banking Authority (EBA) conducted stress tests of ninety banks in the European Union, including twenty-four in Spain, and announced the results in July 2011. Only a few banks were rated short of capital and the shortfall appeared easily filled.[29] But these results masked deeper problems: while the two large internationally active banks, Santander and BBVA, were reasonably strong, a large number of cajas were, in fact, quite weak.[30]

Spanish banks lost access to capital markets and then interbank funding over the course of 2011 and the first half of 2012. The funding problems were aggravated by deposit withdrawals, which accelerated in the first half of 2012. Spanish banks drew heavily on the LTROs in winter 2012. But by spring 2012, they had become extraordinarily heavily dependent on the ECB.[31] The main question was how long the ECB would allow this to continue before insisting that the Spanish government turn to the Eurogroup for financial assistance, as it had done in the case of Ireland.

Bankia, under the management of former IMF Managing Director Rodrigo Rato, turned to the government for a capital infusion in the amount of €23.5 billion in May. The Rajoy government's initial reaction to Bankia's request was to propose recapitalizing it by issuing government bonds. Bankia would then be able to present the bonds to the ECB in regular refinancing operations.[32]

---

[27] Willem Buiter, "Spain: Prospects and Risks," *Global Economics View*, Citigroup Global Markets, March 28, 2012.

[28] IMF, "Spain: Financial Stability Assessment," *Country Report* No. 12/137 (June 2012), Figure 1, p. 8.

[29] EU-wide stress test results at <http://www.eba.europa.eu/risk-analysis-and-data/eu-wide-stress-testing/2011/results>.

[30] European Commission, "The Financial Sector Adjustment Programme for Spain," pp. 15–28.

[31] IMF, "Spain: Article IV Consultations," July 2012.

[32] "Spain Hopes to Draw European Central Bank into Funding Bankia Bailout," *Guardian*, May 27, 2012.

Confirming the fears of the ECB that the new government was attempting to use it to delay or avoid essential restructuring, the proposal was quickly quashed.[33]

By late spring 2012, it was becoming clear that Rajoy would have to seek official help. He placed a formal request to the Eurogroup for access to €100 billion for the purpose of recapitalizing Spanish banks.[34] The stated objective of the program was to "increase the long-term resilience of the banking sector as a whole, thus restoring its market access." This would be accomplished by overhauling the weak banks through an asset quality review and stress test, segregation of impaired legacy assets, and recapitalization of banks as necessary with either privately raised equity or loans from the EFSF and ESM. The program also included strengthening the regulatory and supervisory framework, including transparency, corporate governance and review, and enforcement of capital requirements—"horizontal conditionality."[35]

ROLE OF THE IMF AND CROSS-CONDITIONALITY

Owing to the domestic political stigma associated with borrowing from the IMF, Rajoy and his government placed supreme importance on avoiding a "full program." Madrid indeed proclaimed that the financial assistance it was seeking was not a full program because it was limited to restructuring the banking system, conditionality applied only to that sector, and the IMF was not involved financially. But the program, while different from those for Greece, Ireland, and Portugal, contained many elements of a full program and the institutional arrangement was a variation on, rather than a rejection of, the troika.

Under the Spanish program, the Fund staff would monitor the financial sector, assess progress against program conditions and, considering the macroeconomic context, write quarterly reports. The restructuring of individual financial institutions was explicitly outside the IMF's mandate. The Fund staff would participate in monitoring missions with the Commission, as would the ECB, but it would make its assessment independently. A form of technical

---

[33] Patrick Jenkins, "ECB rejects Madrid plan to boost Bankia," *Financial Times*, May 29, 2012; Jeff Black, "ECB Wasn't Consulted on Spanish Recapitalization Plan," *Bloomberg*, May 30, 2012.

[34] The Eurogroup issued three statements on Spain around the initiation of the program, on June 9, June 27, and July 20, 2012. Rajoy placed the request on June 25; see Kincaid, "The IMF's Role in the Euro Area Crisis," p. 18.

[35] European Commission, DG Ecfin, "The Financial Sector Adjustment Programme for Spain," *European Economy*, Occasional Papers 118 (October 2012), pp. 30–49.

assistance under the Fund's articles, the monitoring reports were a product of the Fund staff alone and were not approved by, nor necessarily reflective of, the views of the Executive Board.[36] They were informed by, but distinct from, the Financial Sector Assessment Program (FSAP), which had been completed earlier, and the regular Article IV consultations, which continued in parallel to the monitoring procedure.[37]

Notwithstanding the primary focus of program conditionality on banks and regulatory authorities, Spain undertook obligations to its European partners in all of the policy areas that are covered in a full program. Those obligations were simply organized under three different processes rather than a single program. Spain had been under the Excessive Deficit Procedure (EDP) since the global financial crisis and was brought under the Macroeconomic Imbalances Procedure (MIP) in May 2012. These procedures, conducted by the Commission, established commitments with respect to fiscal policy and structural reforms, including in the labor and product markets and local government administration, respectively. The Spanish government took comfort in the fact that it was not being singled out for special treatment under these procedures, because they applied to the other states by virtue of their membership in the monetary union. But the adjustment required under the EDP, a fiscal effort of 7.1 percent of GDP, was equivalent to program austerity. Creditor governments accepted these commitments as adequate complements to the financial sector obligations under the formal program.

Moreover, the program's memorandum of understanding stated clearly that the targets for deficit reduction would be satisfied in parallel with the banking program and were subject to the EDP.[38] In addition, although it did not actually do so, the Eurogroup could halt disbursements for bank recapitalization if it were not satisfied with Madrid's adherence to the EDP. The Eurogroup, and key creditor governments, could thus coordinate the three elements of the adjustment process—banking, fiscal, structural—with financing. Furthermore, by the reading of this author, the European Court of Justice (ECJ) November 2012 ruling on the ESM makes the linkage to EU fiscal rules a requirement for financial assistance.[39]

---

[36] IMF, "Terms of Reference for Fund Staff Monitoring in the Context of European Financial Assistance for Bank Recapitalization," July 20, 2012.

[37] For further treatment of the role of the IMF, Nicolas Véron, "The IMF's Role in the Euro Area Crisis: Financial Sector Aspects." *IEO Background Paper* BP/16–02/10; Kincaid, "The IMF's Role in the Euro Area Crisis," pp. 18–19.

[38] Memorandum of Understanding, preamble, and paragraphs 29, 30 and 31, in DG Ecfin, "Financial Sector Adjustment Programme for Spain," October 2012. Although the actual deficits overshot their targets, the Commission deemed the fiscal effort, as measured by the reduction in the structural balance, to be in compliance with the EDP.

[39] C-370/12 *Thomas Pringle* v. *Government of Ireland* [2012] ECLI:EU:C:2012:756.

Spain's financial sector program was also "full" in the sense that the IMF was integrally involved in its design. Having completed the FSAP in spring 2012, the IMF was up to date and well informed on the Spanish banking system and its vulnerabilities. Notwithstanding the formal designation of the Fund's role as monitor and the absence of a financial contribution, therefore, the troika functioned de facto as three.

This informal arrangement was carefully negotiated between the Spanish and German governments. Bilateral contacts between Chancellor Merkel and Prime Minister Rajoy and between Wolfgang Schäuble and Luis de Guindos, the Spanish Minister of the Economy and Competitiveness, intensified during the approach to the program, and remained frequent afterward. Two important decisions were made bilaterally. First, officials of the two countries agreed that the program would be limited to the financial sector. Second, Ministers Schäuble and de Guindos established the size of the program, €100 billion. The size of the program, for example, was not discussed in the Eurogroup prior to the decision.[40]

As one participant in these bilateral discussions later said, it is "only normal" that a program should be teed up in this way prior to a decision in the broader forum. Officials want to become aware of, and resolve, any major sticking points in advance.[41] Berlin wanted tighter commitments on the fiscal side and more progress on labor market reforms. Madrid wanted to avoid introducing structural reforms into the memorandum and thus preempted with its own reform plan. They agreed on the "parallelism" between the financial sector reform, on the one hand, and obligations under the Excessive Deficit Procedure and Macroeconomic Imbalances Procedure, on the other hand.

The political transition in Spain from the Socialist government to the center-right government was critical in paving the way for managing the rescue without a full, formal program. Rajoy's government was more politically compatible with the conservative–liberal coalition government in Berlin. Chancellor Merkel had tried to persuade Prime Minister Zapatero to take a precautionary program from the IMF prior to the election. Had Zapatero remained in office, Chancellor Merkel would have almost certainly insisted that Spain take a full program in the formal sense.[42]

[40] Interviews with European officials, Washington, D.C., March 19, 2014, and April 18, 2015; Brussels, July 22, 2014. See, also, Eurogroup, "Eurogroup Statement on Spain," Brussels, June 9, 2012.

[41] Interview, July 15, 2015.

[42] This counterfactual, which admittedly cannot be known with certainty, reflects the consistent, collective judgment of very well-informed German and European officials. Interviews, Brussels, July 22, 2014; Washington, D.C., March 19, 2014, and April 18, 2015; Berlin, July 15, 2015.

GETTING AHEAD OF THE CURVE, FINALLY

Even after the financial sector program was announced and initially implemented, there were even odds that the Spanish government itself, not simply
the banks, would also eventually lose access to the capital markets and be
pushed into a second, full program. Rajoy was able to avoid this fate thanks to
faithful implementation of the financial sector program, a robust response by
the ECB, and ultimately, support from German policymakers for the actions
taken by the ECB and, critically, for banking union.

The launch of the Spanish banking program coincided with dramatic developments elsewhere in the euro area. Political turmoil in Greece (discussed in
Chapter 10) weighed on the financial situation of Spain and Italy and introduced "redenomination risk" into the markets. Spain's situation and the general
deterioration of the bond markets contributed to a shift in the German position
with respect to banking supervision and bank resolution in Europe. At a critical
European Council meeting in late June, Chancellor Merkel and her colleagues
agreed to the broad outlines of the banking union. The communiqué stated
explicitly their determination to break the link between the sovereign and the
banks once and for all.[43] But even the European Council agreement failed to
stem the growing sense of panic in the financial markets.

The ECB responded in two ways. First, Draghi announced in London,
"Within our mandate, the ECB is ready to do whatever it takes to preserve
the euro. And believe me, it will be enough."[44] Second, Draghi announced the
Outright Monetary Transactions (OMT) program in early September.[45]
OMT would provide for ECB purchases of sovereign bonds similar to the
Securities Market Programme, which was being retired.[46] But the ECB would
activate OMT only after the country in question agreed to an ESM financing
program with governments and European Commission on the basis of strict
conditionality. The Eurogroup would have to purchase on the primary market

---

[43] Banking union and the politics surrounding it are addressed in Nicolas Véron, "A Realistic
Bridge Towards European Banking Union," *Bruegel Policy Contribution* No. 2013/09; Ángel
Ubide, "How to Form a More Perfect European Banking Union," *Peterson Institute Policy Briefs*
No. 13–23, Washington: Peterson Institute, October, 2013; Lorenzo Bini Smaghi, *Austerity:
European Democracies against the Wall*, Brussels: CEPS, 2013, 87–92; and Rachel Epstein and
Martin Rhodes, "International in Life, National in Death? Banking Nationalism on the Road to
Banking Union," in *The Political and Economic Dynamics of the Eurozone Crisis*, eds James
A. Caporaso and Martin Rhodes (New York: Oxford University Press, 2016). See also, Euro Area
Summit Statement, Brussels, June 29, 2012.

[44] Speech by Mario Draghi, President of the European Central Bank at the Global Investment
Conference in London, July 26, 2012.

[45] Press Conference with Mario Draghi, President of the ECB, Vítor Constâncio, Vice-
President of the ECB, Frankfurt am Main, September 6, 2012.

[46] Decision-making leading to the announcement of OMT, as well as the London speech, are
discussed in Neil Irwin, *The Alchemists: Three Central Bankers and a World on Fire* (New York:
Penguin, 2013), pp. 279–84.

via the ESM and the country in question would have to retain access to international capital markets. Euro-area governments would thus have political responsibility for designing the adjustment programs of the borrowers.

The OMT program was controversial in Germany. The Bundesbank opposed the program and its president, Jens Weidmann, voted against it in the Governing Council meeting in September. But Chancellor Merkel supported the ECB's decision publicly and Finance Minister Schäuble criticized Weidmann for his opposition.[47] Although the program was later challenged in the Constitutional Court, the statements of these key German officials boosted the credibility of the program in the financial markets.

The commitment to banking union, Draghi's famous statement, and announcement of OMT mark the decisive turning point in the euro crisis. More than two and a half years after the onset of the Greek crisis, euro-area authorities were finally getting ahead of the curve. The acute phase of the crisis would continue and Cyprus would soon succumb. But these measures brought sovereign spreads down, setting the stage for Spain to exit its program.

SPAIN EXITS

Spain's eighteen-month package was concluded in January 2014, at a moment when conditions in the European capital market were benign and the European banking system was preparing for the transfer of supervision to the ECB. Madrid had drawn on €41.5 billion of the total €100 billion that had been made available.

A comparison of the exit reports of the IMF and European Commission highlighted the analytical areas of agreement and disagreement between the two institutions.[48] Both reports applauded Spanish compliance with the terms of the program and the restructuring of the banking system and bank regulation. While underscoring the success in stabilizing Spanish finance, the reports stressed the importance of post-program follow-through in light of the asset quality review and stress tests that were being conducted later in the year. In contrast to the Commission report, though, the IMF projected the debt ratio rising to 107 percent in 2017–18 (the Commission report declined to project beyond 2014, when a ratio of 99.9 percent was expected), supported

[47] "Merkel: Germany's Share in ECB Bond Buys Not Capped at €190 Billion," *Market News International*, September 17, 2012. Brian Blackstone and Marcus Walker, "How ECB Chief Outflanked German Foe in Fight for Euro," *Wall Street Journal*, October 2, 2012.

[48] IMF, "Spain: Financial Sector Reform—Final Progress Report," *Country Report* No. 14/59, February 2014; European Commission, "Financial Assistance Programme for the Recapitalisation of Financial Institutions in Spain Fifth Review—Winter 2014," *European Economy* Occasional Papers 170 (January 2014).

a slower pace of deleveraging, and advocated smaller dividend payouts to preserve bank capital.

While stating that "further substantial structural adjustment will be necessary over the medium term to put the debt-to-GDP ratio to a downward path," the IMF report observed that doing so would constrain domestic demand and growth. The Commission report specified that the structural deficit would have to be reduced by about one percent of GDP each year during 2013–16 to reach the established targets for reduction in the nominal deficit to 2.8 percent in 2016. The IMF projections for a return to weak growth during 2014 and 2015 were premised on these targets being missed![49] The two institutions agreed on the desirability of further monetary easing on the part of the ECB and finalizing a robust agreement on banking union—but the IMF report was more explicit about the need for both of these important measures to stabilize Spain's finances on a permanent basis. In the end, the fiscal targets were indeed missed and Spain's economy returned to three percent growth in 2015.

ITALY ESCAPES

The postwar pattern of frequent turnover in Italian government continued through the euro crisis. During 2012 and 2013, Italy experienced a deep recession similar to Spain's. After seventeen months in office, Mario Monti conceded the prime ministership to Enrico Letta in April 2013 after elections that were narrowly won by the center-left Democratic Party. Matteo Renzi replaced Letta in February 2014, after a reshuffling of the party leadership, inspiring hope that political deadlock on economic reform could finally be overcome. Throughout this period, Italy maintained access to capital markets as euro-area policies, especially the ECB's, brought down the borrowing rates. The government maintained a relatively tight rein on the fiscal deficit and was rewarded with graduation from the Excessive Deficit Procedure in autumn 2013. However, fiscal probity came at the cost of long-term economic stagnation and a rate of unemployment of thirteen percent. Structural reform appeared to be the only way out of the low-growth trap.

The sustainability of Italian debt was not an acute problem, but, as a long-term proposition, appeared to teeter on a knife edge.[50] At the end of 2013, according to the Italian Treasury, the debt ratio was 132.6 percent[51] and it has

---

[49] Compare Table 1, p. 52, of the IMF Article IV report to p. 28 and Annex 7.1, p. 31, in the Commission report (January 2014) cited immediately above.

[50] See, for example, Domenico Lombardi, "Italy," in *Europe's Crisis, Europe's Future*, eds Kemal Dervis and Jacques Mistral (Washington, D.C.: Brookings, 2014).

[51] Lorenzo Totaro and Andrew Frye, "Renzi's Government Sees Debt-to-GDP Ratio Rising This Year," *Bloomberg*, April 8, 2014.

remained roughly constant since then. Whether this could be reduced over time was largely a function of real growth and inflation. Structural reform could be expected to generate an increase in the long-term potential growth rate only with a lag. The rate of inflation was in the hands of the ECB, outside Rome's control, and it was declining. At the end of 2013, price increases were running well below one percent and the euro area would sink briefly into outright deflation in December 2014. Owing to the size of the country, its importance in European politics, and the precariousness of its debt position, the future of the euro could well be decided in Italy. But that decision lies beyond the focus on the institutional interaction in the crisis programs here and the present book thus leaves further treatment of Italy to other studies.

SOURCES OF VARIATION ON THE TROIKA

As in the previous cases, the role of the IMF remained contested and the creditor governments and Madrid decided the institutional mix for the Spanish program. They chose an institutional arrangement for the program that had both similarities and contrasts with the other crisis programs. A comparison reveals the importance of the domestic politics in both the creditor and borrower countries and of Spain's economic size, which placed a premium on the policies of the euro area as a whole in the solution to the country's crisis. The Spanish program differed from those for Greece, Ireland, and Portugal, first, in that the IMF did not contribute financially. Second, the ECB's actions in the form of unconventional monetary policy and Outright Monetary Transactions, while still not formally under the umbrella of the program, were decisive. As far as fiscal policy is concerned, third, Madrid could claim that it had not been singled out because its obligations under the Stability and Growth Pact and Macroeconomic Imbalances Procedure were, in principle, similar to all of its partners by virtue of their membership in the monetary union. Spain's fiscal commitments were enforced not by suspension of disbursements, as they would otherwise have been under a regular program, but by the more leaky Excessive Deficit Procedure. In the event, Spain overshot the deficit targets by a wide margin—registering not 2.8 percent of GDP in 2014, as originally specified, but 5.9 percent, then 5.1 percent in 2015, and 3.9 percent in 2016.[52]

Despite overshooting the fiscal targets, cross conditionality was never triggered because the creditor countries were basically content with these arrangements. Banking-sector restructuring was successful, banks' access to markets

---

[52] European Commission, "European Economic Forecast," Spring 2016, pp. 82–4. The figure for 2016 was a forecast. In that year, with the credibility of the SGP at stake, the Commission decided formally to fine Spain but set the fine at zero.

was restored, and Spain no longer needed financial assistance. Critically, the lenience afforded Spain under the fiscal arrangements enabled a robust recovery. Spain grew 3.2 percent in 2015, more than the other large countries in the euro area, and unemployment, while high, was expected to decline below twenty percent after 2016. With growth, the country had good prospects for repaying the debt incurred under the program. The recovery also helped Rajoy's Popular Party fend off challenges to the orthodoxy from the Socialist Party and Podemos in national elections in December 2015 and June 2016.

The Spanish program was similar to other programs, however, in that all of the institutions of the troika were involved in designing and monitoring the program and the government undertook a reform agenda that covered all of the policy areas that are usually included in an IMF program, including fiscal policy and structural reform. The Spanish government was desperate to differentiate its travails from other crisis cases, for reasons of domestic politics and market confidence, and conventional wisdom thus understates the similarities among the various institutional arrangements for the country rescues. Nevertheless, the institutional mix in the Spanish case is best understood as a variation on, rather than an alternative to, the troika.

This interpretation challenges an argument that is commonly advanced for explaining why the Fund's role did not include a financial contribution to the Spanish program. While the IMF can and does lend to governments to enable them to recapitalize their banks, it has no facility to do so without also bringing fiscal and other government policies under the program. Given that the Spanish government did not lose access to the financial markets, the argument goes, the Fund's lending facilities were not "fit for purpose." While the statement is not wrong as far as it goes, it is a narrow reading of the episode that obscures more fundamental reasons for the roles chosen for the institutions.

The question as to why the Spanish government was able to retain access to the capital markets holds the key to a deeper understanding. The answer is *not* that problems were confined to the banking sector and the government accounts were sound. Spain's general government deficit was unsustainably large and the country was on its way toward losing market access. The crises in Ireland and Cyprus were also primarily banking-sector problems, yet those crises were allowed to deteriorate until the sovereign was fully involved and thus required a regular program with fiscal and structural conditions and IMF financial participation. Why did the creditor states lend to Spain comparatively early in this process and not push the country into a Fund program?

Domestic politics are the key to understanding the choice of the institutional arrangement for Spain. Because Mariano Rajoy replaced Zapatero as prime minister and his center-right party held an outright majority in parliament, Merkel, Schäuble, and most of the rest of the German government had a relatively high level of confidence in their Spanish counterparts to implement a tough program—a level of confidence that had not applied to the governments in other program countries. Under these circumstances, drift on the part of the European Commission was less problematic from the perspective of Germany and other creditor countries and thus the IMF's financial participation was less valuable in constraining it.

The ECB kept the Spanish government in the markets by purchases of sovereign bonds first through the Securities Market Programme and then Long-Term Refinancing Operations. Chancellor Merkel's acceptance of the banking union agenda and her subsequent endorsement of the OMT program were almost certainly deeply influenced by Spain's financial predicament. Her position and the German government's posture on the ECB's unconventional monetary policy were vital to alleviating stress in the markets, reducing bond spreads, and thus probably decisive in enabling Madrid to avoid a second program that would have been openly full. Sovereign access to the markets in the Spanish case did not determine the choice of the institutional form of the program but rather was *endogenous* to the rescue, broadly understood to include the ECB's actions.

Spain's economic size bound the solution to its crisis to changes not only in the ECB's policies but also in other euro-area-wide policies. Specifically, it required a commitment from euro-area governments to banking union as well. (Creditors could afford to rescue smaller countries without these broader reforms.) The United States, other non-European countries, and the IMF strongly favored banking union and an ECB commitment to expand unconventional monetary policies. They viewed these measures to be essential to the success of the Spanish program and to stabilizing the euro area generally. But, while euro-area governments and the ECB proved willing to take large, important steps in these directions, neither was prepared in mid-2012 to make such commitments to the IMF in order to secure its financial contribution when they already had its participation in program design and monitoring.

The Spanish case tells us that the IMF is included even when its financing is not needed and that the Fund nonetheless remains influential in shaping programs. But the Fund's role in this case did not allow it a veto over the program or leverage over euro-area policies on the part of non-Europeans, when modifications of those policies would otherwise have been a plausible quid pro quo for IMF involvement financially. The euro-area decision against direct recapitalization of Spanish banks illustrates the pivotal position of the member states relative to the three institutions. Key European creditors could best organize the rescue to their preferences by keeping the IMF as a "shadow" member of the institutional team.

8

United States and International Monetary Fund

The United States played an active role in the euro crisis and the decisions about the extent and nature of the involvement of the IMF. Both debtor and creditor countries within the euro area appealed to the U.S. government for support in overcoming deadlocks that arose during European deliberations. The United States sought to use the institution strategically to advance its goals in Europe, while seeking to prevent the IMF from being used as a substitute for European governments' contributing their own financial resources. To understand the posture of the IMF in the euro crisis fully, we must understand the posture of the U.S. government.

The U.S. position was by no means the *only* influence behind the IMF's stance. Beyond the euro-area countries themselves, China, Japan, and a small number of other non-European countries also affected the course of the policies of the Fund. Brazil and India, for example, were publicly and privately critical of the Fund's policies in Europe, as were some executive directors from European countries that had not adopted the euro. The managing director and staff of the Fund exhibited a degree of autonomy on a number of decisions. But, among the membership, the United States was the single most important country influencing the course and strategy of the Fund and the most important non-European country mediating among the protagonists in the crisis.[1]

This chapter examines the U.S. posture on the role of the IMF within the context of Washington's broader strategy in addressing the euro crisis. It begins by discussing basic U.S. preferences and the channels of influence

---

[1] Whether the United States is becoming less influential within the IMF is a question we leave for treatment elsewhere. Randall W. Stone, *Controlling Institutions: International Organizations and the Global Economy* (Cambridge: Cambridge University Press, 2011); Kathryn C. Lavelle, *Legislating International Organization: The US Congress, the IMF, and the World Bank* (New York: Oxford University Press, 2011); and Daniel W. Drezner, *The System Worked: How the World Stopped Another Great Depression* (New York: Oxford University Press, 2014), from different perspectives, emphasize U.S. dominance. Jonathan Kirshner, *American Power after the Financial Crisis* (Ithaca, NY: Cornell University Press, 2014) emphasizes decline.

over the management of the crisis in Europe. The chapter then traces the evolution in U.S. strategy as the crisis worsened in Europe and officials in Washington were converted to the cause of deepening the euro area. Puzzling from the standpoint of bureaucratic interest, the Fund's advocacy of such deepening reflects the preferences of the United States and other non-European members.

PREFERENCES AND INSTRUMENTS

The fundamental interest of the United States was to resolve the crisis, prevent contagion to the rest of the world, and thereby sustain the U.S. economic recovery from the 2008–9 recession. U.S. officials did not have a sentimental attachment to the success of Europe's monetary union. Many had served in the Clinton administration at the advent of the euro—Lawrence H. Summers, Timothy F. Geithner, David Lipton, Michael Froman, and Lael Brainard, among others. They had been publicly supportive of the euro but reserved judgment, to put it somewhat mildly, on whether European governments would prove to be willing to introduce the economic flexibility required for the success of the euro over the long run.[2] American officials were never particularly worried about the challenge that the euro might pose to the international role of the dollar, but rather about Europe's potential weaknesses. Over the course of the euro crisis, they, like IMF officials, became strong advocates of deeper integration in the form of large rescue facilities, a broad role for the central bank, and banking union with a fiscal backstop.

Although the direct effects of the subprime mortgage meltdown on the U.S. economy had dissipated, aftershocks emanating from Europe threatened the economic recovery. The author Michael Lewis fittingly entitled his 2011 book on the euro crisis *Boomerang*. Indeed, two acute phases of the euro crisis—the negotiations over the first Greek program in spring 2010 and the row in early summer 2011 over what would become Greece's second program—were followed by a marked drop in U.S. job growth.[3] Domestic factors, including political disputes over the debt ceiling in summer 2011, undoubtedly contributed to these setbacks in growth. The euro crisis also had

[2] See, for example, C. Randall Henning and Pier Carlo Padoan, *Transatlantic Perspectives on the Euro* (Washington, D.C.: European Community Studies Association and Brookings, 2000), pp. 6–17.

[3] U.S. Council of Economic Advisors, *Economic Report of the President*, Table B-35, column 3, p. 361. The stall occurred during July, August, and September in 2010 and June, July, and August in 2011. For a discussion of the global effects, see Edwin M. Truman, "Asian and European Financial Crises Compared," Peterson Institute Working Paper 13–9, Washington, D.C., October 2013, pp. 45–6; IMF, *2012 Spillover Report*, Washington, D.C., April.

some positive countervailing effects, as capital retreated from Europe across the Atlantic. At that stage of the recovery, however, the U.S. economy needed demand from Europe more than it needed its capital. Alan Blinder thus concluded in autumn 2012 that the euro crisis appeared to be "the biggest threat to continued economic recovery" in the United States.[4]

U.S. policymakers were caught by surprise by the Greek crisis and frustrated by the disputes within the euro area. "I couldn't believe that Europe's governments would set themselves on fire and risk another worldwide inferno so soon after we put out the flames of the initial crisis," Timothy Geithner writes in his account of his tenure as Secretary of the Treasury. Geithner urged his counterparts in Europe to put aside fears of moral hazard, make financing available in preemptive quantities, and stimulate growth in the strong countries as the crisis-stricken were undergoing adjustment. During a G7 conference call on May 7, 2010, for example, he scorned the €50 billion that the Europeans offered for what would become the European Financial Stability Facility (EFSF) and European Financial Stabilisation Mechanism (EFSM) and pushed finance ministers to increase the size by an order of magnitude—which they later did.[5]

U.S. policymakers played the role of an "interested broker." Key players on all sides of the intra-euro-area debates appealed to the Obama administration when stymied in European forums. The administration entertained appeals from Prime Minister Papandreou in spring 2010, President Sarkozy in autumn 2011, and Prime Minister Monti in the first half of 2012, for example. Meanwhile, administration officials also worked closely with the creditor countries, Germany in particular. By most European accounts, President Obama was surprisingly knowledgeable about and attentive to the euro crisis. He and officials in the White House and Treasury simultaneously urged discipline and adjustment on the crisis countries and accommodation on the creditor governments. American officials had their own preferences with respect to how the euro-area problem was solved—balanced adjustment in Europe that did not foist unemployment or financial instability on the United States and the rest of the world. But, most of all, they sought to bring the Europeans together around credible plans to arrest the crisis and on this essential matter American preferences coincided with those of both European creditors and debtors.

In seeking to influence European policymakers, the U.S. President, the Secretary of the Treasury, and the Chairman of the Federal Reserve had a number of tools available. They made public declarations of confidence or

---

[4] Alan S. Blinder, *After the Music Stopped: The Financial Crisis, the Response and the Work Ahead* (New York: Penguin Press, 2013), pp. 379–81, 409–28.

[5] Timothy F. Geithner, *Stress Test: Reflections on Financial Crises* (New York: Crown Publishers, 2014), pp. 442 and 446.

concern, which affected markets, applied diplomatic pressure, and arbitrated disagreements among their European counterparts. The effectiveness of moral suasion was conditioned on U.S. policymakers' willingness to bring resources to the table, however. U.S. contributions took two forms. First, the Federal Reserve could offer foreign exchange swap agreements. Second, the U.S. could influence the use of the IMF for euro-area programs.

Federal Reserve Chairman Ben Bernanke and his colleagues in the Federal Open Market Committee had provided swap agreements to several foreign central banks during 2008–9. The ECB was the largest swap user by far during the seizing up of international capital markets at that time.[6] These operations had been effective in providing dollar liquidity to European banks. With respect to monetary policy, however, Bernanke disagreed with the ECB's approach and its support for fiscal austerity in Europe. Bernanke had led the Federal Reserve into uncharted waters with quantitative easing, but ECB President Trichet had been reluctant to follow and would even raise interest rates in 2011.[7] The Fed's monetary diplomacy addressed the policies for the euro area as a whole, though; U.S. activism over bailouts and rescue programs was the province of officials in the Obama administration.

U.S. officials worked through several avenues: transatlantic telephone conversations and video-conferencing, bilateral meetings, and meetings of the G7 finance ministers, G8 summits, and G20 finance ministers and sum-mits. By one count, Secretary Geithner held 168 meetings or phone calls with euro-area officials and 114 with IMF officials between January 2010 and June 2012. Of these, Secretary Geithner met or spoke with the President of the ECB (Jean-Claude Trichet, followed by Mario Draghi) fifty-eight times, German Finance Minister Wolfgang Schäuble thirty-six times, and the French Finance Minister (Christine Lagarde, followed by François Baroin) thirty-two times. These contacts were concentrated around the episodes of particularly intense European negotiations.[8] President Obama was similarly engaged in calls to and meetings with other heads of government, especially, but by no means

[6] Federal Reserve officials testified to Congress several times about the swap arrangements. See, for example, Daniel K. Tarullo, "International Response to European Debt Problems," testimony before the Subcommittee on International Monetary Policy and Trade and Subcom-mittee on Domestic Monetary Policy and Technology, Committee on Financial Services, U.S. House of Representatives, Washington, D.C., May 20, 2010; Steven B. Kamin, "The Economic Situation in Europe," testimony to the Committee on Oversight and Government Reform, U.S. House of Representatives, Washington, D.C., December 16, 2011.

[7] Ben S. Bernanke, *The Courage to Act: A Memoir of a Crisis and Its Aftermath* (New York: W. W. Norton, 2015), especially pp. 474–80, 505–9, 524–6.

[8] Jean Pisani-Ferry, *The Euro Crisis and Its Aftermath* (Oxford: Oxford University Press, 2014), p. 165. Those episodes were the initial Greek crisis in winter 2010, negotiations over the Irish program in autumn 2010, renegotiation of the Greek program in late spring and early summer 2011, the Greek referendum and Italian problem in autumn 2011, the Spanish banking crisis of spring 2012, and the banking union declaration at the EU summit in June 2012.

limited to, German Chancellor Merkel. His contacts also tended to coincide with European summit decisions.

The IMF was thus one of several channels through which U.S. policymakers could weigh in on European decision-making during the crisis. U.S. strategy for the role of the Fund evolved through two main periods: the introduction of the IMF into the solution for Europe and then establishing limits to its involvement and financial exposure.

INITIAL STRATEGY

Obama administration officials had, as mentioned, an abiding interest in a stable solution to the crisis to limit contagion across the Atlantic. As European deliberations over the first Greek package dragged on over the course winter and spring 2010, U.S. policymakers at the Treasury came to believe that Europe would need the IMF in order to formulate and implement the program and hold the Greek government to the conditions. American officials thus endorsed the inclusion of the IMF in the Greek program. Treasury Secretary Geithner, in particular, promoted the Fund's inclusion with his European counterparts, in parallel with Dominique Strauss-Kahn.[9]

At the same time, the U.S. government wanted euro-area policymakers to act decisively to stop the crisis. This entailed among other things commitments of financial resources that would, in the words of the Treasury secretary, "take tail risk off the table." Treasury was concerned about exposure to risk in the absence of a decisive plan on the part of the euro area and did not want the IMF to be providing all or even a majority share of funds for Greece. While they did not propose it, U.S. officials accepted the two-thirds/one-third formula announced by Strauss-Kahn and Salgado.

In spring 2009, the Treasury had secured a large increase in the New Arrangements to Borrow (NAB) to address the global financial crisis and a modest increase in IMF quota resources.[10] In 2010, the Treasury was engaged in a negotiation over a further increase in quotas, which would be agreed at the G20 summit in November and formally adopted by the Fund in December, but still subject to ratification by member countries. While they fought contagion from Europe, therefore, Treasury officials wished to avoid unnecessarily alienating members of Congress, which would be asked to approve the

---

[9] Interviews with U.S. officials and former officials, Washington, D.C., March 18, 2011, January 9 and September 6, 2013, and June 18, 2014.

[10] See, for example, C. Randall Henning, "U.S. Interests and the International Monetary Fund," *Policy Brief* No. 9–12 (Washington, D.C.: Peterson Institute for International Economics, June 2009).

quota increase and could be expected to question the administration about potential costs.[11]

Members' concern about IMF resources being used to "bailout" euro-area governments led to the passage of legislation in the 111th Congress as part of the Dodd-Frank Wall Street Reform and Consumer Protection Act, signed into law in July 2010.[12] Section 1501 of the law requires U.S. representatives at the IMF to oppose loans to high- and middle-income countries with large public debt levels (greater than 100 percent of GDP) if it is "not likely" that they will repay the IMF. The provision proved not to be a barrier to U.S. approval of an active role for the IMF in the crisis but indicated nonetheless that Congress was sensitive to the matter.[13]

Senior U.S. officials were alarmed at the Deauville agreement between Sarkozy and Merkel on private sector involvement. One official thought that pre-announcing creditor haircuts in this way was "a complete disaster" and Obama administration officials pressed the Europeans to backpedal immediately.[14] Secretary Geithner told his G7 counterparts, "You're going to accelerate the run..... You're undermining your own defenses, and it's going to cost you a lot more money in the long run."[15] Obama raised the matter directly with the German chancellor at a bilateral meeting. The result was a statement issued four weeks later on the margin of the Seoul G20 summit qualifying the Deauville terms.[16] The U.S. position closely matched the well-known position of ECB President Trichet on this matter, and both were strongly reinforced by the negative market reaction to the Deauville announcement.

Whether to fund a possibly unsustainable debt position or force a debt restructuring was perhaps *the* critical strategic question for the players in the euro crisis that affected the posture of the Fund and the role that it would play. The U.S. position on this matter was debated internally. President Obama asked David Lipton, then on the White House staff, to prepare a memo on the worst-case scenario for Greece in February 2010. Lipton traced through

[11] See, for example, Martin A. Weiss, "International Monetary Fund: Background and Issues for Congress," *CRS Report*, Washington, D.C., July 17, 2014. In the event, Congress delayed approval for five years.

[12] Public Law 111–203.

[13] In the 112th Congress, continuing concerns about use of IMF resources in the euro crisis likely contributed to the introduction of legislation in the House (H.R. 2313) and Senate (S.Amdt. 501; S. 1276) calling for rescinding the U.S. financial commitments to the IMF that had been approved by Congress in 2009. The Senate voted against the amendment on June 29, 2011. This language was also included in a House draft of the FY2012 State and Foreign Operations Appropriations bill, but the language was not included in the final FY2012 appropriations legislation. The author acknowledges Martin Weiss for the information in this paragraph.

[14] Alan Crawford and Tony Czuczka, *Angela Merkel: A Chancellorship Forged in Crisis* (West Sussex: John Wiley and Bloomberg Press, 2013), pp. 78–9. The official they quote anonymously was probably Secretary Geithner.

[15] Geithner, *Stress Test*, p. 449.　　[16] Crawford and Czuczka, *Angela Merkel*, p. 79.

scenarios for exits on the part of both Greece *and* Germany, among other outcomes, and their implications, which served as the basis for the president's conversations with other leaders. Some officials at the Treasury Department were known to be privately deeply skeptical of Greece's debt sustainability. But Secretary Geithner reportedly had little tolerance for even confidential speculation about extreme scenarios, which risked leaks and could infect the markets. Wanting to avoid a "PSI shock," he and ultimately the rest of the administration opposed debt restructuring and bail-ins, prioritizing financial stability above other considerations.[17]

Ultimately, the U.S. Treasury faced the same dilemma between debt realism and market instability that European governments faced. Given the weakness of the domestic recovery and the lingering fragility of financial markets, it opted to defer the recognition of losses on, for example, Greek government debt—to "kick the can down the road." Treasury was in fact *less* willing to acknowledge doubts about sustainability than some European counterparts. In adopting this position, its rebuke over the Deauville declaration, and its opposition to bailing-in the senior holders of Irish bank bonds,[18] the Department was consistent. (The Treasury had also opposed the 2001 proposal for a Sovereign Debt Restructuring Mechanism put forward by the IMF's Deputy Managing Director Anne Krueger.) The Treasury was not opposed to debt restructuring as a matter of principle: it had supported debt relief for Heavily Indebted Poor Countries (HIPC) in the 1990s and restructuring as a precondition for borrowing in cases of unsustainability in revisions to the IMF lending framework in 2002.[19] But debt restructuring required a credible backstop to prevent contagion and this, senior Treasury officials noted, was lacking in the euro area in 2010 and 2011.

As the crisis worsened, the U.S. Treasury subsequently acceded to the Irish and Portuguese programs, as it had to the Greek program. While they needed large programs, these countries could be accommodated on the basis of the (very rough) two-thirds/one-third contribution ratio within the resource envelope of the Fund.

REVISED STRATEGY

Spain and Italy were another matter, however, their economies and debt being an order of magnitude larger than those of Greece, Ireland, and Portugal.

---

[17] Fed Chairman Bernanke agreed with this position and the U.S. posture was aligned with Trichet's ECB. See Bernanke, *The Courage to Act*, p. 507.

[18] Joint Committee of Inquiry into the Banking Crisis, Houses of the Oireachtas, Witness Statement of Michael Noonan, Minister of Finance, Session 64, September 10, 2015; Donovan and Murphy, *The Fall of the Celtic Tiger*, p. 247.

[19] The Brady Plan of 1989 was another exception to this general posture.

Spain's potential borrowing needs, had it lost access to capital markets, threatened to consume a very large share of the uncommitted resources of the IMF under the two-thirds/one-third formula, while an Italian contingency exceeded them. Moreover, American officials had developed deep misgivings about the governance of the euro area and its ability to respond in a crisis-efficient manner.

European Firewalls

The U.S. Treasury, and U.S. government more broadly, therefore shifted strategy. Secretary Geithner, Undersecretary Brainard, Assistant Secretary Charles Collyns, and Deputy Assistant Secretary Mark Sobel conveyed a disciplined message: the governments of Europe had enough resources to deal with the problem and restoring market confidence was, essentially, a matter of their collective willingness to employ those resources to stabilize the monetary union.[20] Less publicly, senior Treasury officials argued that the euro crisis should be resolved by the governments' taking collective responsibility for debt of the crisis-stricken periphery, including bearing the fiscal cost of losses, while the balance sheet of the European Central Bank should be more fully mobilized.

In taking this position, Treasury officials were advocating the U.S. government strategy during the subprime crisis: having the fiscal authority take the risk, covering any losses from the rescues, while having the central bank provide ample liquidity.[21] The proposal of Daniel Gros and Thomas Mayer (2011) for the ECB to grant a banking license to the European Financial Stability Facility, where any losses on loans to crisis-stricken countries would fall on governments, while effectively mobilizing the ECB as a lender of last resort, was one of several ways in which this could be done, in the Treasury's view.

In this new strategy, a role for the IMF was not out of the question, but it would have to be primarily non-financial, or at least a financial role that was quite small relative to its roles in the previous programs for small countries. The institution specifically could *not* act as a lender of last resort in the

---

[20] Interviews with U.S. officials, Washington, D.C., March 18, 2011, and January 24, March 12 and 21, 2012.

[21] Geithner, *Stress Test*, pp. 473–4. The U.S. government employed this strategy in response to the subprime crisis. The Treasury assumed these risks by injecting capital into banks through the Troubled Asset Relief Program (TARP), while the Federal Reserve introduced innovative new facilities and greatly expanded liquidity operations. More narrowly, the TARP assumed the credit risk associated with the Fed's purchases under the Term Asset-Backed Securities Lending Facility (TALF). Mark Carney and Philipp Hildebrand, then governors of the central banks of Canada and Switzerland, respectively, advocated a TALF for Europe. See also, Bastasin, *Saving Europe*, p. 317.

large-country cases. The Treasury secretary posed a fundamental question: Why should the United States government and other non-Europeans take on risks in order to stabilize the euro area that the governments of the monetary union themselves were not willing to accept? The U.S. position on the use of the IMF thus hardened in mid-2011, which manifest on several occasions.

Wroclaw Ecofin

Secretary Geithner was invited by the Polish finance minister to the informal meeting of the Ecofin Council, which he was hosting in Wroclaw on September 16, 2011. This would be the first time that a U.S. Treasury secretary attended an Ecofin meeting. The secretary told the group that European finance ministers had to act more decisively to build a "firewall," one larger than the perceived scale of the crisis, in order to take the catastrophic risk of Eurozone breakup "off the table" and allow Spain and Italy to be funded at sustainable interest rates. Euro-area governments and the ECB had to work together. Geithner warned against excessive austerity and again advocated a growth agenda. "We would support more financing from the IMF," he said, "but not as a substitute for a more substantial European commitment."[22] In media appearances before the Ecofin meeting, Geithner emphasized, "most importantly," that the Europeans make clear that they stand behind their financial system, for which Europe had ample resources. Seeking a robust reversal of the Deauville doctrine, Geithner referred approvingly to Chancellor Merkel's earlier statements that she would not allow a Lehman-type bankruptcy.[23]

The reactions of the Europeans differed, depending on their position on the tradeoff between financing and adjustment needed in the crisis-stricken periphery. Those who had been clamoring for a more robust response were naturally pleased with the secretary's intervention. Those who had resisted ramping up the firewall and insisted on deeper structural reform resented it.[24] German Finance Minister Schäuble and ECB President Trichet said that there were also growth and debt problems outside the euro area.[25] The tone of the

---

[22] Geithner, *Stress Test*, pp. 474–5; U.S. Treasury, "Readout of Secretary Geithner's Participation in Today's ECOFIN Meeting," Washington, D.C., September 16, 2011.

[23] CNBC Transcript: Jim Cramer Interviews Treasury Secretary Timothy Geithner, September 14, 2011, <http://www.cnbc.com/id/44487020>.

[24] The Bulgarian finance minister found the Treasury delegation "generally obnoxious." "They fulfilled to a tee the American stereotype." Simeon Djankov, *Inside the Euro Crisis: An Eyewitness Account* (Washington, D.C.: Peterson Institute, 2014), p. 95.

[25] Euronews, "Geithner in Poland for Ecofin Crisis Summit," September 16, 2011, <http://www.youtube.com/watch?v=Jj0Is8TRvOs>; Euronews, "Geithner Snubbed at Ecofin Crisis Summit," <http://www.youtube.com/watch?v=u7RxSnOZMVo>.

after-meeting press accounts was dominated by the objections of the Austrian finance minister, who complained of Geithner's rejection of the Financial Transactions Tax (FTT).[26]

Cannes

A few weeks later, in early November, the G20 leaders gathered in the French seaside resort of Cannes. Several critical side meetings were held to grapple with the twin crises in Greece and Italy. After confronting Greek Prime Minister Papandreou over his ill-fated plan for a referendum, the European leaders pressed Berlusconi to accept the precautionary credit line from the IMF along with commitments to policy reforms. But it was President Obama who chaired the critical meeting at which Berlusconi's fate would be decided. He opened the meeting with a proposal, coordinated with the French ahead of time, for a new Special Drawing Rights (SDR) allocation from which the euro-area governments could dedicate €140 billion to the European firewall. Chancellor Merkel was cornered, as Jens Weidmann, the President of the Bundesbank, opposed the proposal. In what stunned observers recall as her most emotional outburst in all of the many meetings surrounding the crisis, a tearful Merkel said, "That is not fair...I am not going to commit [political] suicide." The proposal went nowhere.[27]

At this meeting, President Obama also seemed to let Berlusconi out of the trap that his European colleagues had set for him. Reinforcing the Italian Prime Minister's objections to a precautionary program with the Fund, "I think Silvio is right," he said.[28] Geithner had earlier advised the president, "We can't have his blood on our hands," referring to Berlusconi.[29] The two Americans wanted to bring *both* sides together and, moreover, the U.S. Treasury thought that the precautionary line from the IMF was too small to be credible. The end result was not a precautionary program but an Italian agreement on enhanced monitoring by the Fund, which was allowed to lapse after Mario Monti became prime minister. The episode underscores the limits

[26] "Austrian Minister Criticizes Geithner Intervention," Associated Press, September 16, 2011, at <http://www.utsandiego.com/news/2011/Sep/16/austrian-minister-criticizes-geithner-intervention>. Geithner later observed that the Europeans were continuing a pattern of castigating an American proposal before adopting a renamed version of it; *Stress Test*, pp. 475.

[27] Peter Spiegel, "How the Euro Was Saved," *Financial Times*, May 12, 2014, one of a four-part series on the crisis.

[28] Peter Spiegel, "How the Euro Was Saved," an account which is broadly corroborated by Bastasin, *Saving Europe*. Geithner, on the other hand, reports European officials having asked prior to the summit that the United States deny Italy IMF financing until Berlusconi resigned—which is at odds with European support for precautionary financing at Cannes. *Stress Test*, p. 476.

[29] Geithner, *Stress Test*, p. 476.

beyond which the U.S. government was not willing to let the IMF be used in the crisis—Italy was one program and perhaps a couple hundred billion dollars too far.

Lagarde's Firewall

IMF Managing Director Christine Lagarde was determined to equip the Fund with resources that would allow it to play a financial role in large-country contingencies within Europe. Doing so in the cases of Spain *and* Italy required more funds than the IMF had at its disposal, even after the tripling of resources that had been agreed in 2008. The quota increase that was agreed in 2010, even if implemented, would not add significantly to IMF resources overall. The Fund listed its "forward commitment capacity," although a conservative measure, at slightly less than $200 billion at the beginning of 2012.[30] So Lagarde and the senior management of the Fund decided to ask member countries to enter into bilateral agreements on loans and promissory notes, which, once agreed, would amount to $455.9 billion.[31] These, plus the unused portions of the quota contributions and NAB resources, would in principle allow the IMF to mobilize something on the order of $500–$600 billion if necessary for new contingencies, complementing resources provided through the EFSF and the ESM. Under these arrangements, the IMF would borrow from its members in order to lend to the crisis government. Crucially, the risk of nonpayment would thus be born by the IMF membership as a whole, which would redeem the loan from, say China and Japan, even if the European borrower defaulted. By this mechanism, therefore, the default risk was distributed across all of the members of the IMF in proportion to their quota contributions.

The U.S. government, represented at the Fund by Executive Director Meg Lundsager, declined to contribute through such a bilateral lending agreement (BLA). This refusal was expected, given that the U.S. Treasury had declined to open a similar agreement with the Fund during the previous round of BLAs in 2008–9 and given that congressional approval of the 2010 quota increase was pending. It would have been a considerable uphill battle to secure congressional approval of the loan agreement at a moment when domestic fiscal policy and the debt ceiling were deeply divisive political issues.

---

[30] IMF Financial Activities—Update January 5, 2012.

[31] "IMF Managing Director Christine Lagarde Welcomes Additional Pledges to Increase IMF Resources, Bringing Total Commitments to US$456 Billion," Press Release No. 12/231, June 19, 2012; "IMF to Double Lending Power as Pledges Top $430 Billion," *IMF Survey online*, April 20, 2012.

Secretary Geithner took pains to emphasize that the United States was nonetheless making a substantial contribution through the Fed–ECB bilateral swap, was in a unique position to provide dollar liquidity, and was the only country that was lending into the euro area bilaterally, through the swaps.[32] But, during the previous round of BLAs, even while it declined to participate, the United States supported the effort in general and encouraged other governments to conclude individual agreements. During late 2011 and early 2012, by contrast, the U.S. Treasury conditioned its support for the Lagarde firewall on the Europeans' reinforcing their financial facilities. Rather than encourage other countries to contribute, U.S. officials encouraged them to withhold BLAs until euro-area authorities developed a more robust architecture for the monetary union.[33]

Treasury officials pointed out that European governments were seeking to use the Fund as an "end around" domestic political resistance to augmenting the European firewall—resistance encountered in parliamentary ratification in countries such as Germany, Finland, and Slovakia. Use of the Lagarde firewall would shift risk onto the international community as a whole that the euro-area member states, particularly the creditors, should be bearing instead. The U.S. share of this exposure was proportional to its share in the quota structure of the IMF, 17.69 percent.

By April 2012, however, the Treasury had accepted the establishment of the Lagarde firewall. European decisions on their own firewall in the winter— signing the ESM treaty, allowing lending from the EFSF and ESM to overlap, and Long-term Refinancing Operations by the ECB—were undoubtedly important considerations in the shift.[34] In the end, thirty-seven countries representing three-fifths of the quotas of the Fund, including all of the BRICS and thirteen other non-EU countries, signed bilateral lending agreements with the IMF. The United States and non-European countries secured agreement that these arrangements would be drawn upon only after the regular quota-based resources and the New Arrangements to Borrow (NAB) were largely exhausted. In the event, the IMF did not draw upon the Lagarde firewall over the course of the euro crisis. But the Fund's reliance on borrowed funds through the NAB, as opposed to quota resources, weakens U.S. influence in the Fund in general and the 2012 firewall episode illustrates the limits of U.S. influence over key Fund decisions.[35]

[32] Brookings Institution, "The State of the Global Economy: A Conversation with Secretary of the Treasury Timothy Geithner," Washington, D.C., April 18, 2012, pp. 30–1. This instrument did not support European sovereigns directly, however.

[33] Interviews, Washington, D.C., September 6, 2013, and October 13, 2014.

[34] Brookings, "State of the Global Economy," minute 36.

[35] This made congressional delay in approving the 2010 quota increase and reform all the more self-defeating for the United States. See the testimony of Undersecretary Brainard in U.S. House of Representatives, Committee on Financial Services, Subcommittee on Monetary Policy

Harnessing the European Central Bank

American policymakers were also actively engaged with central bank officials in Europe. Chairman Bernanke and President Draghi had frequent direct contacts on, among other things, the design and implementation of unconventional monetary policy. Fed and ECB officials also discussed their swap facility. This facility had been central to addressing the liquidity needs of European banks during 2008–9, with the ECB having drawn $291 billion at the peak, roughly one-eighth of the Fed's balance sheet at the time.[36] The drawings during the European debt crisis were more modest, peaking at $90 billion in February 2012, but the ECB had at least small drawings outstanding during most of the crisis period.[37] The swap provided important reassurance on liquidity availability during the acute phases.

In earlier decades of international cooperation, central bank governors would talk to fellow governors and finance ministers would talk to fellow ministers—a norm against "cross-talk" generally prevailed. This norm, which had eroded slowly, was buried completely by Geithner and Trichet during the euro crisis—partly owing to the rapport they had established while Geithner was president of the Federal Reserve Bank of New York. And that critical relationship continued after Mario Draghi replaced Trichet at the beginning of November 2011.

Geithner urged his ECB counterpart to adopt the strategy of the Federal Reserve during the subprime crisis—placing the full balance sheet behind the banking system while securing indemnification from governments. Although this advice was economically sensible, even imperative, the ECB presided over a politically fragmented union that contrasted with the institutional environment of the Federal Reserve. The ECB thus delayed committing to further unconventional monetary policies until after governments committed fiscal resources to the firewall.[38]

Geithner had conversations with Draghi before the introduction of LTROs and as the ECB was working up the details of Outright Monetary Transactions (OMT). Speaking of the Bundesbank, which was resisting yet more aggressive

---

and Trade, *Evaluating U.S. Contributions to the International Monetary Fund*, hearing, 113th Cong., 1st Sess., April 24, 2013 (Washington, D.C.: GPO, 2013). See also, Edwin M. Truman, "The Congress Should Support IMF Governance Reform to Help Stabilize the World Economy," Peterson Institute Policy Brief no. 13–7, March 2013; C. Fred Bergsten and Edwin M. Truman, "The IMF Should Move Ahead without the United States," *Financial Times*, April 9, 2014.

[36] Eric Helleiner, *The Status Quo Crisis: Global Financial Governance after the 2008 Meltdown* (New York: Oxford University Press, 2014), pp. 24–53. See also, Eswar S. Prasad, *The Dollar Trap: How the U.S. Dollar Tightened Its Grip on Global Finance* (Princeton, NJ: Princeton University Press, 2013), pp. 201–7.

[37] Federal Reserve Bank of New York, "U.S. Dollar Liquidity Swap Operations," at <http://www.newyorkfed.org/markets/fxswap/fxswap_recent.cfm> [June 30, 2014].

[38] Henning, "ECB as a Strategic Actor."

unconventional measures, Geithner advised Draghi, "You're going to have to leave them behind," in July 2012.[39] The ECB president did exactly that when announcing OMT in September.[40] On this occasion, Chancellor Merkel sided with the ECB and against Weidmann and the Bundesbank—and her support was essential to the new program's positive effects on market confidence.

ADVOCACY OF EURO DEEPENING

As non-Europeans became increasingly frustrated with European decision-making over the course of the crisis, they sought to persuade euro-area authorities to deepen their mutual commitments well beyond the existing treaties. The U.S. government, other member states, and the IMF adopted this approach, while not in unison, broadly together.

U.S. Advocacy

Fundamentally, the U.S. government became increasingly aware that the success of any large-country program would ultimately hinge not simply on the financing package, adjustment program, and implementation, but also on the appropriateness of euro-area-wide policy. U.S. activism also extended to the framework of institutions and policies for the monetary union as a whole—which included streamlining decision-making in the Eurogroup, easing monetary policy by the ECB, advancing the banking union, and introducing greater symmetry of current account adjustment in Europe, a long-standing issue for U.S. policymakers going back to the 1960s and 1970s. The problem was that there was no reliable way to condition international financial assistance on policy and institutional reforms of the euro area as a whole. This underpinned the reluctance of the United States, as well as other non-European countries, to mobilize the IMF for the large countries.

We know that the U.S. government actively encouraged the development of the banking union in order to break the fiscal link between sovereigns and their private banks. This advocacy, and the direct involvement of President Obama, peaked at the Camp David G8 summit during May 18–19, 2012. The summit was especially important because the president hosted it and it preceded the G20 summit in Los Cabos, Mexico, which was followed in turn by the EU summit at the end of the month. With the spreads on Spanish and Italian bonds at new highs, and Greek politics uncertain, it appeared as if the wolf might indeed be at the door of Europe's monetary union. A German

---

[39] Geithner, *Stress Test*, pp. 467–77, 482.   [40] Geithner, *Stress Test*, pp. 476–85.

commitment to banking union—for which the ECB was also calling— appeared to be necessary to calm the crisis and the EU summit was scheduled to discuss it.

At Camp David, the president and other leaders pressed Chancellor Merkel on the issue and broader elements of the solution to the euro crisis. The treatment in the communiqué was limited to one paragraph, which affirmed their "interest in Greece remaining in the Eurozone while respecting its commitments," among other things.[41] But the discussion was broad-ranging, with Obama, Cameron, Monti, Hollande, Barroso, Van Rompuy, Medvedev, Noda, and Harper pressing for some form of debt mutualization, banking union, and reversal of austerity. While Obama and Merkel maintained a personal rapport,[42] tension on the substantive matters was high and the president took pains to reassure the chancellor during a one-on-one meeting after the summit.[43] He urged the chancellor to work with Monti, who had developed a plan for the ECB to purchase the bonds of fiscally prudent governments outright and who the White House viewed as its strongest ally in advancing euro-area reforms.[44] Weeks later, the chancellor did, in fact, agree to proceed with the development of the banking union in the European Council meeting and specifically to break the sovereign-bank link once and for all. Though other political forces and market pressure were also at work, the transatlantic and G8 discussions contributed to the momentum toward this result.

Only the chancellor herself would know exactly how influential U.S. activism had been in prompting the German commitment at the June 2012 Council meeting. President Obama's pressure at Camp David and phone calls over the summer and Geithner's conversations with Schäuble pushed in this direction. But, shortly after the ECB announced OMT, Schäuble led two of his fellow finance ministers in the first of a series of backtracks and slow-walks of the banking union agenda, declaring that "legacy assets" in the weak banks would not be mutualized on a European basis.[45]

---

[41] White House, Camp David Declaration, Camp David, Maryland, May 19, 2012, paragraph 5, at <https://www.whitehouse.gov/the-press-office/2012/05/19/camp-david-declaration>. Greece was at that moment between two national elections, the first of which had been inconclusive.

[42] The relationship between the two leaders in general, and the Los Cabos summit in particular, is described in Crawford and Czuczka, *Angela Merkel*, pp. 95–112.

[43] Reports of the Camp David discussions appear in Mark Landler and Nicholas Kulish, "In Euro Crisis, Obama Looks to Merkel," *New York Times*, June 2012; Tony Czuczka and Margaret Talev, "Obama Seeking Ally on Europe Finds Merkel a Tough Sell," *Bloomberg* News, June 8, 2012. The official press briefing at Camp David was given on May 19, 2012, and appears at <http://www.whitehouse.gov/the-press-office/2012/05/19/press-briefing-press-secretary-jay-carney-mike-froman-deputy-national-se>.

[44] Peter Spiegel, "How the Euro Was Saved: Part Three," *Financial Times*, May 16, 2014.

[45] Ministry of Finance, Government of Finland, "Joint Statement of the Ministers of Finance of Germany, the Netherlands and Finland," Helsinki, September 25, 2012.

The German posture on Grexit was the second critical decision in play over the course of summer 2012. Schäuble reportedly favored severing the "infected leg" in order to restore the rest of the euro area to health. Merkel, after allowing open discussion of this matter among politicians in her coalition through most of the summer, and after meeting with Prime Minister Samaras, decided against Grexit. (This episode is discussed in Chapter 10). The Obama administration had an intense interest: Grexit could have threatened to stall the U.S. recovery for the third time in as many years, at the moment of the 2012 presidential campaign and election! Geithner inveighed against Grexit with Schäuble during the German's vacation on the island of Sylt in July. But neither Peter Spiegel's account of these decisions, nor Geithner's,[46] indicate how important U.S. activism might have been in swinging the chancellor against Grexit.

What was the U.S. government position on the constitution of the troika? Although the Treasury and the White House encouraged and accepted the involvement of the Fund at the outset of the Greek program, as discussed, the involvement of the European Central Bank posed a particular dilemma for them. On the one hand, Geithner and Trichet, then Draghi, spoke frequently and, while they argued some substantive points, shared a number of fundamental interests in common—such as a priority to financial stability and getting the governments of the euro area to collectively accept the costs of bank and sovereign rescues. Together, they goaded the Eurogroup and European Council forward on the financial facilities, Eurobonds, and banking union. On the other hand, they differed on employing the balance sheet of the ECB for the euro crisis in the same way that the Fed had been employed in the subprime crisis. U.S. officials were concerned about excessive protection of the balance sheet on the part of the ECB and mused about placing Frankfurt on the "other side of the bargaining table."

The U.S. government was also interested in the European deliberations over the creation of the ESM and the discussion about its evolution into a "European Monetary Fund." U.S. Treasury officials did not jealously protect the prerogatives of the IMF relative to the regional arrangement, as they had when Japan proposed an Asian Monetary Fund in 1997. To the contrary, they were aggressive in pushing Europeans to endow the ESM with resources and the full range of financial instruments. They were worried by Draghi's suggestion in September 2012 that OMT should be activated in conjunction with an IMF program. Because its main requirement was primary market purchases by the ESM and strict conditionality negotiated collectively by governments, they argued, OMT should be open to access *without* the involvement of the IMF. U.S. officials were generally pleased that the possibility for IMF

---

[46] Spiegel, "How the Euro Was Saved," and, Geithner, *Stress Test*, pp. 440–85.

involvement was written into the formal European arrangements.[47] IMF involvement would be decided on a case-by-case basis and the U.S. would have substantial influence over each decision.

The U.S. thus underwent an important shift over the course of the crisis, one that has not been remarked upon in the scholarly literature to this point. U.S. preferences shifted from being supportive but skeptical of the feasibility of the euro area over the long run at the outset of the monetary union to being enthusiastically supportive of completing the euro area. This shift was driven in large measure by fears of transatlantic spillover from a euro meltdown, as well as concerns over long-term stagnation in the monetary union after the acute phase of the crisis.

IMF Advocacy

European officials often criticized the IMF for a single-country focus in designing programs, failing to take spillover to the rest of the euro area into consideration. While there is some institutional basis for this, it is also true that the IMF became a consistent advocate of completing the institutional architecture of EMU. The Fund was committed to the monetary union and—some contingency planning for exit notwithstanding—accepted the political commitments of its members, even Greece and Cyprus, to remain within the euro area.

Robust support for institutional deepening in the euro area represents a fundamental change from the IMF's predilections during the earlier decades of European monetary integration. During the creation and evolution of the European Monetary System (EMS) in the late 1970s and 1980s, for example, the IMF staff and Executive Board had been skeptical of the merits of the project. That skepticism was based intellectually on the theory of optimum currency areas and the belief that the criteria for optimality under that approach were not satisfied by the countries that were participating in the arrangement. Owing to the European sympathies of the managing directors, a strong plurality of the Executive Board, and the European Department of the staff, this skepticism was not allowed to interfere with the euro project. But it was prevalent; the IMF was certainly not a promoter of the monetary union.

Over the course of the euro crisis, by contrast, the IMF became a persistent advocate. This shift can be seen in a steady drumbeat of formal papers, unofficial papers by members of the staff, and statements by the managing director and other members of the senior management team. Fund officials advocated creative approaches to eurobonds, before that idea was effectively

---

[47] Interviews with U.S. officials and former officials, Washington, D.C., January 24, 2102, January 9 and September 6, 2013, and October 13, 2014.

vetoed by the German government.[48] They advocated faster and more thorough progress toward banking union.[49] The Fund staff, management, and Executive Board encouraged the creation of robust financial facilities in the form of the EFSF and ESM.[50] Behind the scenes, they pointed out the weaknesses in the EFSF (such as in its guarantee structure) in an effort to prod European governments to strengthen them. Basically, the IMF management and staff concluded that, if the monetary union in Europe was to be stabilized and prosper, further deepening in the form of banking union and a fiscal backstop would be necessary.[51]

This shift in posture on the part of the Fund was historic and reflected a strategic shift in the preferences of the key non-European members of the fund, the United States in particular. The European Union had created only half of the institutional architecture necessary to ensure the success of the euro and faced a choice as to whether to advance or retreat. Given the prospect for contagion from exits from the euro area, and given the fact that Europeans themselves would bear the costs of the project, along with garnering the benefits, forward progress was the clear preference of American policymakers. In historical perspective, the change in the American calculus on deepening the euro area was rapid. The IMF did *not* have a bureaucratic interest in completing the monetary union; to the contrary, success could eventually put the IMF out of business in Europe. But, the IMF advocated this position nonetheless, reflecting the balance of preferences among its membership.

CLOSING OBSERVATIONS

The United States confronted a dilemma in addressing the euro crisis. On the one hand, fundamentally, Washington wanted Europe to bear the fiscal costs of maintaining the monetary union, which argued against IMF involvement.

---

[48] Stijn Claessens, Ashoka Mody, and Shahin Vallée, "Paths to Eurobonds," IMF Working Paper 12/172, Washington, D.C., July 2012.

[49] See, for example, Rishi Goyal et al., "A Banking Union for the Euro Area," *IMF Staff Discussion Note* No. SDN/13/01 (Washington, D.C., February 2013).

[50] One example among many is Christine Lagarde, "Global Challenges in 2012," speech, Berlin, January 23, 2012, <https://www.imf.org/external/np/speeches/2012/012312.htm>.

[51] The headline messages from the IMF's annual Concluding Statements on Euro-Area surveillance missions offer a good overview of the progression of staff views on the integration agenda. These can be found on the IMF's website, <www.imf.org>. See also, "IMF Urges Eurozone to Make More Determined, Collective Response to Crisis," *IMF Survey online*, June 21, 2012; Luc Everaert, Aasim Husain, Charles Enoch, and Olga Stankova, "Conference Call on the IMF's 2011 Article VI Consultations," Washington, D.C., July 19, 2011. For an assessment of the IMF's surveillance, See Jean Pisani-Ferry, André Sapir, and Guntram B. Wolff, *An Evaluation of IMF Surveillance of the Euro Area*, Bruegel Blueprint 14, Brussels, Bruegel, 2011.

Given that the European architecture remained incomplete, however, American policymakers had a continuing interest in maintaining a "forward defense" strategy by which the IMF could complement European facilities to fight crises in Europe before they spilled across the Atlantic. Officials in the U.S. Treasury and the White House opted for using the IMF when faced with a serious prospect of contagion, but increasingly conditioned their support on euro-area-wide arrangements.

The staff and management of the Fund were not perfectly aligned with U.S. preferences. Differences arose over the bilateral lending agreements, bailing-in the private sector, especially in the cases of Ireland and Greece, and debt restructuring. From the U.S. perspective, use of the IMF required compromise with the European members and tolerating a certain degree of staff autonomy, "agency drift." But on most elements of program design and virtually every important aspect of euro-area architecture—ECB activism, banking union, avoidance of excessive austerity, internal rebalancing—the United States government, the managing director, and the staff team were well aligned.[52]

By virtue of its influence within the IMF, status in the finance G7, G8 summits and the G20, and bilateral relations with creditors and debtors, the United States had a vital hand in mediating differences among the European governments and the troika institutions when negotiating deadlocks arose. The resolution of the dispute over bailing-in senior bondholders in Irish banks in early 2011, the role of the IMF as discussed around the G20 summit in Cannes, private sector involvement in Greece in early 2012, and bargaining over banking union leading up to the June 2012 European Council meeting provide examples of the U.S. mediating role. U.S. policymakers did not always get their way and their intervention was usually not singularly decisive. Their mediation helped to keep the regime complex for crisis finance from fragmenting when other actors were at an impasse, however, and they would continue to play this critical role, with other key governments, in the years ahead.

---

[52] Undersecretary Brainard cited the posture of the IMF as helpful in her advocacy of the 2010 quota increase in congressional testimony. Lael Brainard, "United States–European Union Economic Relations: Crisis and Opportunity," testimony before the Senate Foreign Relations Committee, U.S. Treasury, Washington, D.C., May 23, 2013. Secretary Jack Lew pressed Congress to approve the quota increase on the grounds that this was essential for maintaining U.S. influence within the Fund. Anna Yukhananov, "Treasury's Lew Presses Congress on IMF Funding," *Reuters*, April 24, 2013.

9

New Facilities and Institutions

As the crisis evolved, euro-area governments constructed first two transitional financial facilities and then a permanent fund. The Euro summit and Eurogroup established these facilities in order to preempt crises, mount financial rescues when crises could not be avoided, and inoculate the rest of the monetary union from the fallout from a restructuring of Greek sovereign debt. This chapter reviews the evolution of the financial facilities of the euro area culminating in the establishment of the European Stability Mechanism. The emergence of the ESM, a new institutional player in crisis finance, prompted a reconsideration of the institutional arrangements under which crisis programs are designed. The chapter thus concludes by reviewing several studies of the troika and some prominent proposals for reform.

EVOLUTION OF EURO-AREA FACILITIES

Augmenting the capacity of the euro area to provide financial assistance was not by any means a streamlined process. The governments debated alternative arrangements and jerry-rigged temporary arrangements on the fly in late-night Eurogroup and Euro summit meetings whose outcomes were subject to ratification risk and delay. Nonetheless, by September 2012 the member states of the euro area had created the European Stability Mechanism, a new, permanent feature of the institutional landscape.

Transitional Facilities

The euro area's capacity to intervene in sovereign finance proceeded through five phases: the original period during which the presumption against assistance to sovereigns prevailed; the creation of the network of bilateral loans to Greece in spring 2010; the establishment of the European Financial Stability Facility (EFSF) and the European Financial Stabilisation Mechanism (EFSM) later in 2010; amendments to the EFSF in 2011 to strengthen the facility and expand its range of instruments; and the negotiation in 2011 and adoption in 2012 of the treaty on the ESM. The EFSF and EFSM served as a bridge between the first, ad hoc facility for Greece and the large permanent mechanism.[1]

The financial structures of these facilities differed importantly, with consequences for the exposure of the contributors and their capacity to underpin market confidence. The EFSF mobilized financing through bond issuance that was guaranteed by all of the member states but on a pro-rata basis. As a consequence, the credit rating of the EFSF itself was only as good as the members backing it. Many of those members suffered rating downgrades as the crisis evolved and had to "step out" from backing the fund when they became borrowers. To satisfy credit-rating agencies, the EFSF had to hold a cash buffer that limited its lending capacity and thus the size of the "firewall" that the euro area could advertise. The bridge thus had to be repaired and reinforced while euro-area governments were also negotiating successive versions of the treaty that would establish the ESM.[2]

The stakes for euro-area governments in negotiating these financial facilities were very high indeed, both financially and politically. Euro-area politics cleaved along multiple dimensions—between private financial institutions and taxpayers, creditors and debtors, and governments and the central banking community, led by the ECB. Euro-area governments secured a limited change to the Treaty on the Functioning of the European Union (TFEU), needed to avoid referenda in some member states, which provided for the establishment of the permanent mechanism.

An especially unsettled moment at the end of 2011 in the planning for the transition between the EFSF and ESM nicely illustrates the connection between the limits of European cooperation on the one hand and the involvement of the IMF on the other. With Italy and Spain hanging precariously on market expectations, which were volatile, the €500 billion lending capacity of the forthcoming ESM did not seem to be sufficient. Creditor governments were not willing to ask their parliaments and electorates to approve larger allocations, however.

---

[1] Although it was created as a temporary facility, the EFSM remains in place and could continue indefinitely. In fact, the EFSM regulation was amended in August 2015 to shield non-euro countries from losses associated with further operations. The EFSF halted new lending when the ESM was created, but will not be retired until Greece repays the thirty-year loans under its second program.

[2] A good analysis of the development and implementation of the EFSF and the handover to the ESM is provided by Ledina Gocaj and Sophie Meunier, "Time Will Tell: The EFSF, the ESM, and the Euro Crisis," *European Integration* 35 (no. 3): 239–53. For contemporary accounts, see Gavin Barrett, *The Treaty Change to Facilitate the European Stability Mechanism* (Dublin: Institute for International and European Affairs, 2011); Bastasin, *Saving Europe*; and European Parliament, Directorate-General for Internal Policies, "The ECB, the EFSF and the ESM—Roles, Relationships and Challenges," Monetary Dialogue, Brussels, December 2011.

European officials thus considered schemes to tap the IMF in order to bypass national parliaments. The first scheme, cooked up between the French finance ministry and the U.S. Treasury, would have supplemented the European firewall with a large new Special Drawing Rights (SDR) allocation. This was effectively vetoed by the German Bundesbank.[3] The second scheme was the set of bilateral lending agreements promoted by IMF Managing Director Lagarde (discussed in Chapter 8). The Lagarde firewall had the advantage that in a number of the members, including Germany, it was the central bank rather than the finance ministry that provided the resources.[4] Those agreements and any credit extended to the IMF through them were thus off the budget of the national governments and not subject to approval or oversight of the national legislature.

Permanent Mechanism

Final agreement on the ESM was reached at the European Council meeting in December 2011 and the treaty was formally signed in Brussels on February 2, 2012.[5] Euro-area finance ministers had negotiated and signed an earlier version of the treaty on July 11, 2011, but this version was not submitted to national parliaments for ratification. Financial conditions deteriorated during the days and weeks following the initial signing, which prompted European officials to go back to the drawing board. Over the autumn of 2011, they negotiated an expansion of the financial instruments, accelerated capital contributions, introduced the emergency decision procedure, and linked eligibility for ESM assistance to adoption of the Treaty on Stability, Coordination and Governance, which contained the Fiscal Compact and was being negotiated in parallel among a broader membership of the European Union.[6] The ESM treaty came into force in September 2012.

The ESM was fully constituted as a public international organization and was established permanently (see Table 9.1). Euro-area member states endowed it with €700 billion in capital,[7] of which €80 billion would be paid in tranches over the following years and the rest of which would be subject to calls if needed. On this capital base, the ESM could borrow on the bond markets. The lending capacity would be €500 billion, available through a

---

[3] Peter Spiegel, "How the Euro Was Saved," *Financial Times*, May 11, 2014.

[4] By statute, U.S. government credits to the IMF must flow through the U.S. Treasury, not the Federal Reserve, and are thus subject to approval by Congress.

[5] Council of the European Union, Treaty Establishing the European Stability Mechanism (T/ESM 2012/en 1), <http://www.consilium.europa.eu/en/workarea/downloadAsset.aspx?id=27068>.

[6] European Parliament, "Troika Report," p. 5.

[7] Later increased to €704.8 billion with the accession of Latvia and Lithuania to the monetary union.

Table 9.1. Evolution of Euro-Area Financial Facilities, 2010–2013

	Legal Structure	Duration	Capital Structure	Purposes	Guarantee Structure	Lending Capacity	Seniority
EFSM May 2010	EU facility under the TFEU.	As long as "exceptional occurrences" in financial markets persist.	Borrowing in capital markets, guaranteed by the EU.	Preserve financial stability of the EU; assistance to members in exceptional circumstances beyond their control.	Collectively through EU budget, no "step out."	€60 bn	Pari passu
EFSF I May 2010	Private company under Luxembourg law.	Temporary, until repaid.	Guarantee of EAMS of €440 bn (120% over-guarantee).	Temporary financial assistance. Intervene in primary debt market. No precautionary line. No secondary market purchases.	Members in a program "step out" of guarantee structure.	€255.5 bn	Pari passu
EFSF II October 2011	Private company under Luxembourg law.	Temporary, until repaid.	Guarantee by members of €780 bn (165% over-guarantee).	Loan disbursements. Precautionary facilities. Bank recapitalization. Purchase bonds in primary and secondary markets.	Members in a program "step out" of guarantee structure.	€440 bn	Pari passu
ESM September 2012	Intergovernmental institution under international law.	Permanent.	Subscribed capital of €700 bn.	Loan disbursements. Precautionary facilities. Bank recapitalization. Purchase bonds in primary and secondary markets.	Members do not "step out," even if in a program.	€500 bn	Preferred creditor (waived in Spain), but subordinate to IMF

Sources: European Commission, "Financial Assistance in EU Member States," at <http://ec.europa.eu/economy_finance/assistance_eu_ms/index_en.htm> and author's assessment.

broad set of instruments: loans, primary and secondary bond market purchases, and precautionary arrangements. Loans could be issued to a member
state to recapitalize their private banks, although such loans would not break
the link between the sovereign and the banks. (In 2014, governments endowed
the ESM with the capacity to recapitalize banks directly, although the terms of
access are quite restrictive.) The ESM was to be tapped "if indispensable to
safeguard the stability of the euro area as a whole and of its Member States"
and "under strict conditionality" (Article 3).

The governance of the ESM parallels the governance structure of the IMF. The
Board of Governors, constituted by the finance ministers of the Eurogroup,
governs the ESM. The Board of Directors, constituted by the finance deputies,
prepares key decisions for the governors and is chaired by the managing director,
who also manages the staff. Decisions within these bodies follow one of three
rules: mutual agreement, qualified majority (eighty percent), and simple majority (fifty percent). Mutual agreement requires unanimity among the members
participating in the vote, which does not include abstentions, and applies to
capital increases, changes in financial instruments, and, notably, provision of
assistance to members. Votes were allocated on the basis of capital subscriptions,
which followed in turn the capital key of the ECB. Under this formula, Germany
controls twenty-seven percent of total votes, France controls twenty percent,
Italy eighteen percent, and Spain almost twelve percent.[8]

Two particular features of the construction of this financial edifice are
especially germane to the choice of the institutional mix for the response to
crises: intergovernmentalism and the facility's relationship to the International
Monetary Fund. First, European governments made a decisive break from
the Community method in favor of intergovernmentalism in the course of
choosing the ESM. Second, governments wrestled with how the IMF should be
involved in the formal legal arrangements of the euro area and their answer
evolved over the course of multiple drafts of the ESM treaty. We examine each
in the following sections.

Intergovernmentalism

Euro-area member states organized mutual financial assistance mainly *outside*
the framework of the EU treaties as an agreement among themselves. The
Commission initially proposed that it be done instead through a mechanism
subject to the Community method.[9] Bringing such assistance within the

---

[8] See, for example, Alessandro Leipold, "Making the European Stability Mechanism Work,"
Lisbon Council Policy Brief, Brussels, February 2012; European Stability Mechanism, "Frequently
Asked Questions on the European Stability Mechanism," January 30, 2014.
[9] Gocaj and Meunier, "Time Will Tell."

Community method remains an aspiration of many within the monetary union. But, when the EFSF was created, this approach was rejected out of a desire for national control and skepticism of the role of the Commission. That basic institutional strategy carried over to the design of the ESM as well.[10]

Under intergovernmentalism, the decision rule is unanimity. Euro-area member states discussed at some length moving all decisions with the ESM to a qualified-majority voting (QMV) basis. Germany rejected this and Finland expressed objections. Adopting QMV for decisions on specific programs was also considered, but Finland was opposed. The result was a compromise under which the eighty-five percent threshold for QMV approval could apply in an emergency, but which was so impractical in its design that it is never likely to be invoked.[11] If some way were found to invoke the clause, the eighty-five percent threshold would still allow the three large countries (Germany, France, and Italy) individual vetoes over programs. The decision rule effectively remains unanimity.

These arrangements keep decisions on ESM rescues ultimately in the domain of national politics. The Dutch parliament must be informed of any member state's request for financial assistance with enough lead-time to form an opinion before the ESM Board of Governors takes any decision. The national parliaments of Germany and Austria reserve the authority to approve not only capital increases and payments—the prerogative of many parliaments—but also the mandate for negotiating financial assistance for a member country as well as the program and memorandum of understanding that is subsequently agreed. The German Bundestag must give prior approval of the plenary when a decision is taken in principle to provide support and its Budget Committee approves the program and memorandum of understanding, unless the plenary decides that it wants to exercise the authority of the Committee on this matter. The German government is obliged to inform the Bundestag comprehensively and the Budget Committee has the authority to demand further information from the finance minister. The government must even consult with the Budget Committee prior to individual disbursements by the ESM under country programs that have already been approved.[12] (Imagine the U.S. Congress approving individual

---

[10] In *Thomas Pringle* v. *Government of Ireland*, the Court of Justice of the European Union ruled that member states of the euro area were allowed under the EU treaties to enter into the ESM Treaty. See C-370/12 *Thomas Pringle* v. *Government of Ireland* [2012] ECLI:EU:C:2012:756.

[11] Interviews with officials involved in these negotiations, Luxembourg, January 31, 2012; and Berlin, February 1–3, 2012. See also, Päivi Leino-Sandberg and Janne Salminen, "Constitutional Change through Euro Crisis Law: Finland," European University Institute, Law Department Project, May 20 2014.

[12] Act on Financial Participation in the European Stability Mechanism, *Federal Law Gazette* No. 43, September 18, 2012, p. 1918. Sections 4 and 5 describe the approval authorities of the full parliament and the Budget Committee, respectively. Available at <https://www.umwelt-online.de/recht/allgemei/wirtschaft/banken/esmfing_ges.htm>.

loans through the Exchange Stabilization Fund or the IMF and being informed in advance of individual disbursements under those programs!)

The Federal Constitutional Court in Germany has mandated this involvement by the Bundestag. In its 2009 decision on the Lisbon treaty and challenges to the euro-crisis programs and the ESM, the Court in Karlsruhe affirmed that further powers could not be devolved to the European Union without the consent of the German parliament, placed (ambiguous) limits on the fiscal resources that could be transferred to European bodies and required Bundestag action on such matters. Some members of the Bundestag might well have wished to avoid political responsibility for the cost of the financial rescues for Ireland, Portugal, Spain, Cyprus, and, most of all, Greece. But the judges in Karlsruhe insisted that this was a responsibility that members could not delegate or relinquish.[13]

Through domestic ratification of European decisions on financial assistance by unanimity, Germany ensured maximum control over the use of common financial facilities, fiscal exposure through them, and equally importantly, the conditions to which borrowers were required to adhere. Other countries could also exercise a veto in principle, and the implementation of the EFSF and changes to it were indeed held up repeatedly by one holdout or another over the course of the crisis. Finland and Slovakia were particularly prominent in this role. However, Germany, as the largest country in the euro area, with a triple-A credit rating, and among the least forthcoming in providing assistance, held the indispensible, critical position in decisions on financial assistance. Its accession was not always sufficient, but it was absolutely necessary.

Pisani-Ferry laments the involvement of national parliaments in the provision of financial assistance in the euro crisis. He observes that this has come effectively at the expense of the involvement of the European Parliament, undermining embryonic federalism of the EU. Under these intergovernmental arrangements the common European interest takes a back seat to the national interests of the member states as articulated through national capitals. Financial assistance was micromanaged by the Eurogroup rather than by the Commission. "Only the imminence of a systemic crisis...can force governments to overcome the calculus of national interests and pursue the common good." "This is a remarkably ineffectual governance regime," he argues.[14]

[13] GFCC, Judgment of the Second Senate of 07 September 2011—2 BvR 987/10—paras. (1–142), <http://www.bverfg.de/e/rs20110907_2bvr098710en.html> (with respect to Greece and the EFSF); GFCC, Judgment of the Second Senate of 12 September 2012—2 BvR 1390/12—paras. (1–215), <http://www.bverfg.de/e/rs20120912_2bvr139012en.html> (with respect to the ESM) among other decisions.
[14] Jean Pisani-Ferry, *The Euro Crisis and Its Aftermath* (New York/Oxford: Oxford University Press, 2014), pp. 165–73. Quotations appear on p. 170.

We return to the question of designing a better institutional framework in the concluding chapter.

Role of the IMF

The role of the IMF as it was written into the legal provisions for the ESM are important to our discussion in two respects. First, as that role changed over the course of successive drafts of the ESM treaty, its evolution illustrates the changes in the collective sentiment on the part of the euro-area member states toward the Fund over the crisis. Second, as the IMF was written into the final treaty, it is now a permanent feature of the institutional landscape of the monetary union. Resistance to inclusion of the IMF notwithstanding, the involvement of the Fund is, while not strictly necessary, presumed in future financial rescues in the euro area. The unanimity decision rule is likely to sustain involvement of the fund—insofar as the European side is concerned—for some time into the future.

The Deauville declaration on private sector involvement coincided with the development of the political consensus within the euro group in autumn 2010 to launch the process of creating a permanent mechanism. At Deauville, recall, Merkel and Sarkozy declared that private investors would be asked to take haircuts on their claims against European sovereigns *whenever* a rescue was mounted with taxpayer money, irrespective of the long-run sustainability of the debt.[15] Chancellor Merkel had developed this conviction earlier in the global financial crisis[16] and it surfaced repeatedly once the crisis migrated to the euro area. The first drafts of the ESM followed this inclination, in keeping with Deauville, the subsequent qualifications of the Deauville statement notwithstanding.

The European Council decided to replace the EFSF and EFSM with a permanent mechanism at its meeting of October 28–9, 2010.[17] The Eurogroup

---

[15] Bastasin, *Saving Europe*, pp. 233–42, helpfully recounts the details of the Deauville meeting. He identifies the 2013 German elections as Merkel's motivation to impose losses on the private sector beginning that year. The intention to impose losses irrespective of long-run sustainability was clear from background briefings at the time, although it was not stated precisely in the Deauville text. See "Franco-German Declaration," Deauville, Monday October 18, 2010. Bastasin also reports Trichet's strenuous opposition and his clash with the leaders, Sarkozy in particular. Pisani-Ferry, *The Euro Crisis and Its Aftermath*, pp. 92–3, contains a good conceptual critique of Deauville.

[16] Crawford and Czuczka, *Angela Merkel*.

[17] The EFSF Framework Agreement mentioned the IMF twice, reflecting the precedent established in the first Greek program. The first mention appeared in recital 1: "It is envisaged that financial support to euro-area Member States shall be provided by EFSF in conjunction with the IMF..." The second appeared in section 2. (1) (a): "[T]he Commission (in liaison with the ECB and the IMF) shall be hereby authorised to negotiate the MoU with the relevant Beneficiary Member State..."

then developed the general features of the mechanism, which were endorsed by the European Council on December 16–17. These features were elaborated in a thirteen-page "term sheet" in the conclusions to the European Council meeting of March 24–5, 2011, and then incorporated, with modifications, into the first full draft of the ESM treaty. That draft served as the basis for the Council's approval in July, after which the draft was amended, eventually finalized at the end of the year and, as noted above, signed at the beginning of February 2012.

The March 2011 Term Sheet provided for a robust role for the IMF:[18]

> The ESM will cooperate very closely with the IMF in providing financial assistance [footnote 5]. In all circumstances, active participation of the IMF will be sought, both on the technical and the financial level. The debt sustainability analysis will be jointly conducted by the Commission and the IMF, in liaison with the ECB. The policy conditions attached to a joint ESM/IMF assistance will be negotiated jointly by the Commission and the IMF, in liaison with the ECB.

The footnote explained: "It is however understood that any IMF involvement will be consistent with its mandate under the Articles of Agreement and by applicable decision and policies of the IMF Board."

Financial assistance was to be accompanied by "[a]n adequate and proportionate form of private-sector involvement" determined on a "case-by-case basis" that would depend on the outcome of a debt sustainability analysis. That analysis was to be "in line with IMF practice," a phrase that, when used in earlier statements, had sent hedge fund and portfolio managers scurrying to Fund documents for precise meaning. A footnote clarified: "In line with the IMF, debt is considered sustainable when a borrower is expected to be able to continue servicing its debts without an unrealistically large correction to its income and expenditure. This judgement determines the availability and the appropriate scale of financing."[19]

If public debt were judged sustainable, then the member state concerned would engage private creditors in a Vienna Initiative-style agreement to maintain their exposures. If debt were not deemed sustainable, then the member state would seek a restructuring in one form or another, agreement on which would be a condition for ESM assistance. The three members of the troika would be involved in either case, with the IMF designing and monitoring the program memorandum of understanding with the Commission and in liaison with the ECB. The term sheet also provided for the introduction of

---

[18] European Council, Conclusions, March 24–5, 2011, p. 26.
[19] The reference was confusing, among other reasons, because that practice was best characterized by the post-2002 lending framework. But that framework had been revised by the introduction of the systemic exemption that permitted lending above access limits in spite of debt nonsustainability to prevent serious contagion. Yet, the ESM document was requiring private bail-in when systemic disruption was threatened.

collective action clauses (CACs) into all sovereign bond issues beginning in July 2013 and specified that the ESM would be senior among creditors to private investors and governments but still subordinate to the IMF.

But several unexpected things happened on the way to finalization of the treaty. European bond markets reacted badly to the notion that private holders would be bailed-in in future restructurings, even if that was delayed until after 2013, and that new investors could be subordinated to older ones by the introduction of CACs. Bond yields rose on all periphery debt, putting Spanish and Italian paper "in play" over the summer—to which the ECB was forced to respond because the EFSF was not equipped to act, prompting in turn an expansion of the EFSF instruments.

Most importantly, from the standpoint of designing the relationship between the ESM and IMF, the Fund clashed with the European partners over the design of the second Greek program in summer 2011 and the restructuring of Greek debt that would be completed at the beginning of 2012. It was thus abundantly clear in mid-2011 that the IMF, Commission, and euro-area member states disagreed fundamentally about how debt sustainability should be defined and assessed. It was also clear that the members of the troika often disagreed on program conditionality—the fiscal multiplier and glidepath for deficits, private bail-in in the banking sector, and the payoff horizon for structural reforms, to name a few elements. European-level policies such as monetary policy were an increasing focus of IMF attention as the basis for program success, but neither European institution nor the Eurogroup were offering formal commitments. Writing mandatory cooperation among the troika institutions into a permanent treaty seemed to be asking for trouble.

The amended version of the treaty thus demoted the IMF from the status of an essential partner to a presumed partner. Governments of the euro area, working on the basis of drafts prepared by the staff of the EFSF, softened the language on IMF inclusion. To some extent, this represented a retreat from ex ante signaling of debt restructuring in unsustainable cases, and the associated shift in emphasis to CACs to provide private-sector bail-in. But the downgrading of the requirement for Fund inclusion also reflected an emerging judgment that the use of the ESM should not be subject to an effective veto by the Fund in a permanent treaty—as well as an increasing realization that non-European governments might block the use of the Fund in Europe, or at least raise the price of its deployment unacceptably high.

The final text of the ESM treaty incorporated the general obligation to "cooperate very closely" with the IMF in recital 8. It added, "A euro area Member State requesting financial assistance from the ESM is expected to address, wherever possible, a similar request to the IMF." The Board of Governors has the authority, not the obligation, to invite representatives of the IMF along with those from other institutions to meetings (Article 5.5) and the ESM is generally entitled to cooperate with the IMF (Article 38). In all, the treaty mentions the IMF thirteen times.

In contrast to the posture taken at Deauville, private sector involvement was to be considered in "exceptional cases," rather than routinely, and in accordance with IMF practice, but not necessarily with the IMF itself (Recital 8). "Whenever appropriate and possible," the debt sustainability analysis would be "conducted together with the IMF" (Article 13.1.b). Negotiations over the memorandum with members requesting assistance would be conducted by the Commission in liaison with the ECB and, "wherever possible, together with the IMF." The same qualification applied to monitoring compliance with conditionality during the program. Although the IMF has its own provisions for post-program monitoring, the treaty provided for post-program surveillance to be carried out by the Commission and Council without reference to the Fund (Recital 17).

The "whenever possible" threshold is vague, and it is not clear whether that hinges on the IMF's willingness to participate alone or whether an inability to reach substantive agreement on program conditionality or debt sustainability could also place the possibility out of reach. The presumption of IMF involvement does not appear to be justiciable in practical terms. Only member states have standing to complain to the Court of Justice of the European Union under the ESM treaty—not private groups or individuals—and no government would be likely to bring a case on IMF exclusion from a program given that any such program would have been approved unanimously. So, the legal text, while expressing a presumption of IMF involvement, essentially leaves the question to a political decision of members in the Board of Governors (the same finance ministers as comprise the Eurogroup). The IMF could be excluded if there were a political consensus to "go it alone" or if the IMF set too high a "price" for participation. But the unanimity decision rule on programs nonetheless means that it takes only one country to call in the IMF. That country has often been Germany and, given the likely dispersion of preferences over programs in the future, Germany or another key creditor is likely to continue to play this role.

New Kid on the Block

The ESM thus became the new institutional player in the regime complex for crisis management and resolution in the euro area. It took over the financing for the Spanish financial sector program and issued the loan on behalf of the union to Cyprus in spring 2013. Its managing director, Klaus Regling, and the members of his staff were involved in designing the programs, their comparative advantage being the financial provisions—just as they advised on the development of programs as administrators of the EFSF. The ESM thus effectively became part of the "troika," broadly defined.

With the introduction of the new institution, the rest of the players jockeyed for position within the European architecture. The ECB welcomed a facility that could relieve it from pressure to provide liquidity to the sovereign through the back door of its banks when the sovereign had deeper problems. Understanding the German motivation in creating the ESM outside the treaty framework, the Commission was alert to efforts to build administrative and analytical capacity in the ESM as a substitute for building its own capacity. The European Parliament, for its part, objected to the decision to create the ESM outside the framework of the Treaty on the Functioning of the European Union and sought to bring the facility back within the Community method over the long term.

The ESM is the first formal, treaty-based institution uniquely for the monetary union as opposed to a broader group of EU members. (The ECB, while it presides over the monetary union, is a creature of the European Union.) Members thus considered whether it might serve as the basis for more complete development of the institutions unique to the euro area. This was a path not traveled in the case of banking union, as the SSM and SRM were open to membership from non-euro countries.[20] But developing a fuller set of institutions and obligations for the monetary union—a new "Community within the Community," so to speak—was now on the agenda.

Regling—who began his career at the IMF, moved to the German finance ministry and later became Director General for Economic and Financial Affairs at the Commission—served as founding chief executive officer of the EFSF and then continued to lead the ESM as managing director. He was principally responsible for building the staffs of both institutions. As a transitional institution, the EFSF's staff was kept relatively small, about twenty-five people in spring 2012. But it was increased significantly in anticipation of, and during the changeover to, the ESM, with sixty staff in January 2013, 120 by January 2013, and 165 over the course of 2015.[21] The EFSF staff, which generally held medium-term contracts, was transferred fairly seamlessly to the ESM in 2013. A Department of Economics and Policy

---

[20] Nicolas Véron, "European Banking Union," statement to the conference on "Banking Union and the Financing of the Portuguese Economy," Lisbon, February 26, 2014; Alessandro Leipold, "Bankng Union," Lisbon Council, December 17, 2013; European Commission, "A Comprehensive EU Response to the Financial Crisis: Substantial Progress Towards a Strong Financial Framework for Europe and a Banking Union for the Eurozone," memo 14/244, March 28, 2014; Christopher Gandrud and Mark Hallerberg, "Who Decides? Resolving Failed Banks in a European Framework," *Bruegel Policy Contribution*, 2013/15, Brussels, November 2013.

[21] ESM, *Annual Report 2012*, pp. 49–51; Matthias Sobolewski, "New Euro Bailout Fund May Not Have Sufficient Staff," *Reuters*, May 23, 2012; EFSF, "European Financial Stability Facility" (FAQs), <http://www.efsf.europa.eu/attachments/2016_02_01_EFSF_FAQ.pdf>.

Strategy was created, headed by Rolf Strauch, but was modest in size at the outset of the ESM.[22]

Whether the ESM would also take on a substantial economic analytical and forecasting capacity, in addition to debt management and financial administration, was an important political and institutional question. Such a capacity could allow the ESM to work relatively autonomously as an intergovernmental institution and lay the basis for what someday might become a full-fledged "European Monetary Fund." The development of such a capacity raises the possibility of overlap with the bureaucratic functions of the European Commission and ECB and larger questions about the institutional basis—intergovernmental or Community method—on which crisis financing in the euro area should be constructed. We now turn to the matter of this institutional division of labor and the future architecture of the euro area.

REVIEWS OF THE TROIKA AND PROPOSALS FOR REFORM

The troika is perhaps the most unloved institutional arrangement in international finance. Borrowing states were certainly unhappy with it; non-Europeans were unhappy with the involvement of the Fund; and the institutions themselves were unhappy with their roles in its division of labor. Once Europe had constructed its firewall in the form of the ESM, therefore, the discourse on crisis governance was fertile ground for reconsideration of the institutional arrangements.

There are several proposals for reforming the troika, altering the role of the IMF, and reconstituting the European arrangements for financial crises. We focus here on reports done by the Brussels-based research institute Bruegel, Alessandro Leipold, European Parliament, and "Five Presidents."

The Bruegel team conducted a preliminary assessment of the Greek, Irish, and Portuguese arrangements around the middle of these programs, publishing the results in May 2013. Its report examined both the economics (financing and adjustment) of these programs and the organization of the troika, detailing the dilemmas faced by the three institutions.[23]

Enumerating the conflicts of interest that plagued the ECB in its participation in the troika, the Bruegel team recommended that the central bank be made a "(mostly) silent partner." That phrase suggested that the ECB should participate in country missions and speak out on matters within the purview

---

[22] ESM, *Annual Report 2012*.
[23] Jean Pisani-Ferry, André Sapir, and Guntram B. Wolff, *EU–IMF Assistance to Euro-Area Countries:An Early Assessment*, Bruegel Blueprint 19, Brussels, May 2013.

of its function as a central bank, including Emergency Liquidity Assistance and Outright Monetary Transactions, but should not participate in program negotiations that extend to fiscal, labor market, and other structural matters.[24] This conclusion coincided with the evolving position of members of the ECB's Executive Board, who were deeply concerned about the ramifications for institutional independence of salient involvement in the troika.[25]

The Commission was caught between its role as an EU institution and guardian of the treaties, on the one hand, and an agent for the Eurogroup in negotiating programs on behalf of the other euro-area member states, on the other hand. The Bruegel report expressed a preference for establishing a European Monetary Fund (EMF) as an EU institution via a change in the treaties. Under that scenario, the resources of the ESM would be folded into the EMF, which would become one pillar of a European Treasury and would operate similarly to the IMF. All of the members of the EU would not automatically be members of the EMF, but the EMF could include non-euro as well as euro states under the proposal.[26] Such a scenario would transcend the dilemma facing the Commission by bringing the function of crisis finance closer to the Community method. The European Parliament, while not approving individual programs, could oversee the EMF and evaluate programs retrospectively. But of course the political barriers to such a treaty change are formidable.

The EMF scenario could possibly also obviate the need for the IMF's involvement. But the Bruegel report advised that the IMF continue to be involved in euro-area programs as long as the governance of the monetary union was incomplete. Here the IMF should function as a "catalytic lender," by which the Bruegel team meant that it would contribute the minimum financing needed to influence conditionality—the report cited the IMF's ten percent contribution to the Cypriot program as about right—but retain the ability to withdraw from the program if disagreement with the European authorities became severe.[27] The Bruegel report informed subsequent thinking in Europe on the troika, particularly at the European Parliament.[28]

Leipold offered a plan to redress the ambiguities of program conditionality, errors in debt sustainability analysis, and operational inefficiency of the troika.[29] He endorsed the idea of transforming the ESM into a Community

---

[24] Pisani-Ferry, Sapir, and Wolff, *EU–IMF Assistance*, pp. 123–4.

[25] Interviews, Frankfurt, December 12, 2012, and Berlin, June 12 and 13, 2013.

[26] Pisani-Ferry, Sapir, and Wolff, *EU–IMF Assistance*, pp. 121–3.

[27] Pisani-Ferry, Sapir, and Wolff, *EU–IMF Assistance*, pp. 120–1.

[28] On program design, see also André Sapir, Guntram B. Wolff, Carlos de Sousa, and Alessio Terzi, "The Troika and Financial Assistance in the Euro Area: Successes and Failures," study at the request of the Economic and Monetary Affairs Committee, European Parliament, Brussels, February 2014.

[29] Alessandro Leipold, "Lessons from Three Years of Euro-Area Crisis Fighting: Getting It Right Next Time," *Lisbon Council Special Briefing* Issue 14/2013, Brussels 2013.

institution and proposed that it be managed by an independent technical body meeting frequently as needed, rather than being managed effectively by the Eurogroup ministers and deputies and thus subject to political interference. In contrast to the Bruegel and Parliament reports, Leipold saw the continued involvement of the IMF as "vital" and advocated clarifying the working relationship among the troika institutions in a public concordat. That agreement would provide for each institution taking the lead on various elements of program design and negotiation, with the IMF specifically responsible for macroeconomic forecasts and debt sustainability analysis. Leipold agreed with Bruegel's advocacy of the ECB becoming a silent partner and urged that national governments refrain from political interference in troika negotiations, and that European governments pledge to protect staff independence of the ESM in particular.[30]

The Committee on Economic and Monetary Affairs of the European Parliament (EP) conducted an extensive investigation of the troika during 2013, publishing its final report in February 2014.[31] Its investigation received questionnaires completed by the Commission, ECB, and the governments of program countries and the Committee traveled to the program capitals to hold public hearings and meet confidentially with national officials. The hard-hitting report criticized the austerity of the programs and scrutinized the roles of the European institutions and the Fund. It found "no appropriate legal basis" under the treaties for the troika, pinned ultimate responsibility for program conditionality on the Eurogroup, questioned the "dual role" of the Commission as an agent of member states and an EU institution (and thus consistency with obligations under the treaties to pursue social and economic goals broader than financial stabilization at any cost), highlighted a similar conflict of interest on the part of the ECB, and inveighed against the absence of democratic accountability at the level of the EU for the operations of the troika. It also "deplored" the way EU institutions were being used as scapegoats for painful adjustment and predicted this would inflame Euroskepticism notwithstanding the fact, it argued, that responsibility actually rested with national governments.[32]

The EP report concluded with a robust affirmation of the Community method. It recommended that the ECB become a "silent partner" (echoing the Bruegel recommendation) to the Commission, which alone would design and negotiate the program, affirmed by the Council. The ESM should be integrated into the legal framework of the European Union over the longer

[30] Compare, as well, to the Fund's own brief assessment of the troika in, IMF, "Greece: Ex Post Evaluation," p. 31.

[31] European Parliament, "Report on the Enquiry on the Role and Operations of the Troika," Othmar Karas and Liem Hoang Ngoc, rapporteurs (2013/2277(INI)), Brussels, February 28, 2014. Hereafter referred to as the "Troika Report" or "EP Report."

[32] European Parliament, "Troika Report," pp. 16–18.

term, which would involve a treaty change. Its financial resources and the human resources of the Commission would eventually be combined into a European Monetary Fund. While the IMF would not be ejected outright, its involvement should be "optional" in the future and could leave a program in cases of disagreement with the Commission and Council. In contrast to the ESM treaty, which established the expectation of IMF involvement, the EP report accepts the Fund's participation (apparently only) if its involvement proves to be "strictly necessary."[33]

The EP report was a smorgasbord of proposals for institutional reform that have informed deliberations since its publication. Jean-Claude Juncker placed troika reform on his agenda for the Commission when he became its President in July 2014.[34] His speech reveals the perceived connection between institutional reform and his political agenda:

> In the future, we should be able to replace the "troika" with a more democratically legitimate and more accountable structure, based around European institutions with enhanced parliamentary control both at European and at national level. I also propose that, in the future, any support and reform programme goes not only through a fiscal sustainability assessment; but through a social impact assessment as well. The social effects of structural reforms need to be discussed in public. I am a strong believer in the social market economy. It is not compatible with the social market economy that during a crisis, ship-owners and speculators become even richer, while pensioners can no longer support themselves.... We must review the Troika and make it more democratic, more parliamentary and more political.

Juncker then set about preparing a report with the other leaders of the European institutions. As input to the process, a team writing for the Jacques Delors Institute also proposed, among other things, that the ESM be converted into a European Monetary Fund. Their proposal would streamline the voting system of the ESM by eliminating unanimity and introduce precautionary financing and graduated policy conditionality, whose intrusiveness would increase with the amount of the loan. Increased risk-sharing by establishing joint and several liability in the EMF would be desirable, the team argued.[35]

Far-reaching changes such as these, however, would require broad-based political consensus for treaty change that seemed unlikely in the mid-2010s. This seemed particularly so after the May 2014 elections to the European

---

[33] European Parliament, "Troika Report," pp. 21–6.

[34] Jean-Claude Juncker, "A New Start for Europe: My Agenda for Jobs, Growth, Fairness and Democratic Change: Political Guidelines for the Next European Commission," Strasbourg, July 15, 2014. The quotation below comes from pages 8 and 18.

[35] Yves Bertoncini, Henrik Enderlein, Sofia Fernandes, Jörg Haas, and Eulalia Rubio, "Improving EMU: Our Recommendations for the Debate on the Five Presidents Report," *Jacques Delors Institute Policy Paper* 137, Berlin, June 15, 2015.

Parliament, which brought a swath of Euroskeptic members into the chamber, and the June 2016 referendum in Britain to leave the European Union. Reversing the choice of intergovernmentalism on the part of the key creditor states was perhaps the greatest barrier to adopting the proposal to create an EMF under the EU legal framework. We return to the normative agenda for institutional reform and some of the political obstacles in the concluding chapter.

10

Greece 2012 and Cyprus 2013

Although it is not large in economic size relative to the euro area, Greece posed the greatest challenge among the program countries. Greece's economic situation was more severe than those of the other stricken countries. Its crisis confronted European governments and their institutions with the questions of how to write down financial claims on Athens and whether Greece should remain in the monetary union. These questions were existential matters for the euro area and exposed sharp differences among the institutions, differences that became more pronounced from one Greek program to the next.

This chapter presents the program for Greece that was agreed in 2012 and that for Cyprus, which was finalized in 2013. The two are presented here together, linked as they were by the restructuring of privately held debt—commonly referred to as "private-sector involvement" (PSI) or private "bail-in." Cyprus had the smallest of the seven programs that are considered in this study but is nonetheless instructive with respect to the roles of the institutions in extreme scenarios. These two cases show that key European creditors adhered faithfully to the IMF as part of the institutional mix and mediated among the institutions when they became deadlocked. These cases also demonstrate the limits and conditions that the IMF placed on its involvement in programs for euro-area countries.

GREECE 2012

Bargaining among the IMF, European institutions, and member states over the *second* program for Greece and its aftermath can be viewed in four phases: the summer 2011 confrontation over the bond exchange and program design; the summer 2012 decision to keep Greece in the euro area and rebase the program; the German elections in September 2013 and debate over restructuring the debt owed to European partners (official-sector involvement, or OSI); and the Fund's broader rethink of debt restructuring.

As the backdrop to considering these phases, we review Greek politics briefly here at the outset. Those politics were fraught, to say the least: successive Greek governments engaged in a continuous process of establishing and re-establishing the parliamentary base of support for the measures to address the crisis and satisfy the troika. Athens cycled through three governments between late 2009 and the middle of 2012. Prime Minister Papandreou led his PASOK government for two years after the onset of the crisis. When the discipline needed to implement the first program eroded, he yielded in November 2011 to Lucas Papademos, under whose technocratic leadership the second program was negotiated and agreed. Greece's adherence to the new program and its future in the euro area was debated nationally during the run-up to elections in May 2012, the results of which were inconclusive.[1] A second election in June established New Democracy as the dominant party and thus the core of a coalition with the remnants of PASOK and the small Democratic Left party. This coalition, led by Antonis Samaras, secured agreement with the European partners that his country would remain in the euro and implemented the reforms in the program—until the fragile consensus behind it unraveled again.

Second Program and Debt Restructuring, 2011–2012

By early 2011 it was apparent that the first program had gone so far off track that it would have to be substantially renegotiated.[2] But the stakes were now even higher and the position of the parties had hardened. Having warned of the unsustainability of Greek debt at the time of the first program in May 2010, a number of the non-European members of the Fund insisted that the institution take a harder line. They did so not in opposition to the Greek government necessarily—because more fiscal adjustment was already being exacted from it than from any other program country—but to the European partners on the questions of what would be realistic in terms of adjustment on the part of Greece, the budget deficits that the country would incur through return to market access, and the financing that would be required to fill the gap.

With a far deeper recession than anticipated, notwithstanding slippage on meeting the fiscal targets, Greece would need substantially more financial assistance than provided under the €110 billion program. Given their criticism

---

[1] This list does not include the government of Panagiotis Pikrammenos, which served as a caretaker administration between the two elections of May and June 2012.

[2] For a critique of the troika programs, see Michael Mitsopoulos and Theodore Pelagidis, "Greece: Tax Anything that Moves!," in *Europe's Crisis, Europe's Future*, eds Kemal Dervis and Jacques Mistral (Washington, D.C.: Brookings Institution, 2014), pp. 21–44; Theordore Pelagidis and Michael Mitsopoulos, *Greece: From Exit to Recovery?* (Washington, D.C.: Brookings Institution, 2014).

of the first program witnessed in the May 9, 2010 meeting of the Executive
Board, however, the non-European members were adamant that the additional
resources would *not* come from the IMF. But the Fund staff also insisted that
the program be fully financed to the point in the future where Greece would
reasonably be expected to borrow again from the capital markets. Under its
rules, the Fund should not agree to a program that was not fully funded to
market access and should not disburse under an existing program unless the
dynamically recalculated twelve-month financing gap was filled. Insistence on
respecting this technical rule triggered a showdown with European governments in summer 2011 and, in the face of their resistance to put up more funds
for Greece, the restructuring of the government bonds held by private banks
and investors.

This negotiation occurred during an extraordinarily sensitive moment for
the leadership of the IMF. In spring 2011, Strauss-Kahn was rumored to be
preparing to tell European leaders that debt restructuring would be necessary
for Greece. On his way to meetings in Europe, with Chancellor Merkel in
particular, he was arrested at Kennedy International Airport on charges of
sexual assault. Although the charges were later dropped, Strauss-Kahn resigned
his post at the Fund during the sensational controversy that erupted during his
detention. John Lipsky thus led the IMF as acting managing director during the
institution's confrontation with the governments of the euro area over Greece
in May, June, and July 2011.

Lipsky attended the Eurogroup meeting on June 20, which on this occasion
was held in Luxembourg. He and his Fund colleagues confronted a fragmented
and discordant set of finance ministers. He told the Europeans that they would
have to fill the financing gap before the Executive Board would agree to
disburse the next tranche[4]—which was necessary to allow Greece to remain
current on bond payments. The prospect of default was, in effect, necessary to
induce the members of the Eurogroup to come together on the plan. But the
Fund was agnostic as to whether the Europeans filled the gap through additional financing from governments or private-sector involvement.[5]

The German government advocated the restructuring of privately held debt
as part of the second program.[6] The U.S. Treasury at this moment thought
that PSI was ill-advised, given that the European firewall was not yet robust.
Thus, the IMF position was closer to the German government view, while the

---

[3] Prime Minister Papandreou, when hearing of the resignation, said, "Greece has lost a friend
at the IMF." Kerin Hope, "Strauss-Kahn's Arrest Costs Greece an Ally," *Financial Times*, May 16,
2011.

[4] "IMF: Need Eurozone Greek Financing for Next Tranche," *Reuters*, June 21, 2011.

[5] Interviews, Washington, D.C., October 27, 2011, and May 12 and 16, 2012.

[6] Noah Barkin and Harry Papachristou, "Germany Sticks to Demand for Greek Bond Swap,"
Reuters, June 10, 2011.

ECB position was closer to the position of the governments of the United States and those in the euro area that were most exposed to contagion.

On July 21, following a European Council and a Eurogroup meeting in early July, a Euro-area summit made the critical decision. Their statement began, "We affirm our commitment to the euro and to do whatever is needed to ensure the financial stability of the euro area as a whole and its Member States." They agreed to support a new program, to extend maturities to fifteen to thirty years with a ten-year grace period, and reduce the interest rate close to the EFSF's cost of funds. Following up on the European Council's endorsement of PSI, the euro-area leaders quantified the private sector's contribution at €50 billion.[7]

The Eurogroup engaged Charles Dallara and his colleagues at the Institute for International Finance (IIF) to organize private bondholders in negotiating the restructuring with Greece. Before private creditors agreed to their contribution to the package, the Fund disbursed the fourth tranche in July and the fifth tranche in December, along with the EFSF disbursements. It did so on the understanding that if PSI came up short, then European governments would augment their contribution.[8]

The first attempt at PSI proved too modest, as conditions deteriorated in the fall, and the Eurogroup sent the IIF back to negotiate deeper "haircuts" with the banks and other investors. Eventually, a 53.5 percent write-off that amounted to a reduction in terms of net present value of between seventy and seventy-five percent was finally agreed in February 2012. A debt exchange was executed in March and April 2012 that applied this haircut to €199 billion of private holdings.[9] This amount was slightly less than sixty percent of Greek government debt, most of the remainder now being owed to official creditors and the ECB.[10]

In tandem, the first program was replaced by a new, second program, final approval of which was announced in March 2012. The new program was expected to be €130 billion,[11] with all of the new money coming from the European side through the EFSF. The IMF portion was shifted to the Extended

---

[7] "Statement by the Heads of State or Government of the Euro Area and EU Institutions," Brussels, July 21, 2011.

[8] Interviews, October 27, 2011, and April 12, 2012; IMF, "Greece: Fourth Review under the Standy-By Arrangement," *Country Report* No. 11/175, July 2011, pp. 26–7.

[9] Jeromin Zettelmeyer, Chiristoph Trebesch, and G. Mitu Gulati, "The Greek Debt Exchange: An Autopsy," *Economic Policy* 28 (75) (July 2013): 513–63; Arturo Porzecanski, "Behind the Greek Default and Restructuring of 2012," in *Sovereign Debt and Debt Restructuring: Legal, Financial and Regulatory Aspects*, ed. Eugenio A. Bruno (London: Globe Business Publishing, 2013). Greek GDP was €193.3 billion in 2012.

[10] By this point, U.S. Treasury officials had withdrawn their objections in consideration of the dramatic fall in bond prices that preceded the debt exchange and the reinforcement of the firewall.

[11] Addition of previously committed funds raises the figure to €164.5 billion.

Fund Facility (EFF) to allow for longer maturity (see Appendix: Financial Rescues for Euro-Area Countries, 2010–2015). Now under the leadership of Christine Lagarde, the IMF was noncommittal about the likely success of the program, warning explicitly that the risks were high. Staff was particularly concerned that financial market access would not be restored by the time the financing under the program ran out. European governments pledged to provide the financing that might be necessary after the program was completed, satisfying the Fund, which noted the commitment explicitly in the documents.[12]

Recommitting to the Euro, Summer 2012

When Sarkozy and Merkel openly discussed the possibility of Grexit at Cannes in November 2011, European officials had decided that it would be prudent to prepare for that contingency, just in case. Peter Spiegel reports the formation of a secret group that included Jörg Asmussen, then at the ECB, Thomas Wieser, chair of the EFC, Marco Buti at the Commission, and Poul Thomsen of the IMF to formulate "Plan Z." Meanwhile, Europeans debated the handling of the second Greek program after the June 2012 election brought Samaras into office at the head of the governing coalition led by New Democracy. Wolfgang Schäuble favored Grexit combined with further strengthening of the firewalls—the "infected leg" strategy.[13] German politicians debated Grexit openly. Philipp Rösler, the chairman of the junior coalition partner, the Free Democratic Party (FDP), said, "For me, Greek exit has long since lost its horrors." Unsure whether Grexit could be managed without serious risk to the rest of the euro area, however, Chancellor Merkel decided not to push Greece out.[14] She announced her decision at a meeting with Samaras in August.[15] While contingency planning was a troika operation, recommitting to Greek membership in the euro area appears to have been a purely European decision.

Having gone off track during the change in government and speculation over Grexit, the program was reset in late 2012. The glidepath to the 4.5 percent primary surplus was pushed out two years to 2016. But the financing gap widened and debt was projected to remain dangerously high. The IMF thus

---

[12] IMF, "Greece: Request for Extended Arrangement," *Country Report* No. 12/57, March 16, 2012. For performance under the program, see also, European Commission, *The Second Economic Adjustment Programme for Greece Fourth Review–April 2014*, European Economy (Brussels), including pp. 67–72 on the disbursement schedule and financing needs.

[13] Peter Spiegel, "Inside Europe's Plan Z," *Financial Times*, May 15, 2014.

[14] Peter Spiegel, "Inside Europe's Plan Z," *Financial Times*, May 15, 2014.

[15] Tony Czuczka and Maria Petrakis, "Angela Merkel Backs Samaras on Greece's Euro-Zone Future," *Bloomberg*, August 24, 2012.

called upon the euro-area governments to make good on their March 2012 reassurances to close the gap and stabilize debt—threatening again to withhold disbursements.[16] The Eurogroup accordingly agreed to relax the terms of its financing further, provide €26 billion in new money, and to advance the timing of program financing to support a debt buyback that would reduce debt by 9.5 percent of GDP. The IMF stated that the Europeans "committed to take further actions, once Greece has further advanced with its fiscal adjustment, to bring debt down to 124 percent of GDP by 2020 and substantially below 110 percent of GDP in 2022."[17] The Eurogroup signaled that commitment at the end of November.[18] "Timely delivery of Greece's European partners' undertakings on debt relief and financing is crucial for program success," the Fund added. Again, the IMF linked its own participation to these assurances.

German Elections and Official Sector Involvement

Over the course of 2013, it appeared that a financing gap might be emerging in 2014 or later. But campaigning for the national elections in Germany, scheduled for September 2013, effectively placed bargaining over what Europeans might do to fill the gap—official sector involvement—on hold. During the campaign, the opposition accused the government of being evasive about the true cost of the euro crisis, with Greece being a sensitive flashpoint.[19] Merkel's Christian Democrats emerged victorious, but their coalition partner, the FDP, lost badly, necessitating the formation of a grand coalition with the Social Democratic Party (SPD) in December.

Meanwhile, debate about OSI continued largely behind the scenes. Christine Lagarde and Poul Thomsen pressed Greek Finance Minister Yannis Stournaras to side firmly with them in the controversy and ask the euro-area partners to write down their official claims on Greece—outright haircuts as opposed to simply maturity extension and interest rate reductions alone.

[16] Interviews, Washington, D.C., December 4, 2012, and Berlin, December 10 and 11, 2011; Peter Spiegel and Alan Beattie, "IMF and Eurozone Split over Greece," *Financial Times*, November 13, 2015, among other public sources.

[17] IMF, "Greece: First and Second Reviews," *Country Report* No. 13/20, January 2013, p. 2. See also European Commission, *The Second Adjustment Programme for Greece–First Review*, European Economy Occasional Papers 123, December 2012.

[18] Eurogroup statement of November 27, 2012. It affirmed, "As was stated by the Eurogroup on 21 February 2012, we are committed to providing adequate support to Greece during the *life of the programme and beyond* until it has regained market access, provided that Greece fully complies with the requirements and objectives of the adjustment programme" [emphasis added].

[19] "Bitter Euro Truths: Crisis Could Damage Merkel's Campaign," *Spiegel Online*, August 27, 2013.

Stournaras reported Wolfgang Schäuble's reaction—"Yannis, forget it"—lamenting to the *Financial Times*, "So it cannot be done, so what can I do?"[20]

Merkel and Schäuble's delaying tactics seemed to pay off as general funding conditions in the markets became quite benign through winter 2013–14. Greece, in particular, benefited from these conditions, returning to the market for short-term financing in February and receiving €8 billion in equity investment in the banking sector. Although anxiety over debt would soon return, investors relaxed in the knowledge that Greece faced light debt service burdens for the moment.

Conflict over Debt Restructuring

The Greek programs placed extreme stress upon cooperation among the IMF, European institutions, and member states. Just as the Argentine default had forced soul-searching at the IMF a decade earlier, the collapse of the first Greek program and PSI with the second forced a reconsideration of lending into cases where debt sustainability was dubious. On this occasion, that reconsideration involved the European institutions as well as the Fund. The questions at the heart of the debate were when debt sustainability should be assessed, who should make the assessment, and whether to lend to a government whose debt is deemed unsustainable.

The IMF began to push back openly in spring 2013 with the publication of its ex post evaluation of the first Greek program, which examined, in particular, the decision to grant exceptional access on the grounds that a restructuring of debt, which could not be certified as sustainable with high confidence, would cause contagion.[21] It supplemented this analysis with a new staff guidance on sovereign debt sustainability paper in May 2013.[22] The ex post

---

[20] Peter Spiegel and Kerin Hope, "Yannis Stournaras Urges 'Troika' to Ease Demands on Greece," *Financial Times*, January 9, 2014. This conversation probably did not literally take place; Stournaras was instead describing the pattern of bargaining among the players over the course of the year. See the commentary on this revelation posted by Yanis Varoufakis, about a year before he became finance minister himself: "Greek Finance Minister Confesses: 'I turned down the IMF's offer of an alliance in favour of a debt restructure,'" January 10, 2014 <http://yanisvaroufakis.eu/2014/01/10/greek-finance-minister-confesses-i-turned-down-the-imfs-offer-of-an-alliance-in-favour-of-a-debt-restructure/>.

[21] IMF, "Greece: Ex Post Evaluation of Exceptional Access under the 2010 Stand By Arrangement", *Country Report* No. 13/156, Washington, D.C., May 2013.

[22] IMF, *Sovereign Debt Restructuring–Recent Developments and Implications for the Fund's Legal and Policy Framework*, Washington, D.C., April 26, 2013 and *Staff Guidance Note for Public Debt Sustainability Analysis in Market-Access Countries*, Washington, D.C., May 9, 2013. These papers were in part a response to the "contractual, market-based approach" advanced by the Institute for International Finance. See Report of the Joint Committee on Strengthening the Framework for Sovereign Debt Crisis Prevention and Resolution, *Principles for Stable Capital Flows and Fair Debt Restructuring & Addendum*, Washington, D.C., October 2012.

evaluation was extraordinary in openly addressing the controversial issues associated with the program, the most sensitive being, "Should debt restructuring have been attempted at the outset?" The evaluation recalled that the euro area had ruled out restructuring notwithstanding the May 2010 projection indicating that the debt trajectory was precarious and a widespread view that restructuring was inevitable. The evaluation answered this question by describing the program as a "holding operation" that bought time for the euro area to build a firewall, concluding:

> However, not tackling the public debt problem decisively at the outset or early in the program created uncertainty about the euro area's capacity to resolve the crisis and likely aggravated the contraction in output. An upfront debt restructuring would have been better for Greece although this was not acceptable to the euro partners. A delayed debt restructuring also provided a window for private creditors to reduce exposures and shift debt into official hands. As seen earlier, this shift occurred on a significant scale and limited the bail-in of creditors when PSI eventually took place, leaving taxpayers and the official sector on the hook.

The evaluation also addressed frontally the question, "How well did the troika arrangement work?" It lamented the lack of clarity in the division of labor among the institutions, in contrast to collaboration between the Fund and the World Bank. The Fund acknowledged a lack of attention to the spillover effects within Europe on its part initially. But, the ex post evaluation continued, the Commission took a consensus approach, had limited success under the Stability and Growth Pact (SGP), and had no prior experience with crisis management. "The Fund's program experience and ability to move rapidly in formulating policy recommendations were skills that the European institutions lacked." The troika nonetheless settled their differences prior to negotiating with program authorities and "coordination seems to have been quite good under the circumstances."[23]

Among the lessons, the evaluation emphasized that its lending framework should be adjusted for countries in a monetary union. Given the absence of the exchange rate instrument, structural reforms play a larger role and these take time to implement and bear fruit. The Extended Fund Facility (EFF) should probably have been offered at the outset in place of the Stand-By Arrangement (SBA). Then the report touched a raw nerve:

> However, advantage could not be taken in the design of the program of one of the country's major strengths, namely the support that Greece might ultimately receive from its euro area partners if it could demonstrate a sufficient track-record of program implementation. Adjusting lending policies to the particular circumstances of monetary unions might allow the possibility of such conditional future assistance to be recognized in program agreements. To some extent this

[23] IMF, "Greece: Ex Post Evaluation," p. 31.

approach is being followed in the EFF-supported program, with euro area partners indicating a willingness to provide additional financing and debt relief conditional on Greece continuing to implement the program.

The evaluation summarized: "A particular challenge is to find ways to translate promises of conditional assistance from partner countries into formal program agreements."[24]

European officials reacted sharply, objecting to both the timing and the substance of the evaluation. The timing was inappropriate, they argued, because the five euro-area countries were still in programs. Fund staff had prepared the evaluation, after all, in anticipation of arguments with European officials over easing the terms of the outstanding official loans. (Recall that this dispute came on the heels of the Cyprus program and during the run-up to the German elections in September.) Europeans also argued that the need for debt restructuring could not have been known in spring 2010 and became clearly necessary only after the crisis worsened and as Athens' implementation proved inadequate.[25]

Commissioner Olli Rehn and ESM Managing Director Klaus Regling delivered the most strenuous public objections. Regling, while acknowledging the need to have the IMF involved in current programs, advocated a Europe-only solution in the long run. The Fund did not understand the rules of the monetary union, he said, "this is a big problem."[26] Discussion of further debt relief for Greece should be pushed back by about a year, he said. Rehn accused the IMF of breaking ranks, "I don't think it's fair and just for the IMF to wash its hands and throw the dirty water on the Europeans."[27]

Regling was specifically critical of the way in which the IMF conducted its debt sustainability analysis and the focus on the debt-to-GDP ratio. That ratio had defined the agreement at the end of 2012—to reduce the ratio from 170 percent to 124 by 2020 and then substantially below 110 percent by 2022—implying that governments would provide relief if necessary. The IMF had agreed to further disbursements on the basis of this agreement. But the ratio is a poor measure of Greece's servicing burden—"meaningless," according to

---

[24] IMF, "Greece: Ex Post Evaluation", p. 2.

[25] But this deterioration—Deauville, market fear, and Greek default on commitments under the program—was endogenous to the absence of an orderly restructuring framework ex ante.

[26] *Frankfurter Allgemeine Zeitung*, June 13, 2013. "The IMF has made a mockery of the stability and growth pact and claims it is responsible for growth. In doing this it is not only creating a false contrast, it is also showing above all it does not understand the rules of our single currency bloc," Regling said.

[27] Peter Spiegel and Kerin Hope, "EU's Olli Rehn Lashes Out at IMF Criticism of Greek Bailout," *Financial Times*, June 7, 2013; "Rehn in Jibe at IMF over Greek Bailout Review as Commission Gets more Criticism," *Kathimerini*, June 7, 2013. However, Rehn objected to Commissioner Viviane Reding's suggestion that the troika be abolished without delay. "Rehn and Reding Clash on Troika's Future," *EurActiv*, July 22, 2013.

Regling—as the interest rates were low and the average maturity stretched out to thirty years.[28] Debt reduction was probably unnecessary, he said, and the ESM could not take losses on loans. ECB President Draghi similarly argued, at this particular juncture, that Greece's debt was sustainable.[29]

From the standpoint of a political scientist, the debate over whether the debt–GDP ratio or the debt service ratio is the best measure of debt sustainability is relevant but woefully incomplete. Neither ratio is a good predictor of the likelihood of default or restructuring. Niall Ferguson's quip is apt: "Default is always and everywhere a political decision."[30] The argument over the appropriateness of the ratios is not merely technical but fundamentally political and institutional—about whose rules will apply, when unsustainability will be acknowledged, and who will take the hit.

In sum, euro-area governments, tied to the fate of their banks, took different positions on when and how that debt reduction should be achieved. Reflecting Chancellor Merkel's inclination to bail-in the banks, Germany pursued PSI for Greece, just as it would soon seek private-sector bail-in for Cypriot banks. The ECB, and to a somewhat lesser extent the Commission, were averse to private-sector bail-in.

The IMF helped to break the logjam and induce the banks and other financial institutions to negotiate haircuts. Having been brought into the first Greek program, the Fund used its debt sustainability analysis as a lever to secure agreement among the euro-area member states to additional financial commitments and private sector involvement. These steps were thus taken both earlier and more extensively than would likely have been the case if the Fund had not been included in the program.

CYPRUS

Cyprus represents another archetypical case of a banking system run amok, like Ireland, dragging its (complicit) sovereign government into the abyss. With political control of the island divided since the 1974 war, only the Greek-Cypriot-controlled portion of the island joined the European Union in 2004. Cyprus, or at least the portion now in the EU, joined the monetary union in

[28] Matina Stevis and Gabriele Steinhauser, "Bailout Fund Boss Says Current Greek Debt Analysis 'Meaningless'," *Wall Street Journal*, September 26, 2013. Willem Buiter characterizes the European creditors' posture toward Greece colorfully: "You have to pay us nothing forever." Peterson Institute, July 10, 2014.

[29] Matina Stevis and Gabriele Steinhauser, "EU Official Questions Need for Debt Forgiveness in Greece," *Wall Street Journal*, September 26, 2013.

[30] Niall Ferguson, Stavros Niarchos Lecture, Peterson Institute for International Economics, Washington, D.C., May 2011. He was playing off Milton Friedman's famous remark, "Inflation is always and everywhere a monetary phenomenon."

2008. The country was closely tied to Greece politically and economically and, with the natural development of the economy limited by partition, pursued a highly skewed "business model" as an international banking center.

Cypriot banks were quite successful in intermediating foreign deposits into investments in Europe and elsewhere. But Nicosia became known as a money-laundering center that was used largely by Russian depositors seeking to evade taxes. With a population of 872,000, the banking system accumulated liabilities amounting to more than $160 billion, more than seven times its $23 billion GDP. The Cypriot case thus resembled a shady, Mediterranean version of Iceland.

Choosing Institutions

As large holders of Greek government bonds, Cypriot banks were hard hit by the restructuring of Greek sovereign debt. During the spring and summer of 2012, when general anxiety in the euro-area sovereign bond market was most acute, the government of Cyprus requested a program from the European authorities and the IMF. Officials in Nicosia anticipated an election in February 2013, however, and resisted negotiations with the troika throughout the autumn. By the time a new center-right government, led by Nicos Anastasiades, replaced the communist government in late February 2013, it had become clear that at least two banks were insolvent. Insolvency rendered these banks ineligible for Emergency Liquidity Assistance (ELA), on which the Cypriot banking system had become dependent,[31] and the ECB lowered the boom in March by threatening to halt the provision of liquidity, forcing the new government into the embrace of the troika.[32]

The politics within the euro area had shifted since the summer of 2012, however. With the ECB announcement of Outright Monetary Transactions (OMT) in September, capital markets had calmed considerably and yield spreads declined substantially. Creditor governments thus became more willing to accept the risks of driving a harder bargain. German Finance Minister Schäuble questioned in January 2013 whether Cyprus met the requirement of systemic significance to qualify for ESM financing. Noting that there had to be "a danger for the stability of the euro zone as a whole," he said, "This has to be

---

[31] Landon Thomas reveals the fierce debate within the ECB over allowing the Central Bank of Cyprus to extend ELA in a series of articles in the *New York Times*. See "E.C.B. Minutes Showed Doubts Over Keeping a Cyprus Bank Afloat," October 17, 2014; "Europe's Central Bank Defies Its Own Rules in Cyprus Bailout," November 18, 2014; "Cyprus Government Report Points Fingers on Bank Collapse," November 18, 2014.

[32] Christopher Lawton, Todd Buell, and James Marson, "ECB Threatens to Cutoff Cypriot Banks," *Wall Street Journal*, March 21, 2013.

met. We will see."[33] ECB President Draghi swiftly retorted that the bankruptcy of Cyprus would indeed pose such a threat, beginning with the recently stabilized but fragile Greek economy.[34] *Der Spiegel* reported that Draghi's view was shared by European Commissioner Rehn and ESM Managing Director Regling.[35]

The overarching question at the outset of the Cyprus program was how to handle the banking system and in particular whether to close the two insolvent banks and bail-in their creditors.[36] During autumn 2012 through early winter 2013, the European Commission was opposed to closing Laiki Bank and the Bank of Cyprus. The ECB was also originally opposed to closing the banks and bailing-in private creditors and depositors. It was especially concerned that the credits that had been extended to the banks from the Cypriot central bank under ELA be repaid. During January and February, nonetheless, key ECB officials came around to the IMF view that bank closure was necessary.[37]

The International Monetary Fund took a different position from the outset, however. With a banking sector that was seven times the size of the economy, officials at the Fund reasoned, no lending program through the sovereign could be consistent with future debt sustainability. The amounts were so large that Cyprus could not repay, and would inevitably follow the pattern of the Greek program, whereby a large loan into an unsustainable situation would have to be restructured later—only in this case by official rather than by private-sector creditors. Given the experience with Greece and the backlash from the non-European countries, IMF staff was not willing to pursue this strategy in Cyprus. It preferred that the ESM recapitalize the banks directly up front and the previous Cypriot government supported this approach. But the finance ministers of Germany, the Netherlands, and Finland effectively vetoed direct recapitalization.[38] As a second-best strategy, the Fund staff argued that depositors and other private creditors of the banks had to be bailed-in and Laiki Bank and Bank of Cyprus closed. If the Europeans were not willing to accept these measures, then the Fund staff was not willing to propose IMF financial participation to the Executive Board.[39]

---

[33] Rebecca Christie and Rainer Buergin, "Schaeuble Says Cyprus Aid Requires Evident Threat to Euro," *Bloomberg News*, January 21, 2013.

[34] "ECB's Draghi, German FinMin at Odds over Cyprus–Spiegel," *Reuters*, January 27, 2013.

[35] "ECB Warns of Euro-Zone Risk," *Spiegel Online International*, January 28, 2013.

[36] The definitive report was prepared by a specialist financial firm for the government of Cyprus. It estimated the cost of recapitalizing the Cypriot banking system to be €8.9 billion. See PIMCO, "Independent Due Diligence of the Banking System of Cyprus," London, March 2013 <http://ftalphaville.ft.com/files/2013/04/reportasws.pdf.pdf>.

[37] Interviews with central bank officials, Berlin, June 12, 2013; Washington, D.C., March 19, 2014.

[38] Although they indicated it might be possible after the SSM were established in November 2014. Christoph Pauly, Christian Reiermann ,and Christoph Schult, "Troika Travails: Split Emerges over Cyprus Bailout Package," *Speigel Online*, January 21, 2013.

[39] Interviews with IMF officials, Washington, D.C., May 29, June 28, and July 9, 2013.

So, the differences among the members of the troika were stark and the solution to Cyprus' crisis hinged substantially on the choice of institutions to be included in the response. The German government again wanted the IMF to be included and was supported by the Finnish and other creditor governments. Officials in the chancellor's office and finance ministry did not take Bundestag support for the Cyprus program for granted; on the contrary, they worried that the chancellor could lose her working majority. Russian involvement, tax evasion, and money laundering had soured members across several parties and the SPD, in particular, had warned that it would not back an ESM loan that did not have safeguards against abuse. The Bundestag and finance ministry thus backed the bailing-in of private creditors, and their position was consistent with that of the IMF[40]—with whom they worked closely on the design of the program, to the chagrin of officials within the Commission.[41]

Debacle over Insured Deposits

The members of the troika calculated that Cyprus would need a total of about €17.7 billion for recapitalizing the banking system and covering fiscal deficits and debt service until it might reasonably expect to access private capital markets again. The troika offered €10 billion—€9 billion through the ESM and €1 billion through the IMF—and asked Cyprus to arrange the remaining €7.7 billion through a combination of domestic debt measures and an extension of a 2011 loan from Russia[42] (see Appendix). Laiki bank was closed and its working assets transferred to the Bank of Cyprus, which was to be restructured.

One of the more spectacular debacles of the euro crisis followed, however. Under the agreement, the government of Cyprus was to come up with €5.8 billion to cover the losses of the two banks and the capital replenishment for the Bank of Cyprus. The question as to how bank depositors were to be treated was critical. Cypriot government guarantees of bank deposits were capped at €100,000, in line with practice across the European Union.[43] Deposits above this amount were, in principle, exposed to losses in the case of a bank failure, while those below the threshold were supposed to be protected. The new

---

[40] Interviews with German officials, Berlin, June 11 and 12, 2013.

[41] Matina Stevis and Ian Tally, "IMF Concedes It Made Mistakes on Greece," *Wall Street Journal*, June 6, 2013. Note, moreover, that the ESM was present as a fourth institution in the "troika meetings," with its director, Klaus Regling, advising the group on the financing arrangements.

[42] IMF, "Cyprus: Request for Arrangement under the Extended Fund Facility," *Country Report* No. 13/125 (May 2013).

[43] European Union, Directive 2009/14/EC of the European Parliament and of the Council, *Official Journal of the European Union*, March 13, 2009 <http://ec.europa.eu/internal_market/bank/docs/guarantee/200914_en.pdf>.

Cypriot government, however, proposed imposing losses not only on the large depositors (of 9.9 percent) but also on the small (6.7 percent), calling the measure a "tax" rather than a "haircut."[44]

The announcement had an explosive impact in Cypriot politics, threatened an outflow of deposits, and necessitated the imposition of capital controls—another example of making a small problem into a very large one. The Cypriot parliament objected and the new government was forced to revise the program by protecting the small depositors at the cost of imposing potentially large losses on the large depositors. Under the final arrangement, 37.5 percent of the holdings of the large depositors in both insolvent banks were converted into equity and 22.5 percent were frozen pending further review of the need for recapitalization. Depositors were tightly constrained in the amounts they could withdraw from the bank and transfer abroad (see Appendix). The revised agreement was approved by a quickly convened special meeting of the Eurogroup on March 25 in Brussels.[45]

But a good deal of damage had been done in the meantime. Critically, the European taboo against imposing losses on small depositors had been broken, and the consequences for depositor confidence in banks across the southern tier of Europe were potentially far-reaching.[46] Moreover, the capital controls violated the single market and would prove to be more difficult to repeal without prompting capital flight than they were to impose.

Eurogroup and troika officials thus engaged in a spirited round of finger-pointing over how this had gone so wrong.[47] The main mistake was the decision in the Eurogroup to allow the Cypriot government the latitude to decide how the depositor bail-in should be configured. Details remain somewhat murky, but it appears that the Russian government played a heavy role. The Russian government jilted the Cypriot finance minister during a

[44] The operative language in the Eurogroup statement read:

The Eurogroup further welcomes the Cypriot authorities' commitment to take further measures mobilising internal resources, in order to limit the size of the financial assistance linked to the adjustment programme. These measures include the introduction of an *upfront one-off stability levy applicable to resident and non-resident depositors.* Further measures concern the increase of the withholding tax on capital income, a restructuring and recapitalisation of banks, an increase of the statutory corporate income tax rate and a bail-in of junior bondholders. The Eurogroup looks forward to an agreement between Cyprus and the Russian Federation on a financial contribution [emphasis added].

See "Eurogroup Statement on Cyprus," Brussels, 16 March 2013. Christine Lagarde, who attended the Eurogroup meeting without Fund staff, issued a supportive statement, IMF press release No. 13/80, March 16, 2013.

[45] Council of the European Union, "Eurogroup Statement on Cyprus," Brussels, March 25, 2013.

[46] See, for example, Anne Sibert, "Deposit Insurance after Iceland and Cyprus," *Vox*, April 2, 2013.

[47] See, for example, James G. Neuger, "Europe Plays I-Didn't-Do-It Blame Game on Cyprus Tax," *Bloomberg*, March 20, 2013.

trip to Moscow, during which he had hoped to secure financing,[48] but sought to protect its depositors in Cyprus, which the German intelligence agency had reported included Russian oligarchs who used Cyprus for money laundering.[49]

During the meeting that took place on March 16 in Brussels and which agreed upon the original program, Russia was effectively the "18th member" of the Eurogroup. But Russian officials were speaking directly to the Cypriot minister on the telephone rather than with the group as a whole. Russia insisted on keeping the "tax" on large deposits to single digits, which meant there had to be a tax on smaller depositors as well. German Finance Minister Wolfgang Schäuble, who was later criticized for the program, objected to the bail-in of the small depositors. But, in the end, he deferred to the Cypriots' presentation of the haircut as a tax and their handling of the domestic politics of the matter. In retrospect, that deference—shared by the Eurogroup as a whole and the troika institutions—was a clear mistake.[50]

The Fund applied the lessons that it was drawing from the experience with the Greek program (discussed earlier in this chapter) when insisting that the insolvent banks be closed, the domestic system recapitalized, and that this had to be accomplished through substantial private-sector bail-in at the outset. The Fund did not suspend its exceptional access standards for Cyprus as it had done in Greece; the €1 billion commitment was less than 600 percent of quota. The small size of the IMF commitment in this case reflected (a) concern of non-Europeans about exposure and (b) concern that the IMF's preferred creditor status would disallow a large portion of debt from being restructured if that proved to be necessary down the line. Furthermore, the troika anticipated that the economic contraction would amount to thirteen percent of GDP during 2013 and 2014, a significantly greater decline than it anticipated at the outset of the Greek program. In applying these lessons, the IMF drove a harder bargain with the European institutions, using the debt sustainability analysis to do so—a tactic that it had employed since spring 2011.

At the same time, the Fund lent again into a program whose risks it acknowledged were high. Staff thought that economic growth might turn out to be worse than anticipated and debt correspondingly higher relative to GDP owing to the uncertain impact of the banking crisis as well as implementation

---

[48] See, for example, Miriam Elder, "Cyprus Loan Talks Constructive," *Guardian*, March 20, 2013; Olga Tanas and Ilya Arkhipov, "Russia Rejects Cyprus Financial Rescue Bid as Deadline Looms," *Bloomberg*, March 22, 2013.

[49] Russian deposits were estimated to amount to $26 billion in mid-2012. Markus Dettmer and Christian Reiermann, "Bailing Out the Oligarchs: EU Aid for Cyprus a Political Minefield for Merkel," *Spiegel Online International*, November 5, 2012.

[50] Interviews with German officials, Berlin, June 11 and 12, 2013, and a former IMF official, February 16, 2016.

and political risk.[51] (In the event, the contraction after the beginning of the program proved to be relatively mild. But by that time the country had been in severe recession for two years and even in 2016 the economic output remained ten percent below its 2008 peak.) The reservations of the Executive Directors were on full display when their board meeting statements were leaked.[52] The Executive Board decided to contribute to the program, calculating that the Fund was adequately protected against loss. But the implication was that, should the program have to be extended, either the Europeans would have to come up with the additional financing, ease the terms of existing loans, or grant outright debt relief in the form of official sector involvement.

Cyprus's crisis underscored the importance of completing the banking union. The euro area would have been spared the threat of serious contagion had the Single Supervisory Mechanism (SSM), a robust resolution regime, and euro-area-wide deposit insurance been in place. A genuine banking union would have broken the link between the sovereign and the banks. Relatedly, the bail-in of uninsured depositors also underscored a new approach to crisis management in the euro area. Although Eurogroup President Jeroen Dijsselbloem was criticized for referring to it as a "model," a number of European officials expected similar bail-ins in future contingencies.[53]

Completion and Exit

Cyprus exited its program quietly in March of 2016 after experiencing a recession that proved to be shallower than expected (see Figure 6.2).[54] Its government regained market access and, in April 2015, withdrew capital controls while also stabilizing the amount of deposits in the banking system. Compared to 2012–13, the country was relatively unaffected by the travails of Greece in 2015 (discussed in Chapter 11) and the institutions celebrated the Cypriot program as a success. However, the unemployment rate, while declining slightly, remained at about fifteen percent. More ominously, non-performing loans were about sixty percent of bank assets, the equivalent of

---

[51] IMF, "Cyprus: Request for Arrangement under the Extended Fund Facility," April 30, 2013, pp. 23–6.

[52] IMF, Statements of Executive Directors on the EFF Arrangements for Cyprus, BUFF/ED/13/62, Washington, D.C., May 10, 2013. This document was posted at <http://www.stockwatch.com.cy/media/announce_pdf/May15_2013_IMF.pdf>.

[53] See, for example, Benoît Cœuré's remarks to the AICGS 30th Anniversary Symposium, Berlin, June 12, 2013, <https://www.youtube.com/watch?v=rPponThNyLQ>.

[54] Council of the European Union, "Eurogroup Statement on Cyprus," Brussels, March 7, 2016; ESM, "FAQs on the Conclusion of ESM Financial Assistance Programme for Cyprus," Luxembourg, March 31, 2016; European Commission, *Economic Adjustment Programme for Cyprus–7th Review*, European Economy, Summer 2015; Eszter Balazs, "Cyprus Turns Economy Around, Successfully Exits IMF Program," *IMF Survey*, March 15, 2016.

150 percent of GDP, and government debt remained above 100 percent (see Figure 6.3) The institutions identified reducing non-performing loans and following through on privatization as priorities in post-program monitoring. Cyprus decided on a "clean exit," without a precautionary program, a point on which all of the institutions were apparently agreed.

KEY OBSERVATIONS

The second Greek program exposed the sharp conflicts among the institutions within the troika arrangements. Much of the conflict owed to differing assessments of the sustainability of debt and the IMF successfully used its debt and sustainability analysis to elicit agreement on the part of the European creditors to fill any financing gaps that might arise in the future. The November 2012 agreement served as a framework for debt discussions for two and a half years thereafter. Creditor governments accepted, even advocated, write-downs of privately held debt. These governments were less receptive to the IMF's position, to put it mildly, when the focus turned toward restructuring their official claims against Greece in 2013 and as it would turn again in 2015.

The case of Cyprus reveals a couple of additional insights about the troika. The IMF can be influential even when it contributes a relatively small share of the financing, ten percent in this case. It is the backing from the creditor governments that gives the IMF influence in shaping program conditionality, not the proportion of financing that it contributes. The IMF had its own analysis and preferences—first for direct recapitalization of the banks, which was dropped, and second for bail-in and bank closure, which prevailed. Creditor states included the Fund as part of the negotiating team because its preferences overlapped with theirs, the preferences of Berlin in particular.

11

Greece, the Crisis Continues

With each program for Greece, the conflicts among the institutions and the Greek government intensified. Whereas the first program ignored debt reduction, and the second program embraced reductions in private claims, the third program witnessed a standoff over restructuring the claims of official creditors to the Greek government. Those official claims had, of course, been accumulated under the first and second programs and their renegotiation was therefore a political minefield for the governments of the creditor countries. But the earlier programs had deferred the tough decisions on debt and the future had now arrived; the IMF staff became determined not to lend into *yet another* program without restructuring debt robustly. The third program thus provided the ultimate test of the Eurogroup's attachment to the involvement of the IMF and the regime complex for crisis finance in Europe.

The confrontation over the third program for Greece during 2015–16 can be considered in three phases: (1) the lead-up to the national election in January 2015, which brought Syriza into government with its demand to renegotiate the program; (2) February through August 2015, when the program was hammered out amid a series of euro-area meetings that surpassed even the brinksmanship of the acute phase of the euro crisis; and (3) the program's first review, which was delayed until late spring 2016.

SYRIZA TAKES CONTROL

In retrospect, Greece came tantalizingly close to following Ireland, Portugal, and Spain in exiting smoothly from their programs. As bond spreads fell across the monetary union in 2013 and 2014, the crisis seemed to have dissipated. Greece was originally scheduled to receive its last disbursements from the European Financial Stability Facility (EFSF) in December 2014[1] and

---

[1] This was extended by two months to February 2015. See EFSF, "Extension of the EFSF Programme and EFSF Bonds for Greece," press release, Luxembourg, December 19, 2014.

from the IMF in March 2016. After five years of contraction, the Greek economy grew slightly in 2014 and the government's budget registered a small primary surplus. Officials in Europe and the troika considered whether Greece should take a precautionary program during the transition in order to hedge, for example, against the possibility of financial turbulence that might accompany an increase in interest rates by the Federal Reserve. Those plans came to naught, however, as the country descended into crisis once again in early 2015. Rather than exiting its second program, Greece faced the possibility of exiting the monetary union altogether.

Trouble began with the review of the second program in the late summer of 2014. The troika objected to the government's missing the program benchmarks on several structural and labor market policies. As a condition for completion of the sixth review and disbursement of the tranche, the institutions insisted on further increases in taxes and reform of the pension system. The position of the IMF in this review was particularly hawkish, but coincided with Berlin's preferences.[2]

Prime Minister Samaras demurred. He faced elections in early 2015, triggered by an inability to muster a three-fifths majority in parliament to confirm a new president of the republic. On the defensive, the governing coalition wanted to avoid the pension reform prior to the election. Notwithstanding the return to modest growth, output remained twenty-five percent below the pre-crisis level and unemployment remained above twenty-five percent. These conditions, which compared to those of the Great Depression in the United States in 1933,[3] fueled the popular backlash against austerity and support for Syriza.

The English name of the Syriza party is the Coalition of the Radical Left and is a good descriptor. It was created in 2004 as a collection of splintered and fringe left-wing and radical groups, led since 2008 by Alexis Tsipras. The party captured nearly twenty-seven percent of the vote in the election of June 2012, a close second to Samaras's New Democracy. But at that point even Syriza members privately acknowledged that the party was not prepared to govern.[4] Tsipras would use the next two-and-a-half years in opposition to organize the party for competing in the next election and governing afterward.

Leading up to the election in late January 2015, Syriza campaigned on a platform of ending austerity, throwing off the troika, and restructuring the debt, which remained in the vicinity of 170 percent of GDP. The party won the election by a large margin, capturing more than thirty-six percent of the

---

[2] Its position was foreshadowed in IMF, "Greece: Fifth Review under the Extended Arrangement," *Country Report* No. 14/151, Washington, D.C., June 2014.

[3] A point underscored by Athanasios Orphanides, "Does Greece Pose a Threat to the Euro?," presentation to the American Enterprise Institute, Washington, D.C., April 17, 2015.

[4] Interviews by the author with members of parliament, Athens, Greece, July 18 and 19, 2012.

vote and 149 of 300 seats in parliament. Tsipras chose the far right-wing populist Independent Greeks party as the coalition partner and appointed Yanis Varoufakis, an academic economist and self-described "erratic Marxist," as his minister of finance. His government then set to work to persuade the European partners and the IMF to tear up the program and replace it with a new one.

The conflict with the European creditors was nearly absolute. The democratic mandates of the new Greek government and those of the triple-A-rated creditor countries were diametrically opposed. Notwithstanding initial foreign sympathy for some of its objectives, such as cracking down on the economic "oligarchs" and enforcing overdue tax payments, the Tsipras government became almost completely isolated in the Eurogroup and European Council.

Finance Minister Varoufakis presented the economic and moral case for ending austerity and restructuring the debt. The programs had failed to restore meaningful growth to the Greek economy. The country had been subjected to an economic depression that imposed extreme hardship on its citizens and fragmented the political system. Greece had borrowed mainly to pay off other creditors—coverage of current government spending had been a minority share—and the debt was higher as a percentage of GDP than it had been before the first program, notwithstanding the restructuring in 2012.[5]

Varoufakis's position resonated with what many outside analysts had argued from the beginning, even before the first Greek program.[6] Advocacy of deep haircuts on European governments' claims on Greece through the original Greek Loan Facility and the EFSF seemed to be consistent with the November 2012 Eurogroup statement on the debt. Moreover, it resonated with IMF staff advocacy of debt reprofiling as a precondition for further loans in cases where debt is probably not sustainable and closing the systemic exemption. Debt reduction was also broadly consistent with the ongoing revision of austerity doctrine to which the IMF Research Department had made important contributions. But these quarters provided little comfort to the Greek finance minister in the end.

The public confrontation with Germany was as sensational as can be in international finance, even lurid. Varoufakis highlighted the emergence of Golden Dawn, inspired by the Nazi Party, to German audiences. Other Greeks claimed reparations from Germany arising from the occupation during the

---

[5] Varoufakis had been criticizing the troika and the bailouts since the beginning of the crisis on his widely read blog. His view as finance minister was presented in "Greek Debt Standoff Awaits a Decisive Move," *New York Times*, February 12, 2015. His interpretation of the political economy of the monetary union is presented in Yanis Varoufakis, *And the Weak Suffer What They Must? Europe's Crisis and America's Economic Future* (New York: Nation Books, 2016), published after his departure from government.

[6] A contemporary example was Martin Wolf, "Greek Debt and a Default of Statesmanship," *Financial Times*, January 18, 2015.

Second World War, with compound interest. Whether these vituperative exchanges were somehow a strategy on the part of Varoufakis and Tsipras is hard to know.[7] But they alienated public opinion in Germany and elsewhere and thereby pushed the parties apart rather than together.

The bitter atmosphere and yawning gap between the positions of the government and the troika revived open speculation about Grexit. A crucial strategic question, as in the previous confrontations, was whether a Greek default in the wake of an exit would infect the rest of the euro area. Recall that Chancellor Merkel had put an end to Plan Z in summer 2012 because she was concerned about the fallout for Italy, which was too big to rescue. But much had been accomplished since then: the ECB had announced Outright Monetary Transactions (OMT), the ESM had been created as a permanent institution, the ECB had taken on the Single Supervisory Mechanism (SSM) as of November 2014, the Single Resolution Board and other elements of banking union had been set up, and the ECB had initiated quantitative easing (the Expanded Asset Purchase Programme) in March 2015. European officials stated bravely that this new architecture would prevent contagion to the rest of the euro area. But these assurances had an air of wishful thinking—none of these officials knew how the market would actually react.

On February 20, the Eurogroup extended the European portion of the program through the end of June 2015 to allow time to negotiate a package of policy measures in exchange for disbursing the remaining €7.2 billion.[8] German Finance Minister Schäuble, among other creditors, insisted that agreement be reached on completing the second program before any new, third program was considered. But the two programs were so closely related that negotiations over them became conflated. By early 2015, Greece's economy slipped back into recession, the budget deficit widened, and the country would thus need financing beyond the second program, combined with some sort of debt operation. A €20 billion bulge in debt repayments during June through September—to redeem the IMF, the ECB, and maturing Treasury bills—established early or mid-June as the effective deadline for agreement. Without new money, Greece would default.

To complicate matters, Alexis Tsipras had become prime minister declaring that the "troika is over," determined to scuttle the arrangement.[9] His government thus rejected negotiations with it and banished the missions from Athens—a point on which Tsipras placed a great deal of political importance. Much time and energy was therefore devoted to hammering out the

---

[7] Varoufakis was sincere in his aversion to right-wing extremism. See Varoufakis, *And the Weak Suffer What They Must?*, especially pp. 198–237.

[8] European Council, "Eurogroup Statement on Greece," Brussels, February 20, 2015.

[9] See, for example, Henriette Jacobsen and Jeremy Fleming, "Tsipras Declares Death of Troika, Agrees to Further Talks," EurActiv.com, February 13, 2015.

alternative modalities by which the technical work could be conducted and the revisions to the program negotiated. The other member states in the euro area refused to negotiate the elements of the program directly with the Greek government in either the Eurogroup or Euro summit, insisting on the troika. Tsipras finally agreed to hold talks with "the institutions"—as the troika was renamed—in Brussels and allow limited technical visits for data collection to Athens.

Perhaps predictably, serious negotiations did not begin until the prospect of default loomed. In a standoff, neither Greece nor its creditors had an incentive to offer concessions before the other. False deadlines surrounding Eurogroup meetings came and went over the remainder of the winter and spring of 2015. The creditors maintained their insistence on pension, labor-market, and tax reform. Athens provided strategy papers that charted its policy reforms in specific terms.[10] But the Greek government also insisted on debt restructuring and by nearly all accounts was for several months unable or unwilling to engage creditors directly on verifiable commitments. European finance ministers became uniformly and completely exasperated with Varoufakis.

DISPUTES WITHIN THE TROIKA

The prolonged standoff between Greece and its creditors also exposed the arguments among the institutions of the troika. These arguments were as intense as those between them and the Tsipras government.

The IMF had been largely responsible for the tough line the troika had taken with the Samaras government during the second half of 2014.[11] The Fund approached these negotiations with an awareness of several factors. First, disbursements of the remaining tranches were the principal leverage over the government in Athens to follow through on reforms that the Fund deemed necessary. Second, European governments had agreed to provide additional financing if that were needed under the second program and the November 2012 framework was the Fund's principal source of leverage over the creditor

---

[10] The first comprehensive set of reforms presented to secure release of the funds remaining under the second program was "Greek Reforms in the Context of the 20/02/2015 Eurogroup Agreement," Ministry of Finance, Athens, March 2015. It can be found at <http://im.ft-static.com/content/images/55b27a7e-d87c-11e4-ba53-00144feab7de.pdf>. It was followed by a succession of revised proposals that were presented prior to Eurogroup and Euro summit meetings, but which were supplanted by documents presented by the creditors as the basis for final agreement.

[11] Interviews with IMF and European officials, Washington, D.C., April 18, 2015; Brussels, May 11 and 12, 2015; Luxembourg, May 13, 2015; and Berlin, July 13–15, 2015.

countries to follow through. Third, the Fund was due to begin receiving repayment of loans under the first program.

The IMF staff encompassed somewhat differing views on how to proceed. The research department had broken from the austerity line with upward revisions of the fiscal multiplier, while the legal department had been pushing for closure of the systemic exemption. Both positions counseled easing up on fiscal adjustment and giving greater emphasis to debt reduction prior to agreeing to programs in cases of unsustainability. But the managing director and senior management sided with the director of the European Department, the position to which Poul Thomsen had been promoted, in adopting the strict stance on fiscal adjustment vis-à-vis Athens. That stance also closely matched the preferences of the most important European creditor, Germany, and frequent interlocutor of Lagarde, Chancellor Merkel.

But Fund officials also had messages for the creditors that were unwelcome. They repeatedly declared in the winter and spring of 2015 that the design of the new program had to "add up." This meant that it should be fully financed to the return to market access—as opposed to again providing a short-term bridge and then looking to fill a financing gap later. Critically, the phrase also meant that the primary surplus target had to be consistent with debt sustainability: with a high primary surplus, debt relief could be modest; with a low primary surplus, debt relief would have to be more generous.[12] But, since the Fund believed that the 4.5 percent long-run target in the second program was no longer politically plausible, some sort of debt relief would have to be provided. Naturally, that relief would have to come from the European side, not the Fund. IMF staff did *not* insist on haircuts on the principal—sometimes referred to as "nominal haircuts" in the European lexicon—but they did insist on a debt operation *prior* to a financial commitment from the Fund to a new program.

The European Commission, as of July 2014, was led by Jean-Claude Juncker. The former prime minister and finance minister of Luxembourg actively campaigned for the position and secured the support of the newly elected European Parliament. Chancellor Merkel, who had originally opposed his appointment, thus relented. The former prime minister of Latvia, Valdis Dombrovskis, served as Vice President of the Commission and the former finance minister of France, Pierre Moscovici, as Commissioner for Economic and Financial Affairs.

With this new team in place, the Commission took a distinctively more political approach to Greece than either the IMF or the ECB. While the

---

[12] This relationship is derived from the standard debt sustainability equation, wherein the difference between the nominal interest rate and nominal growth rate times the ratio of debt to GDP equals the primary surplus expressed as a ratio to GDP. For a textbook treatment, see, among others, Paul de Grauwe, *Economics of Monetary Union*, 9th ed. (Oxford: Oxford University Press, 2012), pp. 211–17.

Commission also insisted on further fiscal adjustment and structural reforms, a number of officials thought that it had been counterproductive to push them on Samaras. They regarded Samaras to be the euro area's best bet for Greek reform and sustainability. Pressing the pension and VAT reforms on his government during the approach to an election, as the IMF and others did, risked his defeat at the hands of Syriza. After hearing the January 2015 election result, one Commission official thus quipped to his IMF counterpart wryly, "Congratulations, you've succeeding in electing Tsipras."[13] The Commission was not opposed in principle to debt restructuring, but was not pushing haircuts on the creditor member states and did not attach the same urgency as the Fund to the matter given the light burden of debt service.[14]

The ESM was now participating in the meetings as well, as one of the "institutions." Klaus Regling regularly spoke to the joint press conferences after the Eurogroup meetings along with Dijsselbloem and Moscovici. He generally highlighted the payoffs to adjustment that was being undertaken in the country programs. He had objected to the Fund's position on programs and called for Europe-only solutions. With respect to Greece in particular, he pulled no punches in criticizing the IMF's debt sustainability analysis (DSA), with its emphasis on the debt-to-GDP ratio, arguing that low interest rates and long maturities made debt sustainable. Officials in Berlin were more comfortable with the ESM, an intergovernmental institution that was led by someone with whom they could generally see eye to eye, than with the Commission.

The ECB controlled the liquidity of the Greek banking system and, through it, access by the government in Athens to short-term funding. Playing a role similar to that in the Cyprus case, the ECB placed limits on its acceptance of Greek government bonds as collateral in refinancing operations and on the Greek central bank's issuance of Emergency Liquidity Assistance (ELA). As throughout the euro crisis, the ECB was concerned not to allow governments to substitute financing from the central bank for risk-bearing commitments from the ESM. As long as the Greek government stuck to the program, government bonds were acceptable as collateral in regular refinancing operations at the ECB. But Syriza had rejected the program, leading the ECB to suspend their eligibility in early February.[15] Greek bonds were similarly excluded from purchases under the ECB's January 2015 program of quantitative

<hr/>

[13] Interviews by the author with European Commission officials, Brussels, May 11 and 12, 2015.

[14] The Commission's last published analysis on Greece prior to the suspension of the program was, "The Second Economic Adjustment Programme for Greece–Fourth Review," *European Economy*, Occasional Papers 192 (April 2014). See pp. 67–8 of the paper for the treatment of debt sustainability.

[15] ECB, "Eligibility of Greek bonds used as collateral in Eurosystem monetary policy operations," press release, Frankfurt, February 4, 2015. For analysis, see Silvia Merler, "ECB Collateral Damages on Greece," Bruegel blog, Brussels, February 5, 2105.

easing. These actions forced Tsipras and Varoufakis to secure agreement with their European colleagues on an extension of the program. The ECB was criticized for acting in an overtly political manner in this way,[16] but the central bank was a team player of the troika. Had the ECB not exercised this leverage, the Greek government could have strung out negotiations much longer.

As home to the SSM, the ECB now regulated the four largest banks in Greece and could take over direct supervision of the remaining banks if it wished to do so. Greek regulatory authorities no longer had primary jurisdiction. As far as banking supervision was concerned, sovereignty had migrated substantially to the ECB. The Greek banks were the first serious test of the new single supervisor, one which would set precedents for other cases in the banking union, and Frankfurt was thus keen to manage the banks closely.

Two decisions were particularly important in this regard. Nonperforming loans in the banking system were high, and a large fraction of what counted for bank capital was deferred tax assets (DTAs), so the banks would eventually need recapitalization. Not wanting to force the matter, however, the chair of the SSM, Danièle Nouy, repeatedly declared that the banks were solvent.[17] Out of a desire to protect the banks against losses in a restructuring, second, the SSM strictly limited the amount of bills that the banks could purchase from the Greek treasury.

Underlying this balancing act on the part of the ECB was the fundamental institutional conviction that Grexit must be avoided. Benoît Cœuré, a member of its Executive Board, stated this view clearly:[18]

> It is crucial for the stability of the euro area that there is no doubt that participation in the euro is irreversible. Now there is such doubt. The discussion about Grexit has undoubtedly caused instability in this respect. It is like a fine hairline crack that can lead to a major fracture. Consequently, it has to be repaired now. This is particularly important for us as a central bank. We do not decide who belongs in the euro area. That is a political decision. But the ECB's working assumption is that a country's participation in the euro is irreversible. This is also how we have dealt with Greece and why the provision of liquidity to Greece could be sustained.

If Grexit could not be avoided, it was imperative that the ECB *not* be responsible for Greece's expulsion. The president, Executive Board, and Governing Council were determined that, should Grexit come to pass, the governments

---

[16] Karl Whelan emphasizes the discretion with which the ECB acted, in, "What's Going on with Greece and the ECB?," *Bull Market* blog, February 1, 2015.

[17] See, for example, Viktoria Dendrinou, Todd Buell, and Madelaine Nissen, "Greek Banks Well Equipped for Crisis Says ECB's Nouy," *Wall Street Journal*, May 13, 2015; "ECB's Nouy– Consider Greek Banks to be Solvent," *Reuters*, March 27, 2015.

[18] ECB, "Interview of Benoît Cœuré," Frankfurt, August 14, 2015, at <http://www.ecb.europa.eu/press/key/date/2015/html/sp150814.en.html>.

of the euro area would take responsibility. The experience with Italy and Berlusconi had long since driven home the danger of political exposure for the central bank.

Later, in mid-July, Mario Draghi would defend the ECB's actions with respect to Greece similarly:[19]

> We now have a total exposure of €130bn to Greece, that makes us the biggest depositor. We had to adjust the collateral haircuts when the quality of the assets held by Greek banks deteriorated. But we didn't cut the ELA off altogether, as some people pushed for. That would have been against our mandate. We have always acted on the assumption that Greece was, and would remain, a member of the eurozone.

Who exactly pushed for cutting "ELA off altogether" is a particularly interesting question. We know that German Finance Minister Schäuble was deeply frustrated with Draghi and the ECB.[20] Despite forcing the Greek government to the bargaining table, the ECB had not put the screws to Athens completely. First, the ECB continued to drip feed ELA to the Greek banking system over the course of the winter and spring. In the process, the ECB declined to acknowledge publicly the gaping hole in the capital structure of the banking system—which in October it would find to be €14.4 billion. Second, the ECB made little effort to conceal its view that Greek debt was fundamentally unsustainable.[21] Both stances weakened the bargaining position of the creditor states in these negotiations.

GOVERNMENTS NEGOTIATE

Prime Minister Tsipras continued to try to circumvent the formal negotiating arrangements in the troika and Eurogroup. On March 15, he sent a five-page letter detailing his position and his requests from the European partners to Merkel, Hollande, and other leaders. He and Merkel met in Berlin on the evening of Monday, March 23. This was the Greek prime minister's opportunity to cut through the Gordian knot and secure a deal with the one person in the euro area that mattered most, and save the rest of the European machinery a good deal of time and energy in the process. But the German

---

[19] ECB press conference, Frankfurt, July 16, 2015, about 2:00 p.m., as quoted at Eurozone Crisis Timeline, *Guardian*, for that date.

[20] See, for example, Jan Strupczewski and Alastair MacDonald, "'Kindergarten' as Weary Euro Ministers Divide over Greece," *Reuters*, July 12, 2015.

[21] Draghi would become explicit in the summer: "It's uncontroversial that debt relief is necessary. The issue is what's the best form of debt relief. I think we should focus on this." ECB, press conference, Frankfurt, July 16, 2015.

Chancellor told her Greek counterpart that she would not negotiate the substance of the package with him. She urged Tsipras to negotiate with the institutions instead, which his government then proceeded to do.[22]

Merkel nonetheless negotiated critical details with Tsipras directly on April 23 on the margin of an EU summit on immigration and immediately before a Eurogroup meeting in Riga, Latvia.[23] Specifically, they agreed on a reduction in the primary surplus to 1.2–1.5 percent in 2015 and 2016 from program targets of 3.0 and 4.5 percent respectively.[24]

Bilateral discussions between German and Greek officials were pervasive during this period, frequent if not continuous. These conversations usually took place in preparation for meetings of the Eurogroup and European Council, on the margins of those conclaves, and shortly afterward. Communication between the finance ministers was severely strained and became infrequent as a consequence. Chancellor Merkel and Prime Minister Tsipras, by contrast, seemed to get along reasonably well. Public media document at least six meetings in person between the two of them from mid-February through late June[25]—in addition to the European Council and Euro summit meetings themselves—and at least nine telephone conversations over this period.[26] There were almost certainly further conversations that have not been publicly disclosed.

Note two things about these bilateral contacts. First, while Merkel insisted that Tsipras negotiate a program with the institutions, she was willing to wade into the details selectively, especially when the negotiations between Greece and the institutions were deadlocked. Second, Merkel brought in other European officials, the most important of whom was French President Hollande,[27] whose support would be essential in the final bargain.

On a *competing* track, Commission President Juncker also sought to mediate the conflicts between the Greek government and the rest of the European apparatus. Ostentatiously, he took the young prime minister under his wing, inviting him to bilateral meetings in Brussels in January and February and preparing alternative plans that were less demanding and hence embraced enthusiastically by the Greeks.[28] Juncker's approach soured the Commission's relationship with Berlin, but his stance on Grexit was particularly inflammatory.

[22] Peter Spiegel, "Greek Hopes Dashed over Disputed Funds," *Financial Times*, March 26, 2015.
[23] "Summary: Merkel–Tsipras Meeting Sets Tone for Eurogroup," *Guardian*, April 23, 2015.
[24] Paul Taylor, "Merkel: Must Prevent Greece Running Out of Cash before Deal," *Reuters*, April 23, 2015; "Tsipras, Merkel Fail to Agree on Key Issues," *Kathimerini*, April 23, 2015.
[25] Specifically, on February 12 in Brussels, March 23 in Berlin, April 23 in Brussels, May 21 in Riga, and June 10 and 26 in Brussels.
[26] On February 19, March 16, April 26, May 4, 28, and 31, and June 7, 21, and 28.
[27] President Hollande was included in the three meetings in May and June.
[28] For a striking example of Commission freelancing, see Peter Spiegel, "Dijsselbloem Interview: The Annotated Transcript," *Financial Times*, Brussels Blog, March 1, 2015.

"The European Commission's position is that there will be no Grexit," Juncker said. "I am totally excluding failure."[29] During the winter, the creditor countries had relied on the possibility of Grexit for leverage in bargaining with Athens, knowing that membership in the euro area was popular in Greece. Juncker's statements seemed to weaken that leverage and offered hope to Tsipras and Varoufakis that they might exploit differences between the Commission and creditor states. In the end, however, such hope proved false, reliant as the Commission ultimately was on a green light from Germany to advance any viable plan.

Consistent with earlier iterations of the negotiations with Greece, the conflict among the institutions was strong enough to lead the Commission to propose leaving the IMF behind. Merkel was equally consistent in insisting that all three institutions be included in the negotiations and the final agreement. With the backing of her European colleagues, she reiterated the necessity of including the IMF to Tsipras at a meeting of EU leaders in Riga, Latvia, in late May.[30]

On this occasion, Chancellor Merkel took on the task of personally coordinating the institutions to overcome the deadlock. She convened Juncker, Draghi, and Lagarde with French President Hollande in Berlin on the evening of Monday, June 1. Schäuble was not included in the meeting. On the basis of a paper prepared by the Commission, they hammered out a common position that was then presented to Prime Minister Tsipras and his government.[31]

In this paper, the creditors insisted on reform of the pensions system, the most difficult element for Syriza, plus an increase in the VAT and simplification of the rate schedules. By way of concession, they confirmed a significant reduction in the target for primary surpluses for 2015 and 2016 and to 3.5 percent (compared to 4.5 percent) thereafter—which required new funds beyond what had been anticipated in the existing program. A further reduction in interest rates on the loans and a deferment of payments would secure debt sustainability, but no outright reduction in the principal was offered.

For their part, U.S. officials became increasingly concerned about the lack of progress in the negotiations and the effects on financial markets. President Obama weighed in at the G7 summit, hosted by Chancellor Merkel at Elmau in the Bavarian Alps, during June 7–8. In contrast to previous such gatherings, where he pushed Germany, France, and Italy toward accommodation, Obama placed the onus mainly on the Greek government in his public remarks. "The

---

[29] "Power Struggle in Brussels and Berlin over Fate of Greece," *Spiegel Online*, March 13, 2015.
[30] Peter Spiegel, Alex Barker, Stefan Wagstyl, "Eurozone Tells Greece No Deal without IMF," *Financial Times*, May 23–4, 2015.
[31] "Greece–Policy Commitments," joint position of the institutions, June 1, 2015; Stefan Wagstyl, Peter Spiegel, Claire Jones, "Merkel Calls Emergency Summit in Berlin to Speed Up Deal on Greece," *Financial Times*, June 2, 2015.

Greeks are going to have to follow through and make some tough political choices that are going to be good in the long term," he declared.[32] The public statements of Treasury Secretary Lew at the G7 finance ministers meeting in Dresden at the end of May had been more even-handed. "All parties have to move," he said.[33] Lew emphasized "the need for more demand, particularly in countries with large current account surpluses," a pointed reference to Germany.[34]

The creditors' joint paper was the subject of an intense exchange over the following weeks that culminated in the EU summit of June 24–5 in Brussels and a follow-up meeting of the Eurogroup that was scheduled for Saturday June 27. On the morning of June 26, while still in Brussels, however, Prime Minister Tsipras suspended negotiations and called a national referendum on the troika program for Sunday, July 5. He announced the decision on national television on June 27 shortly after midnight, after returning to Athens.

On June 30, Greece defaulted on a €1.55 billion payment to the IMF. In arrears to the Fund, it was ineligible for Fund financing until the arrears were cleared. The second program, having been extended by several months, expired on the same day.

PEERING AGAIN INTO THE ABYSS

The three months from the end of June through the end of September 2015 witnessed the pinnacle of brinksmanship in the crisis—although one might have thought the euro-area member states had already exhausted their capacity for eleventh-hour drama. To preview a complex series of events, Tsipras, having called the referendum in the hope of strengthening his hand with the creditors,[35] *won* the vote. At a climactic summit a few days later, the European Council agreed in principle to extend a third program to the country. The Greek government and the troika in mid-August concluded the program on austere terms that the electorate appeared to have rejected in the referendum—at which

---

[32] He added, "I also think it's going to be important for the international community and the international financial agencies to recognize the extraordinary challenges that Greeks face. And if both sides are showing a sufficient flexibility, then I think we can get this problem resolved." The White House, Office of the Press Secretary, "Remarks by President Obama in Press Conference after G7 Summit," June 8, 2015, <https://www.whitehouse.gov/the-press-office/2015/06/08/re marks-president-obama-press-conference-after-g7-summit>.

[33] Claire Jones, Stefan Wagstyl, and Kerin Hope, "Lew Calls for Deal in Greece Talks," *Financial Times*, May 30–1, 2015.

[34] Andrea Thomas, "Jacob Lew Urges Swift Resolution to Greece Bailout Standoff," *Wall Street Journal*, May 29, 2015.

[35] Foreign leaders emphasized this interpretation of the referendum. See, for example, Mark Deen, Arne Delf, and Christos Ziotis, "Merkel and Hollande Turn Away from Greece," *Bloomberg Business*, June 29, 2015.

point the left-wing faction split from Syriza and Tsipras called a national election to affirm the program. The prime minister also won this election, in late September. The episode placed the vagaries of democratic governance in stark relief—a profound topic that we leave for another study. We emphasize here the ultimate refusal of the euro-area leaders to countenance the exit of a member, having peered together into this abyss and retreated from the precipice.

Greek Referendum

After Tsipras announced the referendum, the Greek government closed the banks for three weeks. During this time, strict limits were imposed on deposit withdrawals from the banking system, along with other capital control measures, until further notice. With the expiration of the program, the ECB had no latitude to raise the ceiling on ELA further, which effectively ended the banks' ability to redeem deposits. A euro held in the form of a deposit in a Greek bank was no longer the equivalent of a euro deposited elsewhere—one tentative step toward Grexit.

Prime Minister Tsipras campaigned against the troika proposal, asking Greeks to vote "no." His intention was to win a mandate that would strengthen his hand with the creditors, the other governments of the euro area as well as the institutions themselves. The referendum campaign was intense, confused, and relatively brief. On July 5, Tsipras won by an overwhelming majority, sixty-one percent have voted *against* the troika program.

Tsipras's victory was pyrrhic. As an attempt to extract easier terms or debt forgiveness from the European partners, the referendum backfired badly, in two respects. First, the other leaders and ministers in the European Council and Eurogroup no longer trusted the Tsipras government to faithfully implement any program to which they would agree. Second, economic conditions worsened markedly in the meantime, at least doubling the amount of funding that would be required in a third program.

The President of the Council, Donald Tusk, called a meeting of the Euro summit on Tuesday, July 7, to take stock, at which point Tsipras was told to formulate a proposal for consideration by the Eurogroup and then by another Euro summit the following weekend. That summit would be the last chance among a string of "last chances" to reach an accord.

Meanwhile, Tsipras replaced Varoufakis with Euclid Tsakalotos as finance minister. They presented a counterproposal to the European partners that looked very much like the troika proposal that had been *rejected* by the referendum! Not only was this inconsistent with the referendum result, it was out of date, given the deterioration of the economy and the banking system over the three preceding weeks.

Threat of Grexit

Creditors played hardball. "I am strongly against Grexit but I can't prevent it if the Greek government is not doing what we expected," said Juncker. "We have a Grexit scenario prepared in detail; we have a scenario as far as humanitarian aid is concerned," he added. "Our inability to find agreement may lead to the bankruptcy of Greece and the insolvency of its banking system," declared Tusk, adding, "For sure, it will be most painful for the Greek people."[36]

Wolfgang Schäuble drew the most attention by proposing that Greece exit the euro area temporarily.[37] The German finance minister believed this to be Greece's best course of action.[38] Shortly after the proposal was circulated, the Eurogroup convened but without reaching agreement. The Euro summit would finally decide and the outcome was very much in doubt. Speculation about Grexit during 2010 and 2012 had underestimated the capacity for leaders to find agreement in the clutch. But at this moment, the weekend of July 11–12, the risk of Grexit was very real.

As finance minister, Varoufakis had studied exit as an option, which he called "Plan X."[39] He had opposed Greece's entry into the monetary union in 2001. But he concluded that exit would take at least a year, would be greatly disruptive in the meantime, and thus cost far more that would be practical. It would be better to remain in the euro area and continue to battle with the creditors over debt relief and a new program.[40] Tsipras and Tsakalotos seemed to take the same view.

Some of the leaders who gathered for the Euro summit were open to Grexit. But others were vehemently opposed, with Hollande and Renzi criticizing it particularly sharply. Chancellor Merkel never publicly endorsed the Schäuble proposal, giving rise to speculation of a serious disagreement with her finance minister. Ultimately, neither she nor any of the others at the summit wanted to

---

[36] Peter Spiegel, Anne-Sylvaine Chassany, and Duncan Robinson, "Athens Given Bankruptcy Ultimatum," *Financial Times*, July 8, 2015.

[37] John Cassidy, "Grexit: An Indecent Proposal from Germany," *New Yorker*, July 12, 2015. The one-page document, which originated from the German finance ministry, was entitled "Comments on the Latest Greek Proposals," and is posted at <http://www.sven-giegold.de/wp-content/uploads/2015/07/grexit_bundesregierung_non_paper_10_juli_2015.pdf>.

[38] See, among other places, Stephen Fidler, "Fear of the Unknown Binds a Greek Deal with Few Believers," *Wall Street Journal*, July 16, 2015. Varoufakis claimed that the German finance minister was "hellbent" on Grexit.

[39] Peter Spiegel and Kerin Hope, "Yanis Varoufakis Defends 'Plan B' Tax Hack," *Financial Times*, July 27, 2015. Varoufakis provided details in a conference call organized by the Official Monetary and Financial Institutions Forum (OMFIF) in London on July 16, <https://www.youtube.com/watch?v=KXRDoEXrzb8>.

[40] See, for example, Yanis Varoufakis and Hans Werner Sinn, "The Situation in Greece and the Future of Europe," seminar at the University of Munich, October 28, 2015, <http://media thek.cesifo-group.de/iptv/player/macros/cesifo/mediathek>. He did not think a temporary exit was practical either.

take political responsibility for expelling Greece, temporarily or permanently. Note that this aversion particularly applied to Christine Lagarde, Mario Draghi, and Jean-Claude Juncker.

The Euro summit was a marathon negotiation running through the night for almost seventeen hours, probably the longest European summit. At one critical point, Merkel and Tsipras caucused with Hollande and Tusk separately to overcome disagreement on the arrangements for privatization.[41] In the end, all the leaders agreed on the outlines of a third program and what Greece would legislate as prior actions before a memorandum of understanding was finalized in the Eurogroup.

The Euro summit statement declared that a Greek request for IMF financial assistance in parallel with ESM assistance was a precondition for Eurogroup agreement on a new ESM program. The statement said that the Eurogroup stood "ready to consider, if necessary, possible additional measures (possible longer grace and payment periods) aiming at ensuring that gross financing needs remain at a sustainable level," which "will be considered after the first positive completion of a review" of the new program. At the same time, the summit ruled out nominal haircuts on the debt.[42]

In mid-July, U.S. officials took an increasingly explicit position on the need for debt relief for Greece. During meetings with his German and French counterparts, Treasury Secretary Jacob Lew underscored "the importance of achieving debt sustainability in the upcoming negotiations," the Treasury Department said. "Without dealing with some form of debt restructuring this problem will just come right back," a senior U.S. Treasury official said.[43] Schäuble showed his sense of humor, saying, "I offered to my friend Jack Lew that we would take Puerto Rico into the eurozone, if the USA took Greece into the dollar union. He thought I was joking."[44]

Third Program

Launching negotiations for an ESM program required ex ante approval by national governments, several of which required, in turn, parliamentary authorization. Of these, the debate in the German Bundestag, which took place on July 17, was most climactic. Schäuble gave an impassioned presentation. His reservations about a third program were well known—personally he continued to favor temporary Grexit—but as finance minister he backed

[41] Anne-Sylvaine Chassany, Alex Barker, and Duncan Robinson, "'Sorry, But There is No Way You Are Leaving This Room'," *Financial Times*, July 14, 2015.

[42] Euro Summit, "Statement," Brussels, July 12, 2014 (SN 4070/15).

[43] Stephen Fidler, "Fear of the Unknown Binds a Greek Deal with Few Believers," *Wall Street Journal*, July 16, 2015.

[44] "Eurozone Crisis Live," *Guardian*, July 16, 2015, 9:51 a.m.

the chancellor and called for an affirmative vote.[45] Sixty members of the CDU and CSU defected. But with nearly unanimous support of the SPD, the bill passed by a large margin.

Within hours after the Bundestag vote, and with other member states having also backed the launch of negotiations, the Eurogroup convened by videoconference to authorize a bridge loan through the EFSM for Greece. That loan would cover Greece's obligations—including a large payment to the ECB and clearing arrears to the IMF—while the third program was being finalized, approved, and its first tranche disbursed. With bridge financing in place, Greek authorities allowed the banks to reopen on Monday, July 20, while keeping in place the capital controls.

Greece's third program, announced on August 14, made €86 billion available from the ESM over a period of three years (see Appendix: Financial Rescues for Euro-Area Countries, 2010–2015). Of this amount, €54 billion was designated for medium- and long-term debt service, €15 billion for the clearance of arrears with the IMF and other creditors plus the build-up of cash buffers, and €25 billion for the recapitalization of the banking sector. Because Greece was required to run a primary surplus, almost none of the financing would go to cover current deficits.[46]

As a condition for this financing, Tsipras's government agreed to spending cuts and tax increases that would amount to more than four percent of GDP (on a continuing basis) by 2018. These included the reforms to the pension system and VAT increases that Syriza had strongly resisted. In contrast to previous programs, notably, the government was required to adopt many of these measures as *prior actions*, that is, *pre*conditions for the first disbursement.[47] Such was the lack of trust on the part of the creditors with respect to implementation. Greece accepted primary surplus targets of −0.25 percent of GDP in 2015, 0.5 percent in 2016, 1.75 percent in 2017, and 3.5 percent in 2018, and an undefined period beyond that into the future.[48]

---

[45] See, for example, Cerstin Gammelin, "Griechenland Debatte–Nicht Überzeugt, Nicht Überzeugend," *Süddeustche Zeitung*, July 17, 2015.

[46] "Eurogroup Statement on the ESM Programme for Greece," General Secretariat of the Council, Press Office, Brussels, August 14, 2015; "Memorandum of Understanding between the European Commission and the Hellenic Republic," Brussels, August 14, 2015; and European Stability Mechanism, "The ESM Programme for Greece," Luxembourg, August 14, 2015.

[47] European Commission, "Report on Greece's compliance with the draft MOU commitments and the commitments in the Euro Summit statement of 12 July 2015," Brussels, August 14, 2015. On the lessons from prior actions at the IMF, see Alessandro Leipold, "Two (Potentially Fatal) Achilles' Heels: Can a Mythical Greek Accord Be Made to Work?," The Lisbon Council, *Economic Intelligence* Issue 08/2015.

[48] "Memorandum of Understanding between the European Commission Acting on Behalf of the European Stability Mechanism and the Hellenic Republic and The Bank of Greece," Brussels and Athens, August 19, 2015. This and most of the other documents related to the third program can be found on the Commission's website <http://ec.europa.eu/economy_finance/assistance_eu_ms/greek_loan_facility/index_en.htm>.

Athens agreed as well on further structural reforms in labor and product markets, privatization, and, importantly, restructuring of the banking system. The nonperforming loans in the Greek banking system were estimated to be more than thirty-five percent of total loans.[49] The four main systemically important banks, plus the smaller banks, underwent a new round of stress tests that was conducted by the SSM in October 2015, which identified a need for €14.4 billion in new capital.[50] The recapitalization was carried out quickly thereafter to avoid having to bail-in large uninsured depositors under the new rules of the banking union that kicked in at the beginning of 2016.[51] The stabilization of the banking system was expected to pave the way for the elimination of controls on deposit withdrawals, repatriation of deposit flight, and ratcheting back of banks' reliance on ELA.

DUELING DEBT ANALYSES

As with the first and second programs, the sustainability of debt was at the center of the debates, both official and academic, over the third program. The IMF's reservations about the sustainability of debt were known over the course of the winter and spring of 2015,[52] but the Fund did not trumpet them publicly. Frustrated with the resistance to his insistence on debt restructuring, Varoufakis had asked Christine Lagarde in the June 2015 meeting of the Eurogroup whether the IMF could certify that Greece's debt was sustainable. She could not, of course.[53]

The troika presented a paper to the EU summit in late June that presented three scenarios and assessed them on *both* a debt-to-GDP and gross-financing basis. Doing so was itself a concession on the part of the Fund, which had been using the November 2012 framework, centered on the debt-to-GDP measure, as an argument for more generous debt reduction. The document found that debt was likely sustainable on a gross-financing basis under two of the three scenarios. The third scenario, however, did not find debt to be sustainable, and

[49] Eleni Louri-Dendrinou, "Greece, the Euro Crisis and the European Banking Union," presentation at American University, Washington, D.C., October 14, 2015.

[50] ECB, Banking Supervision, "Aggregate Report on the Greek Comprehensive Assessment 2015," and "ECB finds total capital shortfall of €14.4 billion for four significant Greek banks," Frankfurt, October 31, 2015.

[51] Miranda Xafa, "Greece," in *European Banking Supervision: The First Eighteen Months*, eds Dirk Schoenmaker and Nicolas Véron, Bruegel Blueprint 25, Brussels, June 2016, pp. 101–13.

[52] Varoufakis writes that Poul Thomsen was even more eager for debt relief than he was as finance minister in February 2015. Yanis Varoufakis, "Endgame for the IMF–EU Feud over Greece's Debt," *Spiegel Online*, April 3, 2016.

[53] Landon Thomas, "The Greek Debt Deal's Missing Piece," *New York Times*, August 16, 2015. The story is corroborated later by Yanis Varoufakis.

this was the IMF's baseline scenario.[54] Frustrated by the way their analysis was downplayed at the summit, officials at the Fund decided to release their debt sustainability analysis.[55]

The IMF made its analysis public a couple of days before the referendum on July 6. The report observed that in late summer 2014, no further debt relief would have been needed had the program been implemented as agreed. But, backtracking by the new government and the need for new loans changed that picture fundamentally:[56]

> Coming on top of the very high existing debt, these new financing needs render the debt dynamics unsustainable. This conclusion holds whether one examines the stock of debt under the November 2012 framework or switches the focus to debt servicing or gross financing needs. To ensure that debt is sustainable with high probability, Greek policies will need to come back on track but also, at a minimum, the maturities of existing European loans will need to be extended significantly while new European financing to meet financing needs over the coming years will need to be provided on similar concessional terms. But if the package of reforms under consideration is weakened further—in particular, through a further lowering of primary surplus targets and even weaker structural reforms—*haircuts on debt will become necessary* [emphasis added].

The Fund's release noted that this analysis had been prepared before the closing of the banks, imposition of capital controls and arrears to the Fund, all of which would increase the need for debt relief compared to its projections in the report. Releasing the document publicly laid bare the differences among the troika institutions and the euro-area creditors. Posting it during the referendum campaign certainly reflected a view that the Greek electorate's choice to reject or accept a program should be premised on a realistic debt assessment. But it also no doubt reflected a calculation that the institution should disassociate itself from the more optimistic scenarios of the Europeans to limit damage to its credibility in the event that further relief were denied and the third program were to fail.

The Commission responded with the publication of its own DSA on July 10, on the eve of the Euro summit meeting. That document pointed to "serious concerns regarding the sustainability of Greece's public debt."[57] Nearly simultaneously, the IMF updated its DSA for the Euro summit as well. It began, "Greece's public debt has become highly unsustainable," and noted that debt

---

[54] "Preliminary Debt Sustainability Analysis for Greece," June 25, 2015, <http://online.wsj.com/public/resources/documents/eurogroupdebtanalysis.pdf>.

[55] Landon Thomas, "The Greek Debt Deal's Missing Piece," *New York Times*, August 16, 2015.

[56] IMF, "Greece: Preliminary Draft Debt Sustainability Analysis," *Country Report* No. 15/165, June 26, 2015.

[57] European Commission, "Greece—Request for Stability Support in the Form of an ESM Loan," Brussels, July 10, 2015, pp. 6–8.

was now projected to peak close to 200 percent of GDP. "Greece's debt can now only be made sustainable through debt relief measures that go far beyond what Europe has been willing to consider so far." It offered a menu that included maturity extension, a "very dramatic" extension of grace periods on all of the debt, outright transfers, and "deep upfront haircuts," leaving the choice to Greece and its European partners.[58]

Haircuts were, of course, the red line that the German government had said that it would not cross. Finance Minister Schäuble even pronounced them *illegal* under the treaties and the Euro summit of July 11–12 thus ruled them out explicitly. So, planning would consider the other options, further extension of maturities and longer grace periods[59]—but only after the program was faithfully implemented and certified by a review. These could be a reward for good behavior ex post rather than a concession up front.

The Fund therefore *declined* to contribute the financing that it had notionally placed on the table in the troika negotiations. Having declared Greek debt to be unsustainable, it could only lend through activation of the systemic exemption. This was theoretically possible but blocked in practice by two factors. First, nearly every European finance minister, except possibly Yanis Varoufakis, seemed to repeat the mantra that Greece's problems were not a threat to the euro area as a whole. Invoking the systemic exemption was hardly consistent with those assurances. Second, more importantly, some non-European countries in the Fund strongly resisted activating the systemic exemption for a third Greek program.

The Fund's position, articulated in a statement by the managing director, was that Greece could not restore debt sustainability by its action alone and the European partners would have to provide debt relief "well beyond what has been considered so far." With this, plus pension and banking sector reforms, she could recommend a financial contribution from the Fund after the first program review.[60] David Lipton, First Deputy Managing Director, would later elaborate, saying, "We want a debt operation agreed between Greece and its creditors." Lipton said, "For us to go forward, we want more than a general assurance that the matter will be handled, with enough specific details on how it will be handled to assure the fund that Greece's debt service will be on a sustainable path."[61]

[58] IMF, "Greece: An Update of IMF Staff's Preliminary Public Debt Sustainability Analysis," *Country Report* No. 15/186.

[59] For analysis, see William R. Cline, "From Populist Destabilization to Reform and Possible Debt Relief in Greece," *Peterson Institute Policy Brief* 15-12, Washington, D.C., August 2015.

[60] IMF, "Statement by IMF Managing Director Christine Lagarde on Greece," press release No. 15/381, August 14, 2015.

[61] Rebecca Christie and Andrew Mayeda, "IMF Pushes Europe for Formal Restructuring Accord on Greek Debt," *Bloomberg*, November 1, 2015.

Notwithstanding disagreement over debt relief, Chancellor Merkel and her finance minister continued to insist on the IMF being involved in the program, including in a lending capacity.[62] Their attachment to the Fund was reflected in the statement of the Eurogroup at the time of approval of the third program on August 14. The Eurogroup statement described "the continued programme involvement of the IMF as indispensable" and welcomed the intention of the managing director to recommend a financial contribution once "an agreement on possible debt relief to ensure debt sustainability has been reached." The IMF's contribution would reduce the ESM share of the package correspondingly, it said. The Eurogroup described policy conditionality as shared, as it had been developed in parallel among the three institutions.[63] In the meantime, Fund staff would continue to participate in troika missions and quarterly reviews of the program.

The debate in the Bundestag on August 19 over final approval of the third program highlighted the tension between debt restructuring and IMF involvement. Presenting the program, Minister Schäuble insisted that "[f]urther plans will not encompass haircuts," financial participation of the IMF was "unavoidable," and he did not have the "slightest doubt" that the Fund would join on the basis of agreement on debt sustainability.[64] Members from the Left and the Green Party argued that this was a contradiction.[65] But members from the CDU and CSU were adamant that there would be no haircut and IMF participation was necessary.[66]

Spared from defaulting on the July 20 payments, Prime Minister Tsipras set about passing legislation to satisfy his government's commitments under prior actions and the first review. The left-wing faction of his party, led by Panagiotis Lafazanis, continued to resist many of these measures.[67] So, Tsipras called yet another national vote for late September—an election that would serve as a vote of confidence in the program and his government. The Lafazanis faction split from the rest of Syriza, campaigned against the program, and lost. The portion of Syriza that remained loyal to Tsipras polled nearly as well as the party had performed in the previous election in January. Many European officials would have preferred that Tsipras create a more

---

[62] "Griechenlandhilfe: Schäuble und Merkel Ringen um Rettungspolitik," *Der Spiegel*, August 14, 2015.

[63] Eurogroup, "Eurogroup Statement on the ESM Programme for Greece," General Secretariat of the Council Press Office, Brussels, August 14, 2015.

[64] German Bundestag, Plenary Transcript, Stenographic Report, 118th Session, Berlin, Wednesday, August 19, 2015, <http://dipbt.bundestag.de/doc/btp/18/18118.pdf>. The minister's remarks appear at #11457-58.

[65] German Bundestag, Plenary Transcript, August 19, 2015, at 11460–65 and 11473.

[66] German Bundestag, Plenary Transcript, August 19, 2015, at 11471 and 11511.

[67] On the Lafazanis faction's hostility to the third program and willingness to entertain Grexit, see Kerin Hope and Tony Barber, "Syriza's Covert Plot during Crisis Talks to Return to Drachma," *Financial Times*, July 24, 2015.

stable basis for implementing the memorandum by inviting To Potami and/or PASOK to join the governing coalition. Tsipras disappointed them by instead renewing Syriza's partnership with the Independent Greeks.

PROTRACTED FIRST REVIEW

The decisions on the third program in July and August 2015 anticipated a first review in the autumn, on the basis of which European creditors would then decide whether to grant debt relief in the form concessional interest rates and the further extension of maturities. With relief, observers anticipated, the IMF could deem debt to be sustainable and thus contribute to the financial package of the program. That scenario, contingent as it was, would have been uncharacteristically straightforward for a program for Greece. Instead, the first review dragged on for eight months, drawn out by deadlock between the IMF and the European Commission again over Greek policies and the adjustment measures.

Love–Hate Triangle

The first review boiled down to three-way bargaining among Berlin, the IMF in Washington, and Athens. Berlin wanted tough fiscal measures still, to stabilize the Greek government finances over the long term. The Commission did not want to push Athens beyond the measures envisaged in summer 2015; the IMF served Berlin's objectives better in this respect.[68] The IMF continued to press for pension cuts and (with bank restructuring completed at the end of 2015) an expansion of the tax base, arguing that *still more* needed to be done in order to reach the primary surplus targets that were identified in the program. The Fund conceded that haircuts on the outstanding principal would not be necessary in order to achieve debt relief sufficient to warrant its financial participation—that could be achieved through a longer moratorium on interest rate payments and a very long-term extension of maturities. But—and this was the Fund's central position—the primary surplus targets and planned debt relief had to be consistent.[69]

Although Fund officials sometimes appeared to be indifferent among the choices of the arithmetically viable options, the IMF staff was not, in fact, neutral. The officials who were driving the Fund's position did not believe that the 3.5 percent target for the primary surplus was politically realistic over the

[68] Interviews with European officials, Washington, D.C., April 15 and 16, June 2, 3, and 6, 2016.

[69] Poul Thomsen, "Greece: Toward a Workable Program," *iMFdirect*, February 11, 2016.

long term. Some other European governments were running or were expected to run primary surpluses of this magnitude; but none of them had suffered a collapse of the economy on the order of twenty-five percent.[70] Achieving these targets over time would have to survive multiple elections in the face of very high unemployment and political fragmentation. IMF officials therefore recommended a more modest target for the primary surplus of 1.5 percent over the long term.[71]

As a medium-term target for the end of the third program, in 2018, the IMF would nonetheless acquiesce to the 3.5 percent figure. But it rejected the calculations of the Commission and the European Stability Mechanism with respect to the fiscal measures that would be required to achieve that target. The impasse held up agreement on the first review through the end of 2015 and early 2016. Using 2016 as the baseline, the Commission estimated that a 3.0 percent fiscal effort would be needed to reach the target. The IMF expected that Greece would have to undertake spending cuts and revenue increases amounting to 4.5 percent. Eventually, after meeting on the sidelines of the spring meetings of the IMF and World Bank in April 2016, they bridged their disagreement by having Greece prepare *two* sets of measures—one package of legislation equivalent to 3.0 percent of GDP and a "contingency mechanism" that would provide further reductions amounting to as much as 1.5 percent if the IMF turned out to be correct that the first package would be insufficient.[72] Greek Finance Minister Euclid Tsakalotos protested the contingency mechanism but ultimately accepted it.

"Dynamite with a Lighted Candle"

Frustrated at the stance that Poul Thomsen and the Fund management were taking, Prime Minister Tsipras repeated his earlier attempt to jettison the IMF

[70] For a review of country experience, see Barry Eichengreen and Ugo Panizza, "A Surplus of Ambition: Can Europe Rely on Large Primary Surpluses to Solve Its Debt Problem?," *Economic Policy* 31 (85): 5–39.

[71] Christine Lagarde presented this position in a letter she circulated to all of the finance ministers ahead of the May 9, 2016 Eurogroup meeting. She also argued that the point had come where the two issues, the fiscal package and debt relief, must be considered together rather than sequentially. Peter Spiegel, "Leaked: The Annotated Lagarde Letter on Greece," *Financial Times*, Brussels Blog, May 6, 2016. The full letter is reproduced in Marcus Walker, "Lagarde to Eurozone: IMF Won't Budge on Greece," *Wall Street Journal*, May 6, 2016.

[72] Marcus Walker, "Greece Creditors Push for More Austerity," *Wall Street Journal*, April 18, 2016; Council of the European Union, Eurogroup Statement on Greece, Brussels, May 9, 2016; Council of the European Union, "Remarks by J. Dijsselbloem following the Eurogroup Meeting of 9 May 2016," Brussels, May 9, 2016. As later agreed at the Eurogroup meeting of May 25, 2016, the contingency mechanism created a process by which additional measures would be introduced automatically if Greece fell short of the primary surplus targets, but not the particular structural reforms that the IMF had recommended.

from among "the institutions." He did so during the deadlock over fiscal adjustment in late 2015, but was rebuffed by the finance ministers of Finland, the Netherlands, and Germany.[73] Schäuble explained that the German and other parliaments had agreed to aid Greece on condition that the IMF remained engaged in the program. Asking the Bundestag to change that agreement would be like "entering a room full of dynamite with a lighted candle."[74]

Tsipras's next attempt to marginalize the Fund was more sensational—a leak of the transcript of a clandestine eavesdrop of a teleconference among officials in the IMF's troika mission to Athens. The recording was almost certainly made by Greek government security services, although this is not publicly acknowledged or otherwise confirmed. The transcript appeared on Wikileaks on April 2.[75] A record of a conversation among Thomsen, his mission chief Delia Velculescu, and another staff member, it underscored their frustration with the Commission and inability to bring to a conclusion the impasse over the review. They lamented the absence of an action-forcing event until Greece was scheduled to make large payments in the second half of July. The Greek government chose to interpret this passage as an attempt to create a crisis, in order to put the IMF on the defensive.[76]

Managing Director Lagarde responded swiftly with a public letter to Tsipras, saying, "Of course, any speculation that IMF staff would consider using a credit event as a negotiating tactic is simply nonsense."[77] She met with Chancellor Merkel in Berlin on April 4. Speaking together before the press, the two women acknowledged the differences among the players in the negotiations and Merkel repeated her opposition to haircuts. "It is not a demand of the federal government to have no debt haircut, but rather in our opinion this is legally not possible in the euro zone." But they affirmed their determination to work constructively toward a conclusion of the review.[78]

---

[73] Euclid Tsakalotos said, "Alexander Stubb, Jeroen Dijsselbloem and Wolfgang Schäuble made it clear the IMF is a *sine qua non*. Not just in terms of technical assistance but active involvement in the financial package.... But the IMF is also pressurizing countries... on debt relief. On both sides it seems to be difficult. But the involvement of the IMF is agreed. This is our commitment." "Interview: Greek Finance Minister," *Handelsblatt*, January 14, 2016.

[74] "Davos: Tsipras, Schaeuble Discuss IMF Involvement in Greek Bailout," *Kathimerini*, January 21, 2016.

[75] With an article prepared by Julian Assange. See "19 March 2016 IMF Teleconference on Greece," *Wikileaks*, April 8, 2016,<https://wikileaks.org/imf-internal-20160319/transcript/IMF %20Anticipates%20Greek%20Disaster.pdf>.

[76] The Greek government spokeswoman said, "The Greek government is demanding explanations from the IMF over whether seeking to create default conditions in Greece, shortly ahead of the referendum in Britain, is the fund's official position." Rebecca Burn-Callander, "Greece Challenges IMF over WikiLeaks Revelations," *Telegraph*, April 2, 2016.

[77] IMF, "IMF Managing Director Christine Lagarde Letter to Greece Prime Minister Alexis Tsipras," press release No. 16/149, April 3, 2016.

[78] "Merkel–Lagarde: Determined to Continue to Help on Greece," *The Press Project*, April 5, 2016.

Tangled Governance

They would not, in other words, allow the Greek Prime Minister to drive a wedge between them.

The episode revealed a couple of things about the institutional politics of the third program. First, it highlighted the closeness between Berlin and the IMF notwithstanding differences over debt sustainability and debt relief. Tsipras's attack on the IMF had been an indirect attack on Berlin's position on fiscal adjustment measures. Second, it illustrated relative empathy between the Greek government and the European Commission. By attempting to exclude the Fund from the program altogether, the Greek government hoped for more lenience in the adjustment program. That would have required revisiting further measures or debt relief later, if the Fund were right about the program not yet "adding up." But Tsipras's time horizon was not distant: the fiscal bird-in-the-hand in the short term would have been worth two debt relief birds-in-the-bush in the long term.

Debt Showdown, Spring 2016

Deadlock over debt sustainability in winter and spring 2016 repeated in many respects the disputes among the institutions in 2015, but with two important differences. The United States Congress finally approved the quota increase and reforms for the IMF, more than five years after they had been agreed in 2010, allowing them to go into effect. These, first, doubled Greece's quota in the Fund. As a condition for congressional approval, second, the Obama administration sought to close the systemic exemption, to which the Executive Board agreed in January 2016.[79] The closure meant that, in principle, the threat of international contagion was no longer a valid basis for lending to a country whose debt the Fund staff could not deem to be sustainable with "high probability." Debt would have to be restructured before the Fund would be able to grant exceptional access to Greece.

The IMF staff and management thus continued to strike a correspondingly tough negotiating position on the debt, which also coincided with the expressed preferences of many non-European member states.[80] But the global environment posed potential threats to systemic stability. The European Union's complicated relationship to Turkey undermined confidence that the refugee crisis had been resolved. The Federal Reserve had begun to raise interest rates in December 2015 and China and other emerging markets experienced a new

[79] IMF, "IMF Executive Board Approves Exceptional Access Lending Framework Reforms," press release No. 16/31, January 29, 2016.

[80] The former U.S. Executive Director of the Fund opposed financial participation, for example. Meg Lundsager, "Commentary: Why the IMF Must Walk Away from Greece," *Reuters*, May 17, 2016.

wave of financial volatility. The British referendum on membership in the European Union loomed on June 23. The electorate would surprise financial markets by voting to leave, although that outcome was given long odds in the spring.

These threats to stability placed a premium on completing the first review in May even if it did not secure definitive debt relief. The review would be completed in a series of European and international meetings during April and May 2016, the Eurogroup meeting of May 24 being critical. Disbursements were necessary for payments that Greece was scheduled to make in the second half of July and finance ministers wished to avoid any drama over the completion of the review during the run-up to the British referendum.

Eurogroup finance ministers again received dueling debt sustainability analyses prior to their meeting on May 24, one prepared by the ESM in consultation with the other European institutions and another prepared by the IMF. The ESM paper presented alternative scenarios that quantified the benefits of reprofiling the EFSF loans and transferring the €8 billion in profits from ANFA and SMP to Greece.[81] These measures would push gross financing needs (GFN) as a percentage of GDP below twenty percent in the very long term.[82] The European institutions' proposal carried the benefit from the creditors' domestic political perspective of avoiding such requirements.

The Fund's competing DSA was founded on different premises with regard to the primary surplus and long-term growth rate. Emphasizing that the Greek government's policy trajectory fell "well short of what would be required to achieve their ambitious fiscal and growth target" under the program, the Fund reiterated its belief that the target for the primary surplus should be 1.5 percent, rather than 3.5 percent. As far as long-term growth was concerned, the Fund reasoned that the 1.25 percent was the *best* that Greece could expect, given the modest extent of structural reform and prospects for investment and its declining working-age population.[83]

---

[81] These profits stem from holdings of Greek government bonds at the ECB and the national central banks. ANFA refers to the Agreement on Net Financial Assets. See ECB, "What is ANFA?," Frankfurt, February 5, 2016 (updated April 7, 2016).

[82] European Stability Mechanism, "Greece: Proposal for Debt Relief Measures," May 2016. Intriguingly, the paper also floated the possibility of buying out the IMF's share at the end of the program in 2018, a suggestion that was not adopted in the subsequent Eurogroup meeting. Both the European and IMF DSAs anticipated that the ECB would lift inflation to the upper limit of its two percent target, although even the ECB itself could not envisage reaching that target in the medium term.

[83] The European institutions' baseline scenario envisaged growth of 1.5 percent into the second half of the 2020s. Their adverse scenario was closer to the IMF's "best," with growth down to 1.3 percent by 2025. Both DSAs expected growth near three percent during 2017–19. See the European institutions' paper, "Greece: Proposal for Debt Relief Measures," for the May 9 Eurogroup meeting, <http://online.wsj.com/media/greece-debt-measures-05102016.pdf>.

The IMF's baseline scenario thus forecast unsustainable outcomes in the long term on *both* the debt ratio and gross financing requirement. Fund staff proposed that European official creditors extend maturities much further, defer interest payments until 2040, and cap interest rates at 1.5 percent. Such a restructuring would deliver a net-present-value benefit of about fifty percent of GDP and, more importantly, prevent gross financing needs from rising above twenty percent in the out years. With such a restructuring, the Fund staff could assess Greek debt to be sustainable, opening the path for financial participation in the program.[84] Critically, however, it would also have budgetary implications for member states and would have thus required parliamentary approval in many of them.

Between the presentation of the two DSAs and the Eurogroup meeting fell the meeting of G7 finance ministers and central bank governors in Sendai, Japan. This was the moment for the United States, Britain, Japan, as well as Canada to weigh in on the European negotiations, certainly as far as the involvement of the IMF was concerned. Would they nudge the IMF to yield and accept *de minimis* concessions on debt? Or would they reinforce Lagarde's hard-line position on debt relief and push German Finance Minister Schäuble to be more forthcoming?

Greece was discussed in the plenary meeting, though apparently not at length. The more serious consultations took place bilaterally on the margin of the plenary. U.S. Treasury Secretary Lew held bilateral meetings with Jeroen Dijsselbloem and Wolfgang Schäuble. "The Secretary underscored the importance of Europe following through on its commitment to put Greece's debt on a sustainable path through meaningful debt relief," the Treasury Department reported. But, he added, "[A]ll parties need to be flexible to successfully conclude the negotiations."[85] Christine Lagarde held a bilateral meeting with Minister Schäuble as well. The issue was not decided in Sendai, but the bilateral and plenary meetings there helped to pave the way for the bargain that was decided a couple of days later in the Eurogroup. As in previous instances of deadlock among the institutions, the key countries mediated this impasse.

---

[84] IMF, "Greece: Preliminary Debt Sustainability Analysis–Updated Estimates and Further Considerations," *Country Report* No. 16/130, May 2016. The document was leaked to the media then posted on the Fund's website before the Eurogroup meeting of May 25.

[85] Embassy of the United States, "Readout from a Treasury Spokesperson of Secretary Lew's Meeting with German Finance Minister Wolfgang Schäuble at the G7 in Sendai, Japan," Athens, Greece, May 21, 2016. The Secretary's public remarks remained fairly evenhanded. "I also continued to urge the importance of finding a pragmatic and sustainable solution for Greece that includes meaningful debt relief as it continues to deliver on reform implementation," Lew told reporters after the G7 meeting. U.S. Treasury Department, "Treasury Secretary Jacob J. Lew Statement at the G7 Finance Ministers and Central Bank Governors Meeting in Sendai, Japan," press release, Washington, D.C., May 21, 2016.

The German finance minister confronted a domestic political problem that was similar to the problem his government faced at the initiation of the third program: Schäuble and Merkel wanted the IMF on board but did not want to grant debt relief. Their strategy was to defer relief that rose to a level that would require approval of the Bundestag until *after* the federal election in September or October 2017, while promising the minimum necessary to entice the Fund to contribute financially after the first review. Given opposition among many developing and emerging-market countries to the IMF's participation, European creditors' influence in the Executive Board and the posture of the United States would be critical to the success of the German strategy.

In Brussels on May 24, the Eurogroup, perhaps predictably, opted for modest debt relief in the short term. The IMF was represented by Poul Thomsen, who was accompanied by Sean Hagan, the Fund's General Counsel. Sealing the bargain was delayed for four hours by consultations between Thomsen and Lagarde, who was on an official visit to Kazakhstan. German Finance Minister Schäuble reportedly objected to the wait, apparently having expected that the bargain had been substantially settled a couple of days earlier in Sendai. The Europeans in the meeting reported that Thomsen was frustrated and unhappy on his return to the group after consultation with Lagarde.[86]

The Eurogroup committed in its statement to a package of debt measures.[87] In the medium and long term, these could include the EFSF loan reprofiling and capping of interest rates that were in the IMF's DSA, among other measures. But these were contingent on a daunting string of conditions: adverse economic scenarios, new DSAs by the institutions, and, importantly, full implementation of the program by Greece. Even if these conditions were satisfied, a decision would be taken on them only at the end of the program in 2018. Only in the short term was something more definite planned—a smoothing of the peaks in interest payments without changing the average maturity of EFSF loans. The program still targeted a primary surplus of 3.5 percent of GDP for 2018.[88]

For its part, the IMF agreed with the package of policy measures, but not that it would secure the 3.5 percent target for 2018, and did not agree to that target for the duration of the program. Nonetheless, Fund management expressed its "intention" to recommend to the Executive Board approval of

---

[86] Jan Strupczewski, "Lagarde Remote Control Makes Europeans Doubt IMF Role in Greek Deal," *Reuters*, May 27, 2016.

[87] Eurogroup, "Eurogroup Statement on Greece," Brussels, May 25, 2016. See, also, ESM, "FAQ on Decisions Concerning Greece at Eurogroup Meeting on 25 may 2016," Luxembourg, <http://esm.europa.eu/assistance/Greece/index.htm>.

[88] See, also, Alex Barker, Mehreen Khan, and Shawn Donnan, "Greek Debt Deal Leaves Key Points Open," *Financial Times*, May 26, 2016; Viktoria Dendrinou and Gabriele Steinhauser, "Eurozone, IMF Strike Deal on Greek Debt," *Wall Street Journal*, May 25, 2016.

a financial contribution before the end of 2016. The statement was important because the Executive Board could not act on a program except on a proposal from the staff; recommending approval would relinquish the effective veto that management has over the process. The text of the Eurogroup statement was muddled on whether that recommendation would be subject to a finding that debt was sustainable, but the Fund quickly clarified that it would be.[89] The DSA would be updated once the Eurogroup's short-term measures were specified.

Effectively, the Eurogroup and IMF deferred the decision on the Fund's participation until the end of 2016. But, as of summer 2016, it was not at all clear that the IMF would make any definitive decision either to contribute financially or reject financial participation even at the end of the year. The May Eurogroup result opened the prospect that the IMF might *never* declare definitively that it would *not* participate in the program even if debt relief were coming too little too late. Such a declaration would trigger acknowledgments to domestic critics of the program that the governments of creditor states were eager to avoid. The German government, in particular, was thus satisfied with ambiguity about the role of the Fund. President Obama, speaking of the need to accelerate global economic growth, noted "the fact that the Greek debt crisis has been resolved for a reasonable length of time I think should help."[90] As long as the United States acceded to this position—as the swing member between the Europeans and emerging market and developing countries—the door could be kept open indefinitely. Given the constraints, ambiguity about the IMF's financial role best served the key members.

VIABILITY OF THE PROGRAM

The program was widely derided in the summer of 2015 as a repeat of an austerity formula that had already proven to be a failure. This criticism came from across the political spectrum in Europe and the United States. Paul Krugman, for example, called the third program "pure vindictiveness" and a "complete destruction of national sovereignty."[91] (Schäuble responded that

---

[89] IMF, "Excerpt from a Eurogroup Press Conference on Greece: Transcript of Quotes by Poul Thomsen," Brussels, May 24, 2016; IMF, "Transcript of a Press Briefing with Gerry Rice, Director, Communications Department," Washington, D.C., May 19, 2016.

[90] The White House, Office of the Press Secretary, "Remarks by President Obama in Press Availability—Ise-Shima, Japan," press release, Washington, D.C., May 26, 2016.

[91] Paul Krugman, "Killing the European Project," *New York Times* blog, July 12, 2015. See, also, presentations by Ashoka Mody, Anne Krueger, Athanasios Orphanïdes, Plutarchos Sakellaris, and Desmond Lachman at the AEI seminar, "Does Greece Pose a Threat to the Euro?," April 17, 2015, <https://www.aei.org/events/does-greece-pose-a-threat-to-the-euro>.

Krugman "has no idea about the architecture and foundation of the European currency union.") Outrage against the program dominated Twitter the day after the July Euro summit under #ThisIsACoup. The list of conditions was indeed onerous, unprecedentedly so as "prior actions."[92]

However, Grexit would certainly have been costly and would not have enabled Greece to avoid austerity over the medium term. Virtually all of the structural reforms demanded of the government were desirable irrespective of the program—indeed necessary to have a hope of raising Greece's long-term growth rate. In contrast, by remaining within the monetary union and sticking with the program, Greece benefited from bank recapitalization within the context of the banking union, which gave the exercise credibility. These, in turn, enabled Greek banks to regain access to regular refinancing at the ECB and perhaps eliminate capital controls.[93] This strategy is Greece's best hope of making these reforms pay off.

Advocates of Grexit seem to assume that, once outside the euro area, the Greek government would become well functioning. Economic policy would be administered in such a way as to reap the benefits of a currency depreciation: the Bank of Greece would be independent, monetary policy would be stabilizing, and wage and price movements would not offset the competitive advantage gained from the currency adjustment. Privatization would proceed apace and the resources saved through restructuring or defaulting on the debt, rendered definitively unsustainable as a consequence of depreciation, would be well employed. These assumptions are both implicit and heroic.

Notice that those who advocate Grexit with the greatest conviction are generally not Greek. Membership in the monetary union and the European Union has been domestically popular precisely because Greeks recognize the weaknesses in their national governance. The euro-area programs with Greece are a project to radically transform the politics and political institutions of the country, not merely to change the policy settings. Through them, the country has a chance of closing down space for clientelistic politics, reforming the relationship between the state and the economy, and solidifying a new domestic political consensus on these matters.

Success in this transformative project requires transcending austerity and returning to growth. Neither the IMF nor the European Commission seemed to be realistic about the impact of further fiscal contraction on the economy, however. They forecast that the Greek economy would nonetheless grow at a

[92] At a critical moment in July, the Chief Economist and Director of the Research Department at the Fund defended the general approach of the programs. See Olivier Blanchard, "Greece: Past Critiques and the Path Forward," *iMFdirect*, July 9, 2015. See, also, the response by Guntram B. Wolff, "Olivier Blanchard Fails to Recognise Two Major IMF Mistakes in Greece," Bruegel Blog, Brussels, July 14, 2015.
[93] ECB, "ECB Reinstates Waiver Affecting Eligibility of Greek Bonds," press release, Frankfurt, June 22, 2016.

relatively robust rate of nearly three percent on average during 2017–19. Such a rebound would be plausible only with a very robust revival of Greek exports, including tourism, and investment. Although renewing access to regular refinancing facilities at the ECB and dismantling capital controls would surely help, the modest pace of privatization and structural reform, overhang of nonperforming loans in the banking sector, weak demand in the rest of Europe, continuing refugee crisis, and tenuous political position of the Syriza government weighed against optimism about growth.

Restarting growth in this environment would require instead a reduction in the primary surplus targets and a large debt restructuring. Haircuts would not be the most important contribution to this package—the present value of forgiveness on debt that does not mature for thirty years is modest. Reducing interest servicing, including through a moratorium on payments, and extending very long maturities would provide more meaningful restructuring. Sufficient relief should be given to allow the primary surplus to be reduced to the neighborhood of one percent, rather than 3.5 percent. Creditors have argued that several countries have maintained primary surpluses of three to four percent of GDP for some time; but none of them have done so on the back of a Great Depression.

Despite modest concessions on smoothing debt payments, the Eurogroup decisions of May 25 basically deferred the hard decisions until a moment that was expected to be more convenient for creditor governments. The present is rarely a politically convenient moment to admit that debt must be restructured. But the finance ministers almost certainly kicked the can down the road one electoral cycle too far. Doing so was a gamble that was at least as large as front-loading debt relief would have been—a gamble that growth would resume, that Greek politics would permit an implementation of the program,[94] and that legislatures in creditor countries would accept debt relief in 2018. Deferring substantial debt restructuring until then was also a gamble against a serious external shock, such as Brexit, for which the British electorate voted even before the ink was dry on the May agreement.

KEY OBSERVATIONS

We can distill several points from the experience with Greece's third program about the choice of the institutional mix, conflicts among the institutions, and mediation of the conflict by way of closing observations.

---

[94] The Governor of the Bank of Greece and the opposition leader of New Democracy declared that the realistic target for the primary surplus was two percent. See Yannis Stournaras, "Greece Needs a New Deal with Its European Partners," *Financial Times*, June 13, 2016; "Glitch in Bailout Talks Fuels Fears of Delay in Loan Disbursement," *Kathimerini*, May 30, 2016.

First, this case tested more than any other the attachment of the Eurogroup to the troika and the IMF in particular. Tsipras's government came into office declaring that the "troika is over"[95] and repeatedly tried to scuttle the arrangement. Despite the Greek prime minister's strong preference for negotiating directly with other European leaders, his government was nonetheless constrained to negotiate with the same institutions as his predecessor. Syriza's popular mandate in this regard did not trump creditor preference: (small) borrowers cannot be (forum) choosers.

Second, German Chancellor Merkel and her government adhered firmly to their preference for the involvement of the IMF in the institutional mix. European institutions had evolved to the point where all of the functions of a European Monetary Fund had been developed; they were simply spread among three institutions.[96] German officials nonetheless insisted, with the accession of other euro-area governments, that the Greek government reach accommodation with the Fund. Their consistency in this respect carries lessons for their underlying reasons to involve the Fund—lack of institutional capacity in Europe is not primary—which we explore in the next chapter.

Third, creditor governments adopted this position *despite* the IMF's adherence to the November 2012 framework for debt reduction well into 2015 and its insistence that the elements of the program "add up," which significantly constrained their options. They valued the Fund's participation nonetheless in order to soothe the domestic opponents of the programs and counteract the leniency of the Commission. "If the IMF says, 'debt is not sustainable,'...we want it on the table," said one German official, expressing a common view in Berlin. The Fund switched to using gross financing needs, he noted, and this was a fruitful, tough discussion. This "wouldn't have been analytically clear if it had only been the Commission," he said. "It's better to have the three institutions involved."[97]

We might add that any further debt relief to Greece was under the firm control of Berlin and the other national capitals in the euro area. The IMF could withhold a financial contribution or issue pronouncements on debt sustainability, but it could not force creditors to restructure debt. At the end of the day, the decision did not lie with the troika or its individual institutions. By including the Fund in the institutional mix, Berlin and the other creditors foster competition among institutions and elicit alternative analyses and recommendations—without sacrificing decision authority on debt relief.

[95] See, for example, Henriette Jacobsen and Jeremy Fleming, "Tsipras Declares Death of Troika, Agrees to Further Talks," EurActiv.com, February 13, 2015.

[96] Paul Carrel, "Europe Can Handle Future Crises without IMF—Bailout Fund Chief," *Reuters*, August 28, 2015.

[97] Interview with a German official, Berlin, July 15, 2015.

Fourth, it fell to officials from the key countries to mediate the conflicts among the institutions, responsible as they were for choosing the mix. While this informal activism was often hidden behind the scenes, the size of the gaps and the frequency of meetings in the 2015–16 case exposed the extent of such mediation. German officials were especially active in overcoming interinstitutional deadlock. Chancellor Merkel's hosting the critical June 1, 2015 meeting among the three heads of the institutions plus French President Hollande was the apex of this coordination. The United States and finance G7 also played important roles, especially in 2016.

Fifth, German officials were not neutral brokers. Mediation also offered an opportunity to ensure that the substance of the program evolved in such a way as to be capable of being ratified in the Bundestag. Although Merkel insisted that Tsipras reach agreement with the institutions, she also proved willing to negotiate particular elements, which would establish parameters in which the institutions would work. Merkel's agreement to lower the target for the primary surpluses for 2015 and 2016 was a case in point.

Sixth, the outcome of this case differed from most of the others in that the Fund *deferred* the matter of whether to contribute *financially* to the program. The Fund might eventually decide to join the program in this way, if its staff and Executive Board can be satisfied that debt has been made sustainable. But the Fund might also decline to declare whether it is in or out and simply leave its financial role open indefinitely. The IMF *did*, however, participate in virtually all of the other elements of the program, including conditionality design and quarterly program reviews, making the institutional mix similar to that of the Spanish banking sector program. This role owed not to the preferences of the euro-area member states, but rather to those of many of the non-European members of the Fund.

Finally, the Fund's posture created a strong incentive for those within the Eurogroup who were opposed to early restructuring to cut the IMF out of future financial rescues and provided impetus for building a European Monetary Fund on the foundation of the ESM. But such an evolution is by no means certain, as the concluding chapter argues.

12

Lessons and Conclusions

This study reviewed the tangled governance of the financial rescue programs during the euro crisis. It presented the seven program cases, woven through a structured narrative of the overall crisis of the monetary union, beginning with the first program for Greece in 2010 and ending with the third program for that country in 2015–16. These cases examined the initiation, design, and implementation of the programs with particular attention to the institutions—the European Council, Eurogroup, European Commission, European Central Bank, International Monetary Fund and, in the later episodes, the European Stability Mechanism—and the interactions among them. The study also reviewed the involvement of the United States, the most influential of the non-European countries in the euro crisis, and the creation of new European financial facilities.

This concluding chapter draws on these cases to answer the questions that were posed at the outset of the book. The first section explains the choice of the *institutional mix* for countries' financial rescues—why the IMF was included and why its role varied in different configurations of the troika.[1] It separates the explanation for Europe's request for the involvement of the Fund from the explanation for the decision of the Fund itself to participate. For a full explanation of Europe's demand to involve the Fund, we must reach deeper than the rationales that have been offered by policymakers. The second section addresses the *strategies* of key states—arguing that complexity is a consequence of states' efforts to control agency drift—and why Germany, in particular, adhered faithfully to the IMF despite sharp substantive conflicts on particular points of program design. The third section explains why the institutions could cooperate and compete simultaneously and thus why heated conflicts among the institutions did not lead to the demise of the troika. The fourth section recommends institutional reforms to prepare the euro area and the institutions for the next crisis, while the final section proposes an agenda for future research on regime complexity.

---

[1] The regime complex for rescue programs was increasingly referred to as "the institutions" as opposed to simply the "troika" over the course of the crisis because it involved more than three.

EXPLAINING THE INSTITUTIONAL MIX

Why did European governments seek to involve the IMF in one way or another in all of the lending programs for the crisis countries, rather than rely exclusively on their regional institutions? The cases presented in the previous chapters, especially Chapter 5, review the reasons that have been offered by officials of euro-area member states. These officials were sincere in offering them and their reasons have been largely accepted by scholarship to date. But these rationales were more compelling at the outset of the crisis than they proved to be in the later phases. Each is at odds with some of the cases and thus falls short of a satisfactory social scientific explanation for the choice of the institutional mix. In this section, we scrutinize those reasons in light of the programs, identify the sources of attraction to the Fund that were common to all cases, and thereby provide a more fundamental explanation.

To review briefly, officials and commentators openly adduced three principal reasons for involving the IMF. First, euro-area governments expected the Fund to bring expertise and credibility in designing, negotiating, and monitoring the lending programs. Second, the IMF brought additional financial resources, and with them demonstrated the global community's commitment to the success of the programs. Expertise and financial contribution have been the most widely proffered reasons that the Fund has been included, almost conventional wisdom. The third rationale addressed the domestic and international politics surrounding the institutions. Several officials and commentators argued that the key European creditors and European institutions benefited from having the IMF as a scapegoat to share the political heat from the backlash against austerity.

Consider, first, the notion that the IMF's expertise explains its inclusion in the troika. The IMF undeniably possesses extraordinary talent and expertise, and these were motives for involving it initially. Its involvement arguably avoided worse outcomes, perhaps even Greece's expulsion from the monetary union. Nonetheless, the IMF's expertise could not prevent the first Greek program from going off track within six months and it failed to secure confidence in financial markets. The Greek government's inability to implement structural reforms had something to do with this, of course; but so did the troika's failure in 2010 to recognize the full impact of fiscal contraction on growth and to acknowledge that the country's debt was not sustainable. By Greece's second program in 2012, the involvement of Fund's expertise no longer appeared to guarantee success. Moreover, the European institutions (Commission, ECB and EFSF/ESM) developed their own capabilities relatively quickly during the crisis, yet member states continued to choose to include the IMF.

Second, while it is true that the IMF contributed additional financial resources, its share in the country programs declined over time and was nil in some cases. These resources were not a compelling reason to include the

Fund beyond the Portuguese program. The IMF was included in the specification of program conditionality and follow-up monitoring and program reviews even in cases where its financial contribution was unnecessary, such as Spain and the third Greek program through at least late 2016. The creation of robust regional financial facilities in the form of the EFSF and ESM, moreover, did not eliminate euro-area member states' interest in the financial involvement of the Fund.

As for the IMF's value in deflecting backlash against austerity away from creditor member states, consider the Fund's substantive position on program conditionality. From the creditors' perspective, the experience with the Fund was at best mixed. In the early programs, the IMF advocated a more permissive glidepath toward the three percent target for fiscal deficits than the European institutions. The Fund research staff departed from the austerity line in more general terms in 2012. The IMF's stance on the pace of deleveraging and recapitalization in the banking system, private-sector involvement, and certainly restructuring official loans was often unwelcome within the troika. But these stances received applause in the capitals of program countries, Dublin being an outstanding case in point. The celebrity status of the mission chief there was a welcome change for the Fund, which had become accustomed to being demonized in borrowing countries across the globe. But—and this is the important point—the popularity of the IMF rendered it useless as a lightning rod for the political backlash against austerity in Ireland. Quite the opposite, it shone the spotlight back onto the Eurogroup and European institutions as the primary purveyors of austerity. The responsibility of the creditor capitals in this respect became increasingly transparent from one program to the next.

In sum, by 2013, the European machinery had marshaled formidable technical staff and expertise in program design and monitoring, created a robust permanent financial facility of its own (the ESM), and experienced bitter substantive conflict with the IMF. Furthermore, the IMF was known in some program capitals to be on the permissive side of the troika debates over austerity. Yet, the Eurogroup and euro leaders *continued* to seek to include the IMF in the institutional mix for the financial rescues. These facts weaken the value of (a) expertise, (b) financial resources, and (c) deflection of responsibility for austerity as explanations for the Fund's involvement. The argument that European governments included the IMF owing to these factors is not entirely wrong—the programs for Ireland, Spain, and Cyprus showed IMF expertise in a better light that those for Greece—so much as incomplete. As explanations for the institutional mix, these rationales are misleadingly narrow—they are relevant mainly in the context of the broader argument developed below.

There is a less openly acknowledged fourth rationale for involving the IMF, which is that creditor countries lacked confidence in the European Commission to apply strict conditionality. This reasoning, by contrast, survives these cases untarnished. To reach this conclusion is not to judge the trustworthiness of the Commission or its analytical capabilities. Rather, this conclusion acknowledges that creditor states understood that the Commission's preferences diverged from their own; they feared agency drift. Their concerns about the Commission were, in turn, a consequence of its treaty-based mandate in the context of conflicts among member states.

The Commission, like other European institutions, straddled *both* creditor and debtor countries, after all, and these country groups had very different preferences with respect to program design, not to mention the overall response to the euro crisis. Creditor governments even disagreed among themselves. Key decisions on programs, loan disbursements, and the establishment of new financial facilities to address the crisis required unanimous approval of member states. That approval, in turn, required ratification by national legislatures in several countries. The IMF had a reputation for toughness that reassured those constituencies within creditor countries that would have otherwise withheld support for loans, those within the governing coalition in Germany being the most salient.

As the agent of creditor countries in negotiating rescue programs and reassuring domestic political actors who might otherwise withhold approval, the European Commission's usefulness was limited by its construction. Recall that the Commission's mandate is to advance European integration and the interests of the European Union *as a whole*. The Commission is thus a political as well as a technical institution. Serving as the agent of the creditor states in rescue programs sometimes conflicted with its broader mission.[2] German officials, in particular, were disappointed that the Commission had not enforced the fiscal rules of the Stability and Growth Pact (SGP) more strictly.[3] Because the Commission's mandate covered creditor and debtor countries alike, its loyalties were split on decisions that distributed losses across this divide. It could not be expected to side uniformly with creditors against debtors in struggles over program design or indeed the larger issues of internal rebalancing within the monetary union and the reform of its architecture. These considerations prompted creditors to adopt intergovernmental solutions that fell outside the Community method and that redefined the role of the Commission—prime examples being the Stability treaty and ESM treaty.

Substantive disagreement among member states (*preference heterogeneity*, in the lexicon of political scientists) and *intergovernmentalism*, therefore, fundamentally drove European governments to seek the involvement of the

---

[2] This point is emphasized by, European Parliament, "Troika Report."

[3] As discussed in Chapter 3, section on the Commission, the SPD–Green coalition government of Chancellor Gerhard Schröder had violated the SGP in 2003–4 and undermined its enforcement. Pointing this out did nothing to build the trust of German conservatives in the Commission during the euro crisis, however.

IMF. Because member states differed in their preferences for program design, several were not willing to rely entirely on the Commission. Because member states make decisions by *unanimity* under intergovernmentalism, creditors were in a position to insist on the inclusion of the Fund. Given creditor states' clash of preferences with debtors, it was highly likely that a blocking coalition (if not a single influential state) would insist on the IMF's involvement as a condition for approving the program.

This conclusion is important because it suggests that building the technical and financial capabilities of European institutions will not be sufficient to prompt euro-area member states to abstain from involving the IMF in rescue programs. As long as the institutional architecture remains incomplete, in terms of political integration, euro-area member states are likely to seek to include the IMF in crisis programs. A Europe-only solution would require a shift in the governance paradigm away from intergovernmentalism toward collective supranationalism.

Euro-area member states did not seek the financial participation of the Fund in *all* of the programs; the Spanish program was the exception. We now turn to it, the largest country to need a program, then to Cyprus, the smallest, and finally to the third Greek program, the most recent and contentious. In doing so, we glean lessons from the *variation* across the programs.

The institutional arrangement in the Spanish program was a variation on, not a rejection of, the troika. The program financed the banking sector rather than government deficits and the IMF took on the role of advisor in designing policy conditions and monitoring implementation in this context. Spain's commitments extended beyond the financial sector to fiscal policy and structural reform as well, through cross-conditionality, although in the end the country was subjected to less austerity than the countries with regular programs. Although it was euro-area-wide policy and thus not part of the program, formally speaking, the ECB's adoption of more aggressive monetary easing proved to be crucial for Spain.

Assistance for Spain was organized in this fashion *not* primarily because its government opposed the involvement of the Fund: such was the case with every country that European creditors pushed into the arms of the IMF. Nor was it organized in this way because the program was specifically for the banking sector and the IMF lacked an instrument for recapitalizing banks that did not also require fiscal and structural adjustment. Chapter 7 showed that the Spanish government was able to retain access to the financial markets not because its fiscal policy was sound—it was, in fact, on the way toward losing access, just as banking crises in Ireland and Cyprus ensnared those governments. Spain instead retained market access, and thereby avoided a program that included financing from the IMF, ultimately owing to the political affinity between the Spanish and German governments, the economic size of Spain, and the implications of its size for program design.

Political affinity between the Spanish and German governments, first, permitted them to negotiate important parameters of the program bilaterally. Creditors had reasonable confidence in Rajoy's government and its orthodox approach, which neutralized their concerns about the softness of the Commission and rendered the IMF's financial involvement unnecessary. Conscious of Spain's predicament, Chancellor Merkel endorsed the ECB's announcement of Outright Monetary Transactions (OMT), which was decisive in keeping the government in Madrid in the markets. Second, Spain's economic size made euro-area-wide policies, such as banking union and the ECB's monetary policy, essential to the success of its program and the IMF would have required assurances with respect to them that European governments and the central bank would not have been willing to provide. Key creditor governments in Europe could thus best organize the rescue to their liking by keeping the IMF in a non-financial role as a shadow member of the troika.

The case of Cyprus, the smallest of the program countries, reinforces the finding that institutional influence is not associated with the size of its financial contribution. The IMF contributed only ten percent of the financing to the program for Cyprus. Yet its insistence on closing one bank and completely restructuring a second, which required bail-in of large depositors and capital controls, prevailed over the objections of the Commission and, at least initially, the ECB. The IMF prevailed because it was backed by the most influential member state in the euro area, Germany.

Note that Germany was satisfied in this case *only* by involving the Fund. Cyprus could have been easily financed fully, because it was small, but its reputation for money-laundering and tax evasion was a serious political liability for the coalition government during the approach of the German national election in September 2013. So Berlin preferred to cover only part of the financing gap and cover the remainder by bailing-in the private creditors of the problem banks. Because their preferences ran against the wishes of the European institutions, German policymakers faced a problem. Berlin could block a program, but it could not force the Commission and ECB to negotiate the particular program with Cyprus that it wanted. The IMF was Berlin's instrument in this quest.

The inclusion of the IMF solved leaders' *domestic* political problems in organizing rescues. In most of the country programs, the involvement of the IMF protected the right flank of Chancellor Merkel's coalition, helping to sustain a working majority in the Bundestag. In the case of Cyprus, the IMF helped to secure support for the program on the left as well, because Germany's Social Democratic Party was insisting on private bail-in. The Fund played similar roles in the domestic politics of the other creditor countries, including Austria, Finland, Luxembourg, and the Netherlands. Domestic politics explains why the World Bank was not brought into the first Greek program: technically, the Bank could have made a valuable contribution, but as political cover for governments, it would have been next to useless. Berlin and other creditor-country capitals stuck with the IMF despite repeated conflicts over program design. Proposing to the Bundestag that the IMF be dropped, the German finance minister once declared, would be like "entering a room full of dynamite with a lighted candle." (The following section elaborates on the reasons.)

During at least the first half of the third Greek program, the Fund participated only in design and monitoring. Creditor states did not wish to exclude its financial participation; to the contrary, they wanted its contribution almost desperately. Instead, the Fund deliberately withheld its financial contribution in the hope of inducing European creditors to restructure Greece's debt, reflecting the preferences of staff and many non-European member states. The European members had some influence in the matter, but they could not force the Fund's decision. So, whereas the third Greek case matches the argument advanced above, it also highlights the analytical distinction between *demand* for and *supply* of the IMF's participation.

Turning to the question of supply, the Fund's inclusion in euro-area contingencies and its specific role within them also depend, of course, on the approval of its staff and non-European members. The United States confronted a dilemma over the use of the IMF for the euro crisis. On the one hand, the Obama administration wanted to stabilize the monetary union in order to prevent contagion across the Atlantic through financial markets and thus preempt a double-dip recession in the United States. On the other hand, U.S. policymakers wanted the euro-area member states to bear the cost of fighting the crisis and complete the institutional architecture to stabilize the monetary union permanently. Ultimately, the United States supported the use of the Fund, but conditioned its support on euro-area-wide policies to finally extinguish the crisis—the European "firewall," banking union, and robust use of the ECB balance sheet. When the threat of financial spillover declined, the United States and other non-European governments drove a harder bargain with the creditor countries in the euro area—as exemplified by the IMF's insistence on debt restructuring for Greece in conjunction with the third program in 2015. Limiting the IMF's role to design and monitoring during at least the first half of that program shows that the availability of the Fund cannot be taken for granted.

COMPLEXITY FOR CONTROL

These findings carry an important lesson for the political economy of regime complexity more broadly, namely, *complexity is the consequence of a strategy of key states to control their institutions*, to manage agency drift. By gathering

Ellipses describe the locus of outcomes acceptable to each institution

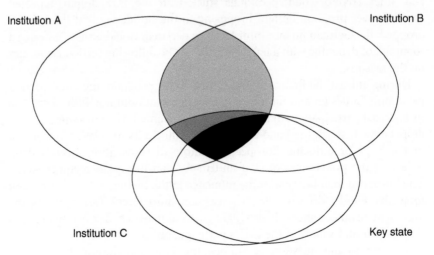

Figure 12.1. Distribution of Preferences among Key Actors.

several institutions to address the euro crisis—and the choice of the institutional mix is made by member states—governments used them to check one
another. A time-honored strategy in the domestic sphere, by which legislatures
control executive agencies, for example, the technique was elevated to the
international level with euro-crisis finance. Specifically, by including the IMF
in the institutional mix, key creditors such as Germany could pull the outcome
toward their preferences.

Figure 12.1 illustrates the strategy in abstract terms. The ellipses in the
figure represent the locus of outcomes that could in principle be accepted by
each of the three institutions. Notice that the intersection of the sets—the zone
of possible agreement—barely overlaps with the preferences of the key member state in the cases of institutions A and B. (The black area is a small subset
of the light gray intersection.) By introducing institution C into the mix, and
thereby narrowing the zone of agreement (to the medium-shaded region), the
key state ensures that the outcome of negotiations among the three institutions will be closer to its preferences. The state's ability to include or exclude
institution C is critical to this formulation.

By substituting the European Commission for "institution A," the ECB for
"institution B," the IMF for "institution C," and Germany for "key state," the
figure would present an idealized picture of the relationship among the
preferences of some of the central actors in the euro crisis. In the absence of
the Fund, the creditor states of the northern tier would have relied upon the
Commission to negotiate the terms of the program, presumably in liaison with

the ECB. The creditors feared that President Barroso, Commissioner Rehn, their fellow Commissioners and DG Ecfin would be more sensitive to domestic political conditions within the borrower country, tweaking the conditions and the program reviews to sustain support for the programs. Creditor governments' preferences did not coincide perfectly with those of the IMF either, of course; in fact they clashed on important points. Creditors nonetheless believed that the triangular bargaining among the institutions would elicit programs closer to their preferences than relying on the Commission and ECB alone.

By introducing multiple institutions into the design and monitoring of country programs, creditors expanded the range of options among which they would ultimately choose. The troika institutions brought competing perspectives and conflicting analysis to the table. This exchange of analysis and information, and the pooling of institutional capabilities, yielded choices that would not have been available had the Commission held a monopoly of these functions. "This wouldn't have been analytically clear if it had only been the Commission," said one key official in commenting on the dueling debt-sustainability analyses of the institutions in the third Greek program. The comment is particularly apt because the Fund's analysis conflicted with his government's substantive position, yet creditor states preferred to include it nonetheless. Creditors benefited from triangulating institutional expertise even when they resisted much of its policy implications.

The strategy of choosing some institutions to check others—whether domestic government agencies or international institutions—has some obvious *dis*advantages. Conflicts among the institutions can render the mix inefficient, even shockingly so. Disputes can even lead to deadlock, which delay or prevent mutually advantageous agreements and which might have been avoided by relying instead on a single institution. But, as we see in the euro crisis, efficiency takes a back seat to control. And when leading member states, the key principals, are themselves the arbiters of interinstitutional conflict, they can better control outcomes.

Time and again the institutions deadlocked on elements of the euro-crisis programs—over bailing in senior bondholders in the Irish banks in 2010–11, Greek private-sector involvement in 2011, closing Cypriot banks and bailing-in depositors in 2013, and debt sustainability for Greece in 2012, 2015, and 2016. Key member states were instrumental in breaking the logjam, sometimes in or on the margins of the G7 finance ministers and central bank governors meetings. At a G7 teleconference in November 2010, for example, the United States weighed in decisively on the side of the ECB to block bailing-in the bondholders in the case of Ireland. Germany was frequently at the center of the mediation process, often with fellow European creditors. German Chancellor Merkel's June 1, 2015 meeting of the heads of the institutions and French President Hollande is a case in point, albeit an unusually visible one.

Almost one year later, meeting at Sendai, Japan, the G7 finance ministers facilitated the agreement that advanced the third Greek program and was announced at the Eurogroup meeting a few days later.

Architects who emphasize efficiency in the design of institutions and global governance generally, and substantive effectiveness in outcomes of cooperation, prefer to endow the institutions with the means to anticipate, preempt, and resolve interinstitutional conflicts themselves. We might envision such mechanisms being set in place among regional financial institutions and the IMF well in advance of crises rather than in the heat of them.[4] Ex ante agreements between the IMF and European institutions, for example, could have avoided the costly delay in invoking the Fund for the first Greek program in winter 2010.

But this book's analysis of the programs in the euro crisis shows how such provisions can threaten member states. Ex ante agreements among institutions can render state mediation unnecessary and rob national capitals of opportunities to influence their work. State governments do not wish to be *disintermediated* by the secretariats of the institutions they create. For this reason, states often do not support injunctions to institutions to cooperate with peer institutions by allocating the resources and bureaucratic means that would be needed to do so. When conflicts arise on matters of importance, key states prefer to mediate the deadlock themselves—and in so doing tilt the outcome toward their preferences.

Understanding *complexity as control* has a number of important implications for interpreting events in the crisis that might otherwise seem paradoxical. First, the usefulness of the IMF to check the European institutions explains why a country such as Germany tolerates the involvement of the Fund even when it disagrees on important substantive questions. Germany had entrée to, and influence within, all of the institutions of the troika. With the other key states in Europe and the G7, German authorities were well positioned to arbitrate the deadlocks that arose. Berlin could do so, moreover, while still holding the veto over, for example, official debt relief for Greece.

Second, this argument about control paints interinstitutional conflict in a new light. Sometimes conflict is interpreted as an indication that the troika is breaking down, that the institutions cannot work effectively together. But the experience of the troika shows that conflict is baked into the control mechanism. States are not likely to abandon the strategy simply because it is

[4] See, for example, Henning, "Coordinating Regional and Multilateral Financial Institutions," *Peterson Institute for International Economics Working Paper* 11–9, Washington, D.C., March 2011; Independent Evaluation Office, "The IMF and the Crises in Greece, Ireland, and Portugal" (Washington, D.C.: IEO–IMF, 2016), hereafter referred to as the "IEO Report"; G. Russell Kincaid, "The IMF's Role in the Euro Area Crisis," Background Paper to the IEO Report (Washington, D.C.: IEO–IMF, 2016).

awkward for international civil servants or because the media have a field day reporting interinstitutional intrigue.

Given these findings, Europeans can be expected to continue to favor inclusion of the IMF in programs for the time being. The presumption of Fund inclusion is written into the ESM treaty. While it is a presumption rather than a requirement, the choice of the IMF continues to be supported by divergent preferences among euro-area member states and unanimity in decisions on financial assistance. The arrangements under the Spanish program, in which the IMF played a shadow role in program design and an explicit role in monitoring, but did not contribute financially, might be replicated in the future. Indeed, the arrangements under the third Greek program through at least late 2016 limited the IMF to design and monitoring. But a sustained refusal of euro-area member states to seek the inclusion of the IMF in sovereign rescues within the monetary union for even design or monitoring, despite persistent conflicts among national preferences and decision-making by unanimity, would be unlikely. Although we could, in principle, envision reforms to the monetary union that might favor Europe-only solutions—discussed below in the section on preparing for the next crisis—such reforms face formidable obstacles of their own.

Is German Power at Work?

Germany was central to European decision-making on the euro crisis in general and sat at the center of the web of institutions that developed the financial rescue programs. Realist theory might ask whether the argument here affirms German power as the explanation for the choice of the institutional mix and, more broadly, the response to the euro crisis. Could we safely explain this choice as a consequence of German control over preponderant financial resources and treat the institutions as a sideshow or epiphenomenal? The answer is "certainly not," for several reasons.

German preferences with respect to crisis programs derive from domestic politics, first of all, and cannot be taken as given. The question of including the IMF, in particular, split the governing coalition; even the finance minister disagreed with the chancellor. Serious opposition to the financial rescues came not from the SPD and Greens but from *within* the CDU/CSU parliamentary group. Merkel lost the "chancellor's majority" in the Bundestag on several occasions during this crisis. Including the IMF in programs limited defection from the right flank of her governing coalitions, curbed the encroachment of the *Alternative für Deutschland* (AfD) party, and reduced Merkel's reliance on the SPD, all of which were valuable to the chancellor. Domestic politics is critical to illuminating the role of the international institutions and cannot be understood within a realist framework; this is an affirmation, instead, of the liberal approach.

Germany was only one of many states that had a formal veto over these arrangements. Many of the others also had serious internal opposition that entailed ratification delay and required accommodation. A realist might point out that Luxembourg, Estonia, and Slovakia, not to mention Finland and the Netherlands, did not have the same sway as the large creditor countries. It is true that, as small countries, they could be bought off or accommodated without undermining the solution. If small states pushed their veto over the ESM treaty too far, for example, the larger states could have found a solution without them; the large countries had "outside options" that were not available to the smaller states. So size did affect the influence that states exercised over these choices.

Nonetheless, relative size does not satisfactorily explain why France and Italy were less influential than Germany. Consider again the relative financial contributions of these countries to fighting the crises. France contributed 20.1 percent and Italy contributed 17.5 percent to the ESM, compared to 27.0 percent from Germany, and all three countries had vetoes under the unanimity rule. Had Germany switched relative shares with Italy, Berlin would almost certainly *still* have had an outsized influence over the negotiations.

The German chancellor and her finance minister were "indispensible Europeans"[5] for two other reasons: their location on the spectrum of preferences and domestic institutions. First, Germany's veto was especially important because, among the large countries, it was the *least* forthcoming. Berlin was, to borrow a phrase from the European integration literature, the "least common denominator," that is, the last holdout that needed to be accommodated.

Second, German preferences were influenced, and Germany's bargaining position constrained, by two important domestic institutions, the Bundesbank and the Federal Constitutional Court (*Bundesverfassungsgericht*). The Bundesbank influenced both the choices of the Governing Council of the ECB, though was sometimes overruled, and public opinion within Germany, including a large swath of the center right that was a core constituency of the governing coalition.

The Constitutional Court set the parameters of decision-making. Through its decisions, the Court required votes to be taken in the Bundestag on the establishment of financial facilities and the individual country programs.[6] Members of the Bundestag did not in general seek this responsibility; most would probably have preferred to avoid it. Indeed, U.S. Congress decides on

---

[5] *Economist*, November 7, 2015, applied this phrase to the chancellor.

[6] The Court also set limits on the amount of fiscal resources that could be transferred to the union level, which, while vague, constrained the size of the ESM to which Germany could consent.

quota contributions to international financial institutions, such as the IMF and multilateral development banks, but does *not* vote on individual programs; none would pass in a timely way if it did! The Court's decision to require votes of the Bundestag was consequential—it forced the government to proceed cautiously, design programs conservatively, and seek the imprimatur of the IMF.

National institutions thus gave Germany a powerful advantage in bargaining over the solutions to the programs, a very credible tying of hands to outcomes that satisfied German preferences.[7] Other large countries did not have this self-commitment mechanism. Occasionally, they attempted to use referenda to shift the outcomes of European bargaining toward their preferences—such was the case with the French referendum on the European Constitution in 2005 and the British referendum on membership in the EU in June 2016. But, thanks to its national institutions, Germany was far more effective in the two-level ratification game and the IMF fit with that strategy.[8]

Consequences of the Choice of Institutions

How might the design and execution of country programs have differed in the absence of the participation of the IMF? A European optimist might be tempted to argue that, without the Fund being involved in the Greek and subsequent programs, the European governments would have stepped up to the plate earlier with more robust funding of new facilities. Continuing this line of reasoning, the ECB—which had withheld its own unconventional measures until governments first made their contributions at several points over the course of the crisis[9]—might not have waited two years to pledge to do "whatever it takes" and provide for conditional assistance through OMT.

But this optimistic scenario gives short shrift to the domestic legal, institutional, and political hurdles to robust financial support for crisis-stricken countries in the euro area. It took time to assuage the sense of betrayal in the north in the wake of Greek fiscal revelations in 2009, develop a strategy to navigate the requirements set by the German Constitutional Court, and make progress on fiscal rules and European banking supervision before political parties and electorates in the north would risk their funds for stabilization of countries in the south. Putting these prerequisites in place required heavy

[7] The framework originated with Robert D. Putnam, "Diplomacy and Domestic Politics: The Logic of Two-Level Games," *International Organization* 42, 3 (Summer 1988): 427–60.

[8] At the subjective level, many German officials, institutions, and segments of the broader public are preoccupied with containing the cost of these programs and of Germany's participation in the monetary union. Actions that might appear to others to be an assertion of power are, for many Germans, an effort to avoid being exploited.

[9] Henning, "The ECB as a Strategic Actor."

lifting over a series of European Council and Eurogroup meetings; they could not have been introduced on the spot in 2010. The IMF helped to bridge the gaps in the architecture of the monetary union in the meantime. In the absence of the IMF, it is more likely that creditors would have refused financing and that Greece would have defaulted or restructured without the benefit of a financial backstop to limit contagion to the rest of the euro area. As a consequence, the monetary union would probably be geographically smaller today, and the damage to European integration much greater, without the involvement of the IMF.

As far as the distribution of the cost of the crisis is concerned, there is no question that the Fund imposed austerity in the program countries as part of the troika. But the IMF pulled the negotiations toward outcomes that were different than those to which the European institutions would have gravitated on their own. The IMF debated the Commission and ECB vigorously on the fiscal glidepath, deleveraging, monetary policy, private sector bail-in, and debt restructuring, among other issues.[10] The Fund was more distant from European banks, which arguably captured national regulators in a number of euro-area countries. Finally, although the financing and credibility of the Fund were not fundamental explanations for the choice to include it, borrowers' adjustment would have been even more severe in their absence.

CONFLICT *WITH* COOPERATION

As it evolved over the course of the euro crisis, the troika was principally an arrangement to coordinate creditor action. Given the choice to include the IMF in the financial stabilization of the crisis countries, the three institutions (with the Commission serving as the agent for the Eurogroup) were bound to form a common position vis-à-vis the program-country governments. They faced an obvious functional imperative: uncoordinated positions or even outright competition could lead to an easing of conditionality to the detriment of adjustment, stabilization, and repayment prospects. The Commission, ECB, IMF, and later the ESM disagreed on many elements of these programs—as amply demonstrated in previous chapters—but the borrowers were generally unable to exploit the differences among them.

The coordination of troika creditors on finance and conditionality did not extend to the *analysis*, as opposed to the *negotiation*, of policy adjustments, debt sustainability, and program design. The institutions competed in these

---

[10] By way of exception, the IMF took a harder line than the Commission on fiscal adjustment in the case of Greece after the middle of 2014. But this was its second-best course of action in the absence of greater debt relief at the time, its first preference.

areas and the debate among them was often intense and sometimes public, even bordering on vitriolic at times. Their competition extended to analysis, surveillance, and assessment of the architectural reform needs of the euro area broadly. At first glance, the coincidence of competition and cooperation might appear to be puzzlingly inconsistent.

The puzzle is explained by the functional nature of the interaction in the two areas of cooperation. Creditor coordination extended as far as necessary given the nature of the spillover from one institution and its regime to the other, a logic similar to Johnson and Urpelaïnen's with respect to regime integration as discussed in Chapter 2. In the area of finance, the spillover was negative: competition undercut the interests of the creditor states and was thus preempted in the troika. In surveillance and analysis, spillover was positive: competition benefited these states by providing a broader range of analysis and forecasts, allowing them to compare and evaluate the best advice and avoid monopolization by one institution. Each institution could provide a check against the other's analysis and forecasts. From the standpoint of the member states, and the key creditors in particular, it was only in finance and conditionality where competition needed to be controlled. International civil servants faced a delicate task in simultaneously cooperating in one sphere while competing in another. But senior national officials were unconcerned with their predicament as long as member states were served.

PREPARING FOR THE NEXT CRISIS

None of the institutions involved in the country programs are particularly happy with their role in the arrangements. Many European officials view the inclusion of the IMF in the mix as not just an embarrassment but also an impediment to faithful application of the rules of the monetary union. They would like to prosecute the next crisis without the IMF.[11] Chapter 9 reviewed the proposals for reform of the troika and reallocation of responsibilities among the institutions, including the review conducted by the European Parliament. Upon becoming president of the Commission in July 2014, Jean-Claude Juncker identified reform of the troika, "based around European institutions with enhanced parliamentary control," as one of his priorities.[12]

---

[11] See, for example, Klaus Regling's remarks quoted in, "Europe Can Handle Future Crises without IMF—Bailout Fund Chief," *Reuters*, August 28, 2015, and Jörg Asmussen and Olli Rehn's statements to the European Parliament, quoted in, "Asmussen and Rehn Sketch Plans for European Body to Replace 'Troika'," *Central Banking*, May 8, 2013.

[12] Jean-Claude Junker, "A New Start for Europe: My Agenda for Jobs, Growth, Fairness and Democratic Change," Opening Statement in the European Parliament Plenary Session, Strasbourg, July 15, 2014, p. 8.

Speaking normatively, what are we to make of these proposals? How should the troika evolve in the future? Should it be redesigned? Should Europe transform the ESM into a full-fledged European Monetary Fund (EMF) and eject the IMF?

One key lesson of this book is that the role of the IMF is inextricably bound up with the evolution of the institutional architecture of the euro area and European Union. The Fund helped to complete some of the missing elements in the architecture of the monetary union—its political role and counterweight to European institutions being especially important—and its role can be expected to change if the euro's institutional architecture were "completed." The main question will thus be whether the euro-area member states can agree collectively on new institutional arrangements for combating crises that would make the Fund superfluous.

Studies, reports, and proposals for the reform of the governance of the monetary union and the European Union are numerous. There is a cottage industry of scholars, officials, task forces, and expert groups working on visions for the future. Among the most important of these, though less ambitious than some, is the Five Presidents' Report, issued by Juncker, Tusk, Shulz, Draghi, and Dijsselbloem in June 2015.[13] They advocated completing the banking union, deepening the fiscal framework, creating a capacity for macroeconomic stabilization, and bringing the ESM into the treaty framework.[14] Their report presented a ten-year, three-stage process for "completing" EMU that will serve to focus the reform debate.[15] But it said nothing further about the role of the IMF, creating an EMF, reforming the troika, or Juncker's ambition to make programs more democratically accountable.

Even these relatively sober recommendations were met with a lukewarm reception on the part of the European Council. The German and French

[13] Jean-Claude Junker, Donald Tusk, Jeroen Dijsselbloem, Mario Draghi, and Martin Schulz, *Completing Europe's Economic and Monetary Union* (Five Presidents' Report), European Commission, June 22, 2015.

[14] To quote: "Finally, the European Stability Mechanism has established itself as a central instrument to manage potential crises. However, largely as a result of its intergovernmental structure, its governance and decision-making processes are complex and lengthy. In the medium term (Stage 2), its governance should therefore be fully integrated within the EU Treaties." Notwithstanding the shift from unanimity to qualified majority voting implied here, it will come as a surprise to some that the governance of the ESM could be simplified and decision-making shortened by bringing them under the Community method! For further analysis, see Guntram B. Wolff, "Euro Area Governance: An Assessment of the 'Five Presidents' Report," *Bruegel blog*, July 24, 2015; Henrik Enderlein and Jörg Haas, "A Smart Move: Why the Five Presidents' Report is Cautious on Substance and Ambitious on Process," *Jacques Delors Institute Policy Paper* 139, Berlin, July 3, 2015; Yves Bertoncini, Henrik Enderlein, Sofia Fernandes, Jörg Haas, and Eulalia Rubio, "Improving EMU: Our Recommendations for the Debate on the Five Presidents' Report," *Jacques Delors Institute Policy Paper* 137, Berlin, June 15, 2015.

[15] European Commission, "Completing Europe's Economic and Monetary Union: Commission Takes Concrete Steps to Strengthen EMU," press release, Brussels, October 21, 2015.

governments had issued a very modest joint position paper a few weeks earlier.[16] Laying down a timetable for consideration of proposals such as the deposit insurance scheme was constructive, but whether political support from member states would materialize very much remained to be seen.

Fiscal Union

Europe could preempt sudden-stop crises and obviate the need for institutionally complex financial rescues by forming a fiscal union. We could envisage the euro area developing its own set of institutions, embedded within the structure of, but distinct from, the institutions of the European Union.[17] A finance minister for the euro area could administer a euro-area budget.[18] A euro-area parliament, or caucus within the European Parliament, would review and pass the budget. Its powers could include the authority to issue debt backed by the union as a whole, eurobonds, and even the authority to tax citizens directly.[19] Fiscal sovereignty would migrate toward the union.

Such a fiscal union would essentially complete the architecture that was left unfinished with the design of the monetary union under the Maastricht treaty and subsequent European treaties. Sovereign crises would become less likely, and when they did occur, financial assistance would be organized within the regular fiscal framework. In such a vision, there would be no need for the IMF to intercede in the rescue of a member state within the euro area. Indeed, with an amendment to the Articles of Agreement at the Fund, the euro area could become a member of the IMF in its own right and be represented there by its finance minister.[20]

Equally importantly, a shift away from intergovernmentalism under a fiscal union would rebalance political influence within it. Once individual member states surrendered a veto, fiscal decisions would not skew toward the

---

[16] *Deutsch-französischer Beitrag zur wirtschafts- und Währungunion*, May 2015, <http://ec. europa.eu/priorities/economic-monetary-union/docs/french-german_contribution_1_de.pdf>.

[17] For a recent, in-depth analysis of the relationship between the euro area and the European Union and further institutional development, see Sergio Fabbrini, *Which European Union? Europe After the Euro Crisis* (Cambridge: Cambridge University Press, 2015). For comparisons to American political development, see, among others, Michelle P. Egan, *Single Markets: Economic Integration in Europe and the United States* (Oxford: Oxford University Press, 2015); Kathleen R. McNamara, "The Forgotten Problem of Embeddedness: History Lessons for the Euro," in *The Future of the Euro*, Matthijs and Blyth, eds, pp. 23–43; and Henning and Kessler, *Fiscal Federalism*.

[18] Benedicta Marzinotto, André Sapir, and Guntram B. Wolff, "What Kind of Fiscal Union?," Bruegel, Brussels, November 23, 2011.

[19] Under such a scenario, but probably only under it, the European Parliament could play the role envisaged in Juncker's July 2014 speech and the preceding report on the troika.

[20] See, for example, C. Randall Henning, *Cooperating with Europe's Monetary Union*, pp. 59–67; Henning, "Regional Arrangements and the International Monetary Fund," pp. 173–5.

preferences of the large-country outlier but toward the political center. The relative influence of creditors and debtors would be more balanced and this rebalancing could, in turn, change substantive outcomes. We might expect that financial assistance that flowed through such a political system would see more bail-in of private creditors, more official financing, and less austerity. The politics of member-state rescues could become less of a morality play between fiscal virtue and vice, and instead cleave between taxpayers, on the one hand, and private banks and other private creditors, on the other.

But such a fiscal union would require a *paradigm shift* to a genuine, full-fledged political union. Europe could conceivably arrive at such a place at some point in the distant future. Notwithstanding significant institutional reform during the crisis, however, the euro area is *not* progressing along this trajectory at the moment. In fact, several basic features of the crisis response—delayed action, program austerity, asymmetry of adjustment, shifting exposure onto governments, and very low inflation in the presence of high debt—contributed to Euroskepticism among electorates across the union. Electorates are less rather than more inclined to support large-scale institutional reform.[21] These features have also left Europe more vulnerable to new shocks than it otherwise would be. While there was a time that one might have thought that a departure of Britain from the European Union would remove an obstacle to deepening within the euro area, that prospect could also fan Euroskepticism on the continent. Major changes to the treaties, let alone another European constitution, will be extraordinarily difficult to ratify for the foreseeable future.

European Monetary Fund

A considerably less ambitious scenario, but a quantum leap nonetheless, would consolidate the institutional capabilities that are presently dispersed across the Commission, Eurogroup, and ESM into a single organization. The Commission would contribute staff and administrative resources, the ESM would contribute financial resources and staff, and the Eurogroup, or the finance ministers meeting as the governing board, would take political responsibility. The board would take explicit responsibility not simply for lending decisions and the management of the facility, but also for the memorandum of understanding with the borrower and thus for the conditionality

---

[21] Pessimism about the prospects for such reform is widely shared. Some of the challenges are examined by, among others, Craig Parsons and Matthias Matthijs, "European Integration Past, Present, and Future," and the volume in which it appears, *The Future of the Euro*, Matthijs and Blyth, eds.

attached to the program. Such an institution would be a veritable European Monetary Fund.

An EMF could be the crisis-finance arm of the euro area under scenarios for partial mutualization that are less ambitious than full fiscal union, including the status quo. It could be equipped with a sovereign debt restructuring mechanism, as Gros and Mayer proposed in 2010, or otherwise support such a mechanism. Removing obstacles in the present ESM for direct bank recapitalization would further erode the corrosive connection between banks and sovereigns. But, an EMF could also take the form of a stand-alone institution for crisis finance that could be created independently of other elements of fiscal integration.

The United States and most of the rest of the world would almost certainly welcome Europe's taking crisis finance entirely inhouse. Although non-Europeans have an interest in how problems of adjustment are resolved within the euro area, and would scrutinize the terms on which an EMF were founded, most outsiders would probably be relieved by the creation of such an institution.

Consolidating these functions within a single institution and bringing it within the EU framework, however, would require a major change to the EU treaties. Securing agreement among member states on the governance, capabilities, and management of such an institution would be equally challenging. Posing these questions would probably resurrect disagreements between the highly indebted and the creditor countries. Creditors would need to have greater confidence in the management of the EMF than they now have in the Commission. Such a scenario would require overcoming all of the reasons that the ESM was set up as an intergovernmental institution in the first place, rather than under the Community method. Efficiency in decision-making would require that creditor states surrender unanimity as the decision rule, but there is little sign of willingness on the part of Germany, the Netherlands, Finland, and the like to do so.

Even the EMF proposal appears to be more than the political traffic can bear for the foreseeable future. So, while the proposal should continue to be pursued, it would be dangerous to assume that such an institution would be in place when the next crisis strikes. Officials of the euro area should plan to fight the next crisis with the institutions that they have, rather than institutions that these officials might wish to have.

Incremental Institutional Change

In the absence of transformative redesign of the architecture, all of the European institutions will probably be engaged in one way or another in any serious financial crisis in the future: the European Council, Eurogroup,

Commission, the ECB, including the SSM, and the ESM, and possibly Euro-stat, the European Banking Authority, and the European Investment Bank.

As long as the financial resources devoted to rescues come through national governments and their parliaments, the European Council, Euro summit, and Eurogroup will remain the central decision-making bodies for crisis programs. The European Commission would be pleased to take command of the programs, but under any scenario of incremental change it will continue to serve primarily as the agent of the Council in negotiations with borrowers. For better or worse, creditor states are not likely to vest substantially greater confidence in the Commission in the near future. Some of the creditors might prefer to augment the ESM staff and its capabilities. Ultimately, though, as argued above, their willingness to jettison the IMF will hinge on abandoning the unanimity decision rule on which the ESM is effectively founded.

How about the role of the ECB? President Draghi and other senior officers of the ECB are deeply uneasy about their association with the programs—including, but not limited to, their association with policy conditionality and periodic efforts on the part of non-Europeans to involve monetary policy.[22] They argue that the political authorities and the Commission should take principal responsibility for designing and implementing these programs. Their posture is understandable from the standpoint of preserving institutional independence.

Functionally speaking, however, the ECB cannot extricate itself from crises or programs. The ECB's decisions on countries' access to regular refinancing, the quality of their collateral, and their eligibility for ELA are critical to triggering recourse to institutional financing. Restructuring the country's banking system is usually an integral part of adjustment programs. The ECB's interest and involvement is even more profound now that it supervises the large banks, as we saw in Greece in 2015. So, whether it is a "silent partner" or a "loud" one, the central bank must remain involved in these elements of crisis programs in the euro area.

One feature of the institutional arrangements that should be changed is the location of political responsibility for the design of programs and their subsequent success or failure. This was obscure to the general public and even many informed observers throughout much of the crisis. But the fundamental responsibility for the programs has always lain primarily with the governments of the euro-area member states, meeting as the Eurogroup, Euro summit, and European Council. This was made abundantly clear at the July 11–13, 2015, Euro summit, where the heads of government negotiated the substantive provisions of the third program for Greece. But, as the European Parliament report on the troika stressed, the Eurogroup, European Council, or

---

[22] Interviews with ECB officials, Washington, D.C., September 14, 2012; Frankfurt, December 12, 2012; and Berlin, June 12, 2013, among other sources.

the Euro summit should take such responsibility in a visible manner in the regular course of announcing a program and the memorandum of understanding.[23] The Council should borrow the famous plaque from the desk of former U.S. President Harry S. Truman and amend it to read "the euro stops here."

International Monetary Fund

To the extent that euro-area member states continue to call upon the IMF to participate in rescue programs, the IMF will continue to have to decide whether to join and, if so, the circumstances under which it would be willing to do so. Within the Fund, the management and staff often take a different view from member states as represented by the Executive Directors and, among member states, non-Europeans can take different views from the European members.

Reservations of the non-European members will condition IMF involvement in euro-area country programs in a couple of ways. First, they will limit the financial contribution to a minority share and could in some cases limit the IMF role to advisory status, as in the Spanish banking program and at least the first half of the third Greek program. Second, IMF involvement will be effectively conditioned on euro-area-wide policies being conducive to successful revival and return to market on the part of program countries.[24]

Nonetheless, if the concerns of non-Europeans can be satisfied, the IMF management and staff are also likely to want to remain involved in the institutional mix. Not the least of reasons for engagement are the Fund's mandate to safeguard international financial stability and the fact that individual euro-area member states remain members of the Fund and retain an equal right to call upon its resources and assistance. Management and staff were never willing to flatly say "no" during the European sovereign debt crisis and remain unlikely to reject outright requests for assistance in the future.

The question has been and will probably continue to be the *price* that the IMF will demand for its participation—in terms of ex ante debt restructuring, private-sector bail-in, official financial contributions from the region, and even perhaps changes to euro-area-wide policies. Fund staff would also seek

---

[23] European Parliament, "Troika Report," paragraphs 101–3.

[24] Assessments by Fund staff of cooperation in the troika include, IMF, "Crisis Program Review," Washington, D.C., November 9, 2015, pp. 57–60; IMF, "Strengthening the International Monetary System—A Stocktaking," Washington, D.C., March 2016, Box 3, p. 30. The IEO Report addresses reforms to troika arrangements in the future, but is not a formal position of the Fund itself. Kincaid's background paper for that report, "The IMF's Role in the Euro Area Crisis," offers the collaboration agreement between the Fund and World Bank as a model for similar agreements between the Fund and European institutions.

a cleaner division of labor among the institutions, in which the Fund in the future would have responsibility for the macroeconomic framework and debt sustainability analysis.[25] For the United States and several other non-European countries, the preferred creditor status of the Fund is non-negotiable. Whether these terms prove to be too steep for euro-area member states, as they were during the first half of the third Greek program, remains an important question.

Despite the *sturm und drang* surrounding "the institutions," the bottom line is that cooperation in one form or another among them is likely to be a durable solution to the problem of organizing crisis programs, albeit a highly contentious one. Substantive conflict among the institutions is not necessarily a sign they are not working well or that the complex is decaying. The purpose of bringing these institutions together, from the perspective of member states, is to have them cooperate in areas where that is essential to substantive effectiveness, while revealing analytical differences in areas where competition is beneficial. Debate, which often becomes public, is simply part of that process.

ORGANIZING REGIME COMPLEXES

This book argues that the preferences and capabilities of the member states, especially creditor states, are an essential point of departure for understanding institutional interaction in the euro crisis—and by extension international finance more broadly. It was the key creditor states that (a) funded and motivated the international institutions, (b) conferred mandates upon them (even when not entirely consistent), (c) decided on the institutional mix, and (d) resolved conflicts among them when that was beyond the staffs and governing bodies of the institutions alone. Simply because some officials in the institutions might be unhappy having to work with other institutions in the mix does not mean that member states should or will choose a simpler arrangement.

The institutions, their design, and adaptability were important to shaping the strategies of states. But the *preferences* of the key creditors, which inhered in their domestic political economy, were fundamental. The particular way in which the troika institutions were brought together—which institution had the lead on which policy sector, which institution served in an advisory capacity—was a distinctly second-order problem. No unique division of labor was necessarily optimal; a couple of alternative formulations were workable as long as the key creditor states could oversee and, when necessary,

---

[25] Interviews with IMF officials, Washington, D.C., May 27 and June 6, 2016.

coordinate them. While the institutions themselves and the officials within them have a lot at stake in the various proposals to reform the arrangements for crisis finance, therefore, architects need not fret over the specific mix. They must ensure, however, that the mechanisms for mediation of institutional disputes, which are largely informal, are robust.

The effectiveness of informal coordination depends in turn on a convergence of preferences among key states, the creditors in particular. Non-European countries—advanced, emerging, and developing alike—acceded to European proposals to tap the IMF for the euro crisis largely because they feared contagion. The integration of international capital and banking markets produced a convergence of preferences among the members of the Fund on avoiding the systemic consequences of a default or a country exiting from the euro. This prospect created a powerful incentive to oversee and coordinate the work of the regional institutions and the IMF.

The coordination worked well enough from the standpoint of the European creditors over the course of the crisis programs. As a model for the crisis-response complex, though, the robustness of mediation seems potentially vulnerable to changes in governments, leaders, and ministers. The legitimacy of back-channel mediation, moreover, is tenuous.[26] Chancellor Merkel managed the process reasonably adroitly in spring 2015, for example, with little or no express opposition to her role. But the acceptance of her mediation might not extend to other government leaders under other circumstances.

These considerations lead to several recommendations. First, when designing institutions and bringing them together in a mix such as that for the euro-crisis programs, we should nurture the mechanisms of *informal* coordination by member states rather than expunge them because they operate in the shadows. We can create space for informalism even within the formal provisions of institutions, legitimizing member-state mediation when institutions are deadlocked. By taking full political responsibility for programs, for example, the Eurogroup and Euro summit would enhance the legitimacy of their presidents in this role. We can bring informal mediation into the open, at least in substantial measure, by announcing meetings and consultations and greater disclosure of their results.

Second, we can confer a mandate for institutions to cooperate with one another in their formal legal provisions. Euro-area member states did so when designing the ESM. The IMF's Articles of Agreement contain a brief, but general, injunction to cooperate (Article X). Cooperation between the IMF and regional financial arrangements is the subject of a G20 protocol, but its

---

[26] A number of officials from countries that are neither in the euro area nor the G7 criticize as insufficient the level of consultation with the Executive Board on important matters early in the euro crisis. See Miguel de Las Casas, "The IMF Executive Board and the Euro Area Crisis," Background Paper to the IEO Report (Washington, D.C.: IEO–IMF, 2016).

guidelines are loose and nonbinding.[27] These guidelines should be updated and strengthened. This can be done without disintermediating national governments and can establish a context in which state mediation could work more effectively in future contingencies.

Third, this book has argued that the institutions involved in the euro programs have coordinated their activities in some areas, such as lending, while competing with one another in other areas, such as analysis and forecasting. This mix of coordination and competition has redounded to the benefit of the principals, member states. But we should not take for granted that institutions will only compete in areas where spillover is positive, such as analysis. States that are common members in these organizations should establish clearer, more explicit directives as to where interinstitutional competition is banned and where it is encouraged.

Finally, this book has several lessons for regime complexity in regions beyond Europe. While it is true that Europe's monetary union accentuates the dilemmas confronting policymakers, the arguments presented here do not hinge on the fact of the common currency. Preference heterogeneity, unanimity decision rules, delegation problems, and agency drift are pervasive elsewhere. This book's argument hinges on these problems, not the functional requirements of the euro, and they will thus likely apply beyond Europe as well.

The experience of Europe serves as a cautionary tale: the wealthiest, institutionally best-equipped region in the world turned to the IMF at its moment of truth in the euro crisis. We would expect other regions to turn to the IMF in the crunch as well—heroic prior statements about regional autonomy notwithstanding. The euro crisis reveals the enduring appeal of the Fund to creditor states.

This study has stressed that the role of the IMF in a region such as Europe depends on the shape and development of regional institutions. When called upon to work with institutions in other regions, therefore, the Fund will complement their work in different ways depending on the contours of the particular regional arrangement. The Fund's role will depend, for example, on the financial capacity of the regional facility, splits among member states on key issues, and their confidence in regional secretariats to operate within their preferences. To retain relevance in a "world of regions," to borrow a phrase from Peter Katzenstein, the Fund will need enough flexibility in lending policies, debt sustainability provisions, and conditionality protocols to straddle different regions simultaneously.

Consider, finally, informal mediation in light of the movement to accommodate emerging-market countries in global institutions. The convention

---

[27] G20 Finance Ministers and Central Bank Governors, "G20 Principles for Cooperation between the IMF and Regional Financing Arrangements," October 15, 2011.

under which the managing director of the IMF has always been a European, while anachronistic, greatly facilitated informal coordination between the Fund and the European institutions. Appointing a non-European to lead the Fund might strengthen the Fund's relationship with institutions in Asia, Africa, or Latin America, but new channels would have to be created in order to avoid deterioration in cooperation with European institutions.

RESEARCH AGENDA ON INSTITUTIONS AND COMPLEXITY

We conclude with considerations for the research program on international regime complexity. This book has addressed questions about the politics of complexity for the euro-crisis rescue programs and has drawn some of the implications for the design of institutional arrangements in future contingencies both in Europe and beyond. But the answers present, in turn, a rich menu of issues for further study.

Comparing regime complexes across regions and across issue areas could be a particularly fruitful path for research. We should examine more deeply institutional complexes for international finance in other regions and the interaction of regional organizations with the IMF. Do preference heterogeneity and unanimous decision-making lead to inclusion of the Fund in crisis rescues there as they do in the euro area? How do patterns of cooperation and competition compare to the complex for crisis finance in the euro area? How do the mechanisms for managing regime overlap and institutional conflict differ?

Similarly, much can be learned from comparisons of complexes for crisis finance with those in other issue areas. The comparative method has been adopted in several of the studies cited above.[28] But more findings can be extracted from this method than have been squeezed to date, especially when the comparisons are structured along important dimensions of variation. One dimension is the degree of fragmentation or cohesiveness of the complex under consideration. A second dimension is the salience of the issue area for core functions of member states. The attention of national governments, the autonomy of international bureaucrats, and mediation of institutional deadlock are likely to vary along the salience dimension.

The comparative method is more difficult with regime complexes than with individual institutions and in other contexts in political science. Examining

---

[28] See, also, Miles Kahler et al., "Global Order and the New Regionalism," Discussion Paper Series, Council on Foreign Relations, New York, September 2016.

regime overlap and institutional interaction requires an intimate understanding of the substance of the issue area—deeper understanding than we can probably expect individual researchers to develop across multiple areas. In-depth comparison thus requires a research program of teams of scholars working collaboratively. But coordinating multiple scholars in the comparative exercise places a premium on achieving a greater degree of standardization of central concepts and nomenclature on complexity.

Comparison of complexes across issue areas can provide further leverage on questions about resolution of interinstitutional disputes, for example. Is institutional conflict and deadlock mediated by a small group of key states that sit at the nexus of the overlap, as in the euro crisis? Or do other actors mediate conflict? What are the informal mechanisms that prevail in other regime complexes? How does informalism differ in those cases and under what circumstances does informalism fail altogether?

In general, studies of institutional interaction can benefit from anchoring institutions in state and social purpose more deeply. This study has done so mainly through the preferences of state members. In other issue areas, however, member states might be more or less central to the anchoring of institutions. Studies of interaction will benefit from locating the strategies of institutions and bargaining among them in a broader political context. More fully "animating" institutions by substantive purpose would engage the interest not only of scholars but also the communities of governance more broadly.

We should know much more about states' strategic use of institutional competition. As a positive matter, when do states deliberately pit some institutions against others? When do they accept competition that arises unintentionally? When do states actively discourage competition? As a normative question, when complexes become too cumbersome or fragmented to manage, is institutional competition a useful tool? Under what circumstances, if any, can institutional competition cut the Gordian knot, help to rationalize the complex, and render it substantively functional? Under what circumstances is such competition instead completely counterproductive?

The accountability and legitimacy of international institutions in the context of complexity deserves greater analysis. International institutions are subject to pervasive scapegoating and credit claiming. Some institutions, such as the IMF, and many national officials have even regarded serving as a scapegoat in the domestic politics of economic reform as one of the institutions' important functions. But, this syndrome obscures accountability and is fundamentally premised on a cynical view of democratic control. The politics of international institutions are long past the point where this syndrome might have ever been functional, and the latitude for evading responsibility is accentuated in a regime complex.

International institutions are proliferating, especially at the bilateral, plurilateral, and regional levels. They are more varied than in the past, in terms of their character as formal and informal organizations, and are sponsored by a variety of actors, national governments, private actors, and even other institutions. Increasingly, they are thrown together to solve substantive problems of global governance—in security, finance, trade, human rights, the environment, energy, and migration, among a host of other issue areas. Given these trends, the study of regime complexity and institutional interaction should be a research priority for the fields of international relations and global governance and for the social sciences more broadly.

Financial Rescues for Euro-Area Countries, 2010–2015

Table A.1. Greece 2010
Total Amount: €110 billion

Institution	Facility and Amount	Terms	Conditionality
International Monetary Fund	Stand-By Arrangement, €30 billion, available over 3 years.	3.5%,[a] repayment due within 3.25–5 years of disbursement.	Primarily fiscal and structural policies, including privatization. General government budget deficit was to be reduced by 11% of GDP over 3 years, to 3% by 2014. Public sector wage cuts, reforms in tax administration, labor and product markets, and privatization in the amount of €50 billion. Bank restructuring was not emphasized. Debt reduction was not required.
European Commission	Greek Loan Facility, €80 billion, available over 3 years.	Euribor plus 3%, rising to 4% on amounts outstanding over 3 years.	
European Central Bank[b]	Outright purchases of Greek government bonds through the Securities Market Programme (SMP) of around €30.8 billion; regular bank refinancing operations; emergency liquidity assistance (ELA).	Vary depending on facility; access requires favorable reviews under the troika program.	

Replaced by a second program in 2012 after disbursing €73 billion.

[a] Surcharge of 200 basis points for large loans, paid on the amount of credit outstanding above 300% of quota. Credit above 300% of quota after three years is subject to a higher surcharge of 300 basis points. Also subject to commitment fee and service charge.

[b] ECB actions are not part of the formal program in this and the other cases below, but nonetheless a substantively important aspect of the financial rescue. The ECB contribution is not included in the total amount.

Sources: IMF, Greece: Staff Report on Request for Stand-By Arrangement, <www.imf.org/external/pubs/ft/scr/2010/cr10110.pdf>; EC Occasional Paper 61, <www.ec.europa.eu/economy_finance/publications/occasional_paper/2010/pdf/ocp61_en.pdf>.

Table A.2. Ireland 2010
Total amount: €85 billion[a]

Institution	Facility and Amount	Terms	Conditionality
International Monetary Fund	Extended Fund Facility, €22.5 billion.	Average rate of 3.85%, repayment within 4.5 years to 10 years of disbursement.	Reform and restructuring of the banking sector, accompanied by fiscal consolidation. Closure of Anglo Irish Bank and Irish Nationwide Building Society, recapitalization of BOI, AIB, EBS, and ILP,[b] and deleveraging of the system. Reduce the deficit to 3% of GDP by 2015. With the exception of a €1 cut in the minimum wage, structural reforms were not central.
European Commission	European Financial Stabilisation Mechanism, €22.5 billion; European Financial Stability Facility, €17.7 billion.	First installment disbursed at 5.51%, reduced to 3.5% in July 2011. Maturity of 7.5 years for both facilities.	
European Central Bank	SMP purchases of Irish government bonds (around €13.6 billion), regular bank refinancing, and ELA.	Vary by facility; access depends on favorable program review by troika.	
Bilateral Loans	UK, €3.8 billion; Sweden, €0.6 billion; Denmark, €0.4 billion.	Annual average interest rate of 5.9%. Maturity of 7.5 years.	

Program was successfully concluded in December 2013. Repayments to the IMF and EFSF began in December 2014.

[a] €17.5 billion was financed by an Irish contribution through the Treasury cash buffer and investments of the National Pension Reserve Fund.
[b] Bank of Ireland, Allied Irish Banks, Educational Building Society Limited, and Irish Life and Permanent Plc.

Sources: IMF *Country Report* No. 10/366, <www.imf.org/external/pubs/ft/scr/2010/cr10366.pdf>; EC Occasional Paper 76, <www.ec.europa.eu/economy_finance/publications/occasional_paper/2011/pdf/ocp76_en.pdf>; NTMA EU/IMF Programme Summary, <www.ntma.ie/business-areas/funding-and-debt-management/euimf-program/>.

Table A.3. Portugal 2011

Total Amount €78 billion

Institution	Facility and Amount	Terms	Conditionality
International Monetary Fund	Extended Fund Facility, €26 billion.	Initially 3.25%, 4.25% on amounts outstanding over 3 years. Repayment period of 9 years.	Primarily structural reforms. Reform of the labor and product markets, with internal devaluation and reduction in labor costs through tax reform. Fiscal deficit reduction by 6.1% of GDP over 3 years to 3% of GDP in 2013. Financial sector reforms to maintain stability, liquidity, and support a balanced and orderly deleveraging in the banking sector.
European Commission	European Financial Stabilisation Mechanism, €26 billion; European Financial Stability Facility, €26 billion.	Rate of 215 basis points (bps) higher than EU cost of funding. Average maturity of 7.5 years.	
European Central Bank	SMP purchases of Portuguese government bonds (around €21.6 billion), regular bank refinancing, and ELA.	Vary by facility; access depends on favorable program review by troika.	

Program was successfully concluded in May 2014. Repayments to the IMF began in March 2015.

Sources: IMF, Transcript of a Conference Call with IMF Mission Chief Poul Thomsen, <www.imf.org/external/np/tr/2011/tr052011a.htm>; IMF, Portugal: Request for a Three-Year Arrangement, <www.imf.org/external/pubs/ft/scr/2011/cr11127.pdf>; Council Press Release on Aid for Portugal, <www.consilium.europa.eu/uedocs/cms_data/docs/pressdata/en/ecofin/122047.pdf>.

Table A.4. Greece 2012
Total Amount €130 billion

Institution	Facility and Amount	Terms	Conditionality
International Monetary Fund	Extended Fund Facility, €28 billion, available over 4 years.	Interest rate of about 3.6% under the EFF. Maturity of 4.5 to 10 years.	Primarily fiscal and structural, including privatization to achieve a primary deficit of 1% GDP in 2012 and a surplus of 4.5% GDP in 2014. Further public-sector wage cuts and reforms in tax administration and the labor market. A longer time horizon applied to the €50 billion privatization revenue target.
European Commission	EFSF contribution of €144.7 billion, including the previously committed €35.5 billion for PSI financing and up to €48 billion for the Hellenic Financial Stability Fund, plus €61.1 billion for government financing.	EFSF borrowing rate plus 150 bps. Also retroactively applied to loans under the first program. Maturity between 25 and 30 years.	
European Central Bank	Eventually restored access to main refinancing operations.	Standard.	
Private Sector Involvement[a]	Exchange covering €177 billion of Greek law bonds, €800 million foreign law bonds, and €9.5 billion state enterprise debt.	Exchanged against new bonds worth 31.5% of the old, cash-equivalent EFSF notes, and GDP-linked securities, for face-value reduction of 53.5%. A present-value reduction in debt of about 70–75%.	
Official Sector Involvement[a]	€3.2 billion.	Reduction of first program interest rate of 150 bps (€1.4 billion). Portfolio income of Greek bonds passed on until 2020 (€1.8 billion).	

Replaced by a third program in 2015 after disbursing €153.9 billion.

a Not included in the total amount.

Sources: EC, *Second Economic Adjustment Programme for Greece, First Review*, <www.ec.europa.eu/economy_finance/publications/occasional_paper/2012/op123_en.htm>; IMF *Country Report* No. 12/57, <www.imf.org/external/pubs/ft/scr/2012/cr1257.pdf>; EC Occasional Paper 94, <www.ec.europa.eu/economy_finance/publications/occasional_paper/2012/pdf/ocp94_en.pdf>.

Table A.5. Spain 2012
Total Amount €100 billion

Institution	Facility and Amount	Terms	Conditionality
International Monetary Fund	Technical assistance only; no financial contribution.	Monitored the financial sector as a whole and prepared independent quarterly reports.	Horizontal conditionality to strengthen the regulatory, supervisory, and bank resolution frameworks. Bank-specific conditionality including bank-by-bank stress tests, segregation of impaired assets, and recapitalization and restructuring of viable banks. Orderly resolution of nonviable banks. No formal full program of conditionality, but cross-conditionality applied.
European Commission	EFSF originally, transferred to the ESM in November 2012; €100 billion.	Cost of funding for each disbursement plus 60.5 bps. Average maturity not exceeding 12.5 years.	
European Central Bank	Technical assistance. Informal financial assistance through SMP purchases of Spanish government bonds (around €43.7 billion) and LTROs.	Vary by facility; access depends on favorable program review by troika.	

Program was successfully completed in January 2014.

Sources: EC, *Financial Sector Adjustment Programme for Spain*, <www.ec.europa.eu/economy_finance/publications/occasional_paper/2012/op118_en.htm>; EC, Post-programme surveillance for Spain, <www.ec.europa.eu/economy_finance/assistance_eu_ms/spain/index_en.htm>; ESM, ESM Programme for Spain, <www.esm.europa.eu/assistance/spain/index.htm>.

Table A.6. Cyprus 2013
Total Amount €10 billion

Institution	Facility and Amount	Terms	Conditionality
International Monetary Fund	Extended Fund Facility, €1 billion.	Basic rate of charge (approx. 1%), plus 200 bps for amounts over 300% of quota, rising to 300 bps if outstanding for over 3 years. 50 bps service fee. 4.5 to 10 year maturity.	Banking sector reforms to restore financial stability, restructure the banking system, and resume the flow of credit to the private sector. Resolution of Laiki Bank, restructuring and recapitalization of remaining viable commercial banks. Fiscal measures to achieve a primary balance of 4% of GDP by 2018.
European Commission	European Stability Mechanism, €9 billion.	Cost of funding plus 10 bps. Upfront and annual service fees of 50 and 0.5 bps respectively. 15 years average maturity.	
European Central Bank	Reopened access to refinancing facilities for banks using Cypriot government debt securities as collateral and ELA.	Standard terms for main refinancing operations.	
Cypriot Government	"Financing assurances" worth €5.2 billion.[ab]	n/a	
Russian Government	€2.5 billion loan restructured.[ab]	Interest rate reduced from 4.5% to 2.5%. Maturity extended 2 years to 2018.	
Private Sector Involvement	€5.8 billion.[a]	Conversion of bank debt and deposits into equity.	

[a] Not included in the total amount.
[b] Contributed to funding the financing gap of €17.7 billion.

Sources: EC, Economic Adjustment Programme for Cyprus, <www.ec.europa.eu/economy_finance/assistance_eu_ms/cyprus/index_en.htm>; ESM FAQ—Financial assistance for Cyprus, <www.esm.europa.eu/pdf/FAQ%20FAQ%20Cyprus%2016052013.pdf>; IMF *Country Report* No. 13/125, <www.imf.org/external/pubs/ft/scr/2013/cr13125.pdf>.

Table A.7. Greece 2015
Total Amount €86 billion

Institution	Facility and Amount	Terms	Conditionality
International Monetary Fund	Decision pending agreement on debt relief.	Pending agreement on debt relief.	Reform of the pension system, VAT schedules, labor and product markets as prior actions. Banking sector reforms to restore financial stability, restructure the banking system (€25 billion). Fiscal measures to achieve a primary balance of −0.25, 0.5, and 1.75% of GDP in 2015, 2016, and 2017 respectively, and 3.5% thereafter.
European Commission	European Stability Mechanism, €86 billion.[a]	Cost of funding plus 10 bps. Upfront service fee of 50 bps for each disbursement and annual service fee of 0.5 bps. Maximum weighted average maturity of 32.5 years.	
European Central Bank	Forbearance on bank solvency until recapitalization; restored access to regular refinancing facilities, June 2016.[b]	Standard terms for main refinancing operations.	
Reprofiling of Debt to the GLF and EFSF	Short-, medium-, and long-term measures to be decided over 2016–18.[b] These include smoothing payments on outstanding EFSF loans; possibly restoring ANFA and SMP profits; possibly further reprofiling EFSF loans, capping and deferring interest payments.	Dependent on debt sustainability analysis. Terms to be decided.	

[a] Amount would be reduced by the amount of any contribution that might be made from the IMF.
[b] Not included in the total amount.

Sources: ESM, ESM Programme for Greece <http://www.esm.europa.eu/assistance/Greece/index.htm>; EC, Memorandum of Understanding <http://ec.europa.eu/economy_finance/assistance_eu_ms/greek_loan_facility/pdf/01_mou_20150811_en.pdf>; Eurogroup Statement, <http://www.consilium.europa.eu/en/press/press-releases/2016/05/24-eurogroup-statement-greece/>.

Bibliography

Abbott, Kenneth W., Philipp Genschel, Duncan Snidal, and Bernhard Zangl, eds. 2015. *International Organizations as Orchestrators*. Cambridge: Cambridge University Press.

Abbott, Kenneth W., Jessica F. Green, and Robert O. Keohane. 2016. "Organizational Ecology and Institutional Change in Global Governance," *International Organization* 70 (2): 247–77.

Aggarwal, Vinod K., ed. 1998. *Institutional Designs for a Complex World: Bargaining, Linkages, and Nesting*. Ithaca, NY: Cornell University Press.

Ahearne, Alan. 2012. "The Political–Economic Context in Ireland," in *Resolving the European Debt Crisis*, eds William R. Cline and Guntram Wolff. Washington, D.C.: Peterson Institute.

Alter, Karen J. and Sophie Meunier. 2009. "The Politics of International Regime Complexity," *Perspectives on Politics* 7 (1): 13–24.

Artis, Michael and Bernhard Winkler. 1998. "The Stability Pact: Safeguarding the Credibility of the European Central Bank," *National Institute Economic Review* 163: 87–98.

Aslund, Anders. 2010. *The Last Shall Be the First: The East European Financial Crisis*. Washington, D.C.: Peterson Institute.

Aslund, Anders and Valdis Dombrovskis. 2011. *How Latvia Came Through the Financial Crisis*. Washington, D.C.: Peterson Institute.

Bakker, Bas B. and Christoph Klingen, eds. 2012. *How Emerging Europe Came through the 2008/09 Crisis: An Account by the Staff of the IMF's European Department*. Washington, D.C.: International Monetary Fund.

Barnett, Richard and Martha Finnemore. 2004. *Rules for the World: International Organizations in Global Politics*. Ithaca, NY: Cornell University Press.

Barrett, Gavin. 2011. *The Treaty Change to Facilitate the European Stability Mechanism*. Dublin: Institute for International and European Affairs.

Bastasin, Carlo. 2012. *Saving Europe: How National Politics Nearly Destroyed the Euro*. Washington D.C.: Brookings Institution Press.

Bastasin, Carlo. 2015. *Saving Europe: Anatomy of a Dream*. Washington D.C.: Brookings Institution Press.

Beach, Derek and Rasmus B. Pedersen. 2013. *Process-Tracing Methods: Foundations and Guidelines*. Ann Arbor, MI: University of Michigan Press.

Bennett, Andrew and Jeffrey T. Checkel, eds. 2015. *Process Tracing: From Metaphor to Analytic Tool*. Cambridge: Cambridge University Press.

Bernanke, Ben S. 2015. *The Courage to Act: A Memoir of a Crisis and Its Aftermath*. New York: W. W. Norton.

Bertoncini, Yves, Henrik Enderlein, Sofia Fernandes, Jörg Haas, and Eulalia Rubio. 2015. "Improving EMU: Our Recommendations for the Debate on the Five Presidents Report," *Jacques Delors Institute Policy Paper* 137, Berlin, June 15.

Biermann, Frank, Philipp Pattberg, Harro van Asselt, and Fariborz Zelli. 2009. "The Fragmentation of Global Governance Architectures: A Framework for Analysis," *Global Environmental Politics* 9 (4): 14–40.

Bini Smaghi, Lorenzo. 2006. "IMF Governance and the Political Economy of a Consolidated European Seat," in *Reforming the IMF for the 21st Century*, ed. Edwin M. Truman. Washington, D.C.: Peterson Institute for International Economics, pp 233–55.

Bini Smaghi, Lorenzo. 2013. *Austerity: European Democracies against the Wall.* Brussels: Centre for European Policy Studies.

Blanchard, Olivier. 2015. "Greece: Past Critiques and the Path Forward," *iMFdirect* (IMF online forum), July 9.

Blanchard, Olivier, Mark Griffiths, and Gertrand Gruss. 2013. "Boom, Bust, Recovery: Forensics of the Latvia Crisis," *Brookings Papers on Economic Activity* 2013 (2): 325–88.

Blanchard, Olivier and Daniel Leigh. 2013. "Growth Forecast Errors and Fiscal Multipliers," *IMF Working Paper* 13/1. Washington, D.C., January.

Blinder, Alan S. 2013. *After the Music Stopped: The Financial Crisis, the Response and the Work Ahead.* New York: Penguin Press.

Blustein, Paul. 2015. "Laid Low: The IMF, the Euro Zone and the First Rescue of Greece," *CIGI papers* no. 61. Waterloo, Ontario, Canada.

Blustein, Paul. 2016. *Laid Low: Inside the Crisis that Overwhelmed Europe and the IMF.* Waterloo, On.: Centre for International Governance Innovation.

Blyth, Mark. 2013. *Austerity: The History of a Dangerous Idea.* New York/London: Oxford University Press.

Boughton, James. 2013. *Tearing Down Walls: The International Monetary Fund 1990–1999.* Washington, D.C.: International Monetary Fund.

Bryant, Ralph C., Nicholas C. Garganas, and George S. Tavlas, eds. 2001. *Greece's Economic Performance and Prospects.* Washington, D.C.: Bank of Greece and Brookings Institution.

Buiter, Willem. 2010. "Games of Chicken between the Monetary and Fiscal Authority: Who will Control the Deep Pockets of the Central Bank?" *Citi Economics Global Economics View*, July 21.

Buiter, Willem. 2012. "Spain: Prospects and Risks," *Citi Economics Global Economics View*, March 28.

Buti, Macro and Nicolas Carnot. 2013. "The Debate on Fiscal Policy in Europe: Beyond the Austerity Myth," *ECFIN Economic Brief* No. 20. Brussels, European Commission, March.

Caporaso, James A. and Martin Rhodes, eds. 2016. *The Political and Economic Dynamics of the Eurozone Crisis.* New York: Oxford University Press.

Carswell, Simon. 2011. *Anglo Republic: Inside the Bank That Broke Ireland.* Dublin: Penguin Ireland.

Chopra, Ajai. 2015. "The ECB's Role in the Design and Implementation of Crisis Country Programs: Ireland and Beyond," *European Parliament, Directorate General for Internal Policies* (IP/A/ECON/2015–07). Brussels, November.

Chopra, Ajai. 2015. Joint Committee of Inquiry into the Banking Crisis, Houses of the Oireachtas, Witness Statement of Ajai Chopra, Session 63 (a), September 10. Dublin, Ireland.

Chwieroth, Jeffrey M. 2010. *Capital Ideas: The IMF and the Rise of Financial Liberalization*. Princeton, NJ: Princeton University.

Claessens, Stijn, Ashoka Mody, and Shahin Vallée. 2012. "Paths to Eurobonds," *IMF Working Paper* 12/172. Washington, D.C., July.

Cohen, Benjamin J. 2012. "The Future of the Euro: Let's Get Real," *Review of International Political Economy* 19 (4): 689–700.

Colgan, Jeff D., Robert O. Keohane, and Thijs Van de Graaf. 2012. "Punctuated Equilibrium in the Energy Regime Complex," *Review of International Organizations* 7 (2) 117–43.

Copelovitch, Mark S. 2010. *The International Monetary Fund in the Global Economy*. Cambridge: Cambridge University Press.

Copelovich, Mark S. and Tonya L. Putnam. 2014. "Design in Context: Existing International Agreements and New Cooperation," *International Organization* 68 (2): 471–93.

Council of the European Union. 2002. "Council Regulation 332/2002," *Official Journal of the European Communities* L 53/1–3.

Council of the European Union. 2010. "Council Opinion on the Updated Stability Programme of Greece, 2010–2013," Document No. 6560/10. Brussels, February 16.

Council of the European Union. 2011. "Treaty Establishing the European Stability Mechanism," *Official Journal of the European Union* L 91.

Council of the European Union. 2012. "Council Decision of 26 April 2012 on a Revision of the Statues of the Economic and Financial Committee," *Official Journal of the European Union* L 121/22–4.

Court of Justice of the European Union. 2012. *Thomas Pringle* v. *Government of Ireland* C-370/12 ECLI:EU:C:2012:756. Luxembourg: CJEU.

Crawford, Alan and Tony Czuczka. 2013. *Angela Merkel: A Chancellorship Forged in Crisis*. West Sussex: Wiley and Bloomberg Press.

Darvas, Zsolt. 2011. "A Tale of Three Countries: Recovery After Banking Crises," *Bruegel Policy Contribution* No. 2011/19. Brussels, December.

Darvas, Zsolt. 2013. "The Euro Area's Tightrope Walk: Debt and Competitiveness in Italy and Spain," *Bruegel Policy Contribution* 2013/11. Brussels, September.

Darvas, Zsolt, André Sapir, and Guntram B. Wolff. 2014. "The Long Haul: Managing Exit from Financial Assistance," *Bruegel Policy Contribution* 2014/03. Brussels, February.

de Grauwe, Paul. 2011. "The Governance of a Fragile Eurozone," *CEPS Working Paper* No. 346. Brussels, May.

de Grauwe, Paul and Yuemei Ji. 2012. "Economic and Monetary Union in Europe," in *Global Economics in Extraordinary Times: Essays in Honor of John Williamson*, eds C. Fred Bergsten and C. Randall Henning. Washington, D.C.: Peterson Institute, pp. 53–83.

de Haan, Jakob, Sylvester, C. W. Eijffinger, and Sandra Waller. 2005. *The European Central Bank: Credibility, Transparency, and Centralization*. Cambridge, MA: MIT Press.

De Las Casas, Miguel. 2016. The IMF Executive Board and the Euro Area Crisis— Accountability, Legitimacy, and Governance. *IEO Background Paper* BP/16-02/02. July 8.

Deutscher Bundestag. 2012. "Act on Financial Participation in the European Stability Mechanism," *Federal Law Gazette* No. 43, September 18, p. 1918.

Dinan, Desmond. 2004. *Europe Recast: A History of the European Union.* London/New York: Palgrave Macmillan.

Dinan, Desmond. 2012. "Governance and Institutions: Impact of the Escalating Crisis," *Journal of Common Market Studies* 50 (2): 85–98.

Djankov, Simeon. 2014. *Inside the Euro Crisis: An Eyewitness Account.* Washington D.C.: Peterson Institute.

Donovan, Donal and Antoin E. Murphy. 2013. *"The Fall of the Celtic Tiger: Ireland and the Euro Debt Crisis."* Oxford: Oxford University Press.

Drezner, Daniel W. 2009. "The Power and Peril of International Regime Complexity," *Perspectives on Politics* 7: 65–70.

Drezner, Daniel W. 2014. *The System Worked: How the World Stopped Another Great Depression.* New York: Oxford University Press.

Egan, Michelle P. 2015. *Single Markets: Economic Integration in Europe and the United States.* Oxford: Oxford University Press.

Eichengreen, Barry. 2007. *The European Economy Since 1945: Coordinated Capitalism and Beyond.* Princeton, NJ: Princeton University Press.

Eichengreen, Barry and Ugo Panizza. 2016. "A Surplus of Ambition: Can Europe Rely on Large Primary Surpluses to Solve Its Debt Problem?" *Economic Policy* 31 (85): pp. 5–39.

Enderlein, Henrik and Jörg Haas. 2015. "A Smart Move: Why the Five Presidents' Report is Cautious on Substance and Ambitious on Process," *Jacques Delors Institute Policy Paper* 139, Berlin.

Enderlein, Henrik, Sonja Wälti, and Michael Zürn, eds. 2010. *Handbook on Multi-level Governance.* Cheltenham, UK/Northampton, MA: Edward Elgar.

Epstein, Rachel and Martin Rhodes. 2016. "International in Life, National in Death? Banking Nationalism on the Road to Banking Union," in *Political and Economic Dynamics of the Eurozone Crisis*, eds James A. Caporaso and Martin Rhodes. New York: Oxford University Press.

Eser, Fabian and Bernd Schwaab. 2013. "Assessing Asset Purchases Within the ECB's Securities Markets Programme," *ECB Working Paper Series* No. 1587. Frankfurt, September.

Eurogroup. 2013. "Eurogroup Statement on Cyprus," General Secretariat of the Council Press Office. Brussels, March 25.

Eurogroup. 2015. "Eurogroup Statement on the ESM Programme for Greece," General Secretariat of the Council Press Office. Brussels, August 14.

Eurogroup. 2016. "Eurogroup Statement on Cyprus," General Secretariat of the Council Press Office. Brussels, March 7.

Eurogroup. 2016. "Eurogroup Statement on Greece," General Secretariat of the Council Press Office. Brussels, May 9.

European Central Bank. 2011. *The Implementation of Monetary Policy in the Euro Area.* Frankfurt: ECB, February.

European Central Bank. 2015. "Interview of Benoît Cœuré," Frankfurt, August 14.

European Central Bank, Banking Supervision. 2015. "Aggregate Report on the Greek Comprehensive Assessment 2015." Frankfurt, October 31.

European Central Bank, Banking Supervision. 2015. "ECB finds total capital shortfall of €14.4 billion for four significant Greek banks." Frankfurt, October 31.

European Commission. 2010. "Commission Assesses Stability Programme of Greece," Document No. IP/10/116. Brussels, February 3.

European Commission. 2012. "Council Recommendation with a View to Bringing an End to the Excessive Government Deficit in Spain," COM (2012) 397 final. Brussels, July 6.

European Commission. 2015. "Completing Europe's Economic and Monetary Union: Commission Takes Concrete Steps to Strengthen EMU," press release. Brussels, October 21.

European Commission. 2015. "Greece–Request for Stability Support in the Form of an ESM Loan." Brussels, July 10.

European Commission. 2015. "Memorandum of Understanding between the European Commission Acting on Behalf of the European Stability Mechanism and the Hellenic Republic and The Bank of Greece." Brussels and Athens, August 19.

European Commission. 2015. "Report on Greece's Compliance with the Draft MOU Commitments and the Commitments in the Euro Summit Statement of 12 July 2015." Brussels, August 14.

European Commission Directorate-General for Economic and Financial Affairs. 2011. "The Economic Adjustment Programme for Ireland," *European Economy Occasional Papers* 76. Brussels, February.

European Commission Directorate-General for Economic and Financial Affairs. 2012. "The Financial Sector Adjustment Programme for Spain," *European Economy Occasional Papers* 118. Brussels, October.

European Commission Directorate-General for Economic and Financial Affairs. 2012. "The Second Adjustment Programme for Greece: First Review," *European Economy Occasional Papers* 123. Brussels, December.

European Commission Directorate-General for Economic and Financial Affairs. 2012. "Macroeconomic Imbalances Country Report–Spain 2012," *European Economy. Occasional Papers* 203. July.

European Commission Directorate-General for Economic and Financial Affairs. 2014."Financial Assistance Programme for the Recapitalisation of Financial Institutions in Spain Fifth Review–Winter 2014," *European Economy Occasional Papers* 170. Brussels, January.

European Commission Directorate-General for Economic and Financial Affairs. 2014. "The Second Economic Adjustment Programme for Greece: Fourth Review," *European Economy Occasional Papers* 192. Brussels, April.

European Commission Directorate-General for Economic and Financial Affairs. 2015. "Economic Adjustment Programme for Cyprus–7th Review," *European Economy.* Summer.

European Commission Directorate-General for Economic and Financial Affairs. 2015. "Macroeconomic Imbalances Country Report–Italy 2015," *European Economy Occasional Papers* 219. June.

European Commission Directorate-General for Economic and Financial Affairs. 2016. "European Economic Forecast," *European Economy Institutional Paper* 025. May.

European Commission, European Central Bank, and European Stability Mechanism. 2016. "Greece: Proposal for Debt Relief Measures," (unofficial paper). May 9.

European Council. 2011. "Conclusions–24/25 March 2011," EUCO 10/1/11 REV 1. Brussels, April 20.

European Council. 2015. "Eurogroup Statement on the ESM Programme for Greece," General Secretariat of the Council, Press Office. Brussels, August 14.

European Court of Auditors. 2016. "Financial Assistance Provided to Countries in Difficulties," *Special report* no 18/2015. January 26.

European Parliament. 2011. "The ECB, the EFSF and the ESM–Roles, Relationships and Challenges," Directorate-General for Internal Policies, Monetary Dialogue. Brussels, December.

European Parliament. 2014. "Report on the Enquiry on the Role and Operations of the Troika," Othmar Karas and Liem Hoang Ngoc, rapporteurs, 2013/2277(INI). Brussels, February 28.

European Stability Mechanism. 2012. *Annual Report 2012*. Luxembourg.

European Stability Mechanism. 2014. "Frequent Asked Questions on the European Stability Mechanism." Luxembourg.

European Stability Mechanism. 2015. "The ESM Programme for Greece." Luxembourg, August 14.

European Stability Mechanism. 2016. "FAQs on the Conclusion of ESM Financial Assistance Programme for Cyprus." Luxembourg, March 31.

European Union. 2009. "Directive 2009/14/EC of the European Parliament and of the Council," *Official Journal of the European Union* L 68: 3–7.

Fabbrini, Sergio. 2015. *Which European Union? Europe after the Euro Crisis*. Cambridge: Cambridge University Press.

Featherstone, Kevin. 2011. "The JCMS Annual Lecture: The Greek Sovereign Debt Crisis and EMU," *Journal of Common Market Studies* 49 (2): 193–217.

G20 Finance Ministers and Central Bank Governors. 2011. "G20 Principles for Cooperation between the IMF and Regional Financing Arrangements." October 15.

Gandrud, Christopher and Mark Hallerberg. 2013. "Who Decides? Resolving Failed Banks in a European Framework," *Bruegel Policy Contribution* 2013/15. Brussels, November.

Gehring, Thomas and Sebastian Oberthür. 2004. "Exploring Regime Interaction: A Framework of Analysis," in *Regimes Consequences: Methodological Challenges and Research Strategies*, eds A. Underdal, and O. R. Young. Dordrecht: Kluwer Academic.

Gehring, Thomas and Sebastian Oberthür. 2009. "The Causal Mechanisms of Interaction between International Institutions," *European Journal of International Relations* 15 (1): 125–56.

Geithner, Timothy. 2012. "The State of the Global Economy: A Conversation with Secretary of the Treasury Timothy Geithner." Washington, D.C., Brookings Institution, April 18.

Geithner, Timothy F. 2014. *Stress Test: Reflections on Financial Crises*. New York: Crown Publishers.

George, Alexander L. and Andrew Bennett. 2005. *Case Studies and Theory Development in the Social Sciences*. Cambridge, MA: Belfer Center for Science and International Affairs.

German Bundestag. 2015. Plenary Transcript, Stenographic Report, 118th Session, Berlin, Wednesday, August 19.

German Federal Constitutional Court. 2011. Judgment of the Second Senate of 07 September—2 BvR 987/10—paras. (1–142).

German Federal Constitutional Court. 2012. Judgment of the Second Senate of 12 September—2 BvR 1390/12—paras. (1–215).

Gillingham, John and Francis Heller, eds. 1996. *The United States and the Integration of Europe: Legacies of the Postwar Era.* New York: Macmillan.

Gocaj, Ledina and Sophie Meunier. 2013. "Time Will Tell: The EFSF, the ESM, and the Euro Crisis," *European Integration* 35 (3): 239–53.

Goldstein, Morris. 2011. "The Role of the IMF in a Reformed International Monetary System," paper for the conference on "The Future of the International Financial System." Bank of Korea, Seoul, May 26-7.

Gould, Erica R. 2006. *Money Talks: The International Monetary Fund, Conditionality, and Supplementary Financiers.* Stanford, CA: Stanford University Press.

Goyal, Rishi, Petya Koeva Brooks, Mahmood Pradhan, Thierry Tressel, Giovanni Dell'Ariccia, Ross Leckow, and Ceyla Pazarbasioglu. 2013. "A Banking Union for the Euro Area," *IMF Staff Discussion Note* No. SDN/13/01. February.

Gros, Daniel and Thomas Mayer. 2010. "How to Deal with Sovereign Default in Europe: Create the European Monetary Fund Now!" *CEPS Policy Brief* No. 202. Centre for European Policy Studies. Brussels, February.

Gutner, Tamar and Alexander Thompson. 2010. "The Politics of IO Performance: A Framework," *Review of International Organization* 5: 227–48.

Hawkins, Darren G., David A. Lake, Daniel L. Nielson, and Michael J. Tierney. 2006. *Delegation and Agency in International Relations.* New York: Cambridge University Press.

Heipertz, Martin and Amy Verdun. 2010. *Ruling Europe: The Politics of the Stability and Growth Pact.* Cambridge: Cambridge University Press.

Helleiner, Eric. 2014. *The Status Quo Crisis: Global Financial Governance After the 2008 Meltdown.* Oxford/New York: Oxford University Press.

Henning, C. Randall. 1994. *Currencies and Politics in the United States, Germany, and Japan.* Washington, D.C.: Peterson Institute for International Economics.

Henning, C. Randall. 1997. *Cooperating with Europe's Monetary Union.* Policy Analyses in International Economics, No. 49. Washington, D.C.: Peterson Institute for International Economics.

Henning, C. Randall. 2002. *East Asian Financial Cooperation.* Policy Analyses in International Economics, No. 68. Washington, D.C.: Peterson Institute for International Economics.

Henning, C. Randall. 2006. "Regional Arrangements and the International Monetary Fund," in *Reforming the IMF for the 21st Century*, ed. Edwin M. Truman. Washington, D.C.: Peterson Institute for International Economics, pp. 171–84.

Henning, C. Randall. 2009. "U.S. Interests and the International Monetary Fund," *Peterson Institute Policy Brief* No. 9-12. Washington, D.C.: Peterson Institute for International Economics. June.

Henning, C. Randall. 2011. "Coordinating Regional and Multilateral Financial Institutions," *Peterson Institute for International Economics Working Paper* 11-9. Washington, D.C.

Henning, C. Randall. 2011. "Economic Crises and Institutions for Regional Economic Cooperation," *ADB Working Paper Series on Regional Economic Integration* 81. Manila, Asian Development Bank.

Henning, C. Randall. 2016. "The ECB as a Strategic Actor: Central Banking in a Politically Fragmented Monetary Union," in *Political and Economic Dynamics of the Eurozone Crisis*, eds James A. Caporaso and Martin Rhodes. New York: Oxford University Press, pp. 167–99.

Henning, C. Randall and Martin Kessler. 2012. *Fiscal Federalism: US History for Architects of Europe's Fiscal Union*. Brussels: Bruegel.

Henning, C. Randall and Pier Carlo Padoan. 2000. *Transatlantic Perspectives on the Euro*. Washington, D.C.: European Community Studies Association and Brookings Institution.

Henning, C. Randall and Andrew Walter, eds. 2016. *Global Financial Governance Confronts the Rising Powers*. Centre for International Governance Innovation (CIGI).

Hodson. Dermot. 2011. "The EU Economy: The Eurozone in 2010," *Journal of Common Market Studies* 49 (1): 231–49.

Hodson, Dermot. 2015. "The IMF as a De Facto Institution of the EU: A Multiple Supervisor Approach," *Review of International Political Economy* 22 (3).

Hofmann, Stephanie C. 2011. "Why Institutional Overlap Matters," *Journal of Common Market Studies* 49 (1): 101–20.

Honohan, Patrick. 2009. "What Went Wrong In Ireland?" Prepared for the World Bank. Manuscript, May.

Houses of the Oireachtas, Joint Committee of Inquiry into the Banking Crisis. 2016. "Report of the Joint Committee of Inquiry into the Banking Crisis." January.

IMF. 2008. *Annual Report for 2008*. Washington, D.C.: IMF.

IMF. 2008. "The FY 09–11 Medium-Term Administrative, Restructuring, and Capital Budgets," Office of Budget and Planning. Washington, D.C., March 20.

IMF. 2008. "Republic of Latvia: Request for Stand-By Arrangement," *Country Report* No. 09/3. Washington, D.C., December 19.

IMF. 2010. "Greece: Staff Report on Request for Stand-By Arrangement," *Country Report* No. 10/110. Washington, D.C., May 5.

IMF. 2010. "Ireland: Request for an Extended Arrangement," *Country Report* No. 10/366. Washington, D.C., December 16.

IMF. 2011. "Greece: Fourth Review under the Standy-By Arrangement," *Country Report* No. 11/175. Washington, D.C., July.

IMF. 2011. "Portugal: Request for a Three-Year Arrangement Under the Extended Fund Facility," *Country Report* No. 11/127. Washington, D.C., June.

IMF. 2012. "2012 Spillover Report." Washington, D.C., April.

IMF. 2012. "Greece: Request for Extended Arrangement," *Country Report* No. 12/57. Washington, D.C., March.

IMF. 2012. "Ireland: Article IV and Seventh Review Under the Extended Arrangement," *Country Report* No. 12/264. Washington, D.C., September 10.

IMF. 2012. "Ireland: Eighth Review Under the Extended Arrangement," *Country Report* No. 12/336. Washington, D.C., December 19.

IMF. 2012. "Spain: Article IV Consultation," *Country Report* No. 12/202. Washington, D.C., July.

IMF. 2012. "Spain: Financial Stability Assessment," *Country Report* No. 12/137. Washington, D.C., June.

IMF. 2012. "Spain: Terms of Reference for Fund Staff Monitoring in the Context of European Financial Assistance for Bank Recapitalization." Washington, D.C., July 20.

IMF. 2013. "Cyprus: Request for Arrangement under the Extended Fund Facility," *Country Report* No. 13/125. Washington, D.C., May.

IMF. 2013. "Greece: Ex Post Evaluation of Exceptional Access Under the 2010 Stand-By Arrangement," *Country Report* No. 13/156. Washington, D.C., May 20.

IMF. 2013. "Greece: First and Second Reviews," *Country Report* No. 13/20. Washington, D.C., January 18.

IMF. 2013. "Ireland: Twelfth Review under the Extended Arrangement," *Country Report* No. 13/336. Washington, D.C., December 19.

IMF. 2013. "Portugal: Eighth and Ninth Reviews Under the Extended Arrangement," *Country Report* No. 13/324. Washington, D.C., November.

IMF. 2013. "Sovereign Debt Restructuring–Recent Developments and Implications for the Fund's Legal and Policy Framework," Washington, D.C., April 26.

IMF. 2013. "Staff Guidance Note for Public Debt Sustainability Analysis in Market-Access Countries," Washington, D.C., May 9.

IMF. 2013. "Statement by Mr. Snel and Mr. Kanaris on Cyprus Executive Board Meeting," BUFF/ED/13/62. Washington, D.C., May 10.

IMF. 2013. *Sovereign Debt Restructuring.* Washington, D.C.: IMF, April 26.

IMF. 2013. *Sovereign Debt Restructuring*, Annex I: Fund Policies on Financing Assurances and External Arrears. Washington, D.C.: IMF.

IMF. 2014. "The Fund's Evolving Approach in Sovereign Debt Crises," *The Fund's Lending Framework and Sovereign Debt–Annexes.* Washington, D.C.: IMF, June.

IMF. 2014. "Spain: Financial Sector Reform: Final Progress Report," *Country Report* No. 14/59. Washington, D.C., February.

IMF. 2014. "Tenth Review Under the Extended Arrangement," *Country Report* No. 14/56. Washington, D.C., February.

IMF. 2015. "Crisis Program Review." Washington, D.C., November 9.

IMF. 2015. "The Fund's Lending Framework and Sovereign Debt–Further Considerations." Washington, D.C., April 9.

IMF. 2015. "Greece: Preliminary Draft Debt Sustainability Analysis," *Country Report* No. 15/165. Washington, D.C., June 26.

IMF. 2016. "Strengthening the International Monetary System–A Stocktaking," Washington, D.C., March.

Independent Evaluation Office. 2016. "The IMF and the Crises in Greece, Ireland, and Portugal: An Evaluation by the Independent Evaluation Office." Washington, D.C.: IEO–IMF, July 8.

Irwin, Neil. 2013. *The Alchemists: Three Central Bankers and a World on Fire.* New York: Penguin.

Issued jointly by the Office of the President and Chancellor's Office, Berlin and Paris. *Deutsch-französischer Beitrag zur wirtschafts- und Währungunion.* 2015. <https://ec.europa.eu/priorities/sites/beta-political/files/french-german_contribution_1_de_0.pdf>.

Jabko, Nicolas. 2011. "Which Economic Governance for the European Union?" *Swedish Institute for European Policy Studies* 2011, Report No. 2.

James, Harold. 2012. *Making the European Monetary Union*. Cambridge, MA: Harvard University Press.

Jinnah, Sakina. 2014. *Post-Treaty Politics: Secretariat Influence in Global Environmental Governance*. Cambridge, MA: MIT Press.

Johnson, Tana. 2014. *Organizational Progeny: Why Governments are Losing Control over the Proliferating Structures of Global Governance*. Oxford: Oxford University Press.

Johnson, Tana and Johannes Urpelainen. 2012. "A Strategic Theory of Regime Integration and Separation," *International Organization* 66 (4): 645–77.

Johnson, Tana and Johannes Urpelainen. 2014. "International Bureaucrats and the Formation of Intergovernmental Organizations: Institutional Design Discretion Sweetens the Pot," *International Organization* 68 (1): 177–209.

Jones, Erik. 2016. "Competitiveness and the European Financial Crisis," in *Political and Economic Dynamics of the Eurozone Crisis*, eds James A. Caporaso and Martin Rhodes. New York: Oxford University Press.

Jones, Erik. 2012. "Italy's Sovereign Debt Crisis." *Survival: Global Politics and Strategy* 54 (1): 83–110.

Jones, Erik, Anand Menon, and Stephen Weatherill, eds. 2012. *The Oxford Handbook of the European Union*. Oxford: Oxford University Press.

Juncker, Jean-Claude. 2014. "A New Start for Europe: My Agenda for Jobs, Growth, Fairness and Democratic Change: Political Guidelines for the Next European Commission." Strasbourg, October 22.

Juncker, Jean-Claude, Donald Tusk, Jeroen Dijsselbloem, Mario Draghi, and Martin Schulz. 2015. *Completing Europe's Economic and Monetary Union* (Five Presidents' Report), European Commission.

Jupille, Joseph, Walter Mattli, and Duncan Snidal. 2013. *Institutional Choice and Global Commerce*. Cambridge: Cambridge University Press.

Kahler, Miles. 2001. *Leadership Selection in the Multilaterals*. Washington, D.C.: Peterson Institute.

Kahler, Miles. 2013. "Rising Powers and Global Governance: Negotiating Change in a Resilient Status Quo," *International Affairs* 89 (3): 711–29.

Kahler, Miles and Andrew MacIntyre, eds. 2013. *Integrating Regions: Asia in Comparative Context*. Palo Alto, CA: Stanford University Press.

Kahler, Miles, et al. 2016. "Global Order and the New Regionalism," Council on Foreign Relations Discussion Paper Series. New York, September.

Keohane, Robert O. 1984. *After Hegemony: Cooperation and Discord in the World Political Economy*. Princeton, NJ: Princeton University Press.

Keohane, Robert O., Jeff D. Colgan, and Thijs Van de Graaf. 2012. "Punctuated Equilibrium in the Energy Regime Complex," *Review of International Organizations* 7 (2): 117–43.

Keohane, Robert O. and David G. Victor. 2011. "The Regime Complex for Climate Change," *Perspectives on Politics* 9 (1): 7–23.

Kincaid, G. Russell. 2016. "The IMF's Role in the Euro Area Crisis: What are the Lessons from the IMF's Participation in the Troika?" *IEO Background Paper* BP/16-02/06. July 8.

Kirkegaard, Jacob F. 2010. "The To-Do List in Ireland," *RealTime Economic Issues Watch*. Washington, D.C.: Peterson Institute, November 19.

Kirkegaard, Jacob F. 2013. "Why the Irish Bank Deal Matters–Especially for Cyprus," *RealTime Economic Issues Watch*. Washington, D.C.: Peterson Institute, February 12.

Kirshner, Jonathan. 2014. *American Power After the Financial Crisis*. Ithaca, NY: Cornell University Press.

Kleine, Mareike. 2013. *Informal Governance in the European Union: How Governments Make International Organizations Work*. Ithaca, NY: Cornell University Press.

Lane, Philip R. 2011. "The Irish Crisis," *CEPR Discussion Paper* No. DP8287. March.

Larres, Klaus. 2009. *Companion to Europe Since 1945*. Malden, MA/Oxford: Wiley-Blackwell.

Lavelle, Kathryn C. 2011. *Legislating International Organization: The US Congress, the IMF, and the World Bank*. New York: Oxford University Press.

Leino-Sandberg, Päivi and Janne Salminen. 2014. "Constitutional Change through Euro Crisis Law: Finland," European University Institute, Law Department Project. May 20.

Leipold, Alessandro. 2012. "Making the European Stability Mechanism Work," *Lisbon Council Policy Brief*. Brussels, February.

Leipold, Alessandro. 2013. "Banking Union: Getting the Big Picture Right," *Economic Intelligence* 05/2013. Lisbon Council, Brussels, December.

Leipold, Alessandro. 2013. "Lessons from Three Years of Euro-Area Crisis Fighting: Getting It Right Next Time," *Lisbon Council Special Briefing* Issue 14/2013, Brussels.

Leipold, Alessandro. 2015. "Two (Potentially Fatal) Achilles' Heels: Can a Mythical Greek Accord Be Made to Work?" Lisbon Council, *Economic Intelligence* Issue 08/2015.

Lewis, Jeffrey. 2012. "Council of Ministers and European Council," in *The Oxford Handbook of the European Union*, eds Erik Jones, Anand Menon, and Stephen Weatherill. Oxford: Oxford University Press, pp. 321–35.

Lombardi, Domenico. 2014. "Italy: Strategies for Moving from Crisis to Growth," in *Europe's Crisis, Europe's Future*, eds Kemal Dervis and Jacques Mistral. Washington, D.C.: Brookings Institution, pp. 64–93.

Lundestad, Geir. 2005. *The United States and Western Europe Since 1945*. London/New York: Oxford University Press.

Mabbett, Deborah and Waltraud Schelkle. 2016. "Searching Under the Lamp-Post: The Evolution of Fiscal Surveillance," in *The Crisis in the Eurozone*, eds James A. Caporaso and Martin Rhodes. Oxford: Oxford University Press, pp. 122–44.

Martha, S. J. Rutsel. 1990. "Preferred Creditor Status under International Law: The Case of the International Monetary Fund," *International and Comparative Law Quarterly* 39 (4): 801–26.

Martinez Oliva and Juan Carlos. 2013. "The EMU versus the EPU," *World Economics* 14 (April–June): 127–43.

Marzinotto, Benedicta, André Sapir, and Guntram B. Wolff. 2011. "What Kind of Fiscal Union?" *Bruegel blog*, June.

Matthijs, Matthias and Mark Blyth, eds. 2014. *The Future of the Euro*. New York: Oxford University Press.

McNamara, Kathleen R. 2014. "The Forgotten Problem of Embeddedness: History Lessons for the Euro," in *The Future of the Euro*, eds Matthias Matthijs and Mark Blyth. New York: Oxford University Press, pp. 23–43.

Merler, Silvia, Jean Pisani-Ferry, and Guntram B. Wolff. 2012. "The Role of the ECB in Financial Assistance: Some Early Observations," European Parliament, Directorate-General for Internal Policies, Department A: Economic and Scientific Policy. Brussels, June.

Mitsopoulos, Michael and Theodore Pelagidis. 2011 "Understanding the Greek Crisis," *World Economics* 12 (1): 177–92.

Mitsopoulos, Michael and Theodore Pelagidis. 2014. "Greece: Tax Anything that Moves!" in *Europe's Crisis, Europe's Future*, eds Kemal Dervis and Jacques Mistral. Washington, D.C.: Brookings Institution, pp. 21–44.

Miyoshi, Toshiyuki et al. 2013. *Stocktaking the Fund's Engagement with Regional Financing Arrangements*. Washington, D.C.: International Monetary Fund, April 11.

Moravcsik, Andrew. 1997. "Taking Preferences Seriously: A Liberal Theory of International Politics," *International Organization* 51: 512–53.

Moravcsik, Andrew. 2008. "The New Liberalism," in *Oxford Handbook of International Relations*, eds Christian Reus-Smit and Duncan Snidal. Oxford/New York: Oxford University Press, pp. 234–54.

Mutschick, Johannes. 2012. "Theorizing Regionalism and External Influence: A Situation-Structural Approach," *Mainz Papers on International and European Politics* No. 2.

Oberthür, Sebastian and Olav Schram Stokke. 2011. *Managing Institutional Complexity: Regime Interplay and Global Environmental Change*. Cambridge, MA: MIT Press.

Orsini, Amandine, Jean-Frédéric Morin, and Oran Young. 2013. "Regime Complexes: A Buzz, A Boom, or a Boost for Global Governance?" *Global Governance* 19: 27–39.

Ovodenko, Alexander and Robert O. Keohane. 2012. "Institutional Diffusion in International Environmental Affairs," *International Affairs* 88 (3): 523–41.

Padoa-Schioppa, Tommaso. 2004. *The Euro and Its Central Bank: Getting United after the Union*. Cambridge, MA: MIT Press.

Papaconstantinou, George. 2016. *Game Over: The Inside Story of the Greek Crisis*. Athens: Provopoulos.

Pauly, Christoph, Christian Reiermann, and Christoph Schult. 2013. "Troika Travails: Split Emerges over Cyprus Bailout Package," *Speigel Online*. January 21.

Pelagidis, Theordore and Michael Mitsopoulos. 2014. *Greece: From Exit to Recovery?* Washington, D.C.: Brookings Institution.

Petrakis, Panagiotis. 2012. *The Greek Economy and the Crisis*. Berlin/Heidelberg: Springer.

Piattoni, Simona. 2010. *The Theory of Multi-Level Governance: Conceptual, Empirical, and Normative Challenges*. Oxford: Oxford University Press.

Pisani-Ferry, Jean. 2014. *The Euro Crisis and Its Aftermath*. Oxford: Oxford University Press.

Pisani-Ferry, Jean, André Sapir, and Guntram B. Wolff. 2011. "An Evaluation of IMF Surveillance of the Euro Area," *Bruegel Blueprint* 14. Brussels.

Pisani-Ferry, Jean, André Sapir, and Guntram B. Wolff. 2013. "EU–IMF Assistance to Euro-Area Countries: An Early Assessment," *Bruegel Blueprint* 19. Brussels.

Polak, Jacques J. 1977. "The IMF and Its EMU Members," in *EMU and the International Monetary System*, eds Paul R. Masson, Thomas H. Krueger, and Bart G. Turtelboom. Washington, D.C.: International Monetary Fund, pp. 491–511.

Porzecanski, Arturo. 2013. "Behind the Greek Default and Restructuring of 2012," in *Sovereign Debt and Debt Restructuring: Legal, Financial and Regulatory Aspects*, ed. Eugenio A. Bruno. London: Globe Business Publishing.

Puetter, Uwe. 2006. *The Eurogroup: How a Secretive Circle of Finance Ministers Shape European Economic Governance*. European Policy Research Unit Series. Manchester: Manchester University Press.

Puetter, Uwe. 2007. "Intervening from Outside: The Role of EU Finance Ministers in the Constitutional Politics," *Journal of European Public Policy* 14 (8): 1293–1310.

Puetter, Uwe. 2012. "Europe's Deliberative Intergovernmentalism: The Role of the Council and European Council in EU Economic Governance," *Journal of European Public Policy* 19 (2): 161–78.

Puetter, Uwe. 2014. *The European Council: New Intergovernmentalism and Institutional Change*. Oxford: Oxford University Press.

Putnam, D. Robert. 1988. "Diplomacy and Domestic Politics: The Logic of Two-Level Games," *International Organization* 42 (3): 427–60.

Raustialia, Kal and David Victor. 2004. "The Regime Complex for Plant Genetic Resources," *International Organization* 58 (2): 277–310.

Regling, Klaus and Max Watson. 2010. *A Preliminary Report on the Sources of Ireland's Banking Crisis*. Dublin: Government Publications Office.

Rhee, Changyong, Lea Sumulong, and Shahin Vallé. 2013. "Global and Regional Financial Safety Nets: Lessons from Europe and Asia," *Bruegel Working Paper* 2013/06. Brussels, November.

Rompuy, Herman Van, José Manuel Barroso, Jean-Claude Juncker, and Mario Draghi. 2012. *Towards a Genuine Economic Monetary Union* (Four Presidents' Report). Brussels: European Council, December 5.

Ruggie, John G. 2014. "Global Governance and 'New Governance Theory': Lessons from Business and Human Rights," *Global Governance* 20: 5–17.

Salines, Marion, Gabriel Glöckler, and Zbigniew Truchlewski. 2012. "Existential Crisis, Incremental Response: The Eurozone's Dual Institutional Evolution 2007–2011," *Journal of European Public Policy* 19 (5): 665–81.

Sapir, André, ed. 2007. *Fragmented Power: Europe and the Global Economy*. Brussels: Bruegel.

Sapir, André, Guntram B. Wolff, Carlos de Sousa, and Alessio Terzi. 2014. "The Troika and Financial Assistance in the Euro Area: Successes and Failures," Study on the Request of the Economic and Monetary Affairs Committee. Brussels: European Parliament, February.

Sargent, Thomas J. and Neil Wallace. 1981. "Some Unpleasant Monetarist Arithmetic," *Federal Reserve Bank of Minneapolis Quarterly Review* 5 (3): 1–18.

Savage, James D. and Amy Verdun. 2016. "Strengthening the European Commission's Budgetary and Economic Surveillance Capacity since Greece and the Euro Area Crisis: A Study of Five Directorates-General," *Journal of European Public Policy* 23 (1): 101–18.

Schadler, Susan. 2013. "Unsustainable Debt and the Political Economy of Lending: Constraining the IMF's Role in Sovereign Debt Crises," *CIGI Papers* No. 19. Waterloo, Ontario, October.

Schadler, Susan. 2014. "The IMF's Preferred Creditor Status: Does It Still Make Sense after the Euro Crisis?" *CIGI Policy Brief* No. 37. Waterloo, Ontario, March.

Schmidt, Susanne K. and Arndt Wonka. 2012. "European Commission," in *The Oxford Handbook of the European Union*, eds Erik Jones, Anand Menon, and Stephen Weatherill. Oxford: Oxford University Press, pp. 336–49.

Schwarzer, Daniela and Sebastian Dullien. 2010. "Policy Options for Greece—An Evaluation," *Stiftung Wissenschaft und Politik Working Paper* 2010/01. Berlin, March.

Sedelmeier, Ulrich and Alasdair R. Young, eds. 2008. *JCMS Annual Review of the European Union in 2007*. Oxford: Wiley-Blackwell.

Sibert, Anne. 2013. "Deposit Insurance after Iceland and Cyprus," *VOX*, Centre for Economic Policy Research, April 2. <http://www.voxeu.org/article/deposit-insurance-after-iceland-and-cyprus>.

Sinn, Hans-Werner. 2015. *The Euro Trap: On Bursting Bubbles, Budgets, and Beliefs*. Oxford: Oxford University Press.

Smits, René. 1997. "The European Central Bank: Institutional Aspects," *International Banking and Finance Law Series* 5. The Hague: Kluwer Law International.

Steil, Benn. 2013. *The Battle of Bretton Woods: John Maynard Keynes, Harry Dexter White, and the Making of a New World Order*. Princeton, NJ: Princeton University Press.

Stone, Randall. 2013. "Informal Governance in International Organizations: Introduction to the Special Issue," *Review of International Organization* 8: 121–36.

Stone, Randall W. 2011. *Controlling Institutions: International Organizations and the Global Economy*. Cambridge: Cambridge University Press.

Telo, Mario, ed. 2007. *European Union and New Regionalism: Regional Actors and Global Governance in a Post-Hegemonic Era*. Burlington, VT: Ashgate.

Truman, Edwin. 2010. "The G-20 and International Financial Institutions Governance," *Peterson Institute Working Paper* 10-13. Washington, D.C., September.

Truman, Edwin. 2013. "Asian and European Financial Crises Compared," *Peterson Institute Working Paper* 13–19. Washington, D.C., October.

U.S. House of Representatives, Committee on Financial Services. *The Role of the International Monetary Fund and the Federal Reserve in Stabilizing Europe*. Hearing, 111th Congress, 2nd Session, May 20, 2010. Washington, D.C.: GPO.

U.S. House of Representatives, Committee on Financial Services, Subcommittee on Monetary Policy and Trade. *Evaluating U.S. Contributions to the International Monetary Fund*. Hearing, 113th Congress, 1st Session, April 24, 2013. Washington, D.C.: GPO, 2013.

Ubide, Ángel. 2013. "How to Form a More Perfect European Banking Union," *Peterson Institute Policy Brief* No. 13–23. Washington, D.C., October.

van de Graaf, Thijs and Ferdi de Ville. 2013. "Regime Complexes and Interplay Management," in *Insights from Global Environmental Governance*, eds Jean-Frédéric Morin and Amandine Orsini. Special Issue of *International Studies Review* 15 (4): 562–89.

Varoufakis, Yanis. 2016. *And the Weak Suffer What They Must? Europe's Crisis and America's Economic Future*. New York: Nation Books.

Vaubel, Roland. 2006. "Principal-Agent Problems in International Organizations," *Review of International Organizations* 1 (2): 125–38.

Véron, Nicolas. 2013. "A Realistic Bridge Towards European Banking Union," *Bruegel Policy Contribution* No. 2013/09.

Véron, Nicolas. 2014. "European Banking Union," Statement to the conference on "Banking Union and the Financing of the Portuguese Economy." Lisbon, February.

Verón, Nicolas. 2016. "The IMF's Role in the Euro Area Crisis: Financial Sector Aspects," *IEO Background Paper* BP/16–02/10. July 8.

Volz, Ulrich. 2012. "The Need and Scope for Strengthening Cooperation between Regional Financial Arrangements and the IMF," *Discussion Paper* 15/2012. Bonn, Deutsches Institut für Entwicklungspolitik, December.

Weiss, Martin A. 2012. "Multilateral Development Banks: General Capital Increases," *CRS Report*. Washington, D.C., January 27.

Weiss, Martin A. 2014. "International Monetary Fund: Background and Issues for Congress," *CRS Report*. Washington, D.C., July 17.

Whelan, Karl. 2012. "ELA, Promissory Notes and All That: The Fiscal Costs of Anglo Irish Bank," *Economic and Social Review* 43 (4): 653–73.

Wijnholds, Onno de Beaufort. 2011. *Fighting Financial Fires: An IMF Insider Account.* New York/London: Palgrave Macmillan.

Wolf, Martin. 2014. *The Shifts and the Shocks: What We've Learned—and Have Still to Learn—from the Financial Crisis.* New York: Penguin Press.

Wolff, Guntram B. 2015. "Euro Area Governance: An Assessment of the 'Five Presidents' Report," *Bruegel blog*. Brussels, July 24.

Wyplosz, Charles and Silvia Sgherri. 2016. "The IMF's Role in Greece in the Context of the 2010 Stand-By Arrangement," *IEO Background Paper* BP/16-02/11 July 8.

Xafa, Miranda. 2016. "Greece," in *European Banking Supervision: The First Eighteen Months*, eds Dirk Schoenmaker and Nicolas Véron. *Bruegel Blueprint* 25. Brussels, June, pp. 101–13.

Zapatero, Jose Luis Rodriguez. 2013. *El dilema: 600 días de vertigo.* Barcelona: Grupo Planeta.

Zettelmeyer, Jeromin, Christoph Trebesch, and G. Mitu Gulati. 2012. "The Greek Debt Exchange: An Autopsy." Manuscript, September.

Index